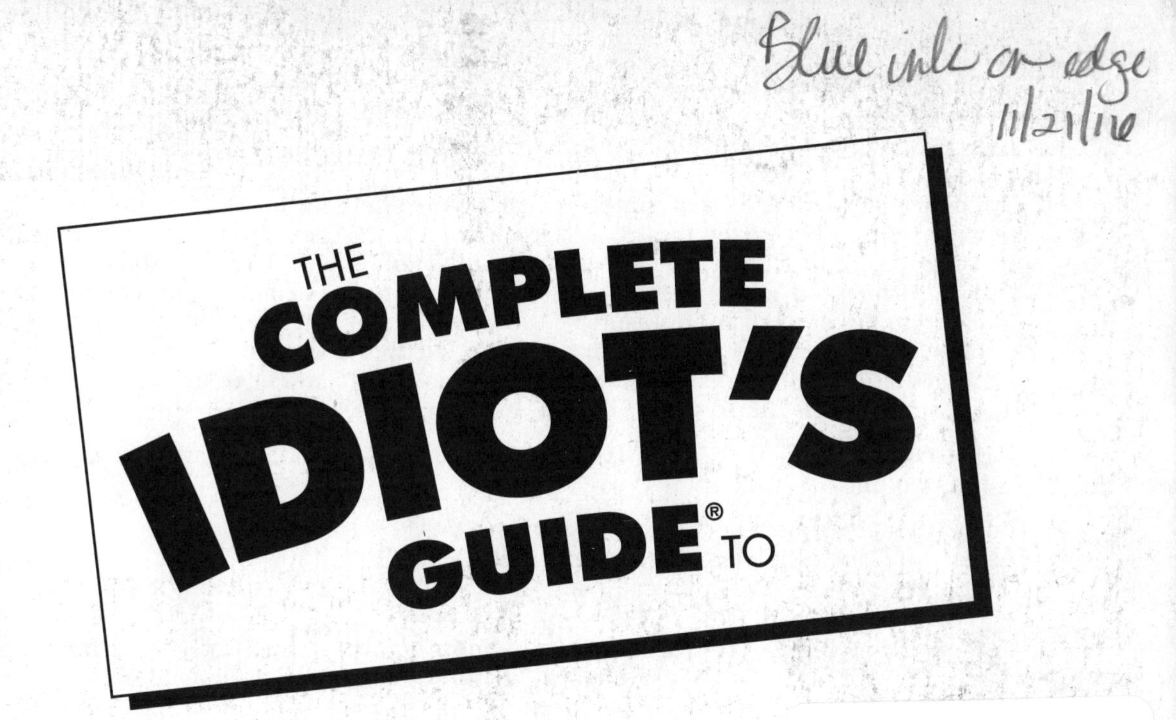

by Paul Baldwin and John Malone

International Standard Book Number: 0-02-864153-1
Library of Congress Catalog Card Number: 2001089691

03 02 8 7 6 5 4 3

Interpretation of the printing code: The rightmost number of the first series of numbers is the year of the book's printing; the rightmost number of the second series of numbers is the number of the book's printing. For example, a printing code of 00-1 shows that the first printing occurred in 2000.

Printed in the United States of America

For marketing and publicity, please call: 317-581-3722

The publisher offers discounts on this book when ordered in quantity for bulk purchases and special sales.

For sales within the United States, please contact: Corporate and Government Sales, 1-800-382-3419 or corpsales@pearsontechgroup.com

Outside the United States, please contact: International Sales, 317-581-3793 or international@pearsontechgroup.com

Publisher
Marie Butler-Knight

Product Manager
Phil Kitchel

Managing Editor
Jennifer Chisholm

Senior Acquisitions Editor
Randy Ladenheim-Gil

Development Editor
Suzanne LeVert

Senior Production Editor
Katherin Bidwell

Copy Editor
Jan Zunkel

Illustrator
Jody Schaeffer

Cover Designers
Mike Freeland
Kevin Spear

Book Designers
Scott Cook and Amy Adams of DesignLab

Indexer
Lisa Wilson

Layout/Proofreading
John Etchison
Lizbeth Patterson
Gloria Schurick

Contents at a Glance

Contents

Appendixes

Foreword

Here it is—*The Complete Idiot's Guide to Acting*. Now there are many out there, never bitten by the acting bug, who have a terrible tendency to believe that anyone who wants to be an actor (in any capacity) is indeed a complete idiot. However, through my years of experience as an actor, from university to community to professional theater, I have had the good fortune to work alongside many actors—from the celebrated to the unsung—and I would like to take this opportunity to say that the vast majority of them are witty, well-read, resourceful, capable, and intelligent people.

There is also a tendency to think of actors as children in constant need of approval and applause. Now, we do like to hear the sound of hands clapping at the end of a performance. (It does beat hearing the thud of over-ripe vegetables and fruit hitting the backdrop.) And while it is very true that the actor must nourish the child inside who wants to "play," it is also true that an actor must learn to keep his wits about him and develop a mature approach to the craft. How many times have you heard someone say—or even said yourself—while watching an actor at work, "Oh, I could do that"? Well, perhaps you could. But what authors Paul Baldwin and John Malone show you clearly in this book is how much preparation and thought have gone into that deceptively simple moment.

In the following pages, Baldwin and Malone carefully guide you through the entire process and tell you what you need to know in order to create that deceptively simple moment for yourself—from where to go to get started all the way through to the reviews and how to deal with them. They give you the basic definitions of the craft and its terms, along with the unwritten rules of the craft—those little secrets and helpful tips that have been learned, usually the hard way, by those who have gone before. They share other actors' stories and experiences, many of them quite hilarious. You will soon realize why wise actors arm themselves with a healthy sense of humor and a philosophical attitude.

We have all experienced situations where we could have profited greatly from just being let in on the secret—something akin to the classic actor's nightmare when one finds oneself centerstage but speechless and nude (because we haven't yet seen the script or been issued a costume). I can't guarantee you'll never have that dream but read on and you will find that you're not alone. More importantly, you will be exposed (in the instructive sense of the word) to an array of situations you might possibly encounter—from costume fittings to final tech rehearsals—that when you find yourself in the spotlight, you'll be glad you're there because you'll be prepared.

Break a leg!

—Carole Monferdini

The theatrical experience of Obie Award–winner Carole Monferdini spans Broadway, Off-Broadway, and regional theaters across the country, including the Williamstown Theater Festival, Philadelphia Theatre Company, and the Barter Theater. She's acted in several Off-Broadway hits for more than a year's run, worked with the National Theater of Great Britain on Broadway, and is a founding member of the Abingdon Theater Company in New York City.

Introduction

In Henry Fielding's great novel *Tom Jones,* the young hero and his friend Partridge go to see a production of Shakespeare's *Hamlet*—a play that had been around for less than 50 years at that point. Partridge, always opinionated and usually wrong, is not impressed by the actor playing Hamlet: "Why, I could act as well as he myself. I am sure, if I had seen a ghost, I should have looked in the very same manner, and done just as he did ..."

Partridge could be right that he would have behaved the same way, if he had indeed seen a ghost, but he has missed the point entirely. The actor who played Hamlet hasn't seen a ghost, just another member of the cast playing a ghost. The wonder is that the actor playing Hamlet can make Partridge think, "That's just what I would have done!"

Acting is pretending. Actors pretend to be people they aren't, caught up in fictional circumstances that sometimes take place in the distant past or the far future. Pretending like this isn't easy to do in a way that will convince an audience of the truth of what's happening. Even critics, who ought to know better, sometimes forget how much pretense is involved. Many movie critics were excited by the special effects in 1999's *The Matrix,* but tended to dismiss its star Keanu Reeves as just okay. They forgot that Reeves had to act a lot of his scenes in front of a blue screen, with the actual effects added much later. Reeves knew what he was supposed to be seeing, but it wasn't there in front of him. He needed to be thoroughly believable, because otherwise no audience would ultimately accept the reality of the special effects. You believe in them because Reeves behaves as though they are indeed real, just as an actor playing Hamlet does when he sees the ghost acted by his good friend Bob.

How do they do it? And—perhaps more important—how do they get the chance to show they can do it? Do you want to play Hamlet? Do you dream of becoming a movie star? Do you think you'd be a wonderful Maria in *West Side Story,* or have your eye on Shakespeare's Cleopatra? Would you be excited to get cast in a small role in your high school play or at the local community theater? Would singing in the chorus of a big musical give you a thrill?

If so, you've been bitten by the acting bug. You may have first appeared on stage in grade school, in a Christmas pageant, but now you want to know more about acting. (You may also be the parent of a grade school kid and want to understand what your child is so excited about.) You may be in junior high or high school, at college, or an adult with a full-time job who still wants to act. Some of you may be thinking seriously about making acting a career.

This book is for all of you. We'll be covering the world of acting from that fourth grade school play to the verge of a professional career, telling you what it's like to be in a high school musical, to become a star actor on a large college campus, or to become a leading light with your local community theater. We'll be giving you the details of every step from auditions and early rehearsals to the problems of dress rehearsals and the thrill of opening night. You'll find out about taking classes to improve your skills, and how to put together an impressive resumé and picture package. We'll warn you of common mistakes, and give you tips about making the most of your abilities. We also think you'll have a lot of fun—this book is packed with backstage stories about actors of every kind, and at every level, actors just like yourselves as well as many who are world-renowned.

What You'll Learn in This Book

We've divided this book into six sections that cover, step by step, every aspect of the acting world. Whether you want to know more about how to succeed at auditions, the best ways to learn your lines for a play, or the rules of backstage behavior during the run of a show, you'll find the answer in these pages. Here's a preview of what you'll discover in each section:

Part 1, "The Acting Bug," focuses on the fact that you can get interested in acting at any stage of your life. We'll tell you about the excitement of a young child playing his or her first role in the fifth grade. We'll explain how you can be a sports star in high school and still act in the school musical. And we'll show you how acting in college can be a big plus both at the time and in terms of your future. Finally, we'll introduce you to the rich world of community theater, a place where you may start acting at the age of 15 or 50.

In Part 2, "Skills of the Theater," you'll find out how to make the most of your natural skills. We'll discuss the basic techniques and knowledge you'll need, from vocal development to stage presence, and give you tips on taking lessons in acting, singing, and dancing. You'll find out how to go about learning a lot on your own and discover why even small parts are important to gaining the experience that counts in the long run. And we'll explain why you can be a big success as an actor even if you don't look like a movie star.

Part 3, "Oh, Those Auditions," will take you through every aspect of the audition process. We'll give you tips on creating a dynamic picture and resumé, and we'll explain how to figure out what directors look for at auditions. You'll learn how to choose the right song for a musical audition and how to mark your sheet music so that the audition pianist can follow you. You'll find out what to wear to auditions—and what to leave in your closet. We'll guide you through the etiquette of the audition process, so you'll know exactly what to expect. Finally, we'll explain how to cope with waiting to find out if you've been cast, and help you to understand that you can lose out on a part you want for reasons that have nothing to do with your talent.

Part 4, "Rehearsal Rigors," will guide you through the entire rehearsal process. You'll find out how to deal with scheduling problems and why it's so important to make sure you don't have any conflicts during the final week before opening. We'll give you tips on learning your lines and discuss the fundamentals of stage blocking, or your movements onstage. You'll learn the ins and outs of taking direction, how to ask the right questions, and when it's okay to argue. We'll tell you how to deal with other members of the cast, and we'll get down to the brass tacks of how to improve your performance with every rehearsal.

Part 5, "'We Open Next Thursday'," will cover the hectic final week before opening, the thrills of opening night, and the actual run of the play. You'll learn the details of costuming, as well as how to deal with any problems caused by the set or the lighting for the play. We'll emphasize the importance of respecting everyone on the technical crew. You'll find out how to get through the long hours of the technical rehearsal, and what happens during the dress rehearsal. We'll explore the excitement of opening night with you. Finally, you'll learn about how to deal with the problems caused by bad reviews (and good ones, too), and what you need to do to keep your performance on a high level throughout the run of the play.

In Part 6, "What Is a Professional?" we'll explore the meaning of the word "professional," and why it often applies to the amateur actor as well as his or her professional counterpart. You'll find out about when and why some community theater actors get paid at least modest sums, and how to go about getting such a reward for yourself. We'll discuss the pluses and minuses of amateur acting vs. a professional career. You'll find out how to get a taste of the professional life by acting in local commercials or working in summer stock. Finally, we'll give you detailed information about how to get into an acting union if you decide that you want to make acting a career.

Between the Lines

Many actors will tell you that much of the best stuff, the insights that make a character really come to life, lies between the lines. In this book, you can find a lot of the best stuff under the following headings, separated from the main text:

Backstage Tales

In this box, we'll tell you great acting stories of all kinds. Some are theatrical legends, others enticing Hollywood lore. We also offer stories about our own experiences, covering what we've learned firsthand, either onstage or as audience members on particularly memorable occasions.

Performance Notes

Directors or stage managers give you performance notes during rehearsal to point out the pitfalls of your performance. That's just what you'll find here: warnings about things you should avoid in your journey through the acting world.

Places, Everyone!

When the stage manager calls out, "Places, everyone," it's time to take your place so that the show can begin. We've used that term here to indicate that you'd better pay close attention to these tips if you want to make the most of your career on the stage.

Stage Directions

Stage directions are the instructions (usually italicized) that appear in published plays to describe specific actions, from "Curtain rises," to Shakespeare's famous, "Exit, pursued by a bear." Here the phrase is used to signal the definition of a theatrical term.

Acknowledgments

We would like to thank Carole Monferdini, Pam Paul, and Jan Buttram for reading the original outline of this book and making many useful suggestions. A book like this draws on the experiences and "backstage tales" of many people, and we take great pleasure in acknowledging the following "theater folk" for being good friends and bearers of many a wonderous tale over the course of several decades: Bob Arnold, Liz A. Biondi, Marcie Brooks, Rob Brock, Joe Centini, Bruce Coyle, Jerry DePuit, Mary and Jim Gilleran, Virginia C. Green, Terry Kerwin, Carolyn Marlowe, R.G. Moore, Beverly Robinson, John Scott, Michael Glenn Smith, and Ralph Symonds. We also want to thank Alpha Books acquisitions editor Randy Ladenheim-Gil for suggesting that we write this book in the first place; development editor Suzanne LeVert for her steadfast support; and our agent, Bert Holtje, for taking such good care of us.

Trademarks

Part 1

The Acting Bug

The acting bug can bite you no matter where in the world you live. Its habitat ranges from Omaha, Nebraska, where Henry Fonda grew up, to Paris, France, the hometown of Juliette Binoche. Morgan Freeman was born in Nashville, Tennessee, Bette Midler in Honolulu, Hawaii, Sophia Loren in Naples, Italy. It doesn't matter where you come from, what language your parents speak, or what kind of accent you have. The acting bug lives near you! The stars we've mentioned above all went on to become household names, but that happens to only a small number of those bitten by the acting bug. There are boys and girls, men and women, in small towns and big cities all across America who get the acting bug but don't really want to become movie stars. At some point in their lives, however, they're encouraged to get up on stage and perform, and they find that the pleasures and challenges of acting add a great deal to their daily existence.

In grade school, high school, or college, they appear in plays and musicals because doing so fulfills them and makes them stand out from out their peers. Many of those who start acting in school appear in community theater productions later in life. Others may not even begin until they are middle-aged or even older. This book is for all of you bitten by the acting bug, wherever you come from and at whatever age you discover the pleasures of performing onstage. And while it's a book dedicated to the amateur actor, those of you who dream of a professional career will also find a great deal of information to guide you along the way.

Chapter 1

Lifelong Susceptibility

In This Chapter

- Discovering what it means to be in your first play
- Understanding why acting is for guys, too
- Exploring the world of college theatrics
- Learning about community theater productions

Some people begin acting very early, in grade school Christmas pageants or historical playlets. Others take up acting in high school, joining their friends in class musicals. Most colleges offer numerous opportunities to act in classic plays, and many institutions are well known for their academic theater programs as well. Also, a surprising number of people don't start acting until adulthood, when they're recruited to perform at charity benefits or encouraged to take on "the perfect role" for a local community theater. Hidden acting talent can surface at any point in life.

If you're reading this book, we'll assume that you or someone you love is susceptible to the acting bug, and now you want to know what it's all about. In this chapter, we'll show you the various ways that people get involved in acting at different stages of life. If you're a parent, we'll give you a glimpse of the thrill of seeing your child make his or her first stage appearance at the age of eight. You'll see why even the high school quarterback can find that playing the lead in a musical gives him greater standing among his peers. We'll introduce you to the opportunities for making your mark on a college campus by taking up acting. And you'll learn about the ways in which community theater acting can enrich your life.

Mommy, They Want Me to Be in a Play

Kids often first start appearing in school plays in the fourth grade. By then, at seven or eight, they are old enough to learn lines for a one-act play, or for a small character role in a longer Christmas pageant. A few children may have already appeared in sing-alongs when they were even younger. But now they have real characters to play, requiring kids who can speak up and be heard, smart enough to remember their lines, and responsible enough to take the effort seriously. And suddenly a child comes running home from school to announce that their teacher wants them to be in a play.

Specially Picked Out

Teachers have a kind of sixth sense about which children might be able to play John and Priscilla Alden, or John Smith and Pocahontas, in a 15-minute play about the earliest days of American history. When it comes to animal plays, they know just who to select for the wise old horse, the wisecracking donkey, and the busybody hen.

Some teachers will take a chance, perhaps to fill a smaller role, on a child who is quite shy, who the teacher thinks would benefit from the group interaction and the sense of achievement that come from taking part in a school play. Many professional actors will tell you that they were on the shy side as children, and first began to blossom when a teacher gave them a chance to perform in a play. Just the fact that they'd been asked gave them the confidence to try. They found that on stage they felt secure in a strange way they'd never quite experienced before. On the playground they might not know what to say sometimes when they were asked a question or teased. But in the play, they always had an answer. It was written down, and they learned the words, and it was a great relief to have a ready answer to whatever was being said to them by the other characters.

Not Just a Show-Off

The authors were both regarded as shy when they were given their first-grade school roles, and it helped bring both of them "out of their shells." Of course, every class has its show-offs as well as its shy kids. Teachers are sometimes wary of putting show-offs into plays, because they're not sure they can control them. (Even adult show-offs can be a nightmare for directors.) But given the responsibility of playing a specific role, a class show-off can also learn new behaviors.

If you're like most parents, you'll be astonished when you see your child on the stage for the first time. "Can that really be my shy little Mary?" you might say, while your neighbor thinks, "How in the world did they get my cut-up son to do his job so well?" Curiously, these two kids may be learning opposite lessons. Shy children discover that they can more safely expose their emotions and talents within the framework of a play, while the show-offs learn that acting is not just "acting out," and that their feelings can be expressed more effectively in a more controlled way.

Backstage Tales

The co-authors of this book both made their first appearances as actors at young ages. John Malone appeared as Captain Miles Standish in a fourth-grade play about the competition between Standish and John Alden for the hand of Priscilla Brewster. The fact that he would lose the girl was more than made up for by the fact that he was given armor made of silver-painted cardboard. Paul Baldwin was cast in the lead of the musical extravaganza *The Old Donkey That Could,* and got to sing "Hee-haw, hee-haw, he says I'm too old to work," after being put out to pasture. At the age of 26, in his first season of one-week summer stock, Paul was assigned the role of Colonel Pickering in *My Fair Lady*, and couldn't help thinking, "Hee-haw, I'm too young for this part."

Discovering a New Ability

Do keep in mind that some children—even smart, confident kids like your own—can't act at all. Acting is a talent. Kids can learn some of the vocal and physical skills that go into acting, up to a point. But unless someone has an innate talent for acting, all the lessons in the world won't make him or her into an *actor*.

Because acting ability is a talent, and not one given to everyone, the child who is good at it inevitably acquires a greater sense of self-worth. What's more, acting—like sports—is rewarded with public demonstrations of approval. It has an audience, and when that audience applauds, the child cannot help but think, "I'm good at something." "They liked what I did." "Hey, I am somebody."

Stage Directions

Throughout this book the word **actor** will be used to designate performers of both sexes. Until the 1970s, a distinction was always made between the male actor and the female actress. But the rise of the Women's Rights Movement has changed that. While the sex distinctions are still made in terms of theater, movie, and television award categories in order to avoid confusion, many women in the acting profession, and a majority among younger performers, refer to themselves as actors. We will follow suit.

You Can Still Play Baseball

When kids get to high school, sports take on a major importance for many of them, boys and girls. Can you—or your child, if you're a parent—be the quarterback of your high school football team, or the center on the girl's basketball team, and still act in plays? Of course you can. It may not be possible during the season that the sport is played, especially if the team is one that's headed for the state championship playoffs. But a varsity sport is going to take up little more than a third of the year, leaving more free time during other seasons.

If your teen is an all-arounder who's a star in more than one sport, it could be a problem; but that's not as common a situation as it used to be. And since many high schools put on two or three stage productions a year, there's likely to be a period when your teen will have time to do that, too.

No, the Guys Won't Laugh

Some boys act in school plays in grade school, but then back off from doing that in high school for fear that they'll be regarded as "sissies." In fact, while your son might get teased a little, most of his friends will be very impressed that he can get up on a stage and perform. And if he's a good athlete as well, then there's no problem at all—except for finding the time to do both.

Even if your son isn't an athletic type, encourage him not to let fears of being teased prevent him from acting if he's got the bug. If he does get teased, ask him if the guys giving him a hard time would have the guts to get up in front of the whole school and play a part. That will shut them up, because deep down they know it does take courage to perform in public.

Backstage Tales

An 18-year-old whom we know was the top running back on his high school football team. In the spring of his senior year, Jack was asked to play the lead in a production of *Charlie's Aunt.* In order to pursue the affections of the girl he loves, Charlie disguises himself as his aunt, wearing a long black dress for much of the play. Of course, Charlie is always on the verge of getting caught doing something no maiden aunt would do, like smoking a cigar. Jack's football teammates were falling out of their seats laughing, and he became more of a school star than ever.

One-Up for College Admissions

Acting in high school plays is a bigger plus than some people realize in terms of getting into the college of your choice. Grades and other academic barometers count most, of course; athletics can also be very important, especially at large institutions that have nationally recognized sports programs. But all colleges try to achieve a balanced student body that reflects a broad range of interests. Almost all colleges have a lively theatrical scene, and many, from big state-funded institutions like North Texas University to private liberal arts colleges like Franklin & Marshall, have highly regarded drama departments. An application that includes credits for acting in—or doing technical work for—high school plays is a definite plus, and can make the difference in a college's choice between you and another student with equal academic standing.

College Theatrics

During the high school years, acting opportunities will be mostly in famous American comedies of the past, like *You Can't Take It With You* by George Kaufman and Moss Hart, or musicals with large casts that give a lot of students a chance to participate, like *West Side Story*. Prep schools often put on a yearly Shakespeare production. But at college, the horizons will be greatly extended. Colleges will often mount classic plays from Greek tragedies to the works of George Bernard Shaw, Henrik Ibsen, and Anton Chekhov. One year they may do a translation of a comedy by Moliere, the next a production of Luigi Pirandello's *Six Characters in Search of an Author*. Shakespeare's plays will be heavily represented, as well as those of his contemporaries Christopher Marlowe and Ben Jonson. The works of lesser-known Jacobean dramatists are likely to show up, too. And, of course, colleges with strong musical departments will also have musicals, and even operas.

College productions undoubtedly do more to keep the great dramas of the past alive than all the professional nonprofit theaters in America put together. For the student who wants to act, the scope of college productions is a truly exciting prospect.

Places, Everyone!

Stay alert for audition announcements. In grade school or high school, teachers are likely to recruit students to act in plays, and public address announcements will alert everyone to the fact that auditions are taking place. At college, you'll have to keep your eye on the college newspaper. Or you may want to join the college dramatic club, which is likely to be one of the most informal and accessible student organizations on campus.

More Than a Grind

It is at college that many people take their first steps into the acting world. A student who was too busy being a teenager during high school may see a few college productions and think, "I could do that." Young people who played on a varsity athletic team in high school, but aren't quite skilled enough in the more competitive world of college sports, can find a new outlet for their energies in acting. And some students who have always stuck mostly to their books decide that it's time to make it something more than a grind.

Because so many productions are mounted on college campuses, they have a need for a lot of actors, and the chances of getting a good role are much greater than in high school, where there were only a couple of plays presented each year. College presents many kinds of opportunities to explore new worlds, and acting in a musical or a play is one of the richest and most rewarding.

Undying Friendships

College dramatic productions are a great way of meeting new people. A big campus can seem almost overwhelming to some students. Being in a play gives students the opportunity to get to know a considerable group of people quite well. The length of the rehearsal period gives them time to forge real friendships. Actors meet not only the other actors, but also architecture students getting experience by designing sets, engineering students who are involved in lighting design, and a wide cross-section of young people doing everything from stage managing to handling props. What's more, unlike athletic teams, drama productions bring together students of both sexes. Meeting people while rehearsing a play is a much more pleasant way of getting acquainted than any college "mixer."

If you take part in college theatrics, you will almost certainly make some friendships that will last a lifetime. You might even meet your future spouse—thousands have.

A Community Theater

Community theaters can be found in most small cities, and even in some towns with a population of only 20,000 or so. Even large cities—Cincinnati, Ohio and Mobile, Alabama for example—will have a community theater or two. Many of these amateur groups have been in operation for decades, acquiring loyal audiences, financial patrons, and reputations for excellence that extend far beyond their modest beginnings.

Although usually nonprofit, community theaters often have professional production standards. Because these theaters usually charge for tickets, lead actors may actually earn a little bit of money for their work. Some community theaters occasionally hire a professional actor to come to town for a few weeks and star as Don Quixote in *Man of La Mancha* or Dolly Levi in *Hello, Dolly!*, with the rest of the roles being filled by local residents. There are a few quite large community theaters, seating several hundred people, such as the Fulton Opera House in Lancaster, Pennsylvania, that schedule a mix of productions, some cast almost entirely with professionals, and others largely with local actors.

Community theaters thrive because they provide good productions of well-known plays and musicals, as well as some original plays, far from Broadway and the major regional theaters scattered around the country. There are plenty of actors to audition for productions everywhere, people who hold down regular nine-to-five jobs but got the acting bug in high school or college and want to continue strutting their stuff on the stage. Many community theater actors have the talent to have turned professional, but decided they did not want to live the uncertain life of the professional actor. By day they are teachers and lawyers, work in banks, stores, or local government; but by night and on weekends they are actors.

Performance Notes

Start a community theater yourself if your city doesn't have one already. Many long-established community theaters began when someone put a notice in the paper about the formation of a play-reading group. Such groups eventually may be able to mount productions, initially perhaps only one a year, with a gradual increase in shows taking place as a devoted audience grows.

"We're Always Looking for Talent"

Even if you're a novice, you can enter into the ranks of community theater whenever the acting bug hits you. Maybe you have a friend who participates or maybe you've been asked to join because of the fine singing you bring to the church choir or your reputation for great comic timing.

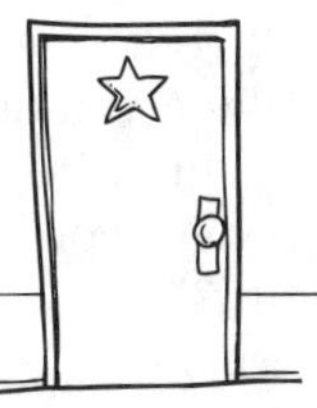

Backstage Tales

The authors have known several people who did not take up acting until later in life, but then became stalwarts of community theater companies. Alicia, for example, had sung in church choirs since she was a child, but had never appeared in a stage production of any kind. In her early fifties, with both children in college, a friend persuaded her that her voice and appearance were perfectly suited to the role of the Mother Superior in *The Sound of Music.* Her rendition of "Climb Every Mountain" was one of the great hits of the show, and she's still up there on stage in both musicals and straight plays a dozen years later. "My son and daughter were astonished at my transformation," she says with some glee.

Circles of Influence

In addition to having loads of fun, you might also find that performing in local productions even enhances your standing in the community as a whole. Over the years, thousands of people will see you perform, and you might even become somewhat of a celebrity. While that may slow down your progress along the supermarket aisles, it's sure to give you a great sense of accomplishment.

In addition, you'll find additional side-benefits to acting in local productions. If you're a lawyer, you're likely to discover that you're getting more clients because audience members start to feel they know you, and think they'd be comfortable having you deal with their legal affairs. As a store owner, you'll find that your celebrity brings more customers through the doors. Stories about such ancillary benefits are common among community theater actors.

At whatever age the acting bug bites you, you'll probably be glad that it did. As a grade school kid, you'll discover a new sense of competence in dealing with the world. If you start acting in high school, it will not only bring you greater popularity among your peers but also prove a valuable credit toward getting accepted by the college of your choice. As a college actor, your place on a large campus will seem more significant. And as a community theater actor, you will find that you are valued as a citizen who contributes something extra to the local scene.

Performance Notes

You may think you don't have time to act in community theater, but that's often a matter of simply making better time-management choices. We know a highly respected cardiologist who made time. He even took on the role of Henry Higgins in a memorable production of *My Fair Lady.* "I gave up golf for acting," he says with a wry smile. "That sits well with my patients, too, I can tell you."

Of course, acting has its difficult moments as well. When you fail to get a role you want, or find yourself coping with a less-than-brilliant director, or get a bad review, you may sometimes wonder, "Why am I doing this?" But the moments of excitement and fulfillment usually far outweigh the occasional letdowns.

In the course of this book, we'll help you learn how to make the most of your talents, how to audition successfully, and how to make the rehearsal period truly count. We'll guide you through the rigors of dress rehearsals and the nervous excitement of opening night. You'll explore the many joys of the acting experience, and learn how to avoid unnecessary problems, as well as cope with the inevitable ones. Whatever your age, regardless of how little acting experience you have, we believe you'll learn a great deal that will enhance your ability to go out on stage and wow an audience.

You've got the acting bug. Now make the most of it.

The Least You Need to Know

- ➤ Acting in a grade school play gives you a chance to discover new talents and to develop self-confidence.
- ➤ High school acting credits will impress college admissions officers.
- ➤ College theatrics enhance your college education and serve as a wonderful way to meet fellow students.
- ➤ Community theater productions not only bring a different kind of fulfillment, they also increase your local standing.

Chapter 2

Proud Parents

In This Chapter

- Discovering the joys of your child's first role in grade school
- Finding out why any part is a great part
- Understanding how much acting can do for a child
- Learning to share a child's triumph

This chapter is mostly for the lucky parents of the grade school children who get up on a stage for the first time at an early age. Some parents tend to worry about whether their child can really handle this kind of experience. Others may over-identify with the child and become upset that their kid isn't playing the most important role. And a few parents may wonder if performing in a play isn't a waste of time, a frivolous expenditure of effort in a world where academic competition seems to start in kindergarten. We'll try to set your mind at ease on all these questions.

In this chapter, we'll be discussing what being in a play means to a young child—and to the parents of that child. We'll explore the ways in which acting helps your child to find new confidence, and expands his or her sense of self. We'll give you guidelines for providing the best support possible for your child in this new experience. And we'll tell you some success stories that put the grade school play in proper perspective.

My Daughter Is the Angel Gabriel

The first stage experience for many kids involves a holiday pageant. Although Halloween and Christmas pageants are not as common as they used to be in public schools, Thanksgiving pageants remain a staple, as are Christmas pageants at many churches. Many public schools around the country also stage historical pageants that celebrate famous local or state events, or folk characters like Johnny Appleseed and Paul Bunyan. Such pageants are ideal theatrical events for young kids because they have many characters and call for plenty of extras, ensuring widespread participation. Even the awkward child who can't carry a tune can find a place on stage in such productions.

"She's Just Adorable"

Your daughter has been asked to play the Angel Gabriel. Or perhaps it's Pocahontas. Maybe it's the star hen of the barnyard. She's very excited. And, as a parent, you can't help getting caught up in the pleasures—and the occasional anxieties—of the experience along with her. She has a dozen lines to learn. It's not like the few short poems she's memorized, because now other characters will speak in between her lines. Can she remember them? She has a quiet little voice. Will she be able to be heard? Then she comes home and tells you about her costume, the wings she gets to wear as Gabriel, the beaded headdress for Pocahontas. As for that hen, well, she's got wings, too, of a slightly different kind.

When you see your child on stage, you will of course be astonished at how pretty or cute or funny she looks. Your heart will skip a beat when she pauses to remember a line. But she does a fine job, and afterward several other parents say, "She's just adorable." My word, you have an actor in the family.

Backstage Tales

Our friends Stan and Marie were a little taken aback when their daughter Sara was asked to play a hen in a fourth-grade play about life on a farm. Sara announced, "I'm going to lay eggs on stage." Her parents looked at one another and struggled to keep a straight face. They managed to say "How exciting," instead of "I hope not." Of course, all Sara had to do was to sit on some plastic eggs nestling in straw, but her cackle each time she laid an egg brought down the house. And when she finally presented a basket of eggs to the farmer, her face glowed with pride. A brilliant performance—a trifle hammy perhaps, but not as overdone as that oinking pig.

More Than a Pretty Face

Young children on stage are indeed adorable. Parental pride is completely justified. But something more important is happening in terms of the child's world. He or she takes on a new kind of responsibility—to learn lines, to get along with and cooperate with a group. The child who tends to hang back will learn how to be a little more assertive within the context of the play, and that can carry over into offstage behavior. Parents often see greater confidence in a child who has appeared in a grade school play. On the other side of the coin, a rambunctious kid who is always interrupting may develop some discipline. If the child doesn't wait for his or her turn to speak in the play, he or she understands that such behavior will ruin the whole thing. Afterward, the overly aggressive child may be better able to contain himself or herself for a change.

Performance Notes

Don't snap pictures or videotape the performance unless you have permission, and even then, do so with discretion. Flash pictures can distract the kids on stage (no adult theater will allow them), and a video camera can create sight-line problems for others in the audience. Take pictures after the performance.

In addition, although the child may not realize it at the time, he or she gets a glimpse of what it means to be an actor. Children absorb the lesson that being in a play involves work as well as fun. They learn what it means to take direction, to move across a stage when they are told to do so and in a way that the director finds effective. They'll learn what being involved in a group endeavor really means because they'll see that it takes a lot of people to make a production happen, people who hammer the sets together, people who work the lights, people who make costumes, and people who furnish props to use on stage. Those costumes and props have to be returned to where they belong after rehearsals, encouraging neatness. The performance itself enables them to experience the magic that occurs when everyone does his or her job in telling a story on stage. Finally, there is all that applause when they take their bows. Wow, they must have really done something right!

No, He's the Front End of the Horse

Joey played a horse in his fifth-grade play. Both his parents took the afternoon off to watch him perform. His great aunt Martha went along, too. "I don't see him," Martha whispered. Joey's father replied, "He's the horse. The front end of the horse. I'd know those hooves anywhere."

Parents need a sense of humor to attend school plays. Your kid may indeed be the front end of the horse, or even the rear end. Actually, the rear end may be the better part, since that kid will probably get a big laugh kicking his or her legs at some point. If they fall down while kicking their legs a little too exuberantly, the laugh will be even bigger.

Don't be embarrassed, no matter what happens, and never criticize a child for missing a line or doing something wrong. This is live theater, where things go wrong quite often, even on Broadway. No actor, no matter how celebrated, hasn't forgotten a few lines at some point, or let out a squawk instead of a musical note. There isn't an experienced actor, alive or dead, who hasn't had a doorknob come off in his or her hand, or suffered some equivalent disaster. So don't expect perfection of your kid. Just have a good time, and keep laughing.

You Gotta Start Somewhere

There's always a parent who is mortified that their adorable child is playing the rear end of the horse. Get over it. It's not you up there, and your kid is probably thrilled. There are also parents who are shamed or angered by the fact that their child didn't get the lead. Don't be. Every actor has to start someplace. Many a Tony or Oscar winner played a messenger with two lines at some point in his or her career. Even most "overnight sensations" have years of small roles or bad roles behind them.

Backstage Tales

The Oscar-winning champ, Katharine Hepburn, managed to get fired a couple of times in her early Broadway career; in the late 1930s, she was dubbed "box-office poison," even though she'd already won her first Oscar for *Morning Glory*. Julie Andrews had been performing professionally in music halls since the age of six, and had already played a lead on Broadway in *The Boy Friend,* before she finally became an "overnight sensation" with *My Fair Lady* in 1957. She didn't even win the Tony for that legendary performance, losing to Judy Holliday in *Bells Are Ringing*. Then the role of Eliza Doolittle went to Audrey Hepburn in the movie. Of course, Andrews trumped the studio bosses by winning the Oscar for *Mary Poppins* that same year.

Some kids, it is true, will be unhappy that they didn't get the lead in their school play. In such cases, they often have an already-existing rivalry with the child who did get the part. If your kid is really interested in acting, that's going to happen a lot over the years. But keep in mind, and tell your kid, that the day will come when the girl or boy who got the lead this time will lose out to your child. You win some, you lose some. That's one of the realities of being an actor, and it's never too soon to learn it.

The fact that it's also a reality of life in general means that the lesson has much broader significance. The child who learns this lesson in the fifth grade isn't going to be scarred for life, but rather ahead of the game in the years to come.

"It's Better Than Halloween"

Most kids will love being in a school play no matter what the size of their part. The costumes have a lot to do with that. It's amazing what can be done with very little, for modest expense. Remember that silver-painted cardboard armor that co-author John Malone wore as Miles Standish? It was made from shirt cardboard by an art teacher. Whether it's cardboard armor, a wig made from yellow yarn, a horse costume fashioned from burlap bags and a cheap mask, or angel wings constructed from chicken wire and tulle remnants, the kids are going to be thrilled. As many children have exclaimed over the years, "It's better than Halloween."

Places, Everyone!

Keep those mementos! Every actor, professional or amateur, has strong memories of the first time he or she ever appeared on stage, no matter how young. As a parent, be sure to save a program if there is one, or any photographs of your child in costume. They'll come to be greatly treasured by your grown child.

If you're a parent known to have sewing or artistic talent, you may well be asked to help make costumes for a school play, perhaps for your own child, or perhaps for another kid. Can Dad or Mom slap together some lightweight wooden swords in his or her workshop? Can he or she bead a headdress for Sacajawea, the Shoshone woman who guided Lewis and Clark? If you have any time to spare at all, you'll find that undertaking such tasks will be enormously rewarding. Fifth-grade actors haven't yet learned to complain about their costumes, although if they continue to act they most certainly will. At that age, they'll be filled with delight and be extremely grateful.

She's Always Been So Shy

As we've mentioned before, teachers will sometimes decide that a part in a school play is exactly what a shy child needs in order to break out of his or her shell, and they're often right. Although the general public tends to assume that actors are extroverts, and were always show-offs to some extent, that's often not the case. Certainly, some "class clowns" end up as actors, but even they often admit that they behaved the way they did in order to compensate for some deficiency they felt they had. Kids who are more shy don't have that outlet, but need for someone or something—like a play—to draw them out. Teachers who direct school plays are generally among the best teachers at any given school, with excellent intuition about what a child can and can't do at any given time. They're not going to expose a shy child to too much pressure by assigning a lead role. But sometimes the shy child may be anxious even about playing one of six angels who sing in chorus.

"You Don't Have to Do This"

If you have a shy son or daughter who's been asked to play a part in a school play, and the child is nervous or reluctant, don't insist that he or she do it. We've known many actors who found themselves in this situation as children, as well as parents whose kids have been anxious about performing. Their testimony suggests that the best approach is to start by telling children that they do not have to be in the play. That relieves a great deal of pressure. With the immediate sense of threat lifted, you can then explore reasons why children might want to do it after all. Because you've already assured them that the choice to perform or not is theirs to make, they'll be more likely to hear good reasons to go ahead and make their stage debuts. Before we suggest some reasons you can give a child for being in the play, let's dispense with the one reason that is least likely to work: "It'll be good for you." Stay away from that altogether. Children—and adult actors, if truth be told—hate being told that something is good for them. Professional actors often start looking for the exit when their agents tell them that a role they dislike will be good for their careers. The child who feels he or she is being shoved on stage is going to react the same way.

Backstage Tales

Famed Hollywood director John Huston persuaded his teenage daughter Angelica to star in his 1969 film *A Walk with Love and Death*, set in medieval France. The film was a flop, and Angelica got dreadful reviews. She didn't return to the screen for seven years, although she went on to win the Best Supporting Actress Oscar for 1985's *Prizzi's Honor*, also directed by her father. He had been right about her talent, but had pushed her too fast to start with—and didn't provide her with a good vehicle, to boot!

Trying to push actors or children on stage doesn't work. They have to decide for themselves that it might work out okay. Not great, necessarily, but at least okay. Does the child have a good friend who is going to be in the show? It might be fun to do it together. Is the child going to get to wear a special costume? That could be a treat. Does the child sing a lot around the house? Here's a chance to do it with a lot of other kids. You could also volunteer your services to help with the show. That way you'll be around some of the time, and the child might feel more secure.

But if your child still doesn't want to do it, let it go. You may even find it necessary to tell a teacher to back off if your child really doesn't want to be in a play—some teachers don't know how to take no for an answer. When the performance takes place, however, your son or daughter may begin to wish he or she was up on stage, and will be more interested the next time around. The acting bug can develop unexpectedly just from watching other people onstage, especially people you know.

Watching a Child Blossom

Many people who eventually become splendid actors don't show any interest in it until much later in life. For every Haley Joel Osment, the extraordinary young star of *The Sixth Sense* and Steven Spielberg's *A.I.*, there's a James Garner, who stumbled into acting in his 20s. The same was true of Paul Newman, who has said he took up acting to "get out of the hardware business," his father's profession. Janet Leigh, although she was signed by MGM at the age of 19, had no thought of becoming an actress before that. An agent saw a photograph of her at her father's ski lodge, and sent a copy to the former MGM star Norma Shearer.

But parents of kids who get interested in acting at a young age are in for some very special moments. While pride in any child's achievements, whether academic or on the playing field, can bring great pleasure, a curious magic occurs when a child gets up on a stage and plays a role. While you may have watched a son who becomes a high school football star throwing the ball in the backyard for years, and are well aware of how hard a daughter studies to make all those A's, a child who gets up on a stage becomes transformed. Yes, you knew that Jenny had a lovely singing voice and that Jason could be very funny. But when they appear as a character in a story, performing a role that is even a little different from themselves, it can come as a considerable revelation. You get to watch your child blossom in an entirely new way.

Places, Everyone!

If your child is in a school play, do everything you can to arrange to take an afternoon off to see it. Countless parents have later lamented the fact that they were too busy to see a child in a school production. And the child whose parents aren't there never forgets it. We've heard a great many actors voice their lingering disappointment, and often resentment, about missing parents at such occasions.

A boy we'll call Rick was the tallest kid in the fifth grade by nearly a foot. The day would come when he would feel good about being a very tall man. But at that age, he felt self-conscious about it, and tended to walk with a stoop, as though trying to make himself shorter and more like everyone else. His parents were always telling him to straighten up, to little avail. But then he was cast in a school play. The play was based on the story of Jack and the Beanstalk, and, of course, Rick got to play the Giant.

Rick became more and more excited about the play, and when his parents saw him on stage, they were astonished. He was standing completely straight. In fact, he seemed to be trying to appear even taller than he was. "Fee, fie, fo, fum," he called out in his biggest voice. And when Jack brought him tumbling to earth, he fell with such abandon that his parents were worried he'd hurt himself. But he hadn't. The gym teacher had helped him work out a spectacular yet perfectly safe fall. And after playing the Giant, Rick didn't stoop anymore. Even though he had been playing the villain, he'd discovered the value of his height.

They Actually Did It!

Many parents go to grade school plays with their hearts in their mouths. It could be said that this is silly because it's just a grade school play, after all. But that's not our view of the situation. A grade school play is of great importance to the kids who are in it. The experience can turn a child into an actor for life—not necessarily a person who's going to make a career of acting, but someone who is going to take pleasure in performing from then on. That's a major development in an individual's life, and it needs to be regarded with proper respect.

Performance Notes

Don't try to stop your child once the acting bug has bitten him or her. People who love to act—even children—find it satisfying in ways too profound to be thwarted. It's not just something they can do—often it's something they must do to be happy.

The parent who attends a grade school performance is naturally going to be a little nervous, simply out of empathy for his or her child. But it's our experience—and the stories told by a great many actors bear this out—that it's not their children these parents are anxious about, but how their child's performance reflects on them. Such parents tend to worry about whether the child is going to embarrass them, rather than how the child will feel if things don't go right. That's unfortunate. The school play is about the child, not the parent. The child who has such parents will usually understand what's really going on, which adds insult to injury. But while this kind of situation is sad, it will also serve as a lesson to the child. Parents who are chiefly worried about themselves and their own reputations are going to be a problem throughout the young actor's life, right on into adulthood. They are the kind of parents who are going to be upset when their son or daughter plays a nasty character. They're going to be distraught when their son or daughter is cast in a controversial play in college. If the child becomes a professional actor, a truce of sorts will eventually be reached, in most cases, but even movie stars tell stories about their parents' discomfort.

You can spot this kind of parent at any grade school play. Don't be one of them. So what if your son is the murderous giant, or your daughter the evil witch? Almost any actor will tell you that evil characters are the most fun to play, and often require the greatest acting ability. Be glad your kid can bring it off. Only fools confuse the character someone plays on stage with the person who's playing it. Relax and enjoy the wicked glint in your kid's eye. We've all got that in us; it's part of being human. And the kid who can act that kind of role has got his or her dark side well under control. That's one of the reasons plays are written, and people flock to see them—the theater enables us to deal with the dark side of being human in a safe context.

When you go to see your child in a grade school play, don't look for flaws in the performances of the children on stage, including your own. It's not going to be perfect. Instead, open up to how much they've accomplished, how amazingly good the kids are after all. They've actually done it!

Congratulations All Round

Let's say your child is just terrific in the play, and you're very proud. You rush backstage to tell your child how wonderful he or she was. But once you've done that, remember that there were a lot of other people, both kids and adults, involved in making the show a success. Make sure you congratulate any other kids standing around. Even if they forgot a line or messed up somehow, muster the generosity to say, "Good job." Some kids may not have parents in attendance. They particularly need some kind words.

Places, Everyone!

Don't take flowers or presents to give your kid after a grade school show. If you want to give them something, save it for later. There will be other kids who aren't getting a gift, whose parents may not even be there. Don't make them feel even more left out, or make your own kid feel uncomfortable receiving a present when other kids aren't getting them.

After you've congratulated your own child, and any others hanging around, make a point of telling the teacher who directed the show how much you enjoyed it. That teacher has worked extremely hard, exercised endless patience, and no doubt wondered at times why in the world he or she took on this difficult task. Give that teacher the kind word that he or she so greatly deserves.

A grade school play should be an occasion for joy. Everyone worked so hard. Everyone did such a great job. It was a group effort and they pulled it off. Good for them!

The Least You Need to Know

- A grade school play is an opportunity for a kid to discover new talents and new confidence.
- The size of the role isn't as important as the fact that a child was given a chance to try something new.
- Children learn a lot about themselves performing in a grade school play, blossoming in unexpected ways.
- Everyone deserves congratulations for a job well done.

Chapter 3

A High School Schedule

In This Chapter

- Learning how to juggle homework and play rehearsals
- Finding out ways your family can help you to develop a role
- Understanding the need to plan ahead in terms of scheduling
- Recognizing how much being in a play can add to your school record

Some kids who started acting in grade school keep right at it when they reach high school, while many others may get involved for the first time in ninth or tenth grade. In grade school, teachers usually select the children who appear in plays, but at the high school level, kids usually have to face auditions. If you're a high school student, that means you have to get out there and show them what you've got! In this chapter, we'll examine how you can fit acting in a play into your busy schedule, and detail the responsibilities involved. You'll find out about ways your family can help you learn your lines and perfect your performance. We'll be emphasizing the need to make sure no conflicts with other activities arise. And we'll discuss the importance that acting can have in respect to college admissions.

Homework and Rehearsals

You may have noticed that you have a lot more homework in high school than in grade school or junior high, and your teachers aren't going to let you slack off just because you have the lead in the school play. In fact, if your grades fall below a certain level, you may not be allowed to take a role in a play. Maintaining a certain level of academic achievement has been increasingly linked to participation in varsity sports in recent years, and the same rules apply to other extracurricular activities as well.

Learning to Use Your Time

Most high schools put on only one or two plays a year. One may be a musical, the other a classic comedy or perhaps one of Shakespeare's most popular works, like *Romeo and Juliet* or *Julius Caesar.* These two plays are the most commonly studied in high school English classes, so playing a part in one of them can increase your understanding of the play and help you ace your exams.

Places, Everyone!

Try to take advantage of any play you're in when it comes to writing papers for various classes. If you're in *Julius Caesar*, for example, you might write a paper on it not only for English class, but also for a history or social studies class by doing a bit more research. Even a comedy like *You Can't Take It With You* gives you an opportunity to write about the 1930s background of the play. And a musical like *Bye, Bye, Birdie* offers insights into 1950s society.

Furthermore, you'll find that you'll spend a lot of rehearsal time just waiting around, so instead of just goofing off, you could get some homework done. If you can't concentrate in the rehearsal hall, try to find a place in a nearby classroom or office. Just make sure the director, stage manager, or an assistant knows where you are, so they don't need to launch a search party when you're needed on stage.

Even though you should be able to get some homework done at rehearsals, you're probably going to need to rearrange your life a little in order to keep your academic work on track. That may mean watching less television, playing fewer video games, or spending less time surfing the Net. Obviously, the bigger your role, the greater the time you're going to have to carve out of your usual schedule. Keep in mind that you're not cutting down on free time just to get homework done—you're doing it because you're in a play, an experience that will bring a lot of fun and rewards in itself.

A Responsible Kid

Acting is a great deal of fun, the rehearsals as well as actual performances. But it's not just fun. It involves hard work. Nobody should accept a part in a play thinking it's just a matter of fooling around on stage. If you're not going to take acting seriously, then you shouldn't be doing it. There's often some guy (and it's usually a boy) in the cast of a high school play who's always telling jokes offstage and breaking up onstage. Everything's a joke to him. But soon enough he'll discover that he's getting dirty looks from his fellow cast members. His lack of responsibility is slowing things down for everyone else. He doesn't know his lines, keeps forgetting his blocking, and pulls a Jim Carrey face every time he makes a mistake. This gets old, fast.

Backstage Tales

Professional actors sometimes start laughing when they make a mistake, too, of course, because rehearsal mistakes can be funny. When co-author Paul Baldwin played Sweeny Todd, he once sang the lines, "Pretty women, standing on the stair ... combing out their hair," as "Pretty women, standing on their hair .... " He didn't even realize he'd done it, but everyone else started laughing, quite naturally. Jim Carrey and Robin Williams are famous for trying to break up their fellow actors on purpose, but you can be sure they also know how and when to get down to business, or other actors would be complaining. And nobody gets paid millions of dollars to hold up production by being cute.

Plenty of moments during the rehearsal of a play bring natural laughter. Wry comments that get a laugh are perfectly okay if things have come to a stop anyway. But trying to get a laugh when real work is being done is out of line. Never try to "stop the show," either in rehearsal or performance, by being funny out of context. The laugh you may get will cost you in terms of popularity in the end. Acting is serious business, even in a comedy, and actors have to be responsible people.

The first responsibility of the actor is to learn his or her lines, the sooner or better. Even beginning actors understand the necessity of that. But beginners sometimes don't recognize how important it is to follow instructions about *blocking*.

You have to learn blocking as thoroughly as your lines, so that it becomes second nature. Otherwise, you'll be colliding with others, and the stage picture will look chaotic to those in the audience. Directors often change blocking as rehearsals continue, so be prepared to accept and learn new instructions.

Several responsibilities are required of actors in any play, even at the high school level. These include the following:

- Being on time for rehearsals
- Learning your lines as soon as possible

Stage Directions

Blocking is the term used to describe stage movements. It's the job of the director, not the actor, to decide how, where, and when you should move onstage. Once the director has made a decision, it will be your responsibility to repeat that piece of blocking at every rehearsal. We'll be going into detail about this subject in Chapter 18, "The Early Stages."

- Learning your blocking
- Paying close attention to anything the director says
- Never holding up rehearsals by playing the clown

Mom, Will You Run Lines for Me?

Depending on the educational approach used in your school system, you may or may not have had to memorize poems in grade school. If you have done a fair amount of that, you'll have a head start when it comes to learning your part, although some people find it trickier to remember lines that are broken up by other character's speeches. While some people have the kind of memory that makes learning lines a snap, others have to spend more time and work at it harder. It's a process that gets easier with practice.

Part of Your Kid's Life

High school kids often look to their parents or brothers and sisters to help them learn lines. While it's certainly something you can do by yourself, simply by studying the sentences and then looking away from the script and repeating them, you might find it easier if someone else reads the lines of other characters. This is particularly useful when it comes to learning the *cue lines* delivered by other characters.

Stage Directions

A **cue line** is the sentence spoken by one character immediately before another character replies or before the second character comes on stage, even if that second character doesn't say anything right away. You have to know cue lines as well as you do your own, because they are the signals that it is time for you to speak or make an entrance.

Let's address the parents of high school actors for a moment. (If you're the high school actor, show your parents the following few paragraphs.) Parents lead very busy lives themselves, but helping a son or daughter learn their lines for a play can be very rewarding in terms of family relationships. You may well throw up your hands when it comes to helping with math or chemistry homework, but running lines with your kid doesn't require expertise or futile attempts to recall what you were taught all too long ago. All you have to do is speak the lines of other characters, and correct any mistakes your kid is making in reciting his or her own lines.

There's more than one approach you can take to deal with any mistakes your kid makes with his or her lines. If your kid has forgotten the first line of a speech, or leaves out an entire sentence in the middle of a speech, it's obviously necessary to give him or her the line that's been left out immediately. But if he or she is getting the lines mostly correct, with just a missing or incorrect word here and there, it's often best to let the young actor complete the speech before pointing out the mistakes. Go over the mistakes, let your kid repeat the correct word or phrase a couple of times, and then start over from the beginning of the speech.

It's important for you to recognize that learning lines takes time. Don't get impatient. There will be a lot of mistakes at the beginning, and even much later on your kid will probably get something wrong that he or she hasn't messed up for several days. Don't overreact when that occurs. It happens to every actor, including very experienced professionals. Your kid may want you always to wait until he or she has completed a speech before noting any mistakes. Some kids may want you to interrupt more often. Go with his or her instructions. Learning lines is a very individual, even quirky, process. There are no hard-and-fast rules, so don't try to pressure the young actor to do it the way you would. That may not work for your son or daughter. The right way is the way that works, even if it seems peculiar.

Shared Success

These days parents often bemoan the fact that they don't get to spend more time with their kids, and teenagers of course can sometimes be difficult to corral for long. Working on the memorization of lines for a play with a son or daughter is a particularly effective way of getting closer because it involves a specific goal, and the achievement of that goal will be visible to all when the play or musical is performed.

Backstage Tales

A high school senior we know, Cathy, played the lead in her school's spring production of the musical *Little Shop of Horrors.* Not only her parents, but also her two younger brothers got involved in helping her learn the role of Audrey. Her mother was proficient at the piano, which made it possible to do a lot of extra work on her songs. Her younger brothers, neither yet in their teens, delighted in growling the part of Mushnik, the man-eating plant. The show was a great success, especially for Cathy, and her whole family was there to share in the excitement, feeling very much a part of the triumph.

When's the Track Meet?

As we noted earlier, being in a high school play may mean cutting back on your other activities for a while, especially free time devoted to sheer entertainment. But some other activities play a more important part in your life that you will have to take into account as well. This is sometimes a "you can't do everything" problem. Amazingly, though, it often ends up being a "you can't be in two places at the same time" problem. This just shouldn't happen if you think and plan ahead.

Say you're on the track team, one of its best runners. You've also accepted the part of Bernardo, Maria's brother in the musical *West Side Story*. This is not a minor role—George Chakiris won the Best Supporting Actor Oscar for it. You're going to have track competitions with other schools every Saturday during the spring, sometimes traveling out of town for them. But that's okay, you think; the two performances of the musical will be at night. Then you discover that the first complete run-through of the show is scheduled on a Saturday afternoon. You can't be in two places at once, can you?

What should you do in a case like this? Let's start with the worst possible thing you can do: avoid facing the problem and just skipping the run-through. You don't tell the director you're not going to be there, you just don't show up. You're supposed to be at the school auditorium at one o'clock.

When you don't show, the director will ask other cast members if they know where you are. A couple may know, and others may have a good idea, but they don't want to rat on you, so they shake their heads. So you've managed to put your friends in the position of having to lie for you—nice guy, aren't you?

Places, Everyone!

Make sure you have the time to meet the responsibilities of the show. It's not just athletic events that create scheduling problems. Many high schools have debating teams, for example, or other activities that can take up lots of free time. And keep in mind that although your activities don't conflict at the beginning of the year, events may crop up—like state finals or other tournaments—that create scheduling problems down the line.

It gets worse. Frantic telephone calls reveal the truth. The director is furious. Usually high school plays have no understudies, but if someone else does in fact know Bernardo's part, you're probably going to be out on your ear. Fired. Great going. You may luck out, of course. You may be very good in the role, and nobody else can really step in. That means that this first complete run-through of the play, when everything's supposed to start falling into place, is going to be something of a waste. It will begin late because of the need to search for you. And with someone, probably the stage manager, reading your lines for you, the scenes you're in aren't going to go very well. You will have succeeded in sabotaging the afternoon's work for a lot of other people as well.

When you accept a role in a play, you're accepting a responsibility. If you fail to live up to that responsibility you're going to let a lot of other people down. Teachers, administrators, and fellow students are all going to be angry. Your parents will certainly be informed, and they'll probably read you the riot act. So, plan ahead when you're offered a role in a play. Sit down with a calendar in front of you and some scratch paper and take a hard look at the whole picture.

Are there any existing conflicts, dates that already place overlapping requirements on your time? It may be possible to work those out, but you need to do it right away, not weeks down the line. Are there potential conflicts that might or might not crop up in the future? When do the dates for the state debating championship, or track championship, take place (should you be successful enough to reach them)? If there's any possibility of a problem, bring it up with the director of the play. He or she may decide to take a chance on you anyway, and if the conflict does materialize, will have had time to plan for it.

Coach vs. Drama Teacher

There is, and probably always will be, a built-in conflict between drama teachers and athletic coaches. It's oil and water all the way. Some coaches feel that acting is a sissy waste of time, and some drama teachers feel that sports have eclipsed educational endeavors. Especially with respect to the more ordinary athlete (one who's not likely to earn an athletic scholarship), the drama teacher will assert that acting in the school play can not only help him or her get into a better college, but will also help develop the kind of poise that corporate recruiters look for. The athletic coach will reply that sports instill courage and loyalty as well as developing the kind of assertiveness necessary in a very competitive society.

Performance Notes

The high school actor, male or female, who is also on a varsity sports team needs to think carefully about the terms he or she uses when approaching a coach about a scheduling conflict. To put this in the broadest possible terms, don't talk about exploring your artistic side, but about how much you're being counted on to pull your weight and help make it a good show. Use the coach's lingo, not the drama teacher's.

Both the coach and the drama teacher are correct about the value of the experience they're touting, up to a point, and it's a shame that they so often fail to recognize that fact. There's no question that team sports provide valuable character grounding. Nor is there any doubt that being in a school play helps develop presentational skills that are also valued by society. And both endeavors emphasize the need to be a "team player." But when it comes to how an individual student is going to invest his or her time, the coach and the drama teacher are likely to go to the mat over the issue.

The coach will usually win. More people go to high school football games than to the school play. But that doesn't mean you can't work out compromises. The quarterback of the football team is not going to be available for the title role in the musical *Li'l Abner* if the show is put on in the fall. In the spring, it could be a different matter. But even in the fall, the bench-warming defensive back who only gets to play every other

Places, Everyone!

If you're at all interested in acting, it's a smart move to audition for high school plays your first or second year. By doing so, you'll not only have more time to enjoy your new activity, but you'll give the director ideas about casting you in favorite roles in future years. When you know that kind of role is coming your way, it can make it much easier to decide how to settle conflicts with other activities.

game might be allowed to be absent from the team for a Saturday or two of final rehearsals. The same applies to members of the girls' basketball or field-hockey teams. Some players can't be excused; others can.

The most important thing for the high school actor to remember, however, is that any scheduling conflicts need to be worked out before you accept a role. Talk about the problem to the teacher who's directing the play. You're likely to be told that you have to talk to the coach, but may also get some good advice on how to approach him or her—the director has been through this before. Then talk to the coach. Both conversations may be difficult, and you may end up having to do one or the other. But being forced to make such a choice will tell you something about yourself and what matters most to you. You'll learn things, even if it does seem like you have to learn them the hard way. What's more, it's not nearly as bad a situation as ending up with everyone mad at you—director, coach, cast members, and team members—when schedules conflict down the line.

The Well-Rounded Student

By participating in both theater and sports, you'll have a chance to become what is known as the "well-rounded student." The phrase itself has been used so often that it's a cliché, of course, but it's one of those clichés that retain a great deal of clout. There's no question that colleges look for well-rounded students.

They want star athletes, too, and they want academically-oriented geniuses who will be in the top 10 in their class. But there are only so many of those to go around. The next best thing is the well-rounded student who has a number of talents and interests. If you play a part in a high school play, it's always a plus with college admissions officers. Your grades are solid, you played a varsity sport, and you're regarded as a good citizen. Very commendable. But there are a great many students whose records are almost identical. Is there anything that sets you apart? Of course, a number of different activities can serve that purpose, from being on the yearbook committee to heading the annual charity drive. But being in a school play is one of the better credits among the extra-curricular activities that separate you out from thousands of other candidates for admission to a particular college.

Lead roles will help most, so you should note any you've played on your application. But for the good student who doesn't have much else in the way of additional credits to boast about, even a small role or chorus part can make a difference. The fact that you appeared in a play suggests that you aren't just a bookworm. Being in a play means you're comfortable working in large groups of fellow students. You have to have some talents beyond being good at taking tests. It's a credit that will at least get you into the "maybe" pile, and may in the end make the ultimate difference that shifts you to the "yes" pile.

There are young people who try out for school plays exactly because they know it will look good on their college admission forms. The authors have both known people who got involved in acting for that very reason. There's often a surprise lying in wait for such students, however. Once they've gone through the experience of rehearsing and performing one play, they want to do it again as soon as possible. They've fallen in love with the theater. They've been bitten by the acting bug.

The Least You Need to Know

- Acting in a high school play is a serious responsibility that you must meet in grown-up ways.
- Helping the budding young actor in your family to learn his or her lines can be an enriching experience for everyone involved.
- Recognize all possible scheduling conflicts before rehearsals begin—and discuss them with your director.
- Acting and sports can co-exist and may well provide a winning combination in terms of college admission.

Chapter 4

College Triumphs

In This Chapter

- Discovering how acting can enrich your college years
- Learning how to make your mark on campus
- Exploring the future benefits of acting experience
- Recognizing the sheer joy that college acting can bring

Because so many productions of plays are mounted every year on most college campuses, you'll have many more opportunities to act in a variety of roles as a college student than you did in high school. What's more, the audience for college theater is more sophisticated, and even experimental plays can draw a considerable crowd. Works that would be considered too controversial to stage at a high school—from bloody Jacobean revenge dramas to foreign plays like Albert Camus' *Caligula*—regularly find a place on college campuses. And while there will be productions of popular musicals like Cole Porter's *Kiss Me Kate* or the operettas of Gilbert and Sullivan, daring works like Stephen Sondheim's *Assassins* are likely to turn up, too.

In this chapter, we'll be introducing you to the rich panoply of acting experiences available on a college campus. We'll explore the ways in which college acting can not only enhance your education but also provide practical benefits in terms of your on-campus and future life experiences. Throughout the chapter, we'll be celebrating the unique opportunities for self-realization that college theatrics present.

Extracurricular Strengths

Even students from very large high schools or top prep schools can feel a bit lost on a major college campus. In high school, you grew up with many of your classmates, but now you may know very few people and are essentially starting over in terms of making friends. You'll make some friends in your dormitory, but the lottery aspect of dormitory assignment means that you might not have a lot in common with your roommates. The big lecture courses you're likely to be taking as a freshman aren't conducive to getting to know people, either. That's why many of the most important friendships students form at college are with people they meet pursuing extracurricular interests, whether sports, the college newspaper, or drama productions.

Most colleges have a Drama Society or Dramatic Club that produces several plays a year. They're always looking for new talent, and few create any roadblocks to membership—you don't have to be chosen or go through an initiation rite. (There may be clubs on campus, like Harvard's famous Hasty Pudding, that are run more like fraternities and sororities, but they tend to put on only original shows or a yearly musical.) With most college drama groups, all you have to do is show up at a meeting, and auditions are usually open to anyone, whether they belong to the drama club or not. They'll be glad to see not only actors but also technical support people of all kinds, whether you're interested in set design construction or lighting design, or merely think it would be fun to get your feet wet by doing props for a show. It's common at colleges for students to act in one show, serve as stage manager for another, and do some other backstage job whenever the need arises.

Places, Everyone!

Keep your eye out for audition notices. In addition to productions mounted by the dramatic club, other groups may produce single plays. If you see a notice in the college paper or a flyer on a bulletin board, and the play interests you, put in an appearance at the appointed times to audition.

For many students, the main reason they appear in college stage productions is because they love to act. They acted in high school, perhaps even in grade school, and being on stage gives them a great deal of pleasure and satisfaction. Others get interested in acting for the first time at college, and discover how exciting and challenging an endeavor it can be. There are also some who decide to try their hand at acting for more practical reasons.

When co-author John Malone was at Harvard, one cast member of a production of Shakespeare's *Troilus and Cressida* admitted that he'd auditioned because he was applying for a Rhodes Scholarship to do graduate work at England's Oxford University. His adviser had told him that although he had a fine academic record and was on the varsity wrestling team, he'd be wise to find another kind of extracurricular activity that would give him a better-rounded profile. So there he was playing Shakespeare, and doing it well. He got the Rhodes Scholarship.

In fact, even those who act just because they love it recognize that there are bonuses for the college actor that go beyond the pleasure of giving a good performance to enthusiastic audiences.

Educational Enrichment

The dramatic literature of the world is a vast repository of fascinating stories and profound insights into the human condition that contains some of the greatest prose and poetry ever written. The surviving works of the Greek tragedians, Aeschylus, Sophocles, and Euripides move and terrify us still, even though they were written more than 2,400 years ago. Aristophanes's comic plays of the same period still make audiences roar with laughter, and his masterpiece about the war between the sexes, *Lysistrata*, can seem as pertinent as ever.

Shakespeare's language and characters are so much a part of Western culture that we sometimes make reference to them without even realizing we're doing it. France has produced some of the greatest playwrights, from Molière's seventeenth-century comedies right down to the present-day works of Yasmina Reza, whose *Art* won the 1999 Tony Award for Best Play. On college campuses, you will find productions of plays from every period, translated from many languages, with such varied fare as Ben Jonson's *The Alchemist* of 1610, Henrik Ibsen's *Peer Gynt* of 1867, and Tennessee Williams's *The Glass Menagerie* of 1945 staged within a single year, sometimes a single term.

Backstage Tales

A young actress we know had quite a year for herself at college in the early 1990s. She played three very different starring roles that many professionals spend half their lives hoping to play: Sally Bowles in John Van Druten's *I Am a Camera,* Rosalind in Shakespeare's *As You Like It,* and Hilda Wangel in Henrik Ibsen's *The Master Builder*. These kinds of opportunities exist at colleges all over the country. Even to play secondary roles in such a range of dramas would be a thrill to most actors.

Reading great plays provides a more intense experience than most novels can provide, and seeing them is even better. And acting in them brings still greater understanding of their meaning and importance. Whether it's a Shakespearean tragedy or a Feydeau farce, the inner workings of a great play become much clearer when you act in it. What you learn, of course, enhances your understanding of other works of literature. Many college actors have found that, despite the time given over to appearing in a play, their grades in literature and even history courses can improve because of the knowledge they've acquired while rehearsing and performing a classic work.

Performance Notes

Don't forget to study—it'll help you to better understand your roles! You've been cast in a college production of the Broadway musical *1776*, playing John Rutledge, who sings the show-stopper "Molasses to Rum." It's a terrific song, but to do it justice you need to understand the historical background of the American slave trade. While this is a popular musical with a generally light-hearted approach to the American Revolution, you're going to learn a lot of history in the process of rehearsing and performing it.

"We're Upping the Scholarship"

You don't get paid anything to appear in a college play, of course, but you might find other kinds of financial rewards. Students on scholarship who keep their grades high and also become known on campus as fine actors who shine in production after production sometimes find that their scholarship stipends are increased in the course of their college careers. The records of all scholarship students are automatically reviewed at the conclusion of each year, and other achievements are also taken into consideration. Your participation in dramatic productions makes you a more significant contributor to the overall life of the college, and that occasionally can help to raise the level of financial assistance the institution is willing to give you.

Making Your Mark on Campus

There will be students on any campus who never attend stage performances. They have other interests. But even they are likely to know who you are if you appear in a number of plays during your own college career, just as students who never attend a hockey game still may recognize the high scorer and the goalie. A college campus is a microcosm of the larger world we live in, where achievers in any field get to be generally known.

"Hey, I'm on the Front Page"

Major dramatic productions quite often get a front-page photo in the college newspaper when they open, to illustrate the review that's published. That photo is likely to be one of a big scene in which many members of the cast are on stage. But there you are, and your name will probably be listed below the photo. This is obviously a candidate for the scrapbook, something to show your kids many years later. What's more, if you've got the title role, you may get a photo of you alone plastered on that front page. That can even happen during the auditions. The director has a friend or roommate who's a photographer for the college paper, and wants some advanced publicity for the actor he or she's chosen to play Richard III or Hedda Gabler. And there you are again, your face dramatically lighted from below. Students you don't even know are suddenly saying hello on the way to class.

Places, Everyone!

Hang in there if you get bad reviews, especially if you're in a lot of shows! The students who write reviews for college papers all think they're going to be the chief critic for *The New York Times* someday, and they need to practice their cutting remarks. That's fine, though, because it helps prepare you for the "real" world you'll soon graduate into.

Prizes to Be Won

Colleges that have a drama department often have an awards ceremony at the end of each year. These are mini-versions of the Tony Awards or the Academy Awards, although the atmosphere is far more informal, the dress fairly casual, and the awards themselves far less spiffy and expensive to produce than a Tony or an Oscar.

But like these nationally televised awards shows, there will be nominees in lead and supporting male and female actor categories, as well as directorial and technical awards. There might be an ensemble award as well, which neither the Tonys nor the Oscars have, but which are particularly appropriate at the college level, since almost everyone plays both leads and smaller roles on occasion.

Since the auditions for college shows are usually open to everyone, whether they are going for a drama degree or not, a lot of students get a chance to win one of these awards. It's a festive occasion, with less riding on the outcome than for professional actors.

Not all colleges have drama departments or this kind of awards ceremony, of course. They may produce many plays each year, but not under a college department umbrella. But they may well have an overall college award for "Contributions to College Drama," or some such title, endowed by a graduate of the college. Such awards may go to an actor one year and to a director the next, and may be given out at a general awards ceremony or commencement exercise. This kind of award can be even more prestigious—and difficult to get—than a drama department award, because it is administrated by a faculty board rather than by other students.

Backstage Tales

Co-author Paul Baldwin was an art major at North Texas State University, but appeared in numerous plays, and was nominated for Best Supporting Actor for his performance as Tulsa in *Gypsy* his second year. He has fond memories of the occasion, since a number of couples decided to dress up as Hollywood stars. One couple came as Rex Harrison and Audrey Hepburn in *My Fair Lady*, looking extremely elegant, as most couples did. But Paul and Toogie Caddell, a Supporting Actress nominee, lowered the elegance quotient by showing up as Fred Astaire and Judy Garland in their tramp outfits for the "We're a Couple of Swells" number from Easter Parade. Oh, yes, Toogie won her award. Paul didn't. They're still great friends 30 years later.

Nice as awards are, most students who act in college plays are more than content simply to have had the chance to perform in so many great plays. Each year a handful of students will graduate from college and embark on a professional acting career. A few will be successful—not always the ones most people expect to make it. Forging a career as a professional actor requires a different kind of ability than starring in college productions, as we'll be discussing in the final four chapters of this book.

Gaining Poise for the Future

Those who do a great deal of acting in college and are much admired for their talent, yet decide not to pursue a professional career, sometimes puzzle their friends. "You're so good," friends will say. "Why don't you at least give it a try?" The answer is often, "Because I don't want to do that with my life," which is not very satisfying to the questioner even though completely sincere. Co-author John Malone loved acting, but he wanted even more to write. An enormously talented friend of his also loved acting, but she wanted to be a lawyer; she started out as a prosecutor, subsequently became a defense lawyer, and ended up a judge. "I've spent a lot of my life giving performances," she says with a smile. "The courtroom is very much a stage." Her greatest success at college, appropriately enough, had been as Portia in *The Merchant of Venice*.

In fact, many professions require that people give performances. That aspect may not be as obvious as it is with a trial lawyer, but the ability to stand in front of groups of people and sway their emotions and opinions can be crucial in numerous professions, from advertising and press relations to corporate boardrooms. Acting in college plays can prepare you for challenges that have nothing, on the surface, to do with theater.

Impressive in Public

A few people are born with the natural instincts that enable a person to be impressive in public. Some clergymen and politicians seem always to have been able to dominate a crowd with little effort. But the most famous religious speaker of twentieth-century America, Billy Graham, reveals in his autobiography how painful his first attempts at delivering a sermon were. He had to learn from scratch how to hold an audience. President Theodore Roosevelt, who coined the term "bully pulpit" to describe the leadership possibilities of the presidency, was a spindly, asthmatic child who remade himself in his early twenties, and became a spellbinding presence.

The child who is a "natural" on stage or in front of the camera all too often loses the ability to command an audience when he or she grows older. Many of the most famous child stars—Shirley Temple, Jackie Cooper, Freddie Bartholomew, Margaret O'Brien, Bobby Driscoll—either retired while still young or struggled to retain a following in adulthood. The very qualities that charm audiences when an actor is a child can become grating in an adult.

There is no one route to learning how to take command of a stage, to project your personality in ways that make people pay attention. But people who act in college plays, whether they began in grade school or started as a college sophomore, usually learn lessons that last about making an impression on an audience. The student who began acting in grade school discovers that what worked back then may have little effect now. They re-learn the art of acting when they are in college. Those who start out at college are old enough so that what they are learning for the first time will be of good use throughout the rest of their lives.

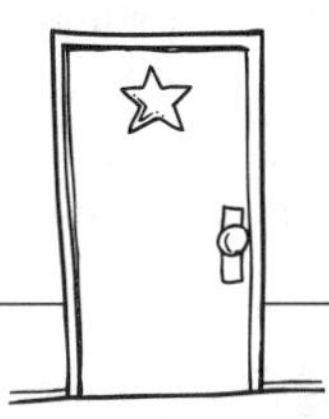

Backstage Tales

Some college-age actors get the idea that being impressive on stage is to be loud, to make every gesture big, and to generally ham it up. Beware of that approach—it can wear thin very quickly. One of the most impressive performances the authors ever saw was that of Alex McCowen as the psychiatrist in the original production of Peter Shaffer's *Equus* at the National Theater in London. He spoke as quietly as any actor we have ever seen on stage (although everyone could hear him perfectly), and his containment was riveting. We later saw Anthony Hopkins and Anthony Perkins in the role on Broadway, and they were both very fine, but not as quietly mesmerizing as McCowen had been.

Ahead of the Corporate Game

Over the last several decades, as the mass media have become increasingly important, and everything sometimes seems to involve public relations of some sort, it has become increasingly difficult for professionals of any kind to hide away behind an office desk. Teaching, of course, has always been a "performing art," but these days even the molecular-research scientist or the corporate treasurer is likely to find it necessary to hold a press conference at some point. Being able to present oneself in public has become essential to promotion and sometimes even to landing a lower-echelon corporate job.

Performance Notes

When you graduate and start filling out job applications or preparing a business resumé, be sure to include your college acting experience. Back in the 1950s or 1960s, some employers may have looked upon acting as a suspect credit, suggesting "bohemian" tendencies and anti-establishment views. But those days are gone, and the ability to perform in front of the public has become a valued skill.

It may be a while before you find yourself dealing with the pressures of a press conference, but chances are good that you will soon enough be asked to present an internal report on some issue, new idea, or problem to groups of colleagues. Experts in public speaking regularly offer expensive training programs in cities large and small. If you've acted in college, however, you're going to be ahead of the game in this regard. You'll be used to performing in public. That sea of faces staring at you won't throw you. You'll know all about the unexpected laugh and the restless guy in the third row. You'll have a solid speaking voice and the poise that goes with it. You'll understand when to increase your volume or speed things up in order to recapture the attention of a restive audience. Your college acting career will have provided you with skills that are highly valued in today's professional world.

Just for the Fun of It

In this chapter we've emphasized several advantages of college acting that go beyond the experience itself, from the educational enrichment to ways in which acting develops skills that have value in the corporate world. But, in conclusion, we'd like to return to the fundamental attraction of acting for so many people: It enables you to express yourself in ways that bring great joy and self-satisfaction.

Never mind that acting in a production of Shakespeare's *King Lear* will increase your understanding of the greatest of English-language playwrights and will help you to write better papers and get better grades. Forget, for the moment, that even a small role in Rogers and Hammerstein's *Carousel* will develop performance skills that can be useful in a future corporate job. Acting is just plain fun.

Of course, there will be down moments—that role you wanted but didn't get, a production that the critics don't much like. There are ups and downs to everything we do in life, but the highs of acting are satisfying in ways that bring people back to it no matter how many problems there were with the last play they appeared in.

Several aspects of the acting experience contribute to the overall sense of satisfaction it brings. Like playing a musical instrument, writing a short story, or painting a picture, acting is a form of self-expression. It makes it possible for you to explore yourself, to give focus to emotions and ideas in new ways, and to convey their significance to others. There is always joy in doing that, no matter what vehicle of expression you employ.

Stage acting brings immediate rewards because of the presence of a live audience. Writers, visual artists, and composers may be great successes, but their sense of achievement is to some degree second-hand, after the fact. That's also true for movie and television actors, which is why many of them return to the stage on a regular basis. Live performances create an excitement that surpasses that of any other art form. As a stage actor, you can feel the audience responding to your efforts, right then and there, in the moment. You hear the laughter, and the muffled sobs when an audience is deeply moved. You can even feel the rapt silence of an audience totally caught up in what's happening on stage.

Backstage Tales

Many movie stars have never performed before a live audience. Some of them are undoubtedly incapable of doing so. They couldn't sustain their performances sufficiently to tell a complete story in two hours on the stage, and because numerous takes can be filmed and then edited together, flaws can be covered up. Stage acting is far more exposed. But movie stars like Glenn Close and Kevin Spacey regularly return to their stage roots exactly because they find the immediacy of the audience response so fulfilling. Both actors have said that live performances recharge their batteries. Even Lana Turner, a studio-made star if ever there was one, found great satisfaction in performing in dinner-theater productions late in her career.

As a college actor, you'll taste the intense joy of making a live audience laugh and cry. You will have the chance to do that in classic plays that are seldom, if ever, revived on Broadway, but which are mounted on college campuses all the time. Make the most of it. Have fun. No matter what you do with the rest of your life, you will always remember, with deep pleasure and pride, the nights spent on a stage in a college town.

The Least You Need to Know

- ➤ Acting in college theater will enrich your educational experience.
- ➤ Acting in college productions will help you make your mark on campus.
- ➤ The skills developed in college theater can be valuable in a great many professions.
- ➤ The joy of self-expression that comes from college acting will be something you remember for the rest of your life.

Chapter 5

A Place in Your Community

In This Chapter

- Learning about becoming an actor as an adult
- Exploring the workings of a local theater company
- Discovering the special rewards of community theater acting
- Finding out why you're never too old to start acting

Community theater is a place where talented actors, often with professional skills, keep their love of acting alive even as they live normal nine-to-five lives. There are hundreds of thousands of people across the country who've always loved to act but—for a variety of reasons—decided against a professional career. Luckily, they knew they wouldn't have to give up acting altogether, since community theaters are everywhere, putting on plays and musicals of all kinds in every season of the year.

Audiences enthralled by live performances support such theaters. Some members of a community theater audience have never been to New York to see a Broadway show, but they know good theater and good acting when they see it. They have their favorites among the local actors, and they see them, quite rightly, as stars.

In this chapter, we'll introduce you to the pleasures of community theater acting. You'll meet people who have acted all their lives and others who became involved as adults because they were asked to give it a try, just for the fun of it. We'll explain how community theater organizations function, and tell you how to become part of the excitement they generate. You're never too old to discover the pleasures of acting in local productions.

The Hospital Fund-Raiser

Many of the actors who regularly appear in community theater productions have been acting since they were teenagers or even younger. Although they hold regular jobs in a variety of professions, community theater gives them an opportunity to continue doing something they love. Those two actors playing the Capulets, the parents of Shakespeare's Juliet? At different colleges, he played Romeo and she played Juliet. They're still on stage a quarter-century later, and enjoying every minute of it. Sometimes they get the starring roles—it depends on the play—but they take great pleasure in smaller character parts as well.

Other community theater performers didn't get involved in theater until their 30s or 40s. Some adults decide they'd like to act because friends are doing it, or because they've always thought they might be good at it but were too busy with other pursuits to give it a try. Still others are recruited for a role because they seem so perfect for it, and then they find that acting satisfies them in surprising ways, so they keep on auditioning for further productions. And then there are those who stumble into acting, often as a result of taking part in a charity performance of some kind.

It's Just One Skit

You're a volunteer at a local hospital, doing your best to spread good cheer one night a week. The hospital wants to spruce up the grounds with some new landscaping, and they make a decision to present an evening of skits and songs to raise money for all those rhododendrons. You've never acted in your life, but it's hard to say no to a request that you make a fool of yourself for charity. You rope your husband into the act as well. You're cast in a skit as a woman who's wheeled on stage on a gurney, crying out, "I'm dying, I'm dying." Your husband gets the punchline, playing a doctor: "The operation was a success, Mrs. Smith. You no longer have that wart on your left arm. Now get some rest." The skit is a big hit with the audience, and you're congratulated on the sincerity of your desperate cries. You protest that you didn't really do anything, but something strange has happened—you want to get on stage again and do more next time.

You Can Count On Me Next Year

A great many people have been roped into performing in a charity skit, or singing in the chorus at a fund-raiser, who have subsequently gone on to bigger and better things as actors. Sometimes all it takes is one appearance on stage for the acting bug to take over. They'll say, "Sure, you can count on me for the next show," but by the time that comes around they may already have auditioned for the community theater, gotten some experience, and feel ready for a bigger role.

Theater is seductive. Once you've gotten a taste of it, you're likely to want more. When there's a good community theater in town, you can have many opportunities to strut your stuff.

Backstage Tales

The authors have known several men and women who appeared regularly with the Metropolitan Opera in New York, not as star singers but as extras in big operas that require a lot of bodies on stage. They've been soldiers in *Aida* or handmaidens in *Turandot*. They get to wear terrific costumes, and even if all they have to do is stand still during a big aria, they get a huge kick out of being on that enormous stage with 3,000 people watching them. Unlike most community theater amateurs, they do get paid—a little—but the spirit in which they perform is similar to that of the amateur performer anywhere: "It makes me feel special," they'll tell you.

A Small Theater Company

Several thousand community theaters are in the United States, some long established and widely known, and others just getting started. In southeastern Pennsylvania, where the authors live, half a dozen such theaters draw audiences from the surrounding area. When a play or musical of particular interest is running, people often drive 30 or 40 miles to see performances in Lancaster, Ephrata, York, and other small Pennsylvania cities and towns. Similar situations exist in most states.

The productions offered in this part of Pennsylvania in the past few years have ranged from popular musicals like *The Sound of Music* to Broadway and movie hits like *A Few Good Men*. Lancaster has outdoor Shakespeare productions every summer. The Theater of the Seventh Sister in Lancaster mounts productions of both classic and experimental plays. Not only is there something to interest almost any theatergoer, but also the diversity of plays performed means that local actors get the chance to display their talents in plays ranging from Jean-Paul Sartre's *No Exit* in the fall to a Neil Simon comedy in the spring.

Performance Notes

You don't have to be part of an "in" group to audition for community theaters. Notices of auditions will appear in local papers, usually the Sunday edition that has the widest circulation. Sometimes one or two lead roles are pre-cast when a play is being produced precisely because those parts can be filled, but that still leaves many other roles open.

Productive Free Time

Most of us fritter away a lot of our free time. Nothing is wrong with that, and you can have a good deal of fun frittering. But some moments you look back and think, "Where did the time go?" "What have I accomplished?" Community theater actors know exactly where their free time goes. They're rehearsing a play and eventually performing it. What's more, they have something very worthwhile to show for it. It's not just a matter of a scrapbook full of pictures, programs, and reviews, either, although those can mean a great deal. Nor is it so much the applause at the curtain call, or the compliments that people pay you in the days and weeks to follow.

If you're like most community theater actors, the greatest satisfaction comes from the laughter and tears of an audience caught up in the play they're watching, the emotional response to a story that you and your fellow cast members are acting out for them. To make other people respond emotionally, whether you are giving them an evening of pure entertainment that's filled with laughter, or a more serious evening that moves them and makes them think—to get through to people in such ways feeds much more than just the ego. It makes you feel that you've done something worthwhile.

Backstage Tales

Co-author Paul Baldwin starred as Charlie Anderson in seven productions of the musical *Shenandoah*. The first time was in 1975 at a pair of dinner theaters in Charlotte and Raleigh, North Carolina. It was Paul's first starring role, and exciting for that reason alone. But, more than anything, he remembers the heavy-set, ruddy-faced men in the audience who cried. They often looked like Army sergeants, and the theater owner said that indeed a number of them had fought in Korea or Vietnam. The fact that the musical was about a family trying unsuccessfully to stay out of the Civil War may also have contributed to the emotion in the theater. But Paul has always said, "When I saw those big guys crying, I knew I was doing something right."

Acting is about communicating with an audience, making them feel, and making them think. And it doesn't matter whether the performance is taking place in the Schubert Theater on Broadway, a dinner theater in North Carolina, or a community theater anywhere in the country, actors at all levels, anywhere, cherish those moments when they know they are getting through to the audience.

It's easy to be cynical when a major star talks about getting through to an audience. "Sure," we tend to think, "and the $10 million you got for that movie, or the $10,000 a week you're getting on Broadway, has nothing to do with it." But community theater actors will talk about the rewards of acting in the same way, and, for the most part, they're not getting paid a dime.

A Lot More Fun Than Bridge

Let's not get too serious here, though. While acting no doubt has its higher rewards, it's also just plain fun. That's probably particularly true for community theater actors. Unlike professionals, your future career isn't riding on every part you play. And even if you acted in college, you've lightened up a little since then. Community theater actors are no less dedicated to doing the hard work that will result in a good performance, but they're less likely than either the professional or the college actor to see everything in make-or-break terms. That means they're freer to enjoy themselves, to simply have a good time.

We've encountered any number of community theater actors who used to spend a lot of time bowling, playing bridge and poker, or meeting for a round of golf every Saturday. That was fun, too, they'll say. But fond as they were of the people they golfed or played cards with, it was the same group that got together week after week. In community theater, they find a much greater sense of adventure. It's a new play, a different cast every time. They may have worked with several of the actors before, but it's always a different mix, and there's usually someone you've never met before. "More adventuring?" says Sancho Panza to Don Quixote in *Man of La Mancha*. "Definitely," is the community theater actor's reply. "I wouldn't miss it for the world."

Performance Notes

Don't bite off more than you can chew! In community theater, as on college campuses, sometimes two overlapping productions may be going on that you'd like to act in, but even two small roles in different plays can lead to scheduling conflicts; directors don't like having an actor on board whose loyalties are divided.

Another Dimension to Life

We live in an extremely fast-paced world. Yet many people, no matter how madly they dash around, feel stuck in a rut. Some may think that to get out of the rut they have to go faster still. Others suspect a change is more to the point. One community theater actor we know—we'll call him Stan—had some wise words on this subject. "I used to have so many so-called priorities in my life that I didn't have the time to realize that, with so many things to get done, I really didn't have any priorities at all."

Then Stan met Carmela. She had agreed to play the temptress Lola in a community theater production of the musical *Damn Yankees*. Stan complained that he'd never see her. She told him he had a good singing voice and was a terrific dancer, and since the cast was short a baseball player, why didn't he join the show? He said he couldn't do that, and then did. That was six years ago. He's been performing in community theater ever since. "A lot of my old priorities went out the window," Stan says. Now he has three: his job, his family (he and Carmela married and have a three-year-old son), and whatever show he's in at the moment. "There's nothing like finding something you really like to do to straighten out your priorities," he says. "Acting added a whole new dimension to my life, and that put everything else into perspective."

Nice to Feel Special Sometimes

When you've been acting in community theater for a while, you'll discover that you're almost as well known as the town mayor. Unlike the mayor, no one wants to vote you out of office. People whose faces you have some memory of, but whose names completely escape you, will stop you in the street or at the mall to say hello and give you a compliment. Sometimes they'll even come over to your table at a restaurant, making you feel like a movie star. And like a movie star, you may occasionally wish they'd leave you alone. It's great to feel special, but that carries some responsibilities with it. Always be nice to your fans. Movie stars who brush people off get a reputation for being stuck-up or nasty, and in a small city you can't afford that. The rewards you get for being admired and recognized have a cost, though: Sometimes you'll have to put on a good act offstage as well as on.

Places, Everyone!

Actors tend to have bad memories for names. That's partly because they work with different people on every production, and just keeping up with those names is tough enough. In addition, actors' heads are stuffed with the names of characters in plays. Don't worry too much if you can't remember someone's name, whether it's a fan or an actor you worked with two years ago. Just say, "Oh, yes, of course," and smile brightly.

"My Kids Are My Biggest Fans"

Rehearsal schedules for community theater productions can mean that you have to rearrange dinner hours, with the actor in the family, or everyone, eating a bit earlier than usual. You will spend a lot of evenings at the theater instead of at home with your family. How do families react to these facts? We've known situations where it caused some tensions, but in the vast majority of cases, both spouses and children are so excited by Mom's or Dad's theatrical ventures that they're more than willing to put up with some inconveniences.

Watching a family member perform on stage not only engenders pride, but also can make it possible for family members to see the actor in a new light. Several community theater performers have said to us that their kids were their biggest fans. Perhaps more important, kids, especially rebellious teenagers, can develop a new respect for the parent they see up there on the stage. Most teenagers are half-delirious about certain music, television, and movie stars. They see performers as very cool indeed, and when Mom or Dad gets big laughs and wild applause in a local show, few kids can remain unimpressed. It's even better when some other kid at school, who's seen the show, says, "You've got a cool Mom."

Backstage Tales

The children of movie stars, growing up in Hollywood, are often pretty blasé about their parents' fame. Jane Fonda, Jamie Lee Curtis, and many others have noted that acting is just what their parents did for a living, and half the other kids they knew had famous parents, too. The children of community theater actors do tend to see their parents as special. Dad or Mom works for a local company, but a lot of other parents in town do the same thing. Very few of them are actors, though!

If You Really Think I Could Do It

Many community theater actors decided to act because a friend persuaded them to try it. We know a man who had never acted in a play until his late 40s. The closest he'd come to performing was to sing in his college glee club. He also happened to play the guitar for his own enjoyment. Several years ago, when a community theater company put on *The Sound of Music*, his teen-aged daughter got the role of Liesl. After the first week of rehearsal, she came home and said that the man playing Captain von Trapp was ill, and they were desperate for a replacement. She'd told the director that her father played the guitar and could sing. Would he please, please, play the part?

Dad was very taken aback. He said he couldn't possibly do it, he had no experience, and he'd make a fool of himself. His daughter begged, the director called up and begged, and his wife said, "Oh, come on, give it a try. After all, you're a sweet man who sometimes behaves like a tyrant. You're a natural." Dad played Captain von Trapp. He was a great success, and he's been acting ever since. He's even done Shakespeare—playing Julius Caesar, no less.

You're Never Too Old to Start

You're 63, and you've never been onstage in your life. Well, that's not quite true; you were president of the garden club and officiated at some awards ceremonies. But that wasn't acting, just saying a few well-chosen words. Nevertheless, your next-door neighbor has gotten it into her head that you ought to be in a play. The part she has in mind is one of the maiden aunts in *Arsenic and Old Lace*. Not the part that Josephine Hull played so famously on Broadway and in the movies long ago, thank heaven; it's the quieter sister they want you for. Even so, it's a lot of lines, and clearly a lot of work. Can you really do this? Can anyone start acting in his or her 60s and do a respectable job?

Of course you can do it, if you have presence and a good speaking voice. You will have to work hard at it, but the rewards will be considerable. Being in a play would certainly liven up your life. And if you're playing one of the charming poisoners in *Arsenic and Old Lace*, it might even cut down on the number of people who ask you to bake a cake for every possible occasion.

Backstage Tales

A surprising number of professional actors didn't get started until quite late in life. John Houseman was deeply involved in the theater, but as a producer, not as an actor. He helped Orson Welles found the Mercury Theater, and then followed him to Hollywood, where he produced such famous films as *The Bad and the Beautiful* and *Lust for Life*. At the age of 71, he became an actor, taking the role of the acerbic law professor in *The Paper Chase*, for which he won the Academy Award for Best Supporting Actor. He acted in another 20 movies, right up until his death in 1988, and became one of the most recognized faces and voices in America with his ads for the brokers Smith Barney.

No matter what your age, if someone tells you you'd be perfect for a part in a play, take it seriously. Give it a whirl. You're likely to find that you love acting. The bug can bite at any time of life.

"With the Kids Gone ..."

While plenty of people act in community theater productions as their kids are growing up, others don't start until their children are fully grown and out of the house. One friend of ours, Miriam, had acted in college but was too busy to even think about community theater while her kids were around, since she and her husband both worked.

"I suppose I was suffering a bit from empty-nest syndrome," Miriam says. "Life seemed awfully quiet and a bit boring. It was my husband who suggested that I audition for community theater. He'd seen me act in college and had been very proud of me back then. In college I'd played Laura in *The Glass Menagerie*, and when auditions for a production showed up in the local paper, I thought maybe I could manage the mother. Even though it's the major role, I knew the play so well that I decided it was worth a try. It hadn't occurred to me, of course, that every older woman in town who'd done any acting would be dying to get their hands on that role. I was called back to read several times, and in the end I got it. That put a few noses out of joint, but I'm friends with all my competitors now. Acting again has done a lot for me. I feel as though I've come full circle."

Places, Everyone!

When you win a role in a community theater production, you may indeed put someone's nose out of joint because he or she wanted the part, too. But that happens even in the fifth grade. It's part of life. Community theater actors seldom let that kind of thing turn into a feud—that would spoil the fun.

Once you do start acting in community theater, you never know what's going to happen. Catherine Coulson began acting with a community theater in middle age. Suddenly, she heard the news that a television series was going to be filmed in the area, and the producers were looking for local people to take small parts. The show was called *Twin Peaks.* Coulson ended up playing a role that brought her fans from around the world: the Log Lady. She didn't pursue a professional career further after *Twin Peaks* had run its course, but she'd enjoyed the experience of a lifetime while it lasted. We'll talk more about how to deal with the kind of professional opportunity Catherine Coulson encountered in the last section of the book. It doesn't happen all that often, but you never know.

Whether you get up on stage as a grade school kid, in high school, at college, or appear in community theater productions much later in life, you'll find that acting enriches your life in both tangible and intangible ways. You've got the acting bug. You've got your eye on bigger and better roles. Now let's find out how to make the most of your natural talents.

The Least You Need to Know

- Even appearing in a skit in a charity show can awaken the acting bug and lead to much bigger things.
- Local theater companies all over the country offer a wide range of shows, and can always use new talent.
- Acting in community theater can give you a new lease on life and increase your standing in your neighborhood.
- You're never too old to explore your hidden acting talents.

Part 2

Skills of the Theater

Some people are born with natural theatrical gifts—a fine speaking voice, a beautiful singing voice, or the grace and strength of a dancer. That is not necessarily enough to make a person a good actor, however. Additional gifts of timing and emotional expression are also required. Still, having a strong natural gift in any of the basic disciplines puts you a big step ahead on the road to being a fine performer.

Most people have really strong natural talent in only one or two areas. Someone with a superb speaking voice may not be much of a dancer, for example. But you can learn the skills of the theater by taking lessons or simply through experience. If you've got basic theatrical talents, you can improve them if you choose. In this section of the book, we'll explore natural skills and the ways you can build upon them.

Chapter 6

Natural Gifts

In This Chapter

- Learning what characterizes a good speaking voice
- Understanding the meaning of natural grace
- Finding out if musicals are for you
- Exploring the basics of good timing
- Discovering how to enhance your self-discipline

What makes someone an actor? It's certainly not just looks. Movie stars are more likely to be exceptionally beautiful or handsome than great stage stars are, but there are a lot of beautiful people who don't make it in Hollywood and plenty of stars who aren't good-looking in the usual way. Bette Davis wasn't beautiful and James Cagney wasn't handsome, but they became Hollywood legends even so. Both started out on the stage, and both had remarkable theatrical skills. Cagney, in particular, was one of those rare actors who had it all. He could play a terrifying gangster or a song-and-dance man with equal success. He had every natural skill in the book and made the most of them all.

In this chapter, we'll be looking at the various kinds of natural skills that help to make a person an actor. We'll cover vocal skills, both singing and non-singing, as well as the qualities of bearing and movement that give some people a head start. But good acting isn't just about physical attributes or talents, so we'll also be examining the mental strengths that contribute to the making of an actor.

What makes an actor an actor? Let's find out.

What a Fine Voice

Having a "nice" voice and having a "fine" voice are not necessarily the same thing. Nice means pleasant, and if your voice is exceptionally pleasing to the ear, it can carry you a considerable ways. A fine voice may also be pleasant, if that is what is required, but it will have other qualities as well. A fine voice has carrying power—it sounds clear and strong without the need to yell or scream—in a child and will acquire resonance when the child becomes an adult. If you listen to a group of eight-year-olds playing outside, some of the voices will stand out because they are loud, but you can always detect the true carrying voice in their midst. It seems to cut right through the babble of childish screeches.

A carrying voice is the result of a combination of physical elements. The larynx, or voice box, is one part of the equation, as is the shape of the roof of the mouth and the size of the sinus cavities and nasal passages. They act as a sounding board, like the cavity of a violin, amplifying and changing the voice according to the way they are constructed. One of the reasons why Barbra Streisand refused to have a "nose job" when she went to Hollywood was that she was worried, with reason, about what a change in her nasal structure might do to her voice.

Backstage Tales

Neither the size of the voice nor how well it carries is of much consequence for movie actors because scenes are so closely miked. In the early days of sound movies, when microphones were primitive, a good voice was imperative, and most of the movie stars of the 1930s were recruited from the New York stage. As movie sound improved, however, vocal power became less important. Even a whispery voice like Marilyn Monroe's can be very effective in the movies. Her voice was alluring, and she was a better singer than critics usually gave her credit for, but it was also a small voice that would not have worked well on stage. Although she studied at the famous Actor's Studio in New York, and there were occasional rumors that she might do a play, people had widespread doubts—which Monroe apparently shared—about whether she would be able to project her voice well enough to be heard in a Broadway theater.

The makings of a fine voice are something you are born with. A modest voice can often be improved, and a good one will get even better with experience. But a fine stage voice is a natural gift.

Such Good Diction

Good diction involves both the way someone shapes sounds and how he or she pronounces the words. A person with good diction will make the consonants ("d," "k," "t," for example) sharp and clear, and will avoid distorting vowel sounds ("a," "e," "i," "o," "u," and combinations of those letters). Many people drop their consonants, so that when they say, "That's a big truck," it comes out as "That's a big truh." Regional accents often distort vowel sounds so that you get the famous Brooklynese, "The oily boid gets the woim," instead of "The early bird gets the worm." Those who speak with a Southern drawl will say "Wha" instead of "Why." People from the Midwest often make several different vowel sounds the same way—"Marry merry Mary," for example, is likely to come out as "Merry, merry, merry."

Regional accents have a long and honorable history, and no one should dismiss them. In fact, some language scholars believe that the twang of people's speech in the Appalachian mountains is the closest-remaining approximation of how English was spoken in Shakespeare's own time, which is very different from the refined accent more often used by actors playing Shakespeare today.

But it's because regional accents are so particular to specific places that most actors try to rid themselves of such distinctive sounds, opting for a clear, all-purpose accent of the kind you will hear television network newscasters use. Of course, if a role calls for a particular kind of accent—a Southern accent for many Tennessee Williams plays, for example—you'll need to learn how to speak that way. Usually, however, the accent won't be terribly heavy because it's more important for the words to be clear than for them to be "regional."

Performance Notes

Lose that accent! You might get away with playing Maria with a Texas twang or a Southern drawl in a high school performance of *The Sound of Music* (especially if you live in Texas!), but beyond that audiences will want to hear you sound as much like Julie Andrews as possible.

A fine voice, then, is a combination of several elements. It starts with the physical equipment a person is born with, which can itself be developed and improved. Good diction sometimes comes naturally, but often has to be worked on. And the accomplished actor will smooth out a regional accent that is too strong, but at the same time will work on his or her ability to use several different kinds of accents, as Meryl Streep is so famous for doing.

She Moves So Well

For some people, moving well is second nature. But this ability has less to do with their physiques than it does with other factors. There are thin people whose movements are stiff and jerky, and heavy people who are extremely graceful. There are short people who have such a spring in their step that they seem much taller, and tall people who tend to stoop awkwardly, hunching their shoulders and looking ill at ease.

Although she was thin to the point of being bony, Audrey Hepburn moved beautifully. The movie *Funny Face* has a sequence during which Hepburn is being photographed for a fashion spread as she comes down a stairway of the Louvre Museum in Paris. As she raises her arms to float a diaphanous scarf behind her head, she manages to upstage one of the world's most famous statues, Winged Victory from ancient Greece.

Hepburn, of course, had been trained as a dancer, and so her grace might be expected. But so, too, was Shirley MacLaine. A more versatile actress than Hepburn, and capable of dancing a hot Broadway number with great pizzazz, MacLaine nevertheless lacked Hepburn's elegance of movement so evident in this scene.

Where does graceful movement come from? And we're talking about grace in men, too. Cary Grant was very graceful in ways that Jimmy Stewart couldn't begin to match. Look at them together in *The Philadelphia Story* (for which Stewart, not Grant, won an Oscar) and you can see the difference immediately. It's in the shoulders. Yes, the shoulders. That's even true of the difference between Hepburn and MacLaine, too, which you can clearly see in *The Children's Hour*, a film in which they co-starred.

A Pleasure to Watch

The shoulders are the key to good posture, and good posture is crucial to the appearance of graceful movement in both women and men. By standing up straight, with the shoulders thrown slightly back, the entire movement of the body is changed. The legs move more freely and smoothly, and when the arms are extended from the body in a gesture, they take on a cleaner, more pleasing line.

Places, Everyone!

Don't hold your shoulders in a stiff position. If you do that, you'll look constricted. Instead, align them properly, so that they appear relaxed as well as straight. The classic exercise for improving posture is to walk with a book on your head, one heavy enough to help it stay in place, but not so heavy that it places pressure on the neck muscles.

While some people have good posture and move well from the start, most of us can stand some improvement well into middle age. When President Clinton, a tall man with big bones, began his first term, he tended to slouch a bit. Many commentators noticed that his posture changed over the next year and a half. He had learned to throw his shoulders back yet keep his posture relaxed. He looked not only more graceful but also more "presidential" when he walked.

The Telling Gesture

Although Audrey Hepburn and Cary Grant may appear more graceful than Shirley MacLaine and Jimmy

Stewart, the latter two had another physical quality that often made them more interesting to watch. Both MacLaine and Stewart's performances are marked by a very telling use of gestures. They use their hands and arms more freely and in a more detailed way than Grant and Hepburn, who gesture less, but in a more stylized fashion. Both approaches work. Interestingly, however, it is unusual to find extraordinary grace and a particularly telling use of gestures in the same performer. Vanessa Redgrave, widely regarded as one of the greatest screen actresses of all time, does combine the two.

Two aspects of gesturing can cause problems. The first problem involves excessive, pointless gesturing. Many amateurs use their hands and arms far too much when they speak. You can see what to avoid simply by turning on the television set and watching a local commercial in which the owner of a car dealership or furniture store extols his own company. His or her hands are a distraction instead of bringing home a particular point. Gestures must have meaning, telling you something beyond what the words convey. Otherwise they blur the meaning of the words themselves.

The second problem is a more sophisticated one, and even professionals can be guilty of it. Everyone has seen a singer put a hand over his or her heart when singing the word "heart." If you're going to do that, why not point to your head when singing that word, or to your feet when talking about walking. You're belaboring the obvious instead of amplifying the meaning of the words. But this problem can also develop into a habit of repeating the same kind of gesture in performance after performance. That is called *mannered* acting, and even great actors can fall into it. Critics often accused Oscar- and Tony-award winners Jack Lemmon and Geraldine Page of using too many of the same mannerisms in each of their films. A strong director will "sit" on such performers, telling the actor to cut it out. In fact, both Lemmon and Page reached the point where they asked directors to stop them when they were up to their favorite tricks. Lemmon, for example, tended to overuse the shrug, while Page played with her hair a lot.

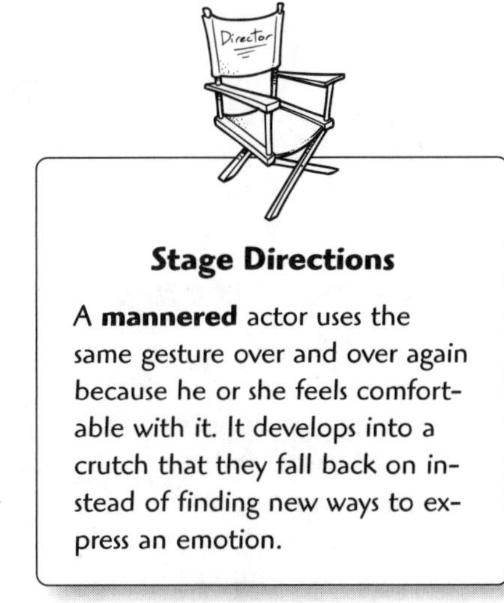

Stage Directions

A **mannered** actor uses the same gesture over and over again because he or she feels comfortable with it. It develops into a crutch that they fall back on instead of finding new ways to express an emotion.

Some people seem to have an instinct for the telling gesture even as children. If you have this natural gift, consider yourself fortunate. It is something that most actors have to work at before they get it right.

All Singing, All Dancing

Children have long held a special place in American musical theater and movies. Shirley Temple, Judy Garland, Mickey Rooney, Eddie Hodges, and Ron Howard—these famous names just scratch the surface. More recently, the young Savion Glover rocketed to Broadway fame in *The Tap Dance Kid*, and 11-year-old Daisy Eagan won a Tony Award as the heroine of the musical *The Secret Garden*. And thousands of children around the country play roles in local productions of *The Sound of Music* and *Oliver!* every year.

Backstage Tales

Andrea McCardle was just another member of the chorus of orphans in *Annie* when it was first produced during the summer of 1974 at The Goodspeed Opera House in Connecticut. But by the time it got to Broadway a few months later, the original Annie had grown too much and McCardle went on to national fame as the Broadway Annie. However, she was a young woman by the time the movie was made seven years later, and the role went to Aileen Quinn. Even the most talented kid is faced with the problem of growing up. Some make it in show business as adults and some don't. Andrea McCardle did, and was starring in *Sleeping Beauty* on Broadway in 2000.

Many kids can sing and dance up a storm, and they do it with a contagious joy. But natural musical talent can lead to the stage much later for other people. They may always have had a good singing voice or been able to dance up a storm from the age of five, but sometimes it isn't until they're adults that the acting bug bites them.

"I've Heard Him in Church"

Community theaters are always on the lookout for new musical talent. Say they're producing *Shenandoah*, the moving hit musical about a Virginia family that gets dragged into the Civil War against their wishes. There may be a regular member of the theater who can play the father, Charlie Anderson, or the company could arrange to hire an actor out of New York to play him. (Co-author Paul Baldwin played Charlie as an Equity guest artist with a New Jersey community theater.) But the musical also calls for four grown sons and two younger ones, so it can be difficult for a community theater to round up enough good male voices. In that situation, someone might say, "I have an idea. There's a young man named Scott who sings at my church. He has a terrific tenor voice and is very good-looking. I bet he could play James."

And so Scott gets a call. Aside from singing in the chorus of a high school Gilbert and Sullivan production, he's never been on stage. But the community theater begs him, and he decides it might be fun. It proves to be so much fun that he, too, becomes a community theater stalwart. This kind of thing happens all the time.

Never Puts a Foot Wrong

You won a dance contest in high school even though you've never had a lesson? Are you one of those people who can pick up the steps of the latest dance craze in a minute, and end up teaching it to all your friends? Obviously, you're a natural. Maybe you should audition for a college or community theater musical.

Performance Notes

If you love to sing, try joining your church choir. Not only will you receive fine vocal training, but singing solo in church will also develop your poise and help you to perform in public.

Many people can dance to popular music at parties and proms with what amounts to professional dazzle. Sometimes other dancers will even stop and form a circle around a couple who's really good. If you've got natural dance ability, you can do a lot more with it besides impressing your friends. The truth is that terrific dancers are harder to find than terrific singers. And you can improve your singing a lot more easily than you can your ability to dance.

Some of Broadway's foremost musical stars—Gwen Verdon, Donna McKechnie, Anne Reinking, Tony winners all—never had singing voices that match their dancing talent. But boy, could they dance. They worked hard on their singing, and while it was their dancing that made them stars, they reached the point where they could more than hold their own as singers, too. Very few people are blessed with equal natural ability in both the vocal and the dance disciplines, but if you're terrific at one, you might not need the other.

A Sense of Timing

Having a wonderful speaking voice (whether speaking or singing), innate physical grace, or a special gift for dancing—any of these can put you ahead of the game as an actor. But, in the end, such natural abilities aren't enough by themselves. To be successful onstage, you also need to have a sense of timing. That, too, is a natural talent, and while you can learn to speak well, sing, and dance, it's not easy to learn good timing. And if you haven't got it, you'll be in trouble onstage.

Can you improve your timing? Certainly. Experience is a great teacher, and your timing is bound to improve unless you have a real blind spot in regard to it. There are many famous actors whose timing is little more than adequate, but who have other qualities that make up for it. Good timing is especially important in comedy, and the audience will indicate who has really exceptional timing: Laughter will reward a performer with superb timing even if the line itself isn't very funny.

Backstage Tales

The late British actor Robert Stephens had many assets. He was ruggedly handsome with a first-rate speaking voice. He starred in many plays in London, both classical and modern, and appeared in numerous movies. But he never reached the highest rank of British actors because he also had a serious failing: His sense of timing was so shaky that it often amounted to what is called "anti-timing." The critics noticed it, and audiences were puzzled by it. Co-author John Malone saw him in the early 1960s in London in a National Theater production of George Farquhar's 1706 comedy *The Recruiting Officer*. Stephens's then-wife Maggie Smith was making her first appearance in a classical play in the same production and scored an enormous hit. But her quicksilver performance only made Stephens look worse. He always seemed to be a beat behind the flow of the play. It was a sad case of anti-timing.

Pausing for Effect

We all take pauses in everyday conversation. We need to take them to decide what we're going to say next. And we tend to tune out people who don't take pauses, because their mouths are usually working faster than their brains. On stage, however, there is a different kind of reality. The actors know their lines, and it would bore the audience to put in a lot of "uh"s or pauses in an entirely realistic way to indicate that they're trying to decide what to say. On stage, pauses are used to make a point. Pausing for effect is quite different from what we usually do in real life, except when we're telling a joke. That pause just before the punch-line serves the same purpose as stage pauses. And that, too, is a matter of timing.

We'll be dealing with pauses in more depth in Chapter 21. For now, just keep in mind that the stage pause must always have a point.

Knowing When to Move

Stage movement—whether in terms of taking a step forward or making a gesture while sitting—is also a matter of timing. We're all aware of other people's body language in real life, at least to some degree. For example, we often can grasp that someone is tense or unhappy without that person saying so, just by looking at how he or she walks or gestures. But on stage, every movement is magnified, and that means that every movement needs to have a point, just as a pause does. Judging when to move or to stand still, when to gesture or to keep the arms still may be indicated by the script or suggested by the director, but it's up to the actor to make them real. The actor creates most gestures him- or herself. Stage movement is a way of saying something, making more explicit the underlying significance of everyday body language. The greatest actors know instinctively when to move, but here again the less naturally gifted can certainly learn to improve with experience.

Performance Notes

Learn to stand still and you'll gain power. If several characters are moving around the stage in a dither, and one is standing stock still, the eyes of the audience will inevitably keep coming back to the actor who isn't moving. Why? Because he or she is creating a terrific moment of suspense. When will that person move?

The Art of Self-Discipline

Natural talent is a great gift, and anyone who has it is fortunate. But, again, natural gifts are seldom enough to achieve real success as an actor. They must be shaped and honed in ways that require a lot of self-discipline. Both authors of this book have known many very talented people who were never able to harness their talents enough to make them reliable as performers. We have known people with big, beautiful voices who could not control pitch properly, so that at some point in a song they would go wildly astray, ruining everything. There are also actors who have great natural presence on stage and are very inventive—so inventive that they seem unable to play a scene (or even read a line) the same way twice. That drives other actors crazy, because they never know what is going to happen on stage from one performance to the next. That lack of consistency also means that one performance may be terrific but the next one dreadful.

Self-discipline means having the ability to be critical of your own efforts and working to improve them. It means being able to take direction, to work toward the kind of line readings and pace that the director feels are necessary.

Controlled but Not Stiff

The art of self-discipline is a matter of controlling and shaping your natural abilities. But that doesn't mean carrying things so far that you stamp out your spontaneity and become stiff. When trying to improve your posture, standing up straight and throwing your shoulders back does not mean holding yourself so rigid that you walk like a robot. Relaxed control is the best kind. When people learn to drive a car, for example, they often overdo their attempts at control, slamming on the brakes so hard that the result is an abrupt or jerky halt. You are actually in most complete control when self-discipline has become second nature, and is thus close to instinctive.

Backstage Tales

Richard Burton became a star of the British Theater in the late 1940s, but then turned to movies in the early 1950s. He was lucky that movie audiences took to him, because he had been virtually thrown out of the Old Vic, the London Shakespeare company that would develop into what is now called the National Theater. Starring in a production of Henry V at the Old Vic, he fought with the director all the way through rehearsals, but appeared to finally agree to do what the director wanted, and the dress rehearsal went very well. On opening night, however, he changed everything, from blocking to line readings, throwing the other actors into total confusion and making a complete hash of the play. This disaster led the board of the Old Vic to inform him that he would never work at the theater again. Burton didn't care, since he had become a movie star with *The Robe* in 1953. Later in his career he did return to the stage several times, but by then had become more responsible and self-disciplined.

Disciplined speech or singing is not constricted. The voice shouldn't be strangled by the need to control it. The same is true for graceful movements. When beginning actors start disciplining their natural talents, it is not uncommon to go through a phase where things become stiff and mechanical. With continued work that problem will pass, and you will be able to make the most of your abilities in a fully relaxed way.

Mentally Sharp

Some people who ought to know better think that actors have an easy life, performing only two to three hours a night, or double that on matinee days. This idea that acting is a lazy kind of activity is wrong on several counts. First, it fails to take into account all the time spent before and after a performance in getting into and out of costume and makeup, not to mention the endless hours spent learning lines and rehearsing. But even more to the point, the intensity required of actors while they are performing must be taken into account.

Few activities demand as much focus and mental sharpness as acting. When you're on stage you're under a microscope. Hundreds of pairs of eyes are taking in your every move. To live up to that kind of scrutiny, you must have the self-discipline to make every moment count. That requires a heightened mental awareness that is extremely draining to maintain. Actors give an enormous amount of themselves to the watching audience. The rewards can be great—there is nothing like cheers from hundreds of people to make you feel good about yourself—but the effort is great, also. Natural skills give you a strong foundation, but you must build upon that foundation in order to succeed.

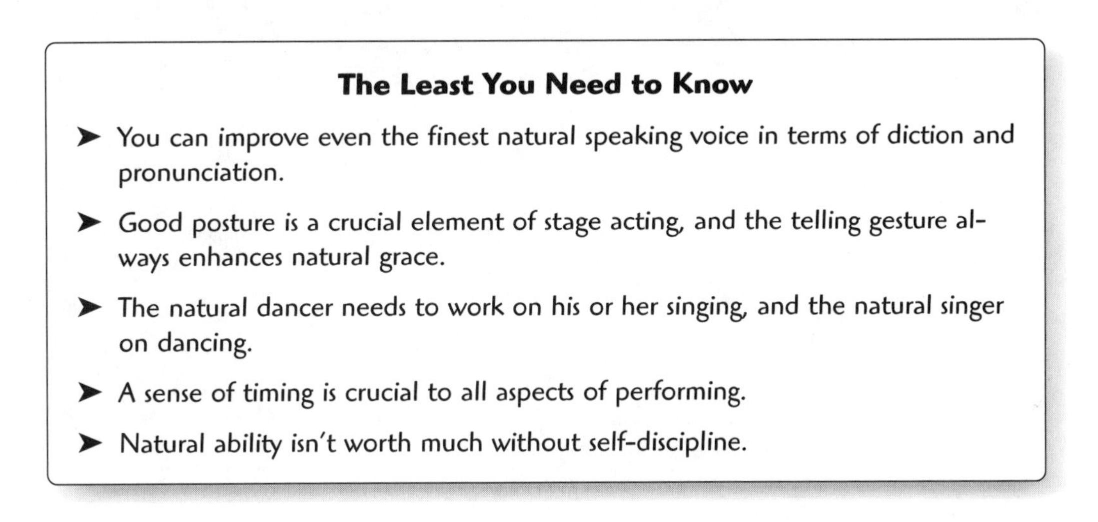

The Least You Need to Know

- You can improve even the finest natural speaking voice in terms of diction and pronunciation.
- Good posture is a crucial element of stage acting, and the telling gesture always enhances natural grace.
- The natural dancer needs to work on his or her singing, and the natural singer on dancing.
- A sense of timing is crucial to all aspects of performing.
- Natural ability isn't worth much without self-discipline.

Lessons Can't Hurt

In This Chapter

- Finding out how to improve your singing voice
- Recognizing the importance of dance lessons
- Exploring the world of acting classes
- Discovering your secondary talents

Every now and then a well-known actor or singer will boast that he or she hasn't "taken a lesson in my life." Congratulations and all that, but few people have such blazing natural talent that a few lessons wouldn't help them. In addition, even those who say they haven't ever had a lesson are forgetting how much they've learned from the directors, music directors, and choreographers of productions with whom they've worked. Beyond that, any actor also learns a great deal from other actors. Despite how much they've learned from experience alone, most actors have taken—and paid for—lessons of one kind or another at various points in their lives. What's more, lessons can be just as valuable to the amateur actor as to the professional. In this chapter, we'll explore the wide variety of lessons available in the singing, dancing, and acting disciplines. We'll guide you in choosing the best kind of teacher. And we'll look at how to make the most of "extra" talents that can help land you a role. We start with how you can learn to improve your singing voice.

Hold That High Note

High notes usually come at the end of a song, providing a climax to the music. They are often held notes as well, doubling the difficulty since the voice must not only rise to hit the note squarely but then hold on to it for several beats. A classic example of a held climatic high note for men is the conclusion to Stephen Sondheim's "Being Alive," from the musical *Company*. An example for women would be "Rahadlakum" from *Kismet*. But numerous songs also have high notes scattered throughout, like Cunegonde's "Glitter and Be Gay," from Leonard Bernstein's *Candide*, or "Corner of the Sky," from *Pippin*.

Stage Directions

The **high note** in a given song will vary according to the kind of voice it is written for. A baritone high note is often an "E," and sometimes an "F," but the high note for a tenor would be a high "C." The same kind of difference exists between songs for soprano and mezzo-soprano (alto) voices.

Improving Your Range

Some people have an extraordinarily wide range of notes at their beck-and-call, but even those lucky few must continually practice to keep their natural ability functioning at peak power. The majority of actor/singers are likely to have a narrower range to start with, and must work hard to be able to produce steady, on-target high notes. Few things are more embarrassing at an audition or in performance than trying to hit a high note and failing, producing instead an off-pitch note or, even worse, a strangled croak. That is why singing lessons can be so important for any actor who aspires to performing in musicals.

Singing lessons can involve many aspects of vocal production and interpretation. With a beginner, a teacher will spend a good deal of time on such basics as proper breathing and diction, making sure that your voice is correctly supported in terms of breath control, and that your use of tongue and lips results in a clear enunciation of the lyrics. With fairly advanced singers, greater attention will be paid to emotional coloring of the voice and the technical details of a vocal score. But at any stage, a good teacher will be concerned with your vocal range—either helping you to extend it so that you can sing higher (or lower) notes with precision and power, or perfecting notes you have already attained so that you can hold them longer.

While you can certainly work on your range by yourself, simply by practicing with songs that lie a bit high or low for your voice, a teacher will speed up the process and see to it that you don't damage your voice in the process.

Backstage Tales

In terms of range, the most extraordinary pop/jazz singer of recent decades has been the British singer and actress Dame Cleo Laine. We attended her first concert in America in 1973, after hearing the recording of a London revival of *Show Boat* in which she had appeared as Julie. The role of Magnolia in the revival was played by Lorna Dallas, an American who had taken lessons from the same singing teacher as co-author Paul Baldwin, Suzanne France. Lorna was terrific, but we were bowled over by Laine, and have followed her career ever since, from Carnegie Hall in 1974 to an outdoor concert during the summer of 1999 in Lancaster, Pennsylvania. She was 72 by then, but still hitting her incredible high notes with complete accuracy. Laine is the only person to be nominated for Grammy awards in the Female Jazz, Popular, and Classical categories. Check out her Web home page at www.quarternotes.com for her lengthy discography.

The Right Teacher for You

Finding the right singing teacher can be a matter of trial and error. In major cities you'll have a great many teachers from whom to choose, so you'll want to ask people you know for their recommendations. In a small town there may be only one singing teacher, and if he or she doesn't work out, you may find it necessary to make a trip to a larger community.

The truest test of a good teacher is whether or not your singing improves as your lessons continue. If you practice faithfully but aren't getting anywhere, then you need someone else. It can also happen that a teacher is right for you only up to a certain point. You may improve dramatically, and then find yourself stalled. That can mean that the teacher doesn't have the advanced expertise to coach you on a higher level—something a fine teacher will admit. Then it's time to move on to someone with a different approach or greater experience.

Places, Everyone!

Be careful when you choose your singing teacher. There are bad singing teachers out there who can do you considerable harm. One sign of a bad teacher is that you find yourself leaving lessons with a sore throat because the teacher insists on increasing the volume without teaching you proper breathing techniques.

You should be wary of a teacher who constantly criticizes your choice of new songs. It's one thing for a teacher to say that you're not yet ready for a particular song, but if the teacher just doesn't like your taste in music, you've got a problem. A good teacher will try to educate your taste, but shouldn't say no to everything you want to sing. That can be a generation-gap problem that arises because the teacher doesn't like anything composed after the 1970s, say. And sometimes a teacher will say no to a difficult song because it is so difficult to play. Stephen Sondheim's songs, for example, are difficult for many pianists; if you think your teacher is rejecting songs because they're hard to play, find someone else.

A Chance to Practice

Singing lessons also give you a chance to practice audition songs, or new songs you're learning for a role, and to receive professional feedback while you are doing it. Many singing teachers also hold musical get-togethers for all their students once a month or so. At each gathering, several students perform songs they've been working to perfect. Doing so can be invaluable experience for beginners who may still be shy about performing in front of an audience. The teachers will usually ask other students to comment on each performance as well. Some may love what you've done, while others may have helpful criticisms to offer.

Performance Notes

When it's your turn to judge a fellow singer, don't be mean! Voice teachers who hold group performance sessions expect to have their students criticize one another sincerely, but to be diplomatic about it. It will quickly become apparent that some of the more accomplished students can take harsher criticism, but go a little easier on the beginners.

Lorraine started taking singing lessons when she was 16. She was a nervous wreck about performing "I Feel Pretty" from *West Side Story* at her first "tea party," as her teacher called these get-togethers. "I soon realized that I wasn't the only one shaking like a leaf," Lorraine recalls. "The feedback from other students was very helpful to me, and when they really liked something, they applauded like mad. I got so I looked forward to those tea parties, and my teacher always had lots of nice things for us to eat afterwards, too. It was a lesson and a party at the same time."

I Didn't Know You Could Tap Dance

Actors who can sing are in demand because many musicals written since the 1960s require both strong acting and good singing. While someone who is more singer than actor can play the male and female leads in a frothy 1950s musical like *The Pajama Game*, you have to be at least as good an actor as singer to play Fredrik and Desirée in *A Little Night Music*. Anyone who can act, sing, and dance well is even more likely to be cast in many shows.

When *West Side Story* was first produced on Broadway, the search for the leading performers went on for a long time because it was so difficult to find performers who were equally strong in all three disciplines. Thus, dance lessons are well worthwhile for anyone who doesn't have two left feet.

Backstage Tales

Christopher Walken won an Oscar for his scary portrayal of a drug-addicted soldier in Vietnam in the 1978 movie *The Deer Hunter*, and since then he has mostly played villains. But he is also a highly accomplished tap dancer, and got to show off that talent in 1981's *Pennies from Heaven*. He can sing as well, and got a chance to do so on Broadway in *James Joyce's The Dead* in 2000. Thus, even those who regard themselves primarily as dramatic actors are well advised to develop any singing or dancing ability they have. Such additional talents can bring you a far greater diversity of roles, and keep you from getting typecast in a particular kind of part.

Tap, Ballet, and Ballroom

Few people are equally good at all kinds of dancing. To start with, your body type may be better suited to one kind of dancing than another. A girl who doesn't have the long limbs and very slender waist necessary to be a first-rate ballet dancer may nevertheless be terrific at tap dancing. And many people who aren't coordinated enough to be top-notch tap or ballet dancers often have the grace to excel in such ballroom dances as the waltz, the tango, and the fox-trot. (Ballroom dance professionals, who compete in contests across the country, are in another category—they usually have tap and ballet backgrounds as well.)

Deborah Kerr was a dramatic star in the movies for three decades and earned six Oscar nominations. Only once did she need to draw on her ballroom dancing ability, but that was in *The King and I*, in which the "Shall We Dance?" waltz with the King is the film's highlight. Another dramatic star, Maureen Stapleton, needed all her ballroom skills to star in the original television production of *Queen of the Stardust Ballroom*, for which she won an Emmy. So, even if your greatest talent is for serious acting roles, any dance ability you have may someday turn out to be essential. Today's lessons may get you a role years in the future that you would otherwise fail to land.

Places, Everyone!

If you do take lessons—of whatever kind—in order to become proficient enough to play a particular role, be sure to tell the teacher exactly what you are trying to do. Although you will always have to learn certain basics, the fact that you have a particular goal will often inspire the teacher to give you some extra tips that will be particularly helpful.

Lessons for a Particular Role

If you are generally well coordinated and graceful, you may be able to dance well enough in a short time to carry off a particular role. When co-author Paul Baldwin was attending North Texas State University, it was announced that a production of the musical *Gypsy* would be mounted later in the year. Paul badly wanted to play Tulsa, the lead boy in Mamma Rose's touring vaudeville act. But Tulsa had to tap dance as well as sing. Paul signed up for several weeks of tap lessons, even though the only class he could work into his schedule was at 8:00 A.M. It meant a lot of hard work, but he got the role.

The Acting Class

Back in the days of the big Hollywood studios, from the 1930s well into the 1950s, there were many stories about beautiful young people being plucked out of nowhere and turned into instant movie stars. The discovery of Lana Turner sitting on a stool at Schwab's Drugstore is the most famous example. But the truth is that all the major studios had training programs for their discoveries. Co-author John Malone once interviewed Lillian Sidney, the head dialogue coach at MGM, who had worked with every young MGM star from Ava Gardner to Jane Powell. She helped Gardner conquer her extreme Southern accent, but refused to go along with the request of the studio bosses to raise the pitch of Gardner's sultry voice. Like any smart teacher, she knew a good thing when she heard it. Nevertheless, movie stars are made, not born. Many of the MGM stars have paid tribute to Lillian Sidney for her patience, skill, and lifelong friendship.

If you want to act, no matter how much natural ability you may have, you'll have a lot to learn. There are few professionals who haven't attended an acting school at some point, and that goes for the majority of amateurs as well.

Even Small Cities Have Them

Even small cities usually have one or two people who give acting classes, and students will make the trip in from the small towns in the surrounding region as well. Many high-school drama or speech teachers also conduct private acting classes. They will cost money, of course, but a group class can be quite inexpensive and well worth it.

Any large city will offer a considerable choice of acting teachers, especially in locales that have one or more notable regional theater organizations in their midst. New York and Los Angeles, as the nation's theater, film, and television capitals, are of course almost as overrun by acting teachers as they are by actors. Many top-acting teachers will require prospective students to audition, and some may even have waiting lists. (Many top acting schools around the country are listed in Appendix A.)

Places, Everyone!

Choose your acting teacher with care, especially if you're young or inexperienced. If a teacher works with the local school system or with a reputable regional or local theater company, you should feel quite secure. However, if you choose a teacher from an ad in the newspaper or from the yellow pages, ask for references and follow up on them. Recommendations from people you know and trust may be your best guide.

Theory and Practice

Not every teacher teaches acting in the same way. Indeed, two different teachers may have nearly opposite approaches. While a number of famous theories of acting exist, they tend to fall into two broad groups. The first is the "outside-in" approach. The most famous exemplar of this approach is the Royal Academy of Dramatic Art (RADA) in London, England.

RADA and others who take the "outside-in approach" place great emphasis on the technical discipline of the voice and body, in the belief that when actors are in full command of their "instruments," they can play any at will.

The other major group of theories takes the "inside-out" approach, commonly called "Method Acting." Based on the ideas developed by Constantin Stanislavsky, co-founder of the Moscow Art Theater, method acting is most famously espoused by the Actor's Studio in New York, put on the map by the young Marlon Brando, and it lists many of America's most famous actors as alumni.

The FADA approach stresses technical skill, while the Method seeks emotional honesty through the exploration of the actor's own experiences and feelings. Some actors believe that the differences between the two approaches are largely a matter of degree, and that the two kinds of training in no way contradict each other. A third "school" of actors champions Spencer Tracy's famous remark that acting is largely a matter of learning your lines and not bumping into furniture. Tracy, of course, was a very great natural actor whose every thought can be read on his face.

Although Method acting is particularly prominent in the United States, plenty of teachers concentrate on technique rather than on soul-searching. That is particularly true among those who teach beginners. If you are not comfortable with the kind of approach a teacher emphasizes, then you should look for another teacher who suits your temperament. The discomfort an actor can feel with the Method approach is eloquently (and amusingly) stated in the song "Feel the Motion" from *A Chorus Line*. And a well-known theater joke manages to put down both the "outside-in" and "inside-out" approaches: "Personally," the actor says, "I come from the Mug-a-slavski school."

Backstage Tales

When Marlon Brando shot to stardom on Broadway and in the movies during the 1950s, his performances created much controversy, especially when less-talented actors began to copy him. Critics accused Method actors of being sloppy; they even called the Method approach the "mumbles" school of acting. In the 1953 film version of *Julius Caesar*, in which he played Mark Antony, Brando proved that he was perfectly capable of enunciating clearly when he wanted to, as many Method actors have done since.

Working on a Group Exercise

One advantage of taking group acting lessons is the opportunity to work on a scene from a play with several other actors. The teacher will pick a scene from a well-known play and assign roles to several students. They will be expected to work on the scene together and then perform it in front of the whole class. Group exercises of this kind can help young actors to discover the importance of relating to other characters, and more experienced ones to hone their skills at listening to every word another character is saying and adapting to the subtleties of how it is being said.

Places, Everyone!

Never complain that the role isn't one you feel comfortable with or would want to play on stage when you're taking group acting lessons. The point of the exercise is to make you "stretch" your abilities to play an uncongenial part. You can sometimes learn more from struggling with such a role—even if you end up playing it badly—than from working on a role you were "born to play."

Perfecting Audition Monologues

When an actor auditions for a production, he or she will be expected to have at least two monologues to perform if asked to do so: a serious one and a comic one. We're not talking about the kind of "monologue" that Jay Leno or David Letterman perform at the beginning of their late night shows, of course. An audition monologue may be a soliloquy, in which an actor addresses the audience, or speaks to him- or herself alone. Many of Shakespeare's characters have soliloquies, as do many characters in modern plays, such as Tom, the son in Tennessee Williams's *The Glass Menagerie*, or Pam Underwood in Peter Nichols's *A Day in the Death of Joe Egg*.

But an audition monologue does not have to be a soliloquy. More often than not, actors use a long speech that would be delivered to other characters in an actual production. You can find thousands of such speeches from hundreds of notable plays. Choose a serious one from a modern play and a comic one from a classic play (or vice versa) to work on in acting class.

Since you are expected to have memorized an audition monologue, working on it for an acting class will help you get it under your belt. And the suggestions of the teacher, as well as of other classmates you may perform it for, will help you to come much closer to perfecting it than you are likely to manage by yourself.

You Can Juggle, Too?

When auditions were announced for the musical *Barnum* in 1980, the producers emphasized that performers not only needed to sing and dance, but that circus skills were also important. Juggling, tightrope walking, and various acrobatic skills would be needed in this extravaganza based on the life of circus impresario P.T. Barnum.

A number of young performers with such special skills ended up winning parts in this major musical over more experienced singers and dancers who had never learned to juggle or perform acrobatic tricks.

Places, Everyone!

Hone any unusual talents you may have—you never know when they'll turn out to be valuable. If you juggle, mime, speak another language, or play a musical instrument, make sure you list it on your resumé under "Special Skills" so that the next time a production requires such talents, you'll be the first one called.

All Kinds of Talent Can Count

Can you play the piano, the violin, or the trumpet? Numerous plays and musicals call for a character to play an instrument onstage. You don't necessarily have to be a very good trumpet player, for example, to give you an edge on getting a role. Provided you are experienced enough to look convincing when you play it, the actual sound may be provided by someone offstage or in the orchestra pit.

Playing a musical instrument is one kind of bonus ability that can help get you a role. But there are many others. The kid who's his neighborhood's yo-yo champion might get a part because of it. Can you walk on your hands, swing a lasso, ride a horse, or do magic tricks? Keep practicing your offbeat talents, whatever they are. You never know when they might turn out to be useful for your acting.

Backstage Tales

Marsha Van Dyke was a very lovely young woman—an "American Beauty Rose" type—who was an extremely promising violinist. The legendary Broadway director George Abbott was casting the musical version of *A Tree Grows in Brooklyn* when he saw Marsha on television. He immediately got in touch with her and asked her to audition for the violin-playing sister. She would also have to sing, however, and did not have a trained voice. But Abbott paid for her to have singing lessons every day for two weeks, and brought her back several times to see how she was doing. In the end she got the role.

You Were a Fencer in College?

Stage sword fights are tricky to pull off. They need to be carefully choreographed to look realistic while making sure that no one gets hurt. Co-author John Malone had to learn to fence for the role of Edgar in *King Lear* while attending Andover. He and the actor playing Edmund spent two months working with the school fencing coach to learn the basics of fencing to perform a short but dramatic fight scene. Many plays, from Shakespeare to Edmund Rostand's *Cyrano de Bergerac,* require fencing skills. Both authors of this book have known young men with a strong interest in Shakespearean roles who chose fencing as a college sport because it would give them a special skill that was pertinent to the kinds of roles they wanted to play.

Whatever special skills you may have, be sure they don't get rusty. Take lessons to improve your ability. And make sure that directors know you're a juggler, or a fencer, too.

The Least You Need to Know

- Find the right voice teacher to help you improve your range and give you a chance to practice audition songs.
- Take dance lessons to increase the variety of roles that you can play.
- Enroll in acting classes to hone your talents on an individual or group basis.
- Keep developing any special skills and make sure directors know about unusual talents you have.

Learning on Your Own

In This Chapter

- Finding out how much info is in your public library
- Learning how to choose which shows to see
- Discovering a new way to watch movies
- Recognizing the importance of your own real-life observations

As we explored in the previous chapter, paying for lessons from a professional teacher can pay big dividends. Unfortunately, not everyone can afford extensive lessons. If that goes for you, does that mean you'll never keep up with the friend who attends numerous private classes? Of course not. There are many ways to learn about acting on your own. What's more, many of these ways of learning on your own are so valuable that even people who take a lot of paid classes should pursue them also.

In this chapter, we'll tell you about the best ways to unearth this information—from your local public library, from the stage shows you see, and the movies you watch. And, we'll be emphasizing the importance of paying close attention to all the real people you encounter in your everyday life, because the ways they talk and move provide the raw material that actors shape into a new reality on stage.

A Library Full of Plays

The more plays you read, the better prepared you'll be as an actor, and the more ideas you'll have about the kinds of roles you want to play. Classic plays, from Greek tragedies to the works of George Bernard Shaw, from Shakespeare to Chekhov, are among the greatest works of world literature, and thus part of high school and college curricula—and part of high school and college theater troupes' repertoires—throughout the country. Reading a selection of them puts any actor ahead of the game.

But there are also many modern classics, particularly comedies, with which you should become acquainted since they are often produced at the high school level and by community theaters. George Kauffman and Moss Hart's *You Can't Take It With You* and *The Man Who Came to Dinner* are presented constantly, as are many Neil Simon plays. Serious plays by such great American playwrights as Arthur Miller, Tennessee Williams, Eugene O'Neill, Edward Albee, and Lillian Hellman are also widely produced by colleges and community theaters.

Places, Everyone!

It shouldn't be necessary to say this, but evidence from library shelves suggests that it must be: DO NOT write in library books! Keep a notebook handy to write your ideas in. It's fine to attach removable gummed notepad sheets to the pages of library books, provided you remove them before returning the books. But the next reader who borrows the library book won't want to read your cute remarks scribbled in the margins, or even what you consider to be wise comments. If you buy a book, of course, you can write in it all you want.

You can find copies of these plays in almost any public library, sometimes in individual editions for each play, and more often in collections of a playwright's major works. If you know a local theater is producing the play, read it before you see it. In terms of a learning experience, seeing a performance of a work that you've read is the next best thing to performing in the play yourself.

Anthology Heaven

In addition to collections of works by authors and individual plays, you can also find anthologies of plays by several different authors on library shelves. For instance, every year since 1920 an anthology of new plays from Broadway (and Off-Broadway, in more recent years) has been published under the title *Best Plays* followed by the year (1998-1999, for example). These anthologies have had different editors and even different publishers over the decades, but they form an invaluable record of the history of the American theater.

Here you'll find the Tony and Pulitzer Prize winners as well as numerous other hits or critically acclaimed theater works. An annual anthology of one-act plays, called *Best American Short Plays*, with the date, has been published for the past 37 years. Numerous other wide-ranging anthologies are also available, including ones devoted to children's plays. (For further information, see Appendix D, "Further Reading.")

All of Shakespeare?

Most American high schools teach at least one or two of Shakespeare's plays, most often *Romeo and Juliet, Julius Caesar,* or *Hamlet.* College English majors will often be required to take a Shakespeare course that covers many more of the major plays. And there are those people who love literature or the theater who have read all 37 plays over the years. But only about 20 of Shakespeare's plays are regularly performed, although it is perfectly possible to see all of them on stage over the years if you live in an area that has an annual Shakespeare festival.

To help you decide which plays you might want to read first, look at the lists below, which focus on specific kinds of roles.

1. **Lead Roles for Younger Men**
    - Romeo (Romeo and Juliet)
    - Hamlet (Hamlet)
    - Henry V (Henry V)
    - Marc Antony (Julius Caesar)
    - Richard II (Richard II)
    - Benedict (Much Ado About Nothing)
    - Petruchio (The Taming of the Shrew)
    - Oberon (A Midsummer Night's Dream)
    - Edgar or Edmund (King Lear)
2. **Lead Roles for Younger Women**
    - Juliet (Romeo and Juliet)
    - Ophelia (Hamlet)
    - Portia (The Merchant of Venice)
    - Rosalind (As You Like It)
    - Viola (Twelfth Night)
    - Beatrice (Much Ado About Nothing)
    - Kate (The Taming of the Shrew)
    - Cordelia (King Lear)
    - Titania (A Midsummer Night's Dream)

Backstage Tales

Keep a notebook of the plays you have read. Write down the title and author of each play, and make a list of the roles in the play that you feel you might be suited for. Add the age and physical description of these characters, and the size of the roles. Make a note of what it is about such roles that caught your attention and made you think they might be right for you. With such a record, you will be able to quickly review the situation if auditions are announced for a production of the play in your locality.

3. **Comic Character Roles for Men**
    - ➤ Puck or Bottom (A Midsummer's Night Dream)
    - ➤ Fool (King Lear)
    - ➤ Gravedigger (Hamlet)
    - ➤ Sir Andrew Aguecheek (Twelfth Night)
    - ➤ Sir Toby Belch (Twelfth Night)
    - ➤ Feste (Twelfth Night)
    - ➤ Dogberry (Much Ado About Nothing)
    - ➤ Jacques (As You Like It)
    - ➤ Ariel (The Tempest)
4. **Ingenue Roles for Women**
    - ➤ Hero (Much Ado About Nothing)
    - ➤ Helena or Hermia (A Midsummer Night's Dream)
    - ➤ Bianca (The Taming of the Shrew)
    - ➤ Celia (As You Like It)
    - ➤ Miranda (The Tempest)

These lists are only a basic guide, and do not include some of the greatest roles for mature actors, like Falstaff and King Lear, or the heaviest dramatic roles for women, like Lady Macbeth and Cleopatra. Shakespeare's plays contain so many wonderful characters that they provide almost limitless stimulation and opportunity for actors. Some of the plays, like *King Lear*, contain at least eight roles that must be played by very accomplished actors. But there are also many, particularly in comedies, that young performers can triumph in. Both younger and older actors can play many of the "clown" roles, from Hamlet's Fool to Sir Toby Belch, successfully. The role that put the great actor George Rose on the map was Dogberry in *Much Ado About Nothing*, whom he played as an old man even though he was only 27 at the time. We have seen most of the roles in the lists above well played by high school or college actors, memorably so on several occasions.

We Have to See That!

All actors, at all ages, love to go to the theater. There is no better audience than one that includes a number of fellow actors, who will empathize deeply with those on stage. When an actor goes to the theater it is always a learning experience. Moreover, you may see a play for the first time and say to yourself, "I'm going to play that role someday." Co-author Paul Baldwin felt that way on first seeing the musicals *Shenandoah*, *On the Twentieth Century*, and *Sweeny Todd*. John Cullum starred in the first two, and Len Cariou in the third, and each performance won the Tony for Best Actor in a Musical. Interestingly, Paul himself was the first actor to play all three of those roles in smaller theaters following their Broadway runs and national tours.

Backstage Tales

One of the pleasures of going to the theater a lot is seeing actors before they become major stars. In the mid 1960s an acclaimed British production of *Romeo and Juliet,* directed by Franco Zefferelli, came to Broadway for a limited run with the British cast intact. Co-author John Malone went to see it and was bowled over by the performance of the 23-year-old actress playing Juliet. More than 30 years later, the British stage star Dame Judi Dench became well known to Americans as Queen Victoria and Queen Elizabeth I in the movies *Mrs Brown* and *Shakespeare in Love.*

Broadway Comes to Town

Tours of Broadway shows are major money-makers for theatrical producers. Quite often a Broadway show, even after running in New York for a year and a half, doesn't make back its original investment until it goes on the road. Seeing Broadway shows on tour gives people who might otherwise never get the chance to see great stars wonderful opportunities.

Some touring productions are as lavish as they were on Broadway. Others have been cut down in scale to some degree because the sets are simply too expensive to transport and can't be rigged quickly enough in new theaters. The "bus-and-truck" tours of shows that play in smaller cities may be quite modest in terms of scenery and may not have big names performing in them. But all three kinds of productions can be well worth seeing. Here are some guidelines about how to make decisions about what to see:

- If a great star is appearing anywhere near you, go. It may not be the best play or musical you've ever seen, but legends are legends for a reason. It's a safe bet that you'll be telling your grandchildren about seeing someone like Bernadette Peters, just as your parents still remember seeing the great stars of their time.
- If a play or musical has won major awards—Tony Awards, critics prizes, or the Pulitzer—it

Places, Everyone!

Don't think every "Tony Award Winner" is a play you must see. That will depend on what the Tony Award was for! If the only award it got was for a star who's no longer with the show, or for sets and costumes they won't be re-mounting, you won't see what won the award.

will be a worthwhile evening whether the original stars are in it or not. In this case, "the play's the thing."

- If it is a "bus-and-truck" tour, it can be worth seeing either because the play or musical is one you've heard a lot about, or simply because some of the young actors in it are likely to be the stars of tomorrow. It's always wonderful to see a play and think, "That girl playing the sister is going to be a star."

A Special Trip

If you live in a smaller city, or a town in a rural area, going to see even touring productions may mean having to make a special trip by car, train, or bus. Many communities have companies that offer theater bus trips, once a month or so, to big cities. The transportation costs and theater tickets are part of a package deal (sometimes a meal is also included), and because it's a large group, the costs can be less than taking a train and buying your own tickets. Many areas of the country have summer theater festivals that can be a great destination for a family excursion. Whether it's the Oregon Shakespeare Festival or the more experimental Spoleto Festival in Charleston, South Carolina, established theater festivals almost always offer first-rate productions that are well worth a special trip.

Places, Everyone!

Never groan when you hear over the loudspeaker that the star of a show is ill and being replaced by his or her understudy. First, that's an extremely rude thing to do. How would you feel if you were the understudy backstage hearing the audience groan? What's more, understudies are carefully chosen. They may in fact be just as good as the star—they're just not as well known yet. Sometimes an understudy will give a better performance than a star who's past his or her peak. Give understudies a break and you may be pleasantly surprised.

Learning from the Mistakes of Others

The more theater you go to see, the more great theater—and the more disappointing—you'll find. Broadway has its hits and its flops, and so does every other theater in the country. Live theater is an art form, and you never know quite what you'll get. Even the best productions occasionally have off-days, when half the cast has colds or everyone's exhausted from traveling.

A bad production is much less of a loss for an actor in the audience than for most other viewers. That's because you, as an actor, can always learn something from other people's mistakes. Instead of just feeling down because someone is playing a role badly, pay attention to what's going wrong. Where is the actor making mistakes? How would you do it differently? If you start asking yourself such questions, it will have been a valuable lesson, even if not the delightful occasion you'd hoped for.

Watching Movies a Different Way

Movies are the most popular form of entertainment worldwide. Rumor has it that when Elizabeth Taylor was at the peak of her career, even people in remote South Sea villages knew who she was. But for the actor, going to the movies is more than just a matter of being entertained. Once again, it should be a learning experience.

Not Just the Story

When people go to a movie, it's mostly for the story that's being told. But while actors love good stories as much as anyone, they usually focus on the acting. They notice details that most audience members may not, and afterwards they talk about the performances more than most people do. Any actor should cultivate the habit of watching the actors closely. Not only will you learn from what they are doing, but you may even get more out of a movie because of that special attention to the details that make a performance ring true.

Favorite Actors

Everyone has favorite actors. One of the reasons for the success of *Titanic* was that teenage girls were besotted with Leonardo DiCaprio, and kept going back to see him again and again. There's nothing wrong with that. When co-author John Malone was a kid, he often went to the westerns that were shown at Saturday matinees in the small town he lived in. Usually he went alone or with a couple of friends. But if it was a Randolph Scott movie, his mother would come along, too. She just loved Randoph Scott, and his father felt the same way about Rhonda Fleming. That's what makes people movie stars.

Actors have favorite movie stars, too. But usually there's a little more to their choices than is the case with average fans. The actor will come to understand his or her favorite star so well that it's as though they know them personally.

Performance Notes

Don't copy your favorite star's style and method. First-rate acting has to grow out of yourself, and using too many of a famous actor's idiosyncrasies can get tiresome. Using a famous actor as a role model is one thing—copycatting is another.

Repeated Viewings

Any first-rate movie is worth seeing again and again over the years, just as great books are worth re-reading. You will discover new things in them at different points in your life, as your own experiences enable you to bring a new perspective to them. But sometimes it is worth seeing a new movie several times in a short period.

Places, Everyone!

Feel free to see movies again and again. Anything in life that makes you think and feel—and from which you can learn—is worth a second look.

The surprise movie hit of 1999—and it was a huge one—was *The Sixth Sense*. Many people went to see it more than once, either because they were fascinated by it or because they wanted to see if the movie had cheated in leading up to its surprise ending. (It hadn't, almost everyone agreed.) But some people, the authors included, went to see it two, even three times, for a different reason: the performances of Haley Joel Osment, Bruce Willis, and Toni Collette. All three of these actors delivered performances of Oscar caliber (only Willis, perhaps because of Hollywood politics, wasn't nominated). After we had seen the movie twice, and got past the excitement of the extraordinary story, we went a third time just to watch the acting. Now we could pick out very small gestures that carried surprising weight, and we came away with even greater respect for what these actors had accomplished.

Can you apply the lessons you learn watching movie acting to stage acting? Certainly. There are some differences between the two, however. On stage, you must project your voice to fill the theater because microphones are not used except in Broadway musicals. You must be more emphatic with your gestures and facial expressions in order to carry them to the back of theater. But these are technical matters, and many important actors who appear regularly on both stage and screen insist that they change what they do only in degree, not in kind.

The People on the Bus

When you're walking around your hometown, or the local mall, or riding on a bus or subway in a city, you glance at the people around you. Some of them are attractive, some not. Some seem a bit peculiar, others so anonymous that they're almost invisible. Well, look closer. That doesn't mean stare, which is rude and intrusive, but subtly watch how they move and talk without making them aware of you. While any performance must come out of you, other people—loved ones, friends, teachers or co-workers, and those strangers on the bus—are the real-life models for your art.

Observing People in Action

When you look at other people, take note of how they move. Everyone walks a little differently. Everyone uses his or her hands in a unique way. Look more closely. When some people laugh, they throw their heads back, while others lower their chins and chuckle into their chests. Some people keep their heads quite still when they're talking intently. Others bob their heads around so much they look as though they might fall off. Watch what people do with their legs when they sit down—you'll notice a great many variations. Now start asking yourself what all these different kinds of body language mean. What do they tell you about the kind of person you're looking at?

Larry, an actor friend of ours, has been making up stories about people since he was a kid. That old lady at the laundromat, the girl on the next block who jogs twice a day even though she's thin, the almost-silent brother of the newsstand owner—Larry notices them and makes up stories about them. He imagines their lives. He doesn't care whether or not what he imagines is correct. It's a way of trying to understand human beings better, and a lot of actors do it. Give it a try.

Whether you just observe what people do, or make up stories to fit their actions as well, you're learning something about what makes people tick. And the more you understand about that, the better actor you will be.

Backstage Tales

Some actors have an extraordinary gift for mimicry. That can lead to a career as an impressionist, one who switches from sounding and looking like one famous person to another at a moment's notice. *Saturday Night Live* has always favored cast members who are good at mimicry, the better to skewer politicians. And some serious actors are amazing mimics, but only do it at parties. Oscar winner Kevin Spacey demonstrated on *Inside the Actors Studio* that he could mimic an extraordinary number of famous stars, and do it so well that you could tell he was turning into Johnny Carson or Katharine Hepburn by the tilt of his head even before he produced their voices. Yet other great actors can't mimic anyone. And many professional impressionists will admit they can't play serious roles. Mimicry is a gift, and a delightful one, but it isn't necessarily related to playing Hamlet or Juliet.

The Actor's Memory

All actors draw on memories of real life. They use their own experiences, both happy and sad, to help create the emotions of the characters they are playing. Some actors do this very consciously; Method actors are trained to do it. Others do it almost unconsciously most of the time. But either way, an actor's memory is always at work during the creation and the performance of a role.

One actor may flip through mental file cards of people he or she has observed when trying to figure out how a character should walk. Another may seem to find a similar answer almost instinctively. But both are drawing on their actor's memory, even though they are doing it in different ways. Everything an actor observes in his or her daily life becomes a part of that memory bank that will be drawn upon in performance. For many that is one of the greatest attractions of acting, beyond the glamour and the applause, because it means that an actor is learning his or her craft every waking minute. And that is an immense source of satisfaction.

The Least You Need to Know

- Make the fullest possible use of your public library, and read as many plays as you can.
- Go to see as many plays and musicals as you can, understanding that you can learn from both good and bad performances.
- See a movie a second or third time if you think you'll discover more secrets about the performances.
- Observe people around you in real life. They are the raw material of an actor's memory.

Chapter 9

Experience Counts

In This Chapter

- Discovering why small parts matter so much
- Exploring ways to stretch your talent
- Recognizing the need to play roles you don't like
- Finding out what you can learn backstage

Few actors start out playing the leading role, though it occasionally happens in high school or college if the director decides to take a chance on a beginner. But even that lucky person is likely to play a smaller part in the next show, and will have to develop his or her talent further before getting major roles on a regular basis. But no matter what size role you play, you will be learning the craft, and the art, of acting every time you appear on stage. Your talent can be exercised and stretched even in small roles. Because experience counts, the more parts you play, the better prepared you will be for a starring role when it does come your way.

In this chapter, we'll be showing you why small parts matter so much, not only as a way to grow, but also in terms of the overall success of a production. You'll learn how to use small roles to stretch your talent. We'll be discussing why even a part you don't much like can be a valuable stepping stone to the roles you really want. And we'll explore the ways in which even an offstage job, like managing props, can be valuable to any actor.

Small Parts Matter

It is an axiom of the theater that "There are no small parts, only small actors." "Small" refers not to physical size, of course, but to talent. An actor whose talent is minimal can fail to impress the audience even if he or she's playing the largest role; indeed, his or her limitations will become clearest in a large part. On the other hand, a fine actor can make even a small role memorable. Beatrice Straight won a Best Supporting Actress Oscar for her performance in the 1976 film, *Network,* even though she appeared in only two short scenes, and Dame Judi Dench won for her role as Elizabeth I in 1998's *Shakespeare in Love,* with eight minutes onscreen. Parts with only a few lines but maximum impact exist in hundreds of plays, ranging from the Gravedigger in *Hamlet* to the telephone repairman in Neil Simon's *Barefoot in the Park.*

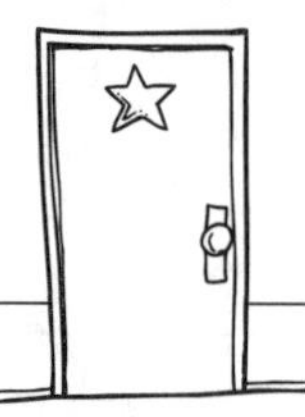

Backstage Tales

Co-author John Malone saw Judd Hirsch as the Telephone Repairman in *Barefoot in the Park* on Broadway. It was Hirsch's first Broadway role and he was hilarious. He went on to an award-winning career, but probably never got bigger laughs in his life. John himself played the part of Bergetto in John Ford's 1627 tragedy *'Tis Pity She's a Whore* while at Harvard College. It was the smallest role he ever played, only 50 lines, but one of the most rewarding. Bergetto is a dim-witted but engaging character who has several major laugh lines (always pleasing to the audience in a tragic play), and then, when he is killed by mistake, has a very moving death scene. No actor can ask for more than to have an audience roar with laughter and end up with tears in their eyes, and if it only takes 50 lines, so much the better.

Even the Messenger Needs to Be Good

Many distinguished actors have started their professional careers playing messengers in Shakespearean or other classic plays. All the messenger usually has to do is go onstage and inform a lead character that something important has happened, like whether a battle has been lost or won. But you'd better get it right or the whole scene may fall apart. In his autobiography, Alec Guinness tells how his career almost ended before it started when he tore onstage and delivered not his own line but the reply to it that was to be spoken by the lead character he was reporting to. Almost every theatergoer has seen a messenger or two who messed up his only line in a way that drew a big laugh, completely undercutting the tension of the scene and forcing the other actors to work twice as hard to get the play back on track.

And bad acting in small parts can ruin a play. The audience may laugh in the wrong place, or get bored listening to secondary characters drone on in a flat voice. Plays create an illusion of reality, and it is easily punctured. It is crucial that small parts be played as convincingly as large ones. So instead of lamenting the fact that you have only five lines, make the most of them. You will not only help make the production a success but also signal that you are ready to take on greater responsibility with a larger role next time around.

Able Support

Many fine actors are seldom cast in starring roles. It may be that they don't have the right kind of looks for romantic leads. Or their voices may have a quality that is better suited to comic relief, or to villains. But there's no shame in being a character actor playing smaller parts. Indeed, a fine supporting actor may get more roles than someone who is made for romantic leads for which there is more intense competition, and there are usually more character roles to fill.

Backstage Tales

Critics often take special note of actors who have a reputation for excellence, saying, for example, "Mary Jones offered her customary able support in the role of the nurse." Having such words as "solid," "reliable," and "dependable" connected to your name is no small accomplishment. Keep in mind that star actors are all too likely to see the word "disappointing" in a review, especially if their previous performance was deemed "dazzling." Smaller character roles offer a chance for steady excellence that lead actors sometimes envy.

Stealing the Show

Actors in smaller roles often end up stealing the show. This has nothing to do with mugging to excess or deliberately drawing attention away from another actor. It's a matter of being so good in a role that the audience remembers your performance more vividly than they do anyone else's. Comic roles are particularly likely to bring such results.

In the Broadway musical *Woman of the Year*, starring Lauren Bacall, there was a scene in which the glamorous Bacall sang a duet with a frumpy housewife played by

Marilyn Cooper. The song was called "The Grass Is Always Greener." In it, the high-powered Bacall character lamented that she was too busy to enjoy the simple things in life, to which the Cooper character kept responding with lists of household drudgeries. Cooper was hilarious in the part and this single song brought her a supporting Tony Award. Was Bacall upset that Cooper got so much attention for this song? Not at all. She told an interviewer that she knew the song was the best in the show, and that she considered herself lucky to have someone as good as Cooper to sing it with.

Performance Notes

Don't *try* to steal a scene. It's something that only happens because you do an extraordinary job. If you try to steal the show, your performance is likely to be hammy.

When she accepted her Tony, Cooper noted that she was a poker player, and suggested that if you stayed in the game long enough, you were bound to win. This is a view that every actor should keep in mind—especially those who find themselves playing smaller roles on a regular basis. Whether secondary roles are a way of gaining experience that leads to bigger ones in the future, or are an actor's destiny, the possibility of major rewards always exists.

Stretching Yourself

As you gain experience as an actor, you'll probably want to take on roles that stretch your talent, roles that present difficulties you haven't faced before. That might mean playing a character considerably older than yourself, or taking on a serious role even though your gift seems to lie more in comedy, or undertaking a major role that you aren't sure you're really ready for.

Playing Older Than Yourself

In high school and college productions particularly, the roles of the older characters must be cast with actors who are in actuality many years—even decades—younger than the part calls for. Some actors have a natural gift for playing older than they are. We've previously mentioned how George Rose scored a great success playing Dogberry as an old man, even though he was only in his late 20s. Both authors of this book played older roles at young ages, John taking on Hero's father Leonato in *Much Ado About Nothing* at 17, Paul playing Colonel Pickering in a summer theater production of *My Fair Lady* when he was 26. Paul went on to play numerous lead characters that were 15 to 20 years older than his actual age.

But even if you don't have a particular gift for age roles, you are likely to find yourself playing one at some point. The requirements of such a role involve using both your voice and your body in different ways. If you've carefully observed all kinds of people in the ways discussed in the previous chapter, you will have a good sense of those differences. A slower or weightier way of carrying yourself when walking will give some sense of age. The voice may need to be pitched a little lower for a middle-aged character, or somewhat higher for an elderly one. Makeup will be important, of course, and it is always fun to add the facial lines and the streaks of gray in the hair that suggest how you yourself may look later in life.

Performance Notes

When playing a character older than yourself, avoid exaggeration. Keep in mind that some people are still quite young in appearance at 50. If you go too far, you will end up with a caricature instead of a character. Be especially careful about age makeup. Accentuate the slight lines that have already appeared on your face rather than painting in dark lines where there are none at all. It takes less than many young actors realize to give the appearance of age.

"I'm Better at Comedy"

Most actors who have played both comedy and tragedy will tell you that comedy is actually more difficult. That's because getting your laughs requires split-second timing. Everyone knows people who simply can't tell jokes properly, no matter how funny the material, and the same is true of some actors. But although comedy may be more difficult, it is usually comic actors who are most reluctant to try something serious, rather than the other way around. Serious actors often think comedy is easier than it looks, while comic actors tend to believe serious acting is more difficult than it looks.

Many of the finest actors can play both kinds of roles with equal conviction. Jack Lemmon started out as a comic actor, and won his first Oscar for his supporting role in *Mr. Roberts* in 1955. But although he was nominated for Best Actor for his hilarious performance in 1959's *Some Like It Hot,* his Oscar in that category came for his dramatic role in 1973's *Save the Tiger.* He has since alternated the two kinds of roles but received his greatest acclaim in serious parts.

A comic actor who undertakes a serious role often gains new respect. Dan Ackroyd, who became a star in the original cast of *Saturday Night Live,* played comic roles in movies for years. When he finally played a dramatic role in 1989's *Driving Miss Daisy,* he was nominated for an Oscar for the first time for his supporting role as Jessica Tandy's concerned son. He took the dramatic plunge rather late, but it's never too late to test yourself. When co-author Paul Baldwin was in college, one of his good friends was a girl who was noted for being very funny, both onstage and off. She was very surprised when a director asked her to audition for the role of the shy, slightly crippled Laura in Tennessee Williams's *The Glass Menagerie.* But the director had seen something in her that she hadn't credited, and she gave a lovely performance in the role.

When you read plays—or go to see them—keep your eye out for roles that are different from what you usually do, but that arouse your interest. If you think, "I wish I

Places, Everyone!

Quite a number of famous actors have said that they often accept a role *because* they fear that it is too much of a stretch. They feel that facing up to such challenges is very important. But sometimes taking a leap into the unknown ends in failure, and critics find the actor "miscast." Thus, while challenging yourself may lead to great things, you also have to be prepared to fall on your face. But it wouldn't be a true challenge if that possibility didn't exist.

Places, Everyone!

Keep in mind that good directors have a gift for seeing possibilities in an actor that he or she hasn't recognized. If you're asked to take a role that you think might not be right for you, trust the director's intuition. You will certainly learn a lot by doing the role and it may open up whole new vistas to you.

could do that," don't leave it as mere fantasy—work on it. Record yourself reading some lines from that role. Listen to the results and then try to improve your performance. You may gain enough confidence, working alone, to eventually audition for a different kind of part.

Hamlet at 18?

Many serious actors regard playing the role of Hamlet as a test of acting skill that every actor should attempt at some point in a career. (Some women have played the role, too, most notably the legendary Sarah Bernhardt.) The role is very complex and open to many different interpretations. The authors have seen many performances of it, and one of the best was also one of the oddest, given by Nichol Williamson using a Scots accent.

Can an 18-year-old possibly hope to play such a difficult role with any success? Of course, and we've both seen it done by different young actors. After all, Hamlet is a university student, and an actor who is the approximate age of the character may be able to bring a freshness to the role that a great actor of 40, for all his or her other strengths, may have trouble matching.

The same goes for extremely difficult female roles. You're asked to play Lady Macbeth while a sophomore at college? Go for it. You probably won't succeed entirely (some of the world's greatest performers have tripped over this part), but you will learn far more by attempting this fiendishly difficult role than by playing something seemingly safer like Juliet.

I Hate This Part, But ...

Professional actors play roles they don't like, or even detest, quite often. In the heyday of the Hollywood studios, from 1930 to the middle of the 1950s, major stars often found themselves stuck with roles they hated. They were under contract and had to do what the studio bosses told them, although a few, most notably Bette Davis, went on strike in order to get better roles. Actors who belong to regional theater companies sometimes have to play roles they don't like even today. And sometimes the working actor simply has to take whatever he or she can get just to pay the rent.

For amateurs it's a little different. They aren't forced to take a role for economic reasons, but they quite often do so out of loyalty to a community theater or to a director friend who desperately need them. In college an actor may take a role he or she isn't thrilled about because many of their friends are in it and they don't want to be left out. But while there's a downside to playing uncongenial roles, you can also gain a great deal from them.

Playing a role you don't much like is often the only way to get cast when you're starting out. But the experience often turns out to be more worthwhile than expected. You will "get into" the role as rehearsals progress, and may come to find it interesting after all. More important, every role enriches your acting vocabulary. Later, playing a part you love, you may well find that you can apply something you learned when you played a role you didn't like.

The Thankless Role

Even Shakespeare wrote a number of thankless roles. Hamlet's friend Horatio is a prime example. He's on stage a lot and has a good many lines, but there's hardly a memorable one in the lot. He asks questions, and tells Hamlet what other characters are up to, and dispenses a little advice, which is never taken. Mostly, he has to stand around and look suitably impressed while Hamlet says famous lines like, "There are more things in heaven and earth, Horatio, than are dreamt of in your philosophy." Take that, you dummy. But Horatio is absolutely necessary to the unfolding of the plot. Hamlet has to have one confidante he can speak frankly to, since he is busy playing emotional and intellectual games with everyone else.

No actor is going to say, "I just can't wait to play Horatio." Still, the role must be filled, and you can learn things while playing it. Let's list a few of them:

- Being able to listen well on stage is crucial to the art of acting, and the role of Horatio will give you a great deal of practice.
- Knowing how to stand still on stage is more important than many young actors realize, and Horatio gets to do a lot of that, too.
- Horatio does get to react to several bizarre situations. There's the appearance of the ghost of Hamlet's father on the battlements to be awed by, and Hamlet's feigned (maybe) madness to be puzzled by, and the deaths of one character after another to be horrified by. What's more, Horatio has to be subtly awed, puzzled, and horrified, which is no easy trick.

Obviously, this list is slightly tongue-in-cheek, but not altogether so. You really will learn quite a lot by playing this kind of "thankless" role that can be applied in more exciting circumstances in another play. There are numerous thankless roles for

Places, Everyone!

Put all your "thankless roles" on your resumé! Directors won't think, "Oh, a bad actor" or "a dull actor," but rather, "Ah, a responsible actor." They'll know that if you've kept working, you're a good actor, or learning to be one, and your experience will be a plus.

women as well. Sonya in Chekhov's *Uncle Vanya*, for example, is similarly self-effacing, a rather ordinary person trapped in a household full of flamboyant nut cases.

When you get cast in a thankless role, give it your fullest attention and learn as much as you can in the process.

The Nasty Character

Many actors love playing villains because such roles are often the most colorful. But some actors, especially those with less experience, don't care for it. Part of the reluctance to play an unpleasant role may be a fear that members of the audience will think that's what the actor is really like. Or, on a deeper level, it may be a reluctance to delve into the darker side of ourselves—and all human beings do have a darker side. Good acting, however, is not just a matter of "showing off." It requires the courage to explore human nature in all its forms. Playing a nasty character can actually make someone a more mature and complete person exactly because it involves exploring that dark side.

One of the curiosities of the theater is that many actors who specialize in villains are often particularly gentle and nice people. On the other side of the coin, there are actors who always play sympathetic roles, and are greatly liked by audiences, yet are difficult to get along with offstage or off camera. The world of the theater, like the world in general, is a complicated place.

So don't be afraid to play nasty characters. Their unpleasantness won't rub off on you, and they offer a great opportunity to show how good an actor you really are. Since nasty characters must also fascinate, playing such roles will inevitably help you grow as an actor.

Okay, I'll Do Props

Professional actors get used to rejection. All but the biggest stars fail to get cast more often than they succeed. For younger actors starting out in high school or college, however, the failure to be cast can be a dreadful blow. "Am I really that bad?" they may ask themselves. But talent may not have as much to do with it as a wide range of other factors, which we'll be discussing in detail in Chapter 16, "The Waiting Game." Directors in amateur theater will often ask an actor who hasn't been cast to take a backstage job of some kind with the production. Let's explore some of the reasons why you should seriously consider such an offer.

Backstage Tales

The musical *Oliver* is a good example of how reality is transformed in the theater. Fagin, the starring role, is a man who runs a gang of urchin thieves—hardly a "nice" man in the usual sense, but he is written and played as an endearing character. Bill Sykes, however, is a murderous villain. He is very important to the balance and plot of the play. Unless he is "hissable," and even a bit frightening, Fagin will seem a darker character than the musical needs him to be. The actor playing Bill Sykes always gets third billing after Fagin and Nancy because he must be played by someone very good, and it often happens that this actor will draw the best reviews of the entire cast. Nasty he may be, but the role is a wonderful one for an actor.

Even Offstage You Learn

While the actors in a play or musical get to take the bows and to bask in audience approval, they can't do their jobs onstage without a great deal of help from the offstage personnel who make the technical side of the show run smoothly. Among the offstage jobs that must be filled are the following positions:

- A stage manager, who will be in charge of everything that goes on backstage during a performance, from seeing to it that the actors are in place to make their entrances, to calling for the rise and fall of the curtain. The stage manager usually has one or two assistants, as well.
- The assistant to the director, who takes on all kinds of administrative duties and may also work with actors who need additional help with their roles.
- A property manager, who is responsible for procuring all the needed props for the show and keeping them organized and ready to use backstage.
- Scenery carpenters and painters, who build and paint the set under the direction of the set designer.
- Lighting technicians, who help to hang, focus, and run the lights according to the specifications of the lighting designer.
- Costume assistants, who help to sew, alter, or go out and buy the costumes sketched or chosen by the designer.

- Prop constructors, who may be asked to create anything from armor to a fake bird.
- Makeup assistants, who may also be needed to help at least some of the actors prepare for each performance.

Places, Everyone!

If you're asked if you'd be willing to work backstage, think about your other abilities aside from acting. If you can draw, you could put that talent to work painting sets or assisting with makeup. Do you build your own bookcases at home? Obviously, stage carpentry would come easily to you. Do you like to tinker with machinery? If so, working as a lighting technician might be the ticket. Are you a "neatnik" who's always got everything organized? That's a quality prop people need. There's an outlet for numerous kinds of ability backstage.

It takes a lot of people to fill all these jobs, every one of which is important in its own way. And you can learn something about the theater by doing any one of them. Both authors worked backstage during high school or college productions, doing jobs that ranged from painting sets to stage managing. We both learned a lot in the process.

Every Aspect of the Theater

All actors should know at least something about every aspect of the theater. Putting on a play is a collaborative effort in every way, and while the actors are the most prominent of those collaborators from the audience's point of view, they need the backup provided by the backstage workers to give convincing and reliable performances. Working backstage teaches actors to fully appreciate the importance of those jobs.

In addition, the backstage view of a production enables an actor to understand the art and craft of acting itself in new ways. When you are onstage playing a part, your focus is narrowed. Observing the flow of a play from backstage gives a better sense of its totality. And there will be details of the actors' performances that will become clear in a new way as well. Every actor we know who has worked backstage feels that the experience taught them something they were able to use as an actor in subsequent productions. Often, in fact, you can learn even more watching actors from backstage than you would as an audience member.

Experience counts in the theater. All kinds of experience. The small role, the part that requires you to stretch yourself, even the role you don't really like, will make you a better actor in the long run. And backstage work is not only a way to be part of a production you wanted a role in, but also will acquaint you with other aspects of the theater that will expand your knowledge and enhance your understanding of what acting is all about.

The Least You Need to Know

- Remember that small roles are vital to the overall success of any production, and may even enable you to steal the show.
- Make an effort to stretch your talents by playing roles that force you to try new things.
- Keep in mind that supposedly thankless or unpleasant roles will enhance your abilities.
- Don't turn up your nose at backstage work; it can be a valuable learning experience.

Looks Aren't Everything

In This Chapter

- Finding out why offbeat looks can be a plus
- Discovering ways to create the illusion of good looks
- Learning how to make the most of the qualities you have
- Exploring the problems that exceptional beauty can create

The movies and television have put a much greater premium on sheer physical attractiveness than was the case before the 1920s. While there were always stage stars who were remarkably beautiful or handsome, to judge by portraits from previous centuries and photographs taken from the 1860s on, many of the greatest stars were not extraordinarily good-looking. Makeup, stage lighting, the distance from which the audience viewed the actors, all enabled many actors with less-than-perfect profiles to create the illusion of beauty.

But film magnified the faces of actors to such a degree, especially in close-ups, that someone with a remarkable face could become a star even though he or she was not a particularly talented actor. On the other hand, great talent could compensate for less-than-gorgeous looks even in the movies. Edward G. Robinson and Bette Davis more than held their own against the likes of Tyrone Power and Lana Turner.

In this chapter, we'll talk about the ways in which physical appearance affect the kinds of roles an actor is likely to get. We'll be exploring the world of the character actor, and the pluses that less-than-perfect looks can bring. Good actors know how to create the illusion of good looks, and we'll give you some tips on how they do it. We'll make clear why neither beauty nor youth is the only path to success. And, finally, we'll deal with the odd truth that exceptional looks can also create problems for an actor.

All Kinds of Characters

The great plays and the merely good but very popular plays that are most often produced by high schools, colleges, and community theaters are filled with *character roles*. The character may be an older man, such as Big Daddy in Tennessee Williams's *Cat On a Hot Tin Roof*, or a young woman, such as Agnes Gooch in *Auntie Mame*. The former is a serious role, the latter a comic one. The comic role could be that of an older woman, like the imperious Lady Bracknell in Oscar Wilde's *The Importance of Being Earnest*, and the serious one a young man such as the befuddled Henrik in Stephen Sondheim's *A Little Night Music*. Thus, character roles run the entire gamut in terms of age and acting style for both men and women.

Stage Directions

Most dictionaries define a *character role* as one that has pronounced or eccentric qualities. Thus, almost every role in *The Wizard of Oz*, except for Dorothy, is a character role, including the Tin Man, the Scarecrow, the Cowardly Lion, the good and evil witches, and the Wizard himself. There are many character roles in realistic movies and plays as well. The mother in Neil Simon's *Barefoot in the Park* is a character role, although she is not eccentric, and the same is true of the doomed young military school student in William Inge's *The Dark at the Top of the Stairs*.

Sometimes even the leads are character roles. There's nothing to suggest that Willy Loman in Arthur Miller's *Death of a Salesman* or Martha in Edward Albee's *Who's Afraid of Virginia Woolf?* should be portrayed by particularly good-looking or glamorous actors. On the contrary, Willy is an ordinary man beaten down by life, and Martha is a middle-aged woman going slightly to seed from too much alcohol. If an exceptionally good-looking person is to play such roles, he or she must work to disguise their physical attractiveness, as Elizabeth Taylor did in the movie based on the Albee play.

Even in musicals, where it is more usual for the leads to be very attractive, numerous star roles require character actors, including Tevya in *Fiddler on the Roof*, Coco Chanel in *Coco*, and both Sweeny and Mrs. Lovett in *Sweeny Todd*. The Phantom in *Phantom of the Opera* is a character role, and so is Norma Desmond in *Sunset Boulevard*.

None of these roles calls for men or women who are especially good-looking, although very handsome men or beautiful women can play them with the proper makeup. What they do call for are superlative actors.

Woody Allen Isn't Handsome

Woody Allen almost always gets the girls in his movies. He is by no means a handsome man, and it might be that he wouldn't be cast in such roles if he wasn't also the writer and director of his movies. But Humphrey Bogart wasn't conventionally handsome, either, and that didn't keep him from playing opposite Ingrid Bergman in what many people regard as the most romantic movie ever made, *Casablanca*. Interestingly, Bogart's initial attempt at a movie career didn't go well. Although he had played romantic leads on Broadway, studio executives didn't think he was handsome enough. But he changed their minds with his combination of charisma and talent.

It's more difficult for women lacking in conventional beauty to get romantic leads in Hollywood, but not in Europe, where Jeanne Moreau, with bags under her eyes at an early age, and Anna Magnani, who was never exactly thin, were two of the greatest women stars for decades.

Backstage Tales

On stage, few of the greatest female stars have been beautiful in the conventional sense. Helen Hayes, Julie Harris, Colleen Dewhurst, and today's Cherry Jones and Stockard Channing, are women with a great deal of character in their faces, but no one ever confuses them with the Ava Gardners or Sharon Stones of the world. Every one of them played a "siren" at one time or another, however. Julie Harris won her first Tony Award for playing Sally Bowles in *I Am a Camera*, on which the musical *Cabaret* was based, and Liza Minnelli won an Oscar for her performance as the enticing Sally.

A Memorable Face of Its Kind

Greta Garbo's beautiful face is unforgettable. But so are many faces that are almost ugly. Charles Laughton was fat and had heavy jowls, Robert Morley had those problems plus a weak chin, Judith Anderson had a huge beak of a nose—and yet all had major careers as actors both on screen and on stage. For many character actors, the strangeness of their faces provided their ticket to a great career. Peter Lorre, short and square with a moon face and saucer eyes, was regarded by many in Hollywood as its most talented actor, and was never out of work for decades. The heavy, jowly Marie Dressler was the top box-office star in the early 1930s, and won an Oscar for *Min and Bill* in 1931. (She also has the most famous double take in the history of the movies to her credit—rent a video of 1933's *Dinner at Eight* and wait for her reaction to the news that Jean Harlow is reading a book. Just thinking about it makes these authors laugh.)

So, if you think you have an odd face, keep in mind that, far from spoiling your chances as an actor, it may be the foundation of your success. Memorable faces, beautiful or not, make for memorable performances.

There's Always a Part for You

Some extremely fine actors have unmemorable faces. They aren't beautiful but they aren't offbeat, either. You'd never give them a second glance on the street. But, once on stage, these faces can take on many different guises. Sheer acting ability lights them up, and the average-looking actor with such acting ability can play an extremely wide range of roles. With the right makeup and costume, they can seem very good-looking, but in another role they can seem thoroughly homely. Because such people look and act so different from role to role, they seldom become stars, but there's always a part for them because they can transform themselves into so many different kinds of characters.

Performers of this sort are likely to be called "an actor's actor," meaning that while audiences tend to take them for granted, other actors realize how tremendously talented they are. It is also sometimes said that such actors are "too good for their own good." They tend to disappear into roles to the extent that audiences sometimes don't realize they saw them playing a totally different kind of part only a few months ago.

Among contemporary performers, Mary Louise Parker is widely regarded as an actor's actor. Her performances in such movies as *The Client, Boys on the Side,* and *Portrait of a Lady* are so different from one another that audiences scratch their heads and say, "Where have I seen her before?" The same is true of Bill Paxton, whose roles as a dangerous drug dealer in *One False Move,* an astronaut with a queasy stomach in *Apollo 13,* and a tornado expert in *Twister* seem to have been played by three entirely different people. Such chameleon-like abilities may not get actors on the covers of magazines, but they do earn the greatest respect from fellow actors and from directors.

Acting as Though You're Beautiful

Few roles in dramatic literature absolutely demand that very beautiful women or extremely handsome men play them. There are exceptions, of course. Helen of Troy crops up in quite a number of plays, including Shakespeare's *Troilus and Cressida,* Christopher Marlowe's *Doctor Faustus,* and Christopher Fry's *Tiger at the Gates.* Marlowe wrote the famous line, "Was this the face that launched a thousand ships," and in all of these plays, therefore, a beautiful woman must play Helen. But most female characters in plays, whether it's George Bernard Shaw's or Shakespeare's quite different Cleopatras or Henrik Ibsen's Hedda Gabler, are described in terms of their allure rather than their sheer physical beauty.

The same goes for male roles; for example, the character of Romeo is traditionally very good-looking. Early in their careers, John Gielgud and Laurence Olivier alternated the roles of Romeo and Mercutio in *Romeo and Juliet* and, even though Gielgud was the less conventionally handsome of the two, critics generally felt that he was more convincing as Romeo, and that Olivier was a better Mercutio.

Backstage Tales

Co-author John Malone was fortunate enough to enjoy the friendship of the late Neville Coghill. An Oxford don who was the leading Chaucer scholar of his time, Coghill was also a man of the theater. He directed countless plays at Oxford, and several in London's West End. He cast Richard Burton in his first role, as Angelo in an Oxford production of *Measure for Measure*. Years later, when Burton was married to Elizabeth Taylor, they appeared in a production of *Doctor Faustus* at Oxford under Coghill's direction, with Burton as Faustus and Taylor in the nonspeaking role of Helen of Troy. Coghill, a very eloquent man, said that all he had to do was look across a dinner table into Taylor's violet eyes to be rendered momentarily speechless. But very few women—Greta Garbo and Ava Gardner also among them—could have that effect on people simply on the basis of their beauty.

But if you are just a moderately pretty young woman or a nice-enough-looking young man, it is still possible to act as though you were the envy of all eyes. If an actor behaves as though he or she were the best-looking person in town, the audience will be convinced that the actor is indeed just that.

Projecting Radiance

Physical attractiveness is not just a matter of having a fine facial structure and a good body. The light in a person's eyes and the way he or she smiles are extremely important as well. How a person moves, whether walking or gesturing, can enhance or diminish the impact of a good build or fine figure. No matter how beautiful a woman or how handsome a man, if their voices are squeaky or monotonous, their attractiveness will seem lessened.

Suzy Parker was the most famous model of her time and her gorgeous face adorned magazine covers all over the world. Then she started to make movies. Her movements were stiff and her voice was flat, and the critics lambasted her in 1957's *Kiss*

Them for Me, in which she played opposite Cary Grant. She worked hard and improved some in *Ten North Frederick* and *The Best of Everything*, but there was still too great a gap between the radiance she had in a still photograph and what happened on the screen. She had no real gift for acting, and soon retired from films.

But just as a world-famous beauty like Parker can fail to connect with an audience, far less beautiful women can often have extraordinary impact. Ellen Barkin has an odd face, with a largish, slightly crooked nose and a certain angularity to her features. Yet she is regarded as one of the sexiest stars to come out of Hollywood in a long time. In movies like 1987's *The Big Easy* and 1989's *Sea of Love*, critics felt she almost burned holes in the screen. And she wasn't just sexy—she was beautiful. Barkin also happens to be a serious actor of great intelligence. She has said flat out that she knows she isn't beautiful but that she gradually learned to act as though she were.

Backstage Tales

Katharine Hepburn was very beautiful as a younger woman, and she was always able to project beauty at any age. But the 1956 movie *The Rainmaker* provides a special acting lesson in creating radiance. Hepburn plays a Midwestern spinster, and used almost no makeup so that her freckles are evident. As she falls in love with the supposed rainmaker who says he can end a drought, she becomes ever more beautiful in the course of the film, without adding makeup or changing her hairdo.

Learning to project the radiance that makes an audience think of you as beautiful or handsome takes work. But if your acting talent is genuine, you will eventually be able to convince audiences that you are as striking as any character is supposed to be.

Handsome Is as Handsome Does

Early in his career, Walter Matthau established himself as a character actor on Broadway, playing mostly comic roles of the kind with which he would later delight millions of moviegoers. A production of a play by the French playwright Jean Anouilh was about to open when the actor playing a crucial role was injured. A desperate search ensued for a replacement, and someone suggested Matthau's name. The producer reacted incredulously, saying that the role was a Count, wealthy and worldly. He said that as good as Matthau might be at stumblebums, he could never play such a role. Matthau's agent told the producer that he didn't know what Matthau could do, and so the young actor was given an audition. The producer couldn't believe his eyes. There was Matthau gliding across the stage as though he were walking on air, the very picture of European elegance. He got the part.

Walter Matthau often said that the key to a character was his walk. If you watch him in a movie like *Plaza Suite*, in which he plays three different roles, you can see what he is doing in this regard. Simply by altering the way in which he moves across a room, he becomes a different person. He almost doesn't need the wigs he uses. If you can walk elegantly, you will become elegant. If you move with the assurance of a very handsome person, you suddenly become more handsome.

Even an actor who is very handsome, like Brad Pitt, can accentuate or downplay that quality depending upon the character he is playing. In *A River Runs Through It*, in which he plays a "golden boy," he is dazzlingly handsome and walks as though he owns the world. But in the thriller *Seven*, in which he plays an arrogant and ignorant detective with a blue-collar background, that dazzle has disappeared. Dazzle would be inappropriate to the character, and Pitt purposely obscures how handsome he actually is, slouching and moving with a certain jerkiness.

Handsomeness—or beauty—is in the eye of the beholder, and any good actor can alter what is seen.

Making the Most of Yourself

What kinds of roles are you best at? What sort of character is particularly well suited to your looks and your personality? Some actors hit their peak when they are quite young, while others do not put everything together until much later in life. If you have genuine talent and you persevere, your time will come. You will find yourself at a moment when everything fits together. But actors must have the patience to wait for that moment, and have the self-knowledge to grasp opportunity when it presents itself.

Finding Your Special Niche

A recurrent fear of star actors is that they will become typecast, and will only be offered parts of a certain kind. Doris Day was the top box-office star for more years than anyone else in movie history, but she was also trapped by her success. In one movie after another in the 1950s, she played essentially the same character, just in different story situations with different leading men.

But many character actors have a different view of typecasting. If you can discover a type at which you excel, you can be assured of a role in numerous different productions. What's more, there are greater differences between one villain and the next, or between one mother and the next, than is sometimes the case for leading ladies like Doris Day. Jack Palance played innumerable villains, as Christopher Walken has also done more recently, but they always managed to find something in each role to make

Places, Everyone!

If you keep getting cast as a villain, the comic maid, or the dumb sidekick, look for the distinctions between one role and another as soon as you start memorizing your lines. Does the latest villain have a special way of saying things that you can accentuate? Can you come up with some physical tick that's new? The situations the character actor may find himself or herself in may be similar from play to play, but you can always find details that can make each role fresh.

that villain distinctive. Palance was so good at villains that he was nominated for Best Supporting Actor in 1952 for the Joan Crawford melodrama *Sudden Fear* and again the next year for the great Western *Shane*. He ultimately won the Supporting Actor Oscar for a comic variation on the theme in 1991's Billy Crystal movie *City Slickers*.

Better with Age

Some actors become famous as teenagers, or even younger. Shirley Temple was the top box-office star of the 1930s, but by her mid-teens her career was over. Judy Garland became a household name with *The Wizard of Oz* as a young teenager, but some of her best work would come as an adult. In recent years we have seen the child and teenage star Ron Howard turn very successfully to directing when he grew up. The jury is still out on whether Anna Paquin, who won an Oscar as a child for 1993's *The Piano*, will have a strong adult career.

But while some actors may be has-beens at 20, many others do not come into their own until their 40s or 50s. John McGiver was a high school teacher in the Bronx until he was in his 40s, when he became a familiar actor in the movies and on television, appearing in everything from 1957's *Love in the Afternoon*, with Audrey Hepburn and Gary Cooper, to 1969's Best Picture, *Midnight Cowboy*. More recently, Olympia Dukakis, who had played tiny roles in movies and on television, and had run her own small New Jersey theater with her husband, burst into stardom in her 50s as Cher's mother in 1987's *Moonstruck*, for which she won the Oscar for Best Supporting Actress. Dukakis was never a stunning woman, but she has a fascinating face that came into its own once she reached a certain age.

Beauty Fades

In some ways, character actors have an advantage over those who play the romantic leads. Lead actors have to worry constantly about their looks. Every new wrinkle, every added pound, is like a warning bell, tolling the passage of the years. "How much longer," the physically gorgeous must ask themselves, "will they let me play the romantic lead?" The character actor, on the other hand, may even welcome wrinkles around the eyes and an expanding waistline—those signs of aging may make them more convincing in the kinds of roles they want to play.

Backstage Tales

In 1981, a friend of the authors—who had won an Obie for her Off-Broadway work—was taking an acting class with an important New York teacher. There was a woman in the class whom everyone felt sorry for. She was almost a dwarf in stature, and not at all pretty. She seemed very talented but she was already in her mid-30s and had never gotten anywhere. "It seemed such a shame," our friend said, "that she was still wasting her time." A year later, the dwarfish woman won the Oscar for Best Supporting Actress in *The Year of Living Dangerously*, playing a male Asian photographer who was so small he could ride on the shoulders of the reporter he worked with, a terribly difficult role to cast. The actress, of course, was Linda Hunt. Hunt has gone on to a very distinguished career and is one of the most-often-heard voices on television doing voice-overs for commercials. "So much for strange looks and being too old to get anywhere," our friend said with a laugh.

Too Pretty to Be Good

Believe it or not, many young actors, male and female, don't get taken as seriously as they would like because they are so very lovely or handsome. For years, critics dismissed Kim Bassinger as just a pretty face. She finally broke through that barrier in 1998 with her Golden Globe and Oscar-winning performance as a soulful high-class call girl in 1998's *L.A. Confidential*. Many critics still do not give Melanie Griffith her due despite her sterling work in a wide range of roles over more than two decades. A pretty face may make you a star and attract moviegoers to the multiplexes, but it often makes critics suspicious.

Being very good-looking can be a special burden for a male actor, too. Tony Curtis was a big star at the box office in the 1950s, but the critics routinely dismissed him as a "pretty face" who couldn't really act. It wasn't until he played a ruthless press agent in 1957's *Sweet Smell of Success* that they began to change their minds. He wore a false nose that coarsened his face as the escaped convict chained to Sidney Poitier in 1958's *The Defiant Ones*, for which both men were nominated for Best Actor. Richard Chamberlain, and more recently Richard Gere, went through similar problems.

Don't Count On Your Looks Alone

While plastic surgery can do extraordinary things to an aging face and body, it cannot completely make members of the moviegoing or theatergoing public forget that someone has been around for a long time. Thus, the actor who has been blessed with extraordinarily good looks needs to start thinking quite early about ways to extend his or her range as an actor, so as to be prepared for the inevitable transition to character roles later on.

Backstage Tales

Marlene Dietrich was one of the first Hollywood stars to put her career in the hands of plastic surgeons. She no doubt extended her film career considerably, and was still glamorous in *Judgment at Nuremberg* in 1961 after more than 30 years as a star. But she paid a price, too. Even during the 1950s, people were joking that Dietrich had had her face lifted so many times that her bellybutton was in the middle of her back. And during the last several years of her life, Dietrich hid out in a Paris apartment, allowing no one to see her face except for servants and her immediate family. The great beauty ended her life in a dark cave of an existence. Her story can make one think that beauty can be a curse as well as a blessing.

Looks aren't everything. The lack of exceptional good looks can in fact make an actor more creative and resourceful. There are so many different kinds of roles for actors that almost anyone with real talent—and the patience and strength to keep learning—can eventually find a worthwhile niche.

The Least You Need to Know

- Remember that few roles demand physical beauty, and that character roles abound.
- Learn how to carry and express yourself so that you seem radiant, and the audience will believe that you are.
- Think about what special niche you can fill, and keep in mind that age may actually bring new possibilities.
- Never count too much on good looks; it's acting ability that matters most in the end.

Part 3

Oh, Those Auditions

Very few actors like auditions. They are nerve-wracking because you have only a few minutes to make an initial impression on the creative team that will decide whether to cast you in a play or musical. That team may comprise just the director and an assistant for a play, but the music director and often the choreographer will also be present for a musical. Depending upon the situation, one or more of the producers, who deal with the financial aspects of a production, may attend as well.

Because auditions are such pressured situations, actors must be thoroughly prepared for them in several different ways. In this section of the book, we'll guide you through every aspect of the audition process. We'll advise you on how to prepare your picture and resumé to make the best impression. It's very important to know what the director is looking for, and we'll suggest ways to clear that hurdle. Special attention will be given to preparing songs to sing at musical auditions. We'll give you tips on how to dress for an audition, and we'll discuss audition etiquette. Finally, we'll suggest ways to keep your cool while waiting to find out if you've been cast.

Chapter 11

Picture and Resumé

In This Chapter

- Discovering how to show your strengths without fibbing
- Learning the basics about good audition photographs
- Recognizing the importance of a clean, updated resumé

At the high school level, all you need at an audition is your own talent—no pictures or resumés are necessary because the director has access to your school records if he or she needs more information about you. By the time you reach college, however, the situation may change, especially if the student body is a large one. The college freshman who has acted in high school, or in some summer productions at a hometown community theater, should make those credits known when auditioning, and the easiest way to do that is with a resumé. In terms of community theater, a picture and resumé are always a good idea, even if you're well known from past productions. The director may have come in from out of town for some productions, and even a director you've worked with before may have forgotten some of your credits—one or two of them might be in roles similar to the one you're now auditioning for.

In this chapter, we'll explore how to put together a picture and resumé that will do you justice. A good picture and resumé will not assure that you are cast in a given production—that will depend on the talent you demonstrate at the audition as well as the abilities of other actors who want the same role—but a bad picture and resumé can certainly cost you a part. We'll be showing you how to make sure that doesn't happen.

Truth in Advertising

A resumé is supposed to be a brief document that tells people who you are in a way that is relevant to the position you are applying for. That means that resumés for different kinds of work sometimes require different kinds of information. In the acting world, the most important aspect of your resumé is the list of roles you've previously played, and where you performed them. Training you have received, whether at a formal school of the performing arts or in a college program, is important. You should always include additional training, whether with an acting, singing, or dancing teacher. And a list of any special skills—from juggling to fencing—can help give you an edge over other candidates for a role.

It is essential that this information be accurate. Truth in advertising applies as much to the acting world as it does to the business one.

Fake Credits Mean Trouble

Quite a lot of people, in all fields of endeavor, are tempted to make their resumés look better than reality would allow. All too often, people lose jobs or are demoted when their employers discover that they do not have the college or post-graduate degree listed on their resumés or never attended the institution named. Recently, the head of a government-funded scientific program, a man widely regarded as a genius, was demoted when it was discovered that he did not have the Ph.D. he had claimed. That incident made headlines. But even if such a transgression doesn't make the papers, it can cause acute embarrassment, and can seriously damage a reputation. That goes as much for your acting resumé as for any other kind.

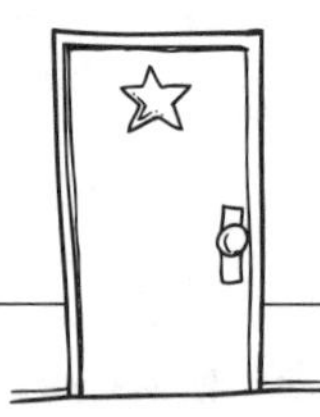

Backstage Tales

During her 1998 international concert tour, culminating with her appearance in New York at Carnegie Hall, Bernadette Peters told a story about false credits. She noted that in the program it stated that she had played Dainty June in a production of *Gypsy* as a youngster. "But that's a lie," she noted. "I was actually the understudy to the girl who played Dainty June." She explained, wryly, that her mother had put it on her resumé, and it had been popping up ever since. As one of Broadway's reigning musical stars, Peters didn't have to worry much about repercussions at this late date. But this story does serve as a reminder that once you put a false credit on a resumé, it is likely to get into a program note, and it can haunt you for a very long time.

We know of one young actor whose entire resumé was mostly imaginary. He had not, in fact, played Hamlet in college. He had not played the lead in Neil Simon's *Broadway Bound* at a summer theater in Ohio. And he had not played Jesus in the musical *Jesus Christ, Superstar.* In reality, he had played Rosencrantz in *Hamlet,* and he had understudied the Neil Simon role but had never gone onstage. And, worst of all, he could barely carry a tune, so he certainly hadn't sung the very difficult role of Jesus.

When this young man gave his resumé with all these lies in it to the director of a community theater production of *Our Town,* he thought he was on safe ground. He had memorized and worked on two of Hamlet's soliloquies, and he knew the Neil Simon role because he had in fact understudied it. If he was asked to perform from either of these plays, he was prepared to do so. Since he was a fairly good actor, the director was interested in him. So much so that he asked him to sing one of the songs from *Jesus Christ, Superstar*—the next production mounted by the theater was going to be *Godspell,* and the director thought he might be able to get a head start on casting that musical. Well, our tone-deaf hero bombed out and had to admit that he hadn't played Jesus. And what about the other roles? Caught. The director told him not to come back until he had actually done something and had a program with his name printed in it to prove it.

Don't put lies on your resumé. No matter how thin your list of actual credits is, stick to the truth. Remember that you'll probably get to show your stuff—at least in amateur theater—even if you've never acted before. If you have genuine acting ability, you may well get a role despite your lack of experience. Everyone has to start somewhere, and it's never a black mark to try. Directors are always looking for new talent.

Of course, some people do put lies on their resumés and get away with it. You may know someone who's done it. But how do you feel about that person? You don't respect them much for doing so, do you? Is that what you want other people to feel about you? Besides, there's no way of telling who's going to get away with resumé lies and who isn't. So, no matter how tempted you may be, tell yourself you're one of the ones who'll get caught, and stick with the truth.

Only the Best Credits?

A different kind of problem arises if you have a lot of theater experience—paring down the credits. If you've been acting since you were a kid, and you're now in your 20s, there's no point in listing every one of your two dozen credits. No one is going to care that you were in a national commercial for diapers at the age of two, or that you played the youngest daughter in a community theater production of *The Sound of Music* in grade school. In fact, putting credits from so far in the past on your resumé can make you look a little silly. Deciding what to put on your resumé and what to leave off is mostly a matter of common sense. But there are exceptions to consider. Take a look at the list below. We have used the musical *Oliver!* to suggest how somewhat different kinds of acting experience could influence whether or not you should include a credit:

- Suppose that Sam had played the title role of Oliver in a community theater production when he was 10. He's now 23, and has played more than a dozen major roles in high school, college, and other community theater productions. The fact that he played Oliver is now no longer very relevant, and can be safely left off his list of credits.
- On the other hand, let's say Sam played Oliver at 10 but then didn't do any acting until very recently, with only a couple of other roles to cite. In this context, his early experience takes on greater significance, and he should list it on his resumé.
- Suppose, once again, that Sam played Oliver at 10, and has played numerous major roles since. But let's add one new fact to this picture. The show he is about to try out for is a new production of *Oliver!* Sam still looks young at 23 and is not very tall. He could certainly play the leader of Fagin's gang, the Artful Dodger; the fact that he once played Oliver, and thus knows the show well, counts for something. He should return that credit to his resumé for this audition, even though he would normally omit it.

Performance Notes

When you go to see a play and look at the program, you will sometimes find that actors playing minor roles have even longer biographical profiles than the star. Even in the professional theater, actors are generally allowed to write their own biographies, but an endless bio about a minor player looks a bit foolish, especially when the star's is far more succinct. Don't go overboard, either in your resumé or in your program biography.

If you have a lot of credits, you need to pare them down simply because a resumé that goes on for pages becomes an annoyance. A resumé is supposed to encapsulate your career, not record your entire life history. You don't want the director to mutter "What's this in here for?" But sometimes the context of the situation will dictate that you should add or delete a particular credit. Think about why each credit you list is there. If it shows your versatility or is particularly relevant to this show, then include it even though it is not very recent. Is it a very difficult role that you played some time ago? Include it to show that you can handle tough assignments. At the same time, delete any credits that don't have a real point.

Picture Perfect?

When a famous actor dies at the age of 80-something, the photograph accompanying the obituary will often have been taken decades ago, showing the performer in his or her prime. That's all very well for obituaries, but it won't do for auditions. The photograph you take to an audition should be recent enough so that it actually looks like you. And it should show you to your best advantage without being so glamorous or retouched that it bears little resemblance to your actual appearance. There is a fine line between the perfect audition photograph and one that is so picture perfect that it's out of whack with reality.

Get a Professional Photo

Professional actors often spend hundreds of dollars a year on photographs, and big stars may spend much more—although the bigger the star, the more likely it is that many photographs will be paid for by the producers of a play or movie.

Amateurs do not have to spend a lot of money on photographs, but it is generally necessary to have them taken by professionals. A cropped photo (to give a close-up of your face) taken by a family member on your trip to Disney World or Yellowstone Park is not going to do the job. You may, however, have a friend who is a very fine photographer, even though not a professional, and someone with that kind of expertise may be able to take some *head shots* that are up to professional standards for little or no money. Unless your photographer friend does his or her own developing, however, you must still pay for the printing of the multiple 8 × 10 copies you will need.

Whether a professional or a skilled friend takes your photograph, you can save money by getting a contact sheet—a single page that shows small "thumbnail" prints of an entire role of film. Professionals will automatically start by giving you a contact sheet. Choose two to five photos that you think are the best, and have 5 × 7 prints made from them. You can then decide which one (or perhaps two) to have blown up to an 8 × 10 size, and printed in multiple copies. You may need to go to a full-fledged photo shop, rather than to your nearest pharmacy, to have all this done properly, if you are not using a professional from start to finish.

Digital cameras, used in conjunction with computers, are beginning to change the way resumé photos are produced. But the technological accessories necessary to get top-quality photos can be expensive, and most amateurs will probably find it best to stick with the tried-and-true contact sheet approach.

Stage Directions

A **head shot** is exactly what it sounds like: a close-up photo of just your head and shoulders. Men can wear turtlenecks or open-collared shirts with or without a sweater. Turtlenecks or a simple blouse are fine for women. Don't wear shirts or blouses with patterns, since they will only distract from your face. The background should be as neutral as possible. Black and white rather than color photographs are most often used, and may be required.

Looking Good, Looking Too Good

Obviously you want to look your best in a resumé photo. A haircut for men, or at least a trim, is in order. (Patrick Stewart–types with bald heads have it easy in this respect, although that shiny top may present a challenge for the photographer.) Some women are experts at doing their own hair; others will want to make a trip to the beauty salon. But the day before having a resumé photo taken is not the time to go for a whole new look in terms of a hairdo. By the time you get the photos back, you may have decided that the new style doesn't suit you after all. Stick with a familiar and well-liked hairstyle.

Generally, men should not wear makeup for resumé photographs, although a few with skin problems use some kind of subtle base as a normal matter. Women have to be careful about the makeup they wear for a photo shoot. Everyday makeup rather than a special-occasion effort is the safest route, for several reasons. One is that a head shot accentuates makeup, and if you apply too much eyeliner or lip gloss, you can end up looking cheap. In addition, you'll use the photo for some time—months, even a year or more for amateur actors—and in that period you may be auditioning for several different kinds of roles. Thus, natural makeup that accentuates your best features makes the most sense. If you use so much makeup that it suggests you play nothing but glamour roles, you may be undercutting your chances of getting a girl-next-door part.

But the main reason to avoid wearing too much makeup is that you may not have time to duplicate that kind of effort before an audition. If your appearance in person is so different from the photo, you will create confusion in a director's mind, and confusion about who you really are can cost you roles. For the same reason, you should say no to suggestions that your photo be heavily retouched. If someday you get to be so famous that you're featured on the cover of *Vanity Fair*, retouching may become a matter of course. But it's a mistake for an amateur.

For both women and men, a photograph that makes you look very good without being unnaturally pretty or handsome is the best bet.

Neatness Impresses

Make your resumé easy to read and well organized. If the design is too cluttered, it not only makes it more difficult to read, but also plants subliminal clues that you aren't completely on top of things. Actors use a variety of formats for resumés, but here is a basic example that will serve for most amateur actors:

Your Name	Age:
Your Phone Number	Height:
Your Address	

LIST OF CREDITS:

Organize your credits by the importance of the role. List the name of the play and its author first, followed by the name of the character you played, and then the name of the theater company that produced the play, as in the following examples:

The King and I Rodgers and Hammerstein	Anna	Mulberry Theater Lancaster, PA
A Midsummer Night's Dream William Shakespeare	Titania	Rand Playhouse York, PA

If you think it's appropriate, you can also add the name of the director, under the author's name. If you've played roles in several different productions at the same theater, it's smart to list them one after another. The fact that a single theater has been so pleased with your work that you have been cast many times over suggests not only that you are talented but also that you are easy to get along with.

TRAINING:

Under this heading, list any special acting, singing, or dance classes you've taken, with the name of the teacher. If you received the training at college or at a professional school, give the institution's name, as in the following example:

Advanced Acting/Mark Sterne/North Texas State University

SPECIAL SKILLS:

List any special skills in the order of your proficiency, as follows:

Piano

Tap Dancing

AWARDS:

List any awards you've received, giving the full name of the award, as well the name of the play and the role for which you received it, and where and when you played it, as follows:

Best Supporting Actress, Theater Department Award, for Gypsy Rose Lee in *Gypsy*, North Texas State University, 1984.

(Professional actors usually list their union affiliations, such as Actor's Equity, immediately under their names, with the home phone or voice mail number below that. Many professionals choose not to list their age and height, but will give the name, address, phone number, and fax number of their agents. Professionals usually do not give a home address.)

Places, Everyone!

When a director or casting agent asks what year you played a certain role, know the answer. It's okay to say "five or six years ago," but don't be so vague that it sounds as though you're hiding the fact that you haven't played a lead since high school.

Revise That Resumé

Obviously you should update your resumé every time you play a new role. If it is a less-important role than some others you have played, you don't have to put it right at the top, but if it's a role particularly relevant to the play you are auditioning for, you might want to put it first. For example, if you just played your first Shakespearean role, and you are about to audition for another play by Shakespeare, you should certainly put that one role at the top, even if it is a relatively small one. The same holds true if you're beginning to branch out into musicals after doing many straight plays.

Backstage Tales

Some actors have the good fortune to play one or two roles many times. Co-author Paul Baldwin, for instance, played Don Quixote in *Man of La Mancha* in six different productions, and the lead role of Charlie Anderson in *Shenandoah* seven times. Listing them all separately takes up too much space. Instead, indicate multiple portrayals of the same role by giving the title, author, and character, and type "(Six productions)" at the end of the line where you would usually put the name of the theater.

As we suggested earlier in this chapter, you should always think about whether you might want to delete a credit that has little relevance to a show you are about to audition for, and substituting with one that does. Even 15 years ago, such revisions could be time-consuming, but in the computer age, it is very simple to make changes. If you use a computer, it is wise to keep a copy of each revised version on a disk, so that you can print out fresh ones as needed with little effort.

Always a Fresh Copy

Every resumé you hand in at an audition should look as though it were hot off the presses. A resumé with crumpled edges or torn corners, never mind coffee stains, is no advertisement for seriousness of purpose. Never just scribble a new piece of information on an old resumé with a ball-point pen. If you can't be bothered to provide a pristine copy of your resumé, why should a director even consider giving you an important role?

The Least You Need to Know

- Never add fake credits to your resumé or you'll always be wondering when you'll be found out.
- Have a professional photograph for your resumé picture, and strive to look your best in it without overdoing the glamour.
- Always hand the director a fresh, clean, recently revised copy of your resumé.

Chapter 12

Know What They're Looking For

In This Chapter

- Learning how to judge which part is right for you
- Understanding the differences between styles of acting
- Finding out how to get hold of scripts ahead of time
- Discovering ways to cope with "cold readings"

One of the main reasons some actors consistently fail to get the roles they want is that they continue to audition for the wrong parts. Such actors may be just as talented as others who are cast on a more regular basis. They run into trouble because they don't have a clear idea about what the director is looking for, or because they misjudge their own strengths and weaknesses. The first problem often arises because they don't know enough about a particular play before they audition for it. The second can occur because they aren't fully honest with themselves about how suitable they are for certain roles.

In this chapter, we'll suggest steps you can take to increase the likelihood of getting cast. How can you figure out which part is right for you? What do you need to know about the style of a given play? How can you get hold of a script before an audition, particularly when the play is a new one? We'll have some answers to all these questions. Finally, we'll give you tips on how to handle a "cold reading" of lines you've never seen before.

You're Not That Small for Sixteen

You've always wanted to play the title role in the musical *Annie*. Not only do you have naturally curly red hair, but you also can belt "Tomorrow" with the best of them. There's just one problem. You're 16 now, and Annie is supposed to be a preteen moppet. You persuade yourself that you still have a good chance—after all, you're not a tall girl. The trouble is that you're not all that small for 16, either. You need to face facts: You are too old and too big for the role.

Stage Directions

"Too short, too tall, too thin, too fat, too young, too old, too pretty, not pretty enough ..." These phrases run through directors' heads when they **type out** an actor with barely a glance. The actor doesn't stand a chance because, in the director's view, he or she doesn't conform to the physical characteristics wanted in the role. What's really discouraging is that an actor can be typed-out as too short at one audition and too tall at the next. Sometimes it seems you can't win.

Most actors make this kind of mistake occasionally, and not just when they're in their teens. Men and women in their late 40s manage to delude themselves that they can play a character who's supposed to be 30. Heavy-set actors are certain they'd be a success as a romantic lead, if just given a chance. These aspirations aren't necessarily foolish, either. After all, good actors constantly play roles that are quite unlike themselves—that's a large part of what acting is about. An actor can indeed succeed in a role for which he or she seems totally wrong on the surface. Nevertheless, actors often get *typed out* at auditions, eliminated just because of their age or physical characteristics.

Because the typing in or out of actors can seem so arbitrary, you should certainly go ahead and try out for roles for which you seem at least fairly well suited. But you can save yourself a lot of disappointment if you stay away from those that are clearly beyond your reach. There is no point in auditioning for the role of Tony in *West Side Story* if you weigh 260 pounds, even if you can sing it beautifully. But there is another Tony, the central character in Frank Loesser's musical *The Most Happy Fella*, which you might be exactly right for since he is supposed to be heavy.

The guy who got the role of Tony in *West Side Story*, however, should stay away from this Tony, although he might well be fine for another role in the show. Within reason, take a few chances. Some directors even like to cast against type. But if a certain kind of physical look is required for a role, don't beat your head against the wall when it just isn't you.

Which Part Is Right for You?

It's a great thrill to read a play and find a character with whom you can really identify, and to say to yourself, "Someday I'll play that part." But identifying with a character psychologically doesn't necessarily mean you will be able to play the role effectively. A great many other factors enter into the picture. Here is a list of questions to ask yourself when you are attracted to a role:

- Am I the right age for the role?
- Am I built right for the role?
- Do I have the right kind of voice for the role?
- Does the role require talents I don't have, like dancing?

You may have to rephrase these questions to fit particular circumstances. For example, in high school and college productions, someone young will usually have to play the roles of the older characters, although occasionally a teacher may take on a difficult older role. So, your age doesn't necessarily rule you out. But by rephrasing the question, you may still see that the role of the grandfather isn't for you. Ask yourself if you really can play an elderly man. If you're 19, but still have a very young face and an obviously athletic build, there's bound to be someone else around who looks older and is either quite thin or quite fat and thus better suited to playing an old codger.

On the other hand, if a community theater mounts the production and you're a good-looking guy of 27, it may be beside the point to audition for an older role. That's because the theater company has a regular pool of men close to the actual age of the character to draw upon.

Backstage Tales

Some actors are geniuses and can play anything. The Broadway debut of Julie Harris came when she was 24, playing 12-year-old Frankie Addams in Carson McCullers's *Member of the Wedding*. She was nominated for an Oscar playing the same role in the movie version two years later. In between, she won the Tony for her second Broadway role, as the sexy, bohemian Sally Bowles in John Van Druten's *I Am a Camera*, which she also played in the movie. She was much too old for Frankie, although small and thin enough, but those qualities might seem wrong for Sally. In other words, the usual rules didn't apply. But then, she was perhaps the greatest actor of her time. Are you?

The Age and Height Ratios

Sometimes you're just right for a role, and the director would love to cast you, but there may be other considerations. If you're a woman and quite tall, say 5'11", your height could rule you out because the best actor for the leading man playing opposite you is only 5'6". The height discrepancy is going to look silly in the big romantic scenes, even if it's true that plenty of short men have tall wives in real life. Such a height discrepancy can work on stage in a comedy perhaps, but if the play is Shakespeare's *Antony and Cleopatra,* it's just not going to make sense to have the great Roman general five inches shorter than the Egyptian queen.

What's more, there may be only one actor available who's really up to the role of Antony. Unfortunately for you, there are two other women, both under 5'6", who could play Cleopatra. Even though the director knows you'd be better, the lack of choice when it comes to Antony usually means that one of the shorter women will get the role. Of course, this could also work the other way around, so that the director will cast a tall, but less talented, Antony opposite you because you're the only one up to the role of Cleopatra.

Similar problems can develop in terms of age. A friend of the authors thought he had landed the role of Fredrik in Stephen Sondheim's *A Little Night Music* in a professional summer theater production. He was 38, a trifle young for the role, but he had a mature bearing and voice, and had played the roles of numerous characters a few years older than he actually was. At the last moment, however, the owner of the theater, a woman in her mid-60s, decided that she was going to play the role of Fredrik's once and future lover, Desirée. A 38-year-old co-star was going to make her look ancient, so another actor in his mid-50s, who was not as good, got the role.

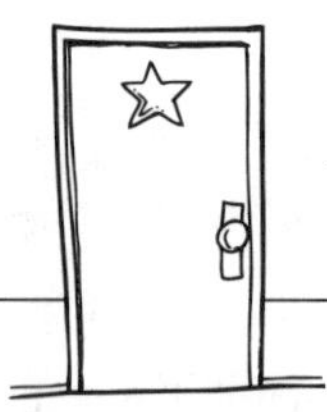

Backstage Tales

In the 1957 movie *Boy on a Dolphin,* Alan Ladd played opposite Sophia Loren. Ladd was one of the shortest actors in Hollywood, while Loren one of the tallest actresses. Much of the movie took place in outdoor seaside settings, filmed on location in Greece. In many scenes between the two stars, a trench was dug that Loren would stand in while acting a scene with Ladd, so that she would not appear taller than him. But you can't do that on stage. In a stage production, one of the stars would have to go, so that the pairing of performers didn't cause this kind of problem.

Whatever aspect of the age/height ratio comes into play, this kind of thing is heart-breaking—and it happens all the time. You never know when it will crop up or which way the chips may fall. Often no one tells you why you didn't get a role, and unless you see a performance of the production, you may never have a clue. The only solace is the recognition that such considerations may sometimes get you a role instead of losing one for you.

It's a Comedy, Not a Tragedy

The most famous of all theater "logos," which dates back to the ancient Greeks, is the juxtaposed masks of comedy and tragedy, the comic mask having a mouth with lips upturned in an exaggerated smile, and the tragic mask having a downturned mouth that expresses the pain of despair. Most playwrights are better at one or the other, and that's been true from the start. Sophocles wrote tragedies, most famously *Oedipus Rex,* while Aristophanes wrote comedies like *Lysistrata.* The greatest of all playwrights, Shakespeare, could write comedies or tragedies with equal success, but no one else has ever had such equal facility in the two forms. What's more, even his tragedies usually have comic characters (the Gravedigger in *Hamlet* and the Porter in *Macbeth,* for example) while the comedies have serious scenes in which misunderstandings appear temporarily disastrous.

Most actors, like most playwrights, are better at either comedy or tragedy, although a few can play both with almost equal conviction. Which are you? Do you feel more adept at making an audience laugh or moving it to tears? Can you do both? When making decisions about what parts (or plays) to audition for, you need to have a firm grasp of the scope of your own talents, as well as the kind of acting a given play or part calls for.

Places, Everyone!

Check out such British sitcoms as *Keeping Up Appearances* and *As Time Goes By* if you want to better understand the difference between the styles of American and English comedy. Most PBS stations around the country show them both fairly regularly. Note, in particular, how controlled the actors' gestures are. Even the simple act of picking up a phone tends to be more character-specific than is the case in most American sitcoms.

Know the Style of a Play

While plays can be generally divided into the categories of comedy and tragedy, each category has many subdivisions. Neil Simon is regarded as one of America's greatest modern comic playwrights, while in England that honor goes to Alan Ayckbourne. Both write domestic comedies about fairly ordinary people in the midst of the kind of turmoil that creates hilarity. But the differences between them are considerable, and are not limited to the differences between British and American English, nor mere social distinctions. An American actor can have a perfect British accent and still have trouble playing Ayckbourne, and the same can be said of British actors in respect to Simon. That's because Simon's plays call for a naturalistic style of acting of the kind usually seen on American television sitcoms, while Ayckbourne's require a style that is at once more exaggerated and more precise.

There are also great differences between various kinds of tragic acting. Shakespeare requires a certain grandeur of style, while an American tragedy like Arthur Miller's *Death of a Salesman* is performed in a far more realistic style. Some plays straddle styles. In Eugene O'Neill's *A Long Day's Journey into Night,* the roles of the senior Tyrones require a grand style, while their sons must be played more naturally—that very difference in style helps to define the chasm between the two generations.

Backstage Tales

In 1961, co-author John Malone saw a renowned French theater company in the 1637 tragic verse masterpiece of Pierre Corneille, *Le Cid.* In the last act, the Spanish princess, played by Maria Casares (who will be known to some for her performance in the film classic *Children of Paradise*), had a very long, enraged speech lamenting her romantic betrayal. Casares hardly raised her voice, and stood stock still at center stage. She indicated her fury by slowly, half-inch by half-inch, raising her arms from her sides until on the final words she clasped them to her breasts with sudden violence. It was electrifying beyond measure, but very few plays can be acted with such steely formal style.

When reading any play that you are thinking of auditioning for, think not only about the characters and the language, but also about the style of acting required. If it is unclear to you what the style should be, go to the library or check the Internet for information about the author. Ask other actors if they've ever appeared in a play by that writer, and find out what their experiences were like. The more you know about the style of acting required, the better you can prepare for an audition.

What's Your Forte?

Emotional truth is more important to an actor when playing tragedy, while timing is more important when playing comedy. Both qualities are necessary to a fine performance in either comedy or tragedy, but the balance between them shifts. Many major actors feel that comedy is more difficult than tragedy, but the latter is more likely to win awards, perhaps because it seems more difficult.

All that huffing and puffing, those heart-rending cries and profusely shed tears, appear to be taking an enormous toll on the actor, and thus are taken as a sign of great seriousness—and talent. Comedy, on the other hand, works best when it appears almost easy. That, of course, is what makes it so difficult—making the hard look simple demands exquisite control.

Most actors know which they're better at. Those who can do both with almost equal proficiency are likely to land many difficult parts, since some of the most taxing roles require aptitude at both. For example, Charlie Anderson, the father in the musical *Shenandoah*, has both songs and dialogue scenes that can make audiences cry, yet in the middle of the play there is a scene in which a suitor pleads to him for his daughter's hand, which is very funny indeed. An actor who can't get his laughs in that scene will not move audiences as deeply either, because the contrast between them is essential to making Charlie so deeply empathetic.

Even if you're not equally good at both, you can still play starring roles. An actor like Charlton Heston has done very well without giving the slightest indication that he can play comedy, and an actress like Lucille Ball could become beloved without ever pulling off a heavyweight dramatic role. Mary Tyler Moore, on the other hand, surprised the world by turning from light comedy to serious dramatic roles later in her life, earning many accolades for her work.

Performance Notes

Don't feel less competent if you're most comfortable playing only comic roles or only serious ones. Later in life you may develop new confidence and abilities. Start with what's most comfortable. You can expand your range later, and even if you don't, there's no shame in being terrific at one style of acting.

Just remember that each of the most important playwrights require a different style. Sometimes the differences are subtle, as between Chekhov and Ibsen, and sometimes very marked, as between Noel Coward and John Osborne. Find out where your strengths lie, audition for roles that play to them, and you'll more often get the part you want.

Can I Read the Play First?

If at all possible, read a play before auditioning for it. You may have seen a movie version of a play, but don't assume that's all you need to know. Most plays are rewritten for the screen. Entire scenes may be dropped—sometimes very important ones. Besides, you need to rehearse any speech from the play that you want to perform at an audition, and that means having a script from which to work.

You should always read the entire play unless time is very short. Your knowledge of a character or event that appears in Act II may change the way you approach a speech for your character in Act I. In addition, the director may see something in you that suggests suitability for a different role than the one you are interested in. If you haven't read the whole play, you'll be unprepared to shift gears and read for another part.

Places, Everyone!

You can ask actor friends if they have a copy of a particular play you can borrow. But don't get annoyed if other actors say that they're sorry but they don't lend their scripts to anyone. Some actors make notes in plays they own that may be as private as a diary. Others may have had bad experiences lending plays that weren't returned. You're asking a favor, and you mustn't take it badly if you are turned down.

Acquiring Published Plays

If you're asked directly by a director to audition for a role, ask him or her if a script is available. He or she may supply you with one, which can save a lot of hunting around.

Most often, though, you'll have to find a copy of the play yourself. Start with the college or public library, and check not only the catalogue listings under the name of the playwright, but also anthologies of plays.

In the end, you may have to buy a copy of a play. Major bookstore chains like Borders and Barnes & Noble will usually stock anthologies of major playwrights, some plays of note in soft cover editions, and hardcover copies of a few recent plays. You can also search the Internet, not only major sites like Amazon.com and bn.com (Barnes & Noble), but also the used book listings at bookfinder.com, Alibris.com, and others. But your best, and least expensive, source is likely to be the performing scripts of plays published by Samuel French (see Appendix C, "Play and Sheet Music Scores"). These editions, with their orange paper covers, are the mainstay of theater companies at all levels.

Backstage Tales

In 1960, Adams House at Harvard College sponsored a playwriting contest, which senior Arthur Kopit won. The play was produced the next fall, directed by a junior named Michael Ritchie. Co-author John Malone was the assistant stage manager of this production of *Oh Dad, Poor Dad, Momma's Hung You in the Closet and I'm Feeling so Sad*. The production was an enormous success, and actresses like Bette Davis and Siobhan McKenna came from New York to see it with an eye on the role of Madame Rosepettle. Kopit went on to become an important playwright, writing such acclaimed plays as *Wings*, while Ritchie would eventually direct such movies as *The Candidate* and *The Bad News Bears*. Local or college playwriting contests can lead to big things and give an amateur actor something to talk about forever.

Ask for Scripts of New Plays

Many colleges have playwright contests, and many community theaters produce the occasional new play by a local or regional playwright. Since these are usually as yet unpublished, all scripts will be xeroxed copies of the original. Copies may or may not be available to actors who want to audition for the production. Always ask if you can get one. You may at least be provided with copies of a few pages containing speeches or scenes that the director wants to hear at auditions. This isn't ideal, but it's a lot better than nothing.

"Cold Reading" Terrors

A "cold reading" is the long-standing theater term for performing a speech or scene you've never seen before. You are more likely to be asked to do this when you audition for a new play than you are for a classic of the theater. But even if you have read the play beforehand, and have come in with a rehearsed speech to perform, the director may ask you to audition for a part you hadn't considered, using a speech or playing a scene you barely recall looking at. The director may have already seen an actor he or she thinks will be perfect for the part you want, but believes that you might be right for another one, and suddenly you are faced with a page full of unfamiliar words.

When asked to do a cold reading, some actors react like a car on a freezing winter morning: The engine stutters and coughs and then stalls altogether. Cold readings are difficult, and can strike terror to the heart. But there are ways to make the situation less frightening.

Performance Notes

Unless you have a photographic memory, don't even try to memorize a speech you're giving for a cold reading. The effort to remember the exact words can just end up confusing you. The director will allow you to have the script page in your hand when you perform, so the brief time you have to look it over is better spent trying to understand the material than trying to memorize it.

Questions to Ask

If a director asks you to do a cold reading, he or she will usually give you a few minutes to read the speech or scene over before you perform. Read it once very quickly to get a sense of what is going on, and then read it again more slowly, thinking about the rhythm of the language and the emotions being expressed.

You probably won't have an opportunity to read the material aloud; other people may be trying to concentrate on the same material or are auditioning while you're preparing. Some people do find it helpful, though, to move their lips silently to the words they're reading. No one will think you're peculiar if you do that.

When you're called to perform your cold reading a few minutes later (you probably won't have more than five minutes), it is perfectly permissible to ask a couple of specific questions. Don't try to initiate a long discussion about the scene or the character you are being asked to portray; there isn't time for that. But you might wonder if a character who's telling another one off is really angry or just being sarcastic, and the answer to that question could keep you from adopting the wrong approach. You might be unsure of how old a character is, and it would certainly help to know. If you don't know how to pronounce a particular word or foreign phrase, by all means ask about it. So long as you keep your questions short and specific and don't ask more than a couple, the director will be happy to answer. He or she knows cold readings are difficult.

Instant Focus

The most important thing you can do when faced with a cold reading is to concentrate absolutely on the speech or scene you are going to perform. Don't start wondering why you're being asked to do this, or lamenting the fact that you have to do it, or, worst of all, worrying about whether you can do a good job. Such thoughts will just make you more nervous, and distract from the task at hand. Nobody is going to expect you to be perfect. Focus on the words on that page, and shut out everything else.

Backstage Tales

Every actor will face a cold reading eventually, so it is time well spent practicing for such an event. Whenever you start reading a new play, open it to the middle, find a longish speech, read it over quickly twice, and then perform it aloud. Joan Crawford used to practice her cold-reading technique simply by opening the telephone book and reading a dozen or so names, addresses, and numbers aloud, absolutely cold.

"Try That Again"

When you do a cold reading, it's a good sign—not a bad one—if the director asks you to give it a second try. That means the director heard something he or she likes, and wants to see if you can improve upon it. The director may ask you to act more or less angry, to take it faster or slower, to relish the humor a bit more, or to be more offhand. Pay close attention and try to do exactly what he or she asks even if it doesn't quite make sense to you.

Sometimes when a director asks you to try it again, it's not so much because what you've done the first time is wrong, but because he or she wants to see if you can take direction. There's a reason for that. Some actors give brilliant cold readings, wowing everybody. That can be because they are exceptionally fine actors and very quick studies. But some people who are very good at cold readings have a fatal flaw. That cold reading is the best they will ever achieve—indeed they may never be able to repeat that moment of excellence again. Even more disturbing, they may be the kind of actor who is incapable of doing anything the same way twice, giving what amounts to a new cold reading every time. One day, that new cold reading will be brilliant, the next, it may be dreadful, and either way the other actors in the cast will be driven crazy not knowing what to expect.

Experienced directors know all about cold-reading geniuses, and have lived through the disaster of casting such actors in crucial roles. By asking an actor to try it again, they are testing to see if the actor can change what he or she does according to specific instructions. If the actor can't change the reading, or does the same things but less well, or changes things radically but not in the ways requested, the director will become very wary. This actor may well be one of those cold-reading stars who never get better and can't take direction.

The Least You Need to Know

- Be honest with yourself in appraising whether a role is really suitable for you physically.
- Know the acting style required by a given play, and stay away from those that aren't your forte.
- Always try to read the entire play before auditioning, or get hold of at least a few pages of a new play.
- Be prepared to deal with cold-reading situations.

Chapter 13

I Feel a Song Coming On

In This Chapter

- Discovering how to choose an audition song
- Learning to avoid common mistakes
- Exploring ways to make a strong impression

Musicals have been the biggest moneymakers on Broadway for decades, and they are also staples as high school and community theater productions. High schools put on musicals because they allow for widespread participation, offering roles in the chorus for good singers who may not yet be strong actors, and giving students in the school orchestra and band a chance to be part of a stage production. Community theaters rely on crowd-pleasing musicals to swell the box-office coffers, providing a budgetary cushion for the production of straight plays that may not draw as large an audience. While colleges are more likely to mount productions of classic dramas and comedies, musicals have their place in this environment also.

Because musicals are so popular with audiences, actors who can sing have many opportunities in amateur theater. In this chapter, we'll explore how to select audition songs that not only show off your voice but are also appropriate to the occasion. Actors often make a number of mistakes in choosing audition material for musicals, and we'll steer you clear of them. You'll also discover ways to stand out from the competition and make a director pleased to have heard you sing.

Are You Really Cher? Or Billy Joel?

Sherry was 17 and although she and her mother disagreed about a lot of things, they were both great fans of Cher. Her mother's affection for the singer went all the way back to the 1960s when Sonny and Cher first made it big with "I Got You, Babe." Sherry had gone bananas over Cher's 1999 hit "Believe." She sang along with it constantly when driving around town, and she thought it was just the thing to sing when she tried out for that year's high school musical, *West Side Story*. But as soon as she started singing, she knew she'd made a mistake. With just a piano and no electronic effects, everything sounded wrong, and she started to lose confidence right away.

This experience taught Sherry a lesson the hard way. Problems can arise when anyone sings a big hit by a top singer, be it Billy Joel, Shania Twain, or Elton John. A simple piano accompaniment just isn't going to have the same kind of "oomph" that the professional recording does. Even if you have a voice that's on par with the star who made the song a hit—and not all stars have great voices—there's going to be a very different effect with a piano. At the very least, it's important that you practice whatever song you're going to sing as you'll sing it at the audition. That way, you won't be surprised at the sound just when it matters most.

Performance Notes

Signature songs are so strongly connected to a particular singer that he or she is said to "own" them. It's foolhardy for a male singer to attempt "My Way," because Frank Sinatra owns it, even though he's no longer with us. Even Liza Minnelli, a great star in her own right, stayed away from her mother's signature song, "Over the Rainbow." Besides, she's got her own: the title song from *Cabaret*.

Don't Invite Bad Comparisons

Even with proper rehearsal, singing the latest hit can be a mistake, because you'll inevitably invite comparisons with the original singer. Everybody—including the director and producers—will have heard a big hit, and they'll notice every way in which your rendition fails to live up to the recorded version.

When auditioning for musicals, it's also wiser to stay away even from older songs that are strongly associated with a particular singer. *Signature songs* may not be on the radio at the moment, but you can be sure that almost any director is going to know exactly how Judy Garland sang "Over the Rainbow," and remember very well how Barbra Streisand belted "People" in *Funny Girl*, the show and movie that made her a star. It's almost impossible to compete with the fond memories of a signature song, so save them for the shower.

Finding a New Way to Sing It

You can still sing a well-known song—just stay away from the top hits of the moment and signature songs. That leaves thousands of great tunes to choose from.

But even with these you can make a better impression if you try to make a song your own in some way. For example, many popular singers, from Barbra Streisand to Cleo Laine to Judy Collins, have recorded Stephen Sondheim's most famous song, "Send in the Clowns," but they all approach it somewhat differently. Streisand gives it a slightly defiant tone, Laine emphasizes its wryness, and Collins adopts a more wistful tone. Any good song leaves itself open to different interpretations. Think about what the words and music mean to you, and shade the song with that emotion. Then the song becomes yours.

You can also change the *tempo* of a song. By singing a ballad in a livelier, more upbeat way, you can make it sound like a different tune. Or you can take a song that is usually treated as a showstopper and slow it down to give it a different feel. You have to use your common sense about this kind of change, of course. Singing the Barry Manilow hit "Feelings" at triple speed just doesn't make sense for such a romantic song. On the other hand, you could turn the Beatles' "I Want to Hold Your Hand," into a ballad to lovely effect. There's a difference between turning a song inside out in a way that sounds peculiar and uncovering aspects of it that lie below the surface.

Another way to make a song your own is to vary the volume of your voice in unexpected ways. While some rock songs are meant for singers to practically scream them from beginning to end, most theater songs demand more subtle treatment. They are often "built," which means you should start at a modest volume and build to a crescendo at the end of the song. If you start out at top volume, there's no place to go, and the song can sound boring.

But you can play with the dynamics of a song. You can make a song that is usually given a top-volume ending more effective by building it up to a crescendo just before the conclusion and then dropping back to a very quiet level at the very end. Many country and pop singers use this technique. It's particularly effective when the last words of the song are a repetition of its title or central refrain. A famous example of this approach is Ray Charles's recording of his own song "I Can't Stop Loving You."

Stage Directions

The **tempo** of a musical composition—be it song or symphony movement—is the rate of speed at which it is supposed to be played. It will be indicated on the sheet music or score by such terms as *allegro,* meaning medium fast, or *presto,* meaning very fast. The marked tempo tells you the intentions of the composer or orchestrator, but in performance, tempos are often changed by the conductor or by a singer in consultation with the pianist or conductor.

"Ave Maria" in River City

You'll also want to avoid choosing an inappropriate song for the role you're aiming for. Learn from Betty's experience: Betty was famous for her rendition of "Ave Maria." When she sang it in church, she was always complimented endlessly for her angelic voice. Because she knew it so well, it seemed like a good choice to sing at an audition for the role of Marian the librarian in a community theater production of *The Music Man*. As usual, she did sing it beautifully. But while Marian needs to have a lovely soprano voice, the role also calls for a good deal of spunk, and the ethereal nature of "Ave Maria" was out of keeping with that image. Betty got a nice role in the chorus, but her choice of audition song made it difficult for the director to see her as Marian.

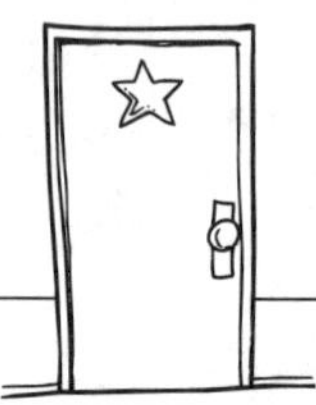

Backstage Tales

In the early years of the American musical, up to 1927, there were two kinds of shows: romantic operettas like Sigmund Romberg's *The Student Prince* or silly comedies like *No, No, Nanette*. Singers were usually suited to one kind or another, which made auditions fairly straightforward. But Jerome Kern's *Show Boat* began to introduce a greater variety of songs, written in different styles for different characters. With *Oklahoma!* in 1943, Richard Rogers and Oscar Hammerstein integrated the songs into the book of the show even further, and they became even more an extension of character. By the end of the century, very dark, sometimes tragic, stories were being made into musicals like Stephen Sondheim's *Sweeny Todd* and Andrew Lloyd Webber's *Sunset Boulevard*. That meant that singers had to have a much greater range of material in their arsenal if they were going to audition successfully.

Choosing Appropriate Songs

Because so many different kinds of musicals are available for production these days, drawn on the output of composers over a period of many decades, entirely different styles of singing may be required even for two musicals produced by the same group in the same year. A community theater might put on the lyrical *Carousel* in the fall and the rock-oriented *Grease* in the spring.

A singer may have the talent to play roles in both musicals, but he or she will have to prove it at the auditions. That means choosing audition songs that are in keeping with the style of the show. Singing "Soliloquy" from the first show, difficult though it is, won't prove you can handle "Summer Lovin'."

Thus, you need to have a repertory of audition songs at the ready, songs that are in the general style of several kinds of musical. Let's look at a possible list of songs for both male and female voices that would show off your ability in different styles:

For soprano voices:

Kind of Show	**Possible Song**
Romantic Comedy	"Ice Cream" (*She Loves Me*)
Serious Musical	"I Dreamed a Dream" (*Les Miserables*)
Rock Musical	"Let the Sun Shine In" (*Hair*)

For baritone voices:

Kind of Show	**Possible Song**
Romantic Comedy	"The Sweetest Sounds" (*No Strings*)
Serious Musical	"Pretty Women" (*Sweeny Todd*)
Rock Musical	"Greased Lightning" (*Grease*)

Know a Song from the Show

Unless it is a brand new musical (written by fellow students at your college, say, or local residents for your community theater), you should always know at least one song from whatever musical you are auditioning for. It doesn't necessarily have to be for the role you really want, so long as it is from the same show—although if you want a lead role that entails singing a very famous song, you'd better know it. No director is going to cast you as Anna in *The King and I* without hearing you sing "Getting to Know You," or as Curly in *Oklahoma!* without you showing your stuff with "Oh, What a Beautiful Morning."

At the audition, you can always start off by singing a song that isn't from the show that's being cast, one you know particularly well that shows off your vocal strengths. In fact, some directors may not want to hear you sing a song from the show at first. They may prefer to get a sense of your talent apart from any role in the musical they're casting. Then, if they like what they hear and see, they will ask you to sing a song from the show itself.

Places, Everyone!

If performing in musicals is your goal, work hard on developing the best singing voice you can. Depending on the part, a person with a terrific singing voice can sometimes win a role over a better actor with more modest musical abilities.

At Home with Your Range

What is the lowest note on the musical scale that you're comfortable singing? What is your highest note? Some people are born with a very wide range, but every serious singer works hard over the years to extend his or her range. Some voices don't "find

Backstage Tales

Those who are trying to land a starring role that requires singing several different kinds of songs sometimes use a secondary song from the musical being produced as their first audition number. For example, the role of Charlie Anderson, the father in *Shenandoah,* requires singing three quite different kinds of songs: tender ballads, a rousing celebration song, and two epic "soliloquies." You'll definitely be asked to sing one of the latter, and it might be smart to start with one of the ballads.

themselves" until well into adulthood. The great operatic tenor Placido Domingo began his career as a baritone, but then developed tenor top notes, and began singing an entirely different repertory; he still retained baritone low notes that give his voice a unique richness. But many singers never develop an exceptional range and still have successful careers—Madonna, for example.

Voice teachers can guide you to developing a greater range, but don't despair if your voice is more limited. Instead, work to develop a personal singing style that makes the best possible use of what you have.

No Time to Experiment

Regardless of what your range is at a given point in your life, never try to exceed it during an audition. The fact that you're beginning to be able to sing a high F instead of just an E-flat doesn't mean that you should give it the old college try when auditioning—even if you can hit that note two times out of three. Auditions are pressure situations, and you're likely to be nervous. That means you're more likely to miss a note you don't quite have under control yet. When you can hit the high F every time, you're ready to show it off at an audition.

Always choose songs that are within your range as regular audition songs. When you're absolutely secure with higher or lower notes, you can move on to a different set of songs. But few things are more likely to kill your chances than a screeched or flat high note, or a low note with so little power that the director can't hear it. Experiment at home or with your voice coach, not at auditions.

Marking Your Sheet Music

If you're planning to sing an audition song in a way that differs from that called for on the sheet music itself, you will need to mark the page in ways that an audition pianist can easily understand.

A change in tempo is often indicated by writing the words "ad lib" (literally meaning "with liberty") at the top left of the first page of music where the usual tempo is indicated by such terms as "allegro," and "presto." The "ad lib" marking informs the pianist that you are not going to adhere to the printed tempo, and that he or she should attempt to follow your lead in playing the piece, speeding things up or slowing them down according to your singing. An experienced pianist should be able to follow you without too much trouble, provided you don't get too eccentric.

Backstage Tales

Some songs are originally written for singers with very special voices. A famous example is "Aldonza" from *Man of La Mancha.* The composer, Mitch Leigh, wrote the song expressly for the original Aldonza, Joan Diener, who just happened to be his wife. Diener had an extraordinary range—it was almost what is called a "trick voice"—and that song, which moves from guttural low notes to scale-topping high notes and puts tremendous pressure on the voice even in the middle range, has been giving other singers, as well as their conductors and directors, fits ever since. "Send in the Clowns" from *A Little Night Music,* on the other hand, was written by Stephen Sondheim for the limited range of Glynnis Johns, who won a Tony for her performance. Emotion, rather than range, is what's important for this song.

If you want to make a long, dramatic pause at some point in the song, draw a diagonal slash (/) at that point in the music. Most pianists will understand this marking, but don't get carried away. One, or at most two, such pauses may be effective, but more will not only lose the element of surprise but chop up the song too much.

Key changes are another matter entirely. Some pianists can take a song down by a third at sight, especially if they know the song well and if the music itself is fairly simple. But more complex pieces, such as songs by Stephen Sondheim, are virtually impossible for anyone but an experienced orchestrator, and are a serious chore even then.

Because the whole purpose of taking a song down is to avoid high notes that are uncomfortable for the singer, it is really the responsibility of that singer to get new sheet music prepared before an audition. Unless you have a talented friend or a generous music teacher who will do this for you, it may be necessary to hire someone to do it. But then, perhaps you shouldn't be using a song that is uncomfortable for you to sing as an audition piece to begin with. Find another that better suits your talents and abilities.

Stage Directions

The **key** in which a piece of music is written, marked at the left hand end of the stave on which the notes appear, defines a system of related notes or tones that form a given scale, such as the key of C or B Minor. A **key change** raises or lowers the pitch of the highest and lowest notes, and requires additional adjustments throughout the piece. Keys are often changed to accommodate the range of a performer during the rehearsal period, but that entails writing new score sheets for the orchestra as well.

Places, Everyone!

Keep in mind that audition pianists are a variable group, so it's important that you make limited changes to your music. Some are extremely talented, while others may be just so-so. Some may know the music to a great many songs, while others a limited number. You probably won't have time to discuss such changes, so clear markings on your sheet music are essential. And always be prepared to change your plans and go along with the pianist if he or she doesn't do what you want.

Performance Notes

Avoid very popular current pop songs when choosing your audition pieces. Contemporary songs given a great deal of radio play can also turn into audition chestnuts with amazing speed, even though they're brand new.

One Too Many Quests

Certain songs get sung a great deal at auditions, either because they are popular with the public, or because they're showy pieces that singers believe will make a vivid impression. But if several singers choose exactly the same audition song, the people conducting the audition will soon be tired of hearing it. They will also inevitably start making comparisons between the numerous renditions of the song. This is another case of singers inviting bad comparisons.

The Sixth "Impossible Dream" Today

Don Quixote's stirring credo from *Man of La Mancha* is one of the greatest songs in the history of American musical theater. It not only shows off technique but also requires acting ability, and many male singers like to use it as an audition song. But it has been performed so often at auditions that stage and musical directors are sick of it, and it takes a truly exceptional rendition of the song to make an impression. We know a musical director who says, "No one who's auditioning should ever sing a song that is played on the loudspeakers in supermarkets," and "The Impossible Dream" is a prime example. Co-author Paul Baldwin played Don Quixote in six different productions of *Man of La Mancha*, performing the song hundreds of times, but he never used it at an audition unless he was specifically requested to sing it. He knew better.

A number of songs are similarly overused at auditions. Music directors groan silently when a female singer starts in with "I Could Have Danced All Night" from *My Fair Lady*, for example. For young girls, the song that's sure to elicit an inward groan is "Tomorrow" from *Annie*. Such songs still work in a full performance of a musical, but in terms of auditions they are chestnuts. Stop roasting them.

In Vogue Is Out

Our music director friend also marvels at how a single song can suddenly start turning up again and again at audition after audition. "You'll hear a song that hasn't been used in a while, and you think, hey, that's a nice choice. But then it starts spreading like the flu. Everybody does it and it gets tired real quick." No one really knows why a particular song gets to be in vogue, and the vogues change fairly regularly, so we can't warn you of specific songs. But if you discover that everyone is suddenly singing your favorite audition song, retire it for a while. A couple of years down the road, you may be able to bring it back, and it will sound fresh again because some other song is in vogue.

Oldies but Goodies

Hundreds of songs come from old musicals, going all the way back to the 1920s, that were hits in their day and can still be magical now. That goes for pop songs of the middle decades of the last century, too. Early in her career Bette Midler revived such old Andrews Sisters songs as "Boogie Woogie Bugle Boy" with dynamite results. Young listeners were astonished at what fun this old song could be, while their parents were delighted to hear a World War II favorite sung again.

Most musicals that have flopped on Broadway over the years have at least one terrific song, and many have several. A good score doesn't necessarily guarantee success on Broadway—the book or the casting may have been the problem, or the show may have been ahead of its time. But that leaves dozens of musical gems, temporarily forgotten by most people, just waiting to be brought back. Co-author Paul Baldwin had great success with a song called "With So Little To Be Sure Of" from the early Stephen Sondheim flop *Anyone Can Whistle*, a show that was far too "different" for its time. This gorgeous ballad seemed to have been written for Paul's voice, and every time he sang it, he got the part he wanted.

Finding Old Songs

How do you go about finding these gems from the past? A good starting point for young performers is to ask older people who are fans of Broadway musicals for ideas. If your parents, or Aunt Mary, or friends of your parents have seen a lot of musicals, pump them for half-remembered favorites. Music teachers, whether private or school professionals, are bound to have some good suggestions.

Does anyone you know have an old record collection that includes Broadway shows? If so, ask to listen to some of them. Even if you don't have a phonograph player, friends of your parents who still do—exactly because they love their old records—will usually be delighted to introduce you to some of their favorites. Your public library might help in this area as well.

Backstage Tales

You can find clues to great old songs at your library. Many public libraries subscribe to *The New York Times*. Once or twice a week, particularly on Saturdays, the *Times* carries reviews of cabaret acts at New York nightclubs. Many of the singers who perform at these venues are older singers who regularly sing songs from past decades. Read the reviews for ideas. And look for old books on the theater in your library stacks, too.

Places, Everyone!

Make sure you bring a legible copy of the sheet music for any old or unfamiliar song. Audition pianists necessarily have to be able to read music at sight, and the fact that the song is different is more likely to inspire them to their best efforts than to upset them. After all, audition pianists get even more bored playing the same songs again and again than the music director does listening to them.

And many old shows are now being re-released on CD, too. Get hold of a catalogue of CDs through your music store, and peruse the listings for Broadway shows.

Finding sheet music for old songs isn't as easy as it once was. It used to be that every music store carried sheet music, but these days you will usually have to go to specialized sources. Take a look at Appendix C, "Play and Sheet Music Scores," for the addresses of a number of companies that stock sheet music to old songs and scores.

"Nice to Hear That Song Again"

Most stage and music directors at schools, colleges, and community theaters have often been involved with musical theater for a long time. Even if they're relative newcomers, they're likely to know a great deal about the history of American musicals; usually they're involved with the production because they love musicals.

That means that when you sing an old song that isn't heard that much anymore, or a great song from a show that flopped, you'll make a real impression. First, they'll be delighted to hear something different from the "in vogue" audition songs of the moment. And they may fondly remember the song, in which case they're likely to tell you how nice it is to hear it again.

Even if they don't know the song, you'll make an impression. A really good song carries its own weight, even when it's unfamiliar. Everyone has had the experience of hearing a song for the first time and thinking how terrific it is. In fact, if the music director doesn't know a song you sing, he or she is likely to ask you what it's from and how you got hold of it. That gives you more time in the spotlight.

Singing an "oldie but goodie" at an audition is a sure way to make an impression. The pianist and the stage and musical directors are going to be hearing singers for hours on end, maybe for several days in a row. It perks them up to hear something different. If they're beginning to get drowsy, you'll wake them up and they'll give you greater attention. What's more, they'll take note of your initiative in seeking out a song that's out of the ordinary. That kind of initiative serves as a sign that you have some imagination, are willing to do some extra work, and are really dedicated to developing your talent. All those qualities are pluses in a performer, and the fact that you seem to have them can make a subtle difference in how you are viewed. It may get you the part you want over someone who's talented but has shown less imagination in choosing an audition song.

Remember, being talented is only half the battle. Being distinctive is just as important.

The Least You Need To Know

- Don't invite bad comparisons by singing the latest hit or the signature song of a great star.
- Choose songs appropriate to the show you're auditioning for and be prepared to sing a song from that show.
- Make certain you are completely comfortable with the vocal range of any song you choose.
- Avoid singing overused songs, looking instead for something different and distinctive.

Chapter 14

Dressing the Part?

In This Chapter

- Learning why you shouldn't overdress for auditions
- Recognizing that sloppiness counts against you
- Finding out how to make the best impression
- Discovering when to break the rules

"What to wear, what to wear?" That's a question that arises for any special occasion, and an audition is definitely such an outing. Cliché would have it that women worry much more about this kind of thing than men, but the latter are far from immune, and when it comes to auditions, everyone needs to think about what he or she is going to wear. The first impression you make at an audition can knock you out of the running almost before you start if how you look doesn't jibe with what the director is looking for.

In this chapter, we'll explain why it's a mistake either to overdress or to show up looking like a slob. We'll give you tips on how to make a good impression using the clothes you've already got in your closet. As with most sets of rules, there are exceptions to consider, and we'll clue you in on those as well.

Dressed to Kill ... Your Chances

In the classic 1948 MGM musical *Easter Parade*, the plot revolves around Fred Astaire losing his long-time dance partner, played by Anne Miller, and choosing Judy Garland to replace her. Anne Miller is dressed to the nines throughout the movie, sweeping in and out of scenes in a million-dollar wardrobe. Judy Garland, on the other hand, is very simply dressed for most of the film. She looks nice enough, but compared to Miller she's drab. The Astaire character tries to make Garland over in the image of Miller. The message might seem to be that fancy plumage is the hallmark of the leading lady. But, in fact, when Astaire relaxes and uses Garland's real gifts, including comedy, they become a greater success than the Astaire/Miller team ever was. The number they perform dressed in tramp costumes, "We're a Couple of Swells," is one of the great treasures of movie musicals.

Many actors, especially women, start out with the idea that if they want to get the lead, they should show up at the audition looking like the Anne Miller character, in the fanciest outfit they can afford. But in the real world, this approach is likely to make a director wary instead of excited.

The Overdressed Prima Donna

A community theater in your area has announced auditions for a production of Noel Coward's *Private Lives*. You'd like to play the star role of Amanda, who wears exquisite costumes throughout the play. Maybe you saw Elizabeth Taylor play the role on Broadway, and you think glamour is the essence of the part. So you go out and spend a small fortune on a satin cocktail gown to wear to the audition. All the other actresses are dressed in a far more ordinary way, and you think you're got it made.

Places, Everyone!

Moderation is your best bet when it comes to dressing for auditions. The Hollywood or Broadway star who's always on the annual "Best Dressed" lists might be able to get away with wearing very expensive, elegant clothes to an audition because that's what she's known for. But keep in mind that such stars seldom have to audition in the first place—they're being begged to play the role.

But let's take a look inside the mind of the director at this point. She's from out of town and has never seen you perform. When you walk out on stage looking like you've just come from a New York champagne brunch, the director is going to say to herself, "Well, who does she think she is?" Because the play itself is set in the 1930s, your fancy new dress is, in fact, out of sync with the period, and instead of making the character come alive, it's getting in the way of your performance. The director is seeing your dress instead of you or the character you are trying to portray. The part ends up going to a young woman who came dressed in a straight wool skirt and white blouse.

The overdressed actor at a college or community theater audition can seem to be saying, "I'm really far too good for this little production, but I'll deign to appear in it." You're all too likely to be taken for a prima donna who thinks she's the cat's meow. And the last thing a director wants to deal with in amateur theater is a prima donna. You see yourself as gorgeous; the director sees you as stuck on yourself and therefore as potential trouble. Play it safe by dressing in clean, simple clothes that enable you to move and that you feel comfortable wearing.

Flaunting Your Body?

Some actors are blessed with great bodies. The voluptuous woman or athletically-built man may have a definite advantage in landing certain roles, provided that he or she also can act. (The annals of show business are littered with sexy women and hunky men who got a chance because of their looks, but disappeared from sight because of their lack of acting ability.)

So, let's assume you're one of the lucky ones and are gorgeous to behold. Does that mean that women should wear very tight sweaters to call attention to their breasts, or that men should wear skin-tight jeans to show off what they've got? That depends on the role you are auditioning for.

If you're auditioning for the role of the sexy social-climbing minx in *Dinner at Eight*, so memorably played by Jean Harlow in the classic 1933 movie, it couldn't hurt to show off your curves. A great body is a requirement for the role, along with spot-on comic timing. Similarly, on the male side of the ledger, if you want to play the young drifter at the center of *Picnic*, it's fine to wear those tight jeans. The character must be a hunk as well as a sensitive actor.

Performance Notes

Beware! Although the casting couch is one of the oldest jokes in show business, it's also a reality. Unfortunately, sleeping with the director or casting agent is more likely to get you a bad reputation than it is a role in his or her next production.

Numerous roles for actors of both sexes call for body-beautiful types. But if the role doesn't really require that kind of blatant sex appeal, then you should probably dress more conservatively for your audition. If the director can't take his or her eyes off your sexual attributes, you may sabotage yourself in terms of less-overtly sexy roles. You could end up seeming wrong for a role even though you can act it with no trouble.

A Slob Is a Slob Is a Slob

While it can be a mistake to overdress for an audition, or to wear clothes that are too sexy, it's almost always a bad idea to show up looking like you've been sleeping in your clothes for the past week. Dirty hair and body odor aren't going to help you either, even if you're trying out for Didi or Gogo, the two tramps in Samuel Beckett's *Waiting for Godot*.

Looking like a slob is going to hurt you for several reasons. The first is psychological: Fairly or not, most people assume that someone who looks like an unmade bed also has a messy, undisciplined mind. If you can't be bothered to put on some fresh clothes, will you take the trouble to learn your lines? Will you show up for rehearsals on time? Can you take direction, since your clothes seem to suggest that you're into flouting authority?

Dirty or wrinkled clothes, an untucked shirt tail or blouse, a missing button, different colored socks, stockings with runs in them—all these details register with a director as signs of mental sloppiness. It's possible, of course, that you may be such a terrific actor that you'll be able to make the director forget what you're wearing. But why create unnecessary obstacles for yourself? That in itself can suggest that you're one of those actors who likes to make things difficult.

Secondly, clothes that are rumpled, or too big (as in the "grunge" look that's been so popular in the past decade) make it difficult to see what you're doing when you perform. A sweater with sleeves that cover most of your hands is going to make your gestures look awkward and ill defined. If you're trying out for a musical, you might be asked to dance a few simple steps, but that's not going to be easy if your pants are hanging around your ankles like paper bags. And it will be difficult to tell whether you have a real problem with posture or if your loose clothes make you look like the Hunchback of Notre Dame.

Bad Impressions Linger

If you show up at one audition looking like a slob, that mistake can haunt you for some time to come. College and community theaters tend to be fairly close-knit groups, and although there will be people who know you well and people who don't, word will get around about your abilities and behavior. What's more, the number of directors is often limited, and you are very likely to find yourself auditioning for the same person more than once. Don't put yourself in the position where a director thinks, "Oh boy, here he (or she) comes again."

Sometimes you may have to show up at an audition looking less than your best because of time factors. The scheduling might mean, for instance, that you have to go directly from coaching little league baseball or girls' soccer to a community theater audition, and there's no place to take a shower and change. So there you are in your sweatsuit, looking grubby. Do yourself a favor and explain your appearance. You don't have to fall all over yourself apologizing; just say "Excuse my appearance," and say why you look unkempt.

Places, Everyone!

Pay attention to footwear when you're dressing for an audition. Think not only about how your shoes look, but also how they feel and if they'll enable you to dance or move quickly if the director calls for it. Very high heels, heavy boots, or sneakers the size of rowboats can all be a problem. If necessary, when the weather is bad, take along an extra pair to change into for your audition.

"Artistic" Doesn't Mean Messy

Some actors, especially younger ones, get it into their heads that since acting is an art form, it's cool to look like they're impoverished artists living in garrets. (Both authors remember that when they were at college, it was usually the classmates with plenty of money who went around looking like bums; the ones who were really struggling financially tended to try very hard to look nice.)

Backstage Tales

In the 1950s, the influence of Marlon Brando was so great that critics and social commentators began to refer to the "torn t-shirt school of acting." In the 1960s, the hippie movement continued to foster the idea that looking disheveled was the sign of the true artist, or at least of the person sensitive enough to understand art. Things calmed down for a while and then the grunge look arrived, which is still with us to some degree. Young people often don't realize that this confusion of artistry and messiness goes in cycles. Anyone a couple of decades older is likely to react with the phrase, "Been there, done that."

Neat, Clean, and Natural

Directors are not usually very impressed by attempts to "look the part" at auditions. When he first auditioned for the role of Charlie Anderson in *Shenandoah*, co-author Paul Baldwin showed up wearing neatly pressed slacks, a white shirt, and a red sweater. His shoes were Bass Weejuns, which he'd been wearing since college. Every other male at the audition was wearing jeans, boots, and plaid flannel shirts, which were in keeping with the Virginia farm setting of the story. But it was Paul who got the starring role on the strength of his ability rather than any costuming. One of the flannel-shirt actors, who was cast as the eldest son, later told Paul that when he saw him at the audition he thought he didn't stand a chance. But then he heard him sing and read a scene and it was Charlie Anderson on stage, no matter what Paul was wearing.

All this goes to say that if you're a good enough actor, you'll be able to capture the character without having to costume for it, and the fact that you don't need to will be all the more impressive. Secondly, as at that *Shenandoah* audition, so many people may be trying to look the part that they become as indistinguishable as if they were all wearing pinstriped suits.

The theater professional arrives at an audition looking nice, but not showy. Neat, clean, and natural is all that's required. There's no need to try to put the costume designer out of work.

Your talent will win you roles, not your wardrobe.

The Look of a Pro?

What does a professional actor look like? Don't answer that question too quickly. True, actors can look extremely glamorous when they arrive for the Academy Awards. That's the night they play the role of movie star. But even among that glittery group, there are a lot of differences. Some have taste, while others clearly do not, and the latter get roasted in the press for their peculiar gowns (and sometimes even for their peculiar tuxedos). A better test is to look at what actors wear when they appear on television talk shows or for an appearance on Bravo's *Inside the Actor's Studio*. The women might wear a pretty dress, a Chanel suit, a pants suit, or something a bit sexier. Men's clothing can range from a jacket and tie, to jeans and an open shirt, to something resembling a caftan. There is no uniform.

Backstage Tales

In Hollywood's old studio days, actors had a dress code. Stars were never supposed to leave the house without looking like stars. But even then, there were some rebels like Bette Davis. But Hollywood mores even got to her briefly. Her mother once arrived by train and was met by Bette in a white convertible wearing jewelry and furs to beat the band. Her mother took one look and asked what Bette thought she was doing. Bette said, "You're right, Mother," and went back to dressing like an ordinary housewife.

Being Yourself

What do you feel comfortable wearing? What would you wear if you were going out to lunch with a friend? Whatever the answer may be, that's probably what you should be wearing to auditions. Don't go to extremes, either by overdressing or by wandering in like a slob. Wear what's natural and comfortable and you'll be just fine.

Making some small adjustments can make sense, however. If you're a woman about to audition for a glamorous role, by all means wear a pair of slightly showy earrings or an elegant pin. A man might want to wear a pair of sharply pressed pants in similar circumstances, and perhaps even a tie under his sweater. But don't get carried away. You should attempt to act elegant or sloppy, depending on the role, and not leave it to your wardrobe. Elegance—or sloppiness—can be acted no matter what you're wearing.

Exceptions to the Rule

Rules can sometimes be broken with great success. That's how most progress is made, in science and business as well as in the arts. But you need to know the old rules very well before you can go beyond them in ways that result in some kind of breakthrough instead of a chaotic mess. Keep that in mind when you're deciding what to wear to an audition, as well as when you're trying to find a new approach to playing Hamlet.

The Anne Bancroft Legend

Perhaps the most famous of the legion of audition stories is about how Anne Bancroft got the role of Gittel in the original stage production of *Two for the Seasaw*. Bancroft had started out as a theater actress in New York, done some good television in the days of shows like *Playhouse 90*, and had been offered a Hollywood contract. Her first role was a small but good one in 1952's *Don't Bother to Knock*, starring Richard Widmark and the young Marilyn Monroe. Monroe was soon a major star in sexy comic roles, but Bancroft's career stalled. She got some leads in B pictures, but her movie career was going nowhere, and five years later she fled Hollywood and returned to New York.

Performance Notes

It's important to recognize that Bancroft pulled off this stunt with a brand new play. No one else had played the role of Gittel yet. The director and the producers knew what they were looking for, and Bancroft hit the nail on the head. But if you try something like this with a well-known play, people may just assume you got your ideas from someone else's performance in the part. A new script is your best bet when taking such chances.

Bancroft managed to get hold of a script of William Gibson's *Two for the Seasaw*, and immediately recognized that she was born to play Gittel, a feisty girl from the Bronx who enters into an affair with a distinguished older man. Her agent got her an audition, although no one was really interested in seeing her, and she showed up dressed in the mismatched clothes and beret Gittel would wear, talking like Gittel and adopting Gittel's "Don't tell me" attitude. She *was* the character, and was handed the role opposite Henry Fonda, the kind of star she couldn't get near in Hollywood. The show was a major hit, she became a star herself, and her next assignment was the utterly different role of Annie Sullivan in *The Miracle Worker*, for which she won the Tony Award, followed by an Oscar for the film version.

Places, Everyone!

Choose with care when to take risks at auditions and with roles. Make certain that the very different role you go after is worth having, and truly within your capabilities. Hold back unless the reward is equivalent to the risk.

Bancroft's story is the kind every young actor dreams of living for him- or herself (although most would gladly forego Bancroft's first miserable years in Hollywood). The trouble is that it only works once in a blue moon.

Great Confidence Required

Dressing as the character for an audition is like taking part in a circus knife-throwing act: You'd better know exactly what you're doing and be extremely sure of yourself. Otherwise disaster can result. Those bad endings don't usually get much publicity, but they circulate through the theater world as cautionary gossip. There's the story about the young woman who was auditioning for a dinner theater production of *The Seven Year Itch*. The play had originally been a hit on Broadway. The movie version starred Marilyn Monroe, and the still photo of her standing over a subway grating with her white dress billowing up around her waist is legendary.

Our dinner theater heroine decided to go to her audition dressed and made up to look as much like Monroe as possible. A brunette, she purchased an expensive blond wig, and paid a seamstress to try to duplicate Monroe's white dress. When she appeared at the audition, jaws dropped. But she had gone too far. Her appearance was so artificial that the director thought for a moment that she was a man in drag. Things got worse when she started speaking. She had practiced speaking in Monroe's whispery voice, forgetting that movie microphones can pick up a pin dropping. On a stage, no one could hear a word 20 feet away. The director asked her to speak up. She tried, but completely lost the Monroe quality when she projected her voice, ending up sounding like she was being strangled. The part went to a girl with a naturally sexy voice who wore a blue cashmere sweater and a simple gray skirt. She had the confidence to be herself instead of hiding behind a disguise.

Greek Tragedy in Business Suits

Another reason to avoid "dressing the part" is that you might not know what that part looks like today, even if it's a well-known, classical role. In the last few decades, many directors have mounted productions of classic plays in which the actors have worn costumes that have nothing to do with the period in which the play is set. There are a number of rationales for taking this approach. Some directors feel that a Greek tragedy performed in business suits forces audiences to see a well-known play in a fresh light. "Ah," the audience member is expected to say, "now I see more clearly how this story is pertinent to my own experience." In other cases, a change of period in terms of costumes, settings, and props is dictated by the belief that a particular modern setting can emphasize the underlying themes of the play—that was the rationale for a production of Richard the III in a Nazi setting.

The authors have seen *Much Ado About Nothing* set in nineteenth-century Texas, *Hamlet* in tuxedos, and *The Tempest* in which young women in cowboy boots and hats, wearing what looked like drum majorette costumes, performed the masque. Some such experiments work, and some the critics tear to shreds. But whether they are successful or not, these productions do underline the fact that dressing for an audition as you expect the character to be costumed can be an exercise in futility. A director planning a modern-dress version of *Antigone* is not going to be impressed by an actress who shows up wearing a long white dress with a band of Corinthian columns around the hem—after all, he's planning to put her into a black silk cocktail dress.

The period changing that goes on in the theater these days can mean that your attempt to dress "in character" is exactly contrary to the ideas the director has in mind. It's better to relax, wear your regular clothes, and take a shower before you get dressed. Then go act your heart out.

The Least You Need to Know

- Avoid dressing like a star unless you really are one.
- On the other side of the coin, don't confuse grunge with artistry.
- Looking your best means looking clean and natural.
- Dressing the character you want to portray is a risk that requires great confidence and is a worthy goal.

Chapter 15

Audition Etiquette

In This Chapter

- Finding out the kinds of attitude to avoid
- Recognizing that auditions are tough on everyone
- Learning why it pays to be nice to the competition
- Discovering how to finish on a gracious note

Having good manners is essential in most situations, but particularly so when everyone is under stress. It's all too easy to behave in a self-centered way at an audition. After all, you're trying to succeed at something that means a lot to you, and you need to do your very best to get the role you want. Since there are other people who want the same thing, your success will mean someone else's failure. But that's no excuse for treating other people badly. If you do, you're likely to regret it later.

In this chapter, we'll discuss how to conduct yourself properly at an audition. We'll clue you in about attitudes you should avoid because they'll do you more harm than good. We'll help you understand why auditions are tough on those involved in casting a show as well as on those seeking to be cast. Even though you are in a competitive situation, there are good reasons to treat your competitors well, and we'll explain what they are. Whether your audition goes well or badly, from your point of view, it's still important to make a polite exit, and we'll give you tips on how to pull that off.

Attitude No-Nos

The phrase "to give attitude" is fairly recent American slang, but it is one that seems likely to last because it sums up a kind of behavior that is unfortunately all too common. People who give attitude make it very clear that only what they feel really counts. Everybody else is a nuisance standing in the way.

You can run into such people in every walk of life, and you'll certainly run across them in the theater world. But while proven stars may be able to get away with a certain amount of attitude, it's likely to make even them unpopular with their peers and even, ultimately, with their audience. But the last place an actor should succumb to the temptation to give attitude is at an audition. "You're not there yet," as the saying goes, and behavior that suggests you're too good for everyone else, or that anybody who disagrees with you is a fool, can mean losing a role even if you're very talented.

You're Not the Star Yet

You may think you are God's gift to the theater. You may, in fact, be terrifically talented. But don't put on airs when you go to an audition. No matter how good an actor you may be, there may be someone else auditioning with equal ability. Or, there may be someone else with a bit less talent who, for one reason or another, is better suited to a particular role (take another look at our discussion of The Age/Height Ratio in Chapter 12, "Know What They're Looking For"). People who go to auditions with the attitude that a role is bound to be theirs only risk deep disappointment.

Performance Notes

Watch your attitude, even after you get the role. When you read in the paper that the star of some incoming Broadway show has departed because of "artistic differences," it's a good bet the star in question was behaving like a prima donna. In amateur theater, directors are particularly wary of prima donnas, and will try very hard to avoid casting them in the first place.

The attitude itself can cost you the part. Although sometimes directors have to cast prima donnas (of both sexes) because there's no one else as good, if a choice exists between two actors, the director is more likely to go with the one who seems easier to work with. If your attitude suggests that you think you're "the star" already, that may be all the director needs to go with the other contender.

If you're a very good actor, and rightly proud of your talent, you can succeed simply by demonstrating your ability while performing during an audition. Confidence is fine; arrogance is not.

That Chip on Your Shoulder

There are a number of reasons why an actor may go to an audition with a chip on his or her shoulder. It may be that the same director didn't cast you the last time you auditioned, or offered you a part you weren't interested in instead of the one you wanted. On the other hand, you might feel a little insulted about having to audition in the first place; the director knows your work well, after all. Or you may have a suspicion that a particular director will cast his best friends before anyone else, and you wonder if you should even bother to show up at the audition at all. All of these can be legitimate beefs. Directors do make mistakes. It could be that you really should have been given the role you wanted last time around and would have done a better job than the actor who got cast. That happens in the theater quite a lot. And it may be a little strange that someone with your experience and success isn't just assigned a role without auditioning. Stars, and even character actors, are often simply offered roles in the professional theater, and it happens all the time in college and community theater, too.

Performance Notes

Try not to audition for every role that comes along or you'll risk developing a chip on your shoulder from all the rejection that'll come your way. Audition for roles or plays that are at least potentially down your alley, and stay away from the others.

But it could be that the role in question is somewhat different from those you usually play, and the director has just enough questions in mind to want to see what you'll do with it. Even professional stars have to audition occasionally. And exactly because some directors do tend to cast their pals ("clique-casting," it's often called), another director may want to avoid giving the appearance of doing that, and will require someone who's really got the part already to audition so that everything looks fair and square to other actors.

It's Rough on the Director, Too

Here is a list of some of the complaints actors often make about auditions:

- I was only given about three minutes. How can they tell anything in that short a time?
- They cut me off in the middle of my monologue/song.
- The director was talking to someone while I was doing my monologue.
- The pianist didn't know my song and made a mess of it.
- The choreographer asked me to do things that were too hard.

All of these things do happen at auditions, whether amateur or professional. But how valid are complaints about them? To start with, college and community theater actors should keep in mind that professionals often have more to complain about than amateurs in all these respects. That's because there are usually many more actors to see at a professional audition, and because the old saying, "Time is money," is more applicable to the professional theater than it is to college or community theater productions. But, in addition, keep in mind that auditions are stressful for directors (and their production colleagues) as well as for those auditioning.

Never Enough Time

The director of a production at any level would often like to give the auditioning actors more time to show their stuff. Directors know that some actors are better at auditions than others, and that the ones who have a knack for it are not always the ones capable of developing the most in the course of rehearsals. They know that some actors need a little time to warm up before they start giving their best effort. And since they need to assemble the best cast possible, it's really in their interest to give people the chance to shine. But only so much time is available, and it's necessary to keep moving along. That sometimes means making snap judgments and cutting an actor off in mid-speech. It's not necessarily a sign that the director thinks the actor is bad, but that he or she clearly isn't right for the available roles.

The complaint that a director talked during your audition is usually unfair. He or she is probably talking about you, and may well be saying to an assistant, or to a producer, "She might work as Gypsy Rose Lee," or some other role, perhaps even one more important than you expected to get. Good directors can talk to an assistant and listen to you at the same time with more care than you might think. That's part of the job. They also may have eyes in the back of their heads, as you will discover in rehearsals.

Time is often the crucial factor as well when a pianist plays an audition song raggedly. It may be an entirely new piece of music to the accompanist, or one that's half forgotten. The pianist doesn't want to play badly—that's embarrassing—but there often isn't time to go over the music with the care necessary to playing well. As for the choreographer who asks for difficult dance steps—well, that may seem cruel, but it does quickly separate the real dancers from the beginners. Sometimes that beginner will be cast anyway, because the director and musical director think he or she is right for the role, can act, and has a fine voice. That means the choreographer will have to put in more time during rehearsals teaching more complicated steps to that cast member.

Everyone Gets Tired

When you go to an audition, you're almost bound to find yourself spending a lot of time sitting around, often on the floor or a flight of stairs, waiting for your name to be called. Even actors who have been given specific appointments are likely to end up waiting a while. It's all too similar to going to an appointment with a doctor or dentist. You show up exactly on time and still find yourself twiddling your thumbs for 40 minutes. And, of course, if you assume things will be running late and don't show up on time, that's exactly the day when, because two other people have cancelled their appointments, you'll lose your turn and have to wait anyway, as well as risk a scolding for being late. So be on time and expect to wait. It's going to be even worse if you show up for a *cattle call.*

Backstage Tales

There are some roles in musicals for which the dance element is paramount, like the title role in *Pal Joey* or the part of Cassie in *Company*. In such cases, the choreographer is likely to get the last word on who is cast. But in many other roles, the acting and singing are primary, and will be the chief determinants. Co-author Paul Baldwin had very little dance training, but early in his career he was cast in *Company*, which has a big dance number for the entire cast, "Side by Side." He had to practice more than most cast members, but got the steps down cold during the rehearsal period. He knew not to even try out for a lead role that required a great deal of dancing, however.

Waiting around is tiring. It's likely to be either too hot or too cold, and since you're nervous to start with, the minutes—or hours, when it's a cattle call—seem to drag by very slowly. It's no fun at all, unless you run into a friend and can spend the time catching up. Some people read a book, others go over their audition speech or scene incessantly, some pace up and down, while others stare at the wall. By the time your name is finally called, you may feel worn out from doing nothing. But, suddenly you've got to be "on." Fortunately, sufficient adrenaline usually kicks in to pick you up.

But the waiting actors aren't the only ones who are tired. The director and his or her assistant are worn out, too. If it's a musical audition, the notes are beginning to blur for the pianist. The choreographer's legs and feet hurt from demonstrating the same audition steps over and over again. These people know they have to stay awake and even-tempered, and they're doing their best to give you a full and fair hearing. What's more, they've had to pay close attention while you sat around. If anything, they're more tired than you are, so give them a break and don't complain.

Stage Directions

A **cattle call** is the derisive term actors use to describe what's advertised as an "open call." In the professional theater, an open call means that anyone who shows up will be seen—sometimes even without a union card. A cattle call was held for the musical *Barnum* because the producers were looking for people who could juggle and walk a tightrope and might never have acted before. In professional or amateur theater, those who go to open calls find themselves being herded like cattle, hence the term.

Competitors Are Also Colleagues

When you show up for an audition, often so many people are awaiting their turns that it may seem as though everyone in the world must be an actor. (We all are, at times, of course, but that's another story.) Yet the world of the theater is in many ways a remarkably small one. There are a lot more plumbers, car dealers, and lawyers than there are actors. And all actors are in the same boat: wanting to show off their talent in the best possible role. Unfortunately, despite the small world of the theater, more actors than roles are always available at any given moment. That means you are always in a competition with others to get those roles. But it pays to remember that your competitors are also your colleagues, deserving of your respect and understanding.

Backstage Tales

The theater world is full of feuds. It is not uncommon for Hollywood stars, when signing a contract for several movies, to have a clause stating that they will not work with a certain director. Bette Midler's contract with Disney had such a clause because of a previous unhappy experience. And there are feuds between actors, too. Even though (or perhaps because) they were sisters, Joan Fontaine and Olivia de Havilland sniped publicly at one another for decades, after Fontaine won the Best Actress Oscar for 1941 in *Suspicion*, beating de Havilland, who was nominated for *Hold Back the Dawn*. But this is "star behavior" that shouldn't be emulated.

You May End Up in the Same Dressing Room

One would hope that everyone auditioning for a play would be at least polite to one another. You can tamp down any temptation to make snide remarks or treat someone coldly if you remember that you might end up one day sharing a dressing room with that very same person. Even leads have to share dressing rooms sometimes, depending on the size of the cast and the backstage arrangement of the theater. That's particularly true in amateur theater, where the theaters are often fairly small and dressing-room space is at a premium.

Even if you don't share a dressing room with someone you've treated badly, you may have to play scenes with him or her onstage. That means working together and not at cross purposes, and if you've antagonized one another while waiting your turn to audition, you can be faced with the extra burden of repairing your personal relationship in order to give good performances. So when you meet new people at an audition, look upon it as a first-day-at-school or first-day-at-a-new-job situation. Even if someone else provokes you, try not to answer back in kind. Someone else's thoughtless or snappish remark may be due to nerves. You may get to like that person a lot down the line. And the chances are good that you will have to work with him or her.

On the Way Up, On the Way Down

There's an old saying that you're likely to run into the same people on the way up as on the way down. We're not talking about staircases here, but career paths. People who've already achieved a good deal of success may think they can get away with treating someone less experienced with disdain. But the day may come when that person is at the top, and you're getting along in years and past your peak. You'll be on your way down, not playing romantic leads anymore, say, but character parts instead. And the person you snubbed when he or she was starting out is now playing the roles you used to get. If you get snubbed now, it's because you asked for it way back when.

Places, Everyone!

Remember where you are, and where you've been. Very few people get to the top and stay there for good in any walk of life, and in the world of show business changes in status can take place with lightning speed. You may get the starring role in one season's production, and find yourself outclassed by a newcomer a year later. So if you are lucky enough to be the "star" for a while, try to behave like Jack Lemmon and Barbara Stanwyck, both famous for their kindness toward younger actors on the way up.

"Thank You for Seeing Me"

Some directors have poker faces. No matter who they're watching, whether it's the most exciting actor they've seen that day or the most dismal, their expression will be one of noncommittal interest. Some directors smile broadly at both the best and the worst. The first kind can seem cold, the second a sweetheart, but translate both expressions with several grains of salt. They're all-purpose, and they mean very little. In rare cases, a director will speak his or her mind, almost always in a positive way, indicating that you've done a very good job. That usually means he's seriously considering you for the role. But no matter how you feel the audition went, or what the director is thinking, it's important to leave the audition with grace and courtesy.

The Gracious Exit

You've just been cut off in the middle of a speech or a song. "Thank you," the director says. "We'll let you know." That means the audition is over. Don't complain that you haven't finished; that's unprofessional. Don't scowl. Don't turn on your heel and stalk off. Don't look as though you're going to burst into tears. None of that is going to get you more time, and it may lose you a chance at a role. Being cut off does NOT

Stage Directions

A **call-back** is just what it sounds like. You will be called to come back and audition again at a set time. A call-back means that the director is seriously considering casting you. But he or she wants to get a more complete sense of what you can do. It's likely that other actors are being called back for the same role, so it's not a sure thing yet. And you may be called back several times before a decision is made, whether it is yes or no.

Places, Everyone!

Never think that returning to the audition to retrieve forgotten belongings will get you positive attention from the director. Is this (a) childish, (b) rude, (c) stupid, (d) all of the above? The answer is d.

always mean you're out of the running. The director has simply seen enough to make a judgment, according to his or her lights. It may be the end of a long day, with a dozen people still to see. The director may be eliminating you, but also might think you could be right for one role or another. If that's the case, you'll get a *call-back*.

Whenever the director says "Thank you," indicating that your time is up, your automatic reply should be, "Thank you for seeing me." Don't add a lot of inflection to the words. Keep them businesslike. If the director has given you quite a lot of time and is smiling, you may be tempted to grin back like the Cheshire Cat, and put a gleeful spin on the words "Thank you." Don't. If you've been cut off before finishing, you might feel like giving your exit line a surly inflection, making it sound like, "Yeah, thanks a whole bunch." Don't.

And no matter what vibes you're getting, avoid being flirtatious or overly intimate. That might suggest a promise you don't really want to keep. Your voice should be even and fairly formal. Sound sincere even if you have to put all your talent into acting that sincerity—even if you'd much rather spit.

There's another aspect to making a gracious exit, which has less to do with manners than it does with appearing organized and competent. When you go to an audition, you're likely carrying things aside from your script—a purse, briefcase, knapsack, or portfolio that contains your resumé, pictures, and sheet music. The audition will likely be crowded, so don't leave any valuables lying around unattended. Take that purse or portfolio into the audition room, or up on stage with you, but leave it in plain sight. Give sheet music to the pianist as soon as it's your turn.

Now comes the important part. When you've finished performing, make sure to collect your sheet music and/or retrieve your purse or portfolio from where you left it. Nothing is more embarrassing than leaving an audition and then having to creep sheepishly back in again to get your belongings, which distracts attention from the person auditioning. How to look like a fool!

There May Be a Next Time

Early in his career, a friend of the authors came across an ad in the New York theater weekly *Backstage* about auditions for non-union production of *Little Shop of Horrors.* Jack, as we'll call him, thought he was right for the male lead. The ad stated, "All Parts Open," meaning that none had been pre-cast, so Jack rushed off during a snowstorm to audition. He sang well and the director and producers were delighted. But then he was told the male lead was already cast. Jack asked when it had been cast. From the first day, they told him. "So," Jack said, "the ad saying all parts were open was a deliberate lie?" The director and producers were no longer delighted.

Jack had every right to be annoyed, of course. The ad was a lie, and it seemed clear that all parts had been declared open in order to attract more talent to the audition, with the hope of getting someone good to take a smaller role. This is unethical, but even so Jack made a mistake in telling everyone off. A year later he auditioned for a different musical, and when he walked out on stage, he realized that the director was the same one he had accused of lying, and that he remembered Jack. Needless to say, Jack wasn't cast in that show, either.

People in the theater have long memories. If you make an enemy, it may be for good. So even if you think you have a right to complain about your treatment at an audition, keep in mind that doing so may lose you future roles, too—all for the sake of making yourself feel better at the moment. In the professional theater, you can report certain kinds of bad behavior by directors, producers, or even other actors to Actors Equity, and the union will investigate the charge. But in amateur or non-union theater, you have no such protection. That means that keeping your mouth shut can be the wiser course, even if you have a legitimate complaint. Sometimes things seem unfair but really are not. Even if they are unfair, you need to think carefully about the consequences before saying so—to open your mouth can lead to greater problems instead of solving the immediate one.

Places, Everyone!

Be patient. No matter how good you are, there are times when you will not be quite right for a role you audition for, or at least someone else will be closer to what the director or producers had in mind. But you will get to show off a considerable range of abilities in the course of these auditions. Eventually, something may click, and you can end up with a bigger reward than you expected.

Another friend, Louise, is a professional with a long list of stage credits. She had never had much luck with television, however. In the 1990s, her agent sent her to several auditions for a major television drama filmed in New York. She was always treated well, and received call-backs a couple of times, but never won any of the roles. She was about to develop a chip on her shoulder, she was so frustrated. "I really wanted to ask them why they kept seeing me," she says. "I felt like they were wasting my time and theirs." But she kept quiet, was always polite, and always thanked them for seeing her. Her sixth audition, which was for the most important role yet, finally led to her being cast.

Following the rules of audition etiquette is not just an exercise in good manners, it's also plain common sense. If you behave like a grownup, that will be remembered, and can serve you well in the long run. If you behave like a spoiled child, that, too, will be remembered, and can come back to haunt you.

The Least You Need to Know

- Don't give attitude when you audition; just show off your talent.
- Keep in mind that auditions are stressful and tiring for everyone, including those judging your abilities.
- Look upon other actors as your colleagues, not just as your competition.
- Learn how to make a gracious exit from auditions regardless of how you think things went.

The Waiting Game

In This Chapter

- Learning how to keep calm until you hear about casting
- Exploring the pros and cons of accepting a smaller role
- Understanding the complexities of assembling a cast
- Discovering how to deal with rejection
- Recognizing the responsibilities that come with a lead role

When it comes to getting a role, the news you're waiting to hear—that you've been cast—only very rarely arrives quickly. Indeed, most actors spend a lot of time waiting for the phone to ring. Days can go by without hearing a word. And when the news does come, it may be less exciting than you had hoped, because although you've been cast, the role is not a big one or, even worse, you don't get a role at all. And even if the news is terrific—you've got the lead—you may not be as thrilled as you might expect, because you realize how much work that's going to take. In this chapter, we'll take you through the psychological ups and downs of the waiting game. We'll explain the good reasons why it often takes so long to let you know whether you've been cast in a play or not. You may be offered a less important role than you wanted, and we'll give you tips on how to decide whether or not you should accept it. We'll provide some guidelines to help decipher the excuses you'll hear if you're not cast. Finally, we'll be looking at the realities that accompany getting a lead role.

Why Haven't They Called?

Few aspects of show business are more frustrating than the wait to hear if you have been cast in a show. With great luck, the director, producer, or your agent will telephone you within 24 hours. But several days may go by before you hear anything, and it is all too easy to drive yourself crazy wondering what's going on during that time. So, let's begin by taking a look at what is likely to be happening during that long silent period. Understanding more completely how the casting process works may help you to live with the delays in announcing a cast list.

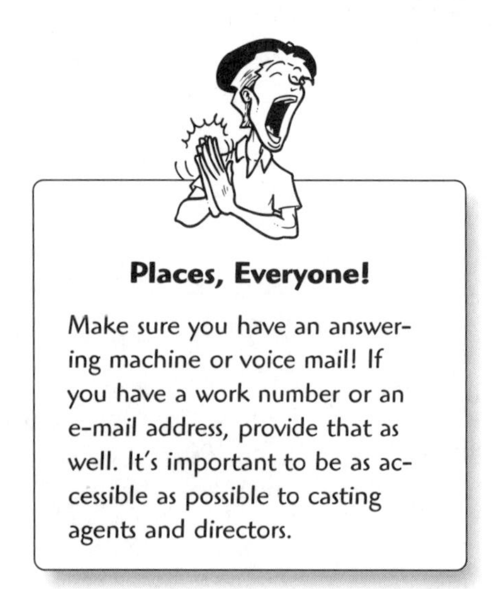

Places, Everyone!

Make sure you have an answering machine or voice mail! If you have a work number or an e-mail address, provide that as well. It's important to be as accessible as possible to casting agents and directors.

Decisions Take Time

Put yourself in the director's shoes. If you were casting a show, would you make up your mind in a couple of hours about who to cast in a dozen roles? Of course not. You might even need to think about it for a couple of days, and the larger the cast, the more thought it may take. That means that a musical is almost always going to require more thought than a contemporary straight play, since the latter tends to have a smallish cast. A play by Shakespeare, with multitudes of characters, is obviously a more difficult casting problem than one by Neil Simon with a quarter as many parts to fill.

What's more, the difficulties that the director faces in making a decision overlap. While the male lead may be a single obvious choice, for example, the female lead could have two or three contenders. Deciding between them isn't often just a matter of concluding which would be best for the lead role. If two actors appear to have nearly equal talent, it would be wise to use one of them as the lead, and the other in a different role. Which of the two seems best suited to that other role? In some plays and musicals, a secondary role is trickier to play than the lead. In *Romeo and Juliet,* for example, Mercutio is in some ways more difficult to pull off than Romeo. And these problems crop up not just in terms of the leads, but also in respect to secondary roles. Often a director is making a decision about two roles simultaneously, and that takes time.

Assigning roles in musicals can be especially complicated because the director must take the opinions of the musical director and the choreographer into account. That can mean as many as three different opinions about a single role, and it can take negotiations and compromises to reach a conclusion. Once again, that is time-consuming.

Backstage Tales

Early in his career, co-author Paul Baldwin auditioned for a dinner-theater production of Stephen Sondheim's musical *Company,* which was scheduled for a 10-week run at two theaters in North Carolina. As a baritone, he knew he couldn't play the tenor lead, Bobby, but he loved the show and just wanted to be in it, regardless of the part. That attitude turned out to be just as well, since the director called to tell him he had been cast, but that the exact role was still to be determined. It wasn't until a week into rehearsal that Paul was assigned the role of Harry, which happened to be the one he had wanted, largely because of the beautiful ballad, "Sorry, Grateful."

Professional actors also have agents, and while that might seem likely to ease the strain of the waiting game, it doesn't always work that way. While theoretically it is the job of an agent to keep after the director or the producers of a show to find out the status of a client, agents can be reluctant to cause a fuss unless the client is a major star. The agent will have to deal with the same director or producer on other shows and needs to remain on good terms with the people who do the hiring. In addition, good agents are often enormously busy because they usually represent a large number of clients. Because your concerns may not always be at the top of his or her list, having an agent can actually slow down the process. At least an amateur actor knows that he or she will get the call directly.

Staying Calm in the Meantime

We're not going to tell you not to worry, because that's the kind of advice that is very easy to give and very hard to follow. Some people are by nature "worrywarts," and if you're one of them, you're inevitably going to get very nervous waiting to hear if you've been cast in a play, and whether you've gotten the part you wanted.

However, here are a few points you should keep in mind:

- Don't try to read tea leaves. As we pointed out in the previous chapter, some directors are extremely poker-faced and rather cool, while others dispense wide smiles by the carload. Trying to figure out the significance of their every word and action during your audition is a waste of time.

Performance Notes

No matter how anxious you're feeling, do not call the director or producer of a show until four or five days have passed. That will only annoy the director and become a mark against you in making a final decision. The only exception to this rule is if you are offered a part in another production after your audition. If so, you have every right to call the show you haven't heard from to tell them why you must know where you stand within 24 hours.

- Don't go over your audition performance again and again in your head. If you start thinking, "I should have emphasized that word more," or "I should have read that line with more anger," you'll agitate yourself for no purpose. It's over, and you can't change anything now. What's more, it's entirely possible that what you thought was a mistake in approach actually caused the director to sit up and take notice. Acting itself, and reactions to what an actor does, are both subjective processes. That means that you really can't know how a director might respond until he or she voices explicit approval or disapproval.
- Even an obvious mistake may not have been fatal. If you were asked to sing a song from the show that lies a bit high for your voice and the climactic note was wobbly, that still may not have ruined your chances. Songs are taken down for actors all the time, and if you are right for the role in many other ways, you could still get it.

A Small but Important Role

When the phone finally does ring, you may not get the news you'd hoped for. Maybe you wanted to play the lead role of Rosalind in *As You Like It*, but have been asked to play Celia instead. Or you wanted the role of Tom in *The Glass Menagerie* and have been offered the part of the Gentleman Caller. Although these are both very good roles that have been played by important actors in the past, you may have had your heart set on the larger role. You're afraid now that you'll feel uncomfortable—and therefore not be good—in the role, perhaps because it will be hard for you to watch someone else play it, or because you don't feel a kinship with the character. What should you do?

Give Yourself Time to Think

If you are offered a role you have doubts about playing—for whatever reason—keep in mind that you can reasonably ask to think it over. The director may behave as though this is an astonishing request, but in fact any experienced director will have encountered this problem many times before. You'll get the good news—that the part is really terrific and you'll be able to do wonders with it—and you'll get the bad news—that the director really needs you for the role and that, if you play it, you'll have the chance at other roles in the future. Of course, this approach also sounds like a veiled threat that if you don't take this role, other roles will be less likely to follow.

As alarming as either approach may sound, keep in mind that it's all standard operating procedure. Say that you know it's a good role, even if you don't think so. If you say you don't like the part, or are not sure you're right for it, or that you're not certain it's worth your time, you'll just open the way for the director to tell you you're wrong. Just say you appreciate the offer, but that you need to mull it over for 24 hours.

Places, Everyone!

If you're absolutely certain you don't want the role being offered, you should of course refuse on the spot. Don't keep the director in suspense just to retaliate for not getting the role you really wanted. Playing that kind of game can hurt you. Instead, make a big deal of how honest you are being in saying no immediately. You don't like the role, period. There's no answer to that and you will at least get credit for your directness.

If you've got 24 hours to make up your mind, you need to buckle down and consider all the factors involved. The size of the role, the significance of the role, your sympathy or lack of sympathy for the character, as well as considerations of the time you will have to dedicate to it are all part of the equation. You should also consider how the role could impact your reputation; if you're known for playing lead roles, a smaller part may put a dent in your reputation. Some people do this kind of thinking in their heads, while others find it helpful to write down a two-column list of specific pros and cons. One actor may come to a decision based on a hardheaded look at the pluses and minuses involved, while another may go with a gut feeling about the situation.

At Least It's Something

In the end, after thinking the matter through carefully, many actors will take a role on the grounds that at least they have been cast. It may be that the play is a favorite of yours and being in it at all will be a pleasure. Perhaps a number of your friends have also been cast, and you'd simply enjoy working with them, regardless of the size of the role you're playing. It may be that having a job—any job—as an actor is a worthy end to the audition process. Those are perfectly valid reasons for accepting a role in amateur theater, and occasionally they make the difference for a professional actor as well.

But consider another aspect of the situation. Say you do play Celia instead of Rosalind in *As You Like It*. It is a good role, and a decent credit for your resumé. An actor learns and grows with any role, so it won't be a waste of time from that point of view. Most important of all, perhaps, is that joining the production will give you a chance to watch another actor develop the role of Rosalind. You may learn quite a lot from that experience, noting things the other performer does that will extend your own ideas about the role. You may also see some mistakes she's making that you will now know how to avoid. There may be another production of the play at some point that you will want to audition for, and what you've learned could get you the part of Rosalind next time.

Backstage Tales

Another reason for taking on a secondary role is that you know you can do a lot with it. A friend of the authors auditioned for the starring role of Sheridan Whiteside in a community-theater production of *The Man Who Came to Dinner.* He was ideal for the role, a bit portly, with great comic timing and a commanding voice. But the director, who was a similar type, decided to cast himself in the lead. (This happens a little too often in community theater.) Our friend was offered the role of Beverly Carlton, based on Noel Coward. He grabbed it and stole the show, getting much better reviews than the director did as Sheridan Whiteside.

Too Tall, Too Short

In Chapter 12, "Know What They're Looking For," we discussed the age and height ratios in terms of being "typed out." It's necessary to bring that subject up again here, since it can be a primary reason why you have to wait so long to hear whether or not you've been cast, and can be the cause of losing a part. As noted before, directors get very nervous about having a leading man who is shorter than the leading lady. But this criterion can apply in other circumstances, too.

Take a play like Neil Simon's *The Odd Couple.* In the original Broadway hit, in the subsequent movie, and on the television show that followed, Oscar the slob was always a bigger man than Felix the neatnik was. Because these characters are so well known to the public, directors are afraid to challenge preconceptions. In fact, however, it could be very funny if the physical embodiment of these two characters were reversed, with a weedy type playing the messy sports reporter Oscar, while the fussy Felix towered over him. But few directors have the imagination or guts to try that, and so many an actor has lost out on one part or the other because he was too short or too tall.

But height and age differentials are only the most obvious of the myriad of excuses directors can come up with for not casting an actor in a given role.

Places, Everyone!

When a director gives you a reason why you haven't been cast in a particular role or been cast at all, don't take it too much to heart. Directors often lie in these situations, telling themselves that they're fudging in order to let you down lightly. Often, however, they're just protecting themselves from second-guessing: The real reason may not reflect badly on you, but it might on the director.

Excuses, Excuses

"We love your work, but you look too much like the woman we're casting in the lead." Or, "I'm sure we'll be using you in the future, but we're looking for someone with more experience in that role." Or, "You sing beautifully, but we've decided to go with someone who's primarily an actor." Or, "We're casting that role with a local audience favorite."

The actor who hears such excuses would like to answer back, of course, since each of these excuses has ready retorts. You look too much like the leading lady? Well, you could dye your hair or wear a wig, and costuming and makeup can effect amazing transformations. More experience? That excuse can make you wonder how you'll ever get that experience unless you're given a chance to attain it. They're stressing acting over singing? Strange, you thought you were auditioning for a musical. The part's going to an audience favorite? Well, last time you saw that favorite on stage, several audience members were wondering at intermission if there wasn't another actor somewhere on the face of the earth who could play her role.

But you know better than to make any of these retorts, since they'd just get you a reputation as "difficult" and hurt your future chances. Still, it can be extremely annoying to hear such excuses when you finally get a call after waiting for several days for the phone to ring. Why, you may think, do you even bother to audition? Of course, if you persevere, the day may well come when some other actor is getting the brush-off because now it's you who have more experience or are an audience favorite.

The Mysteries of Casting

The previous couple of pages may have you muttering darkly about the perfidy of directors. To balance the ledger, keep in mind that few directors play games just for the fun of it. Casting a play is a very difficult job. In fact, many directors have said that getting the casting right is more important than anything they do subsequently in terms of staging and shaping the play during rehearsals. A badly cast show is likely to fail, no matter what happens after that. And badly cast doesn't necessarily mean that bad actors have been chosen. Everyone may be a good actor, but even the best can falter if put into the wrong role.

What's more, good casting is a mysterious process, based on intuition as much as on reason. Critics often talk about the "chemistry" between actors on stage or in the movies, especially in respect to romantic pairings. But chemistry can be important between antagonistic characters of the same sex, too. Sparks are struck between two actors, and no one knows quite why.

Backstage Tales

Spencer Tracy and Katharine Hepburn had legendary onscreen chemistry. They happened to be involved in a long-time affair offscreen, but that doesn't necessarily have anything to do with acting chemistry. Sometimes stars are having torrid affairs offscreen, but fail to catch fire in front of the camera. Other times, surprising combinations work. Julie Andrews and James Garner had tremendous chemistry together in *The Americanization of Emily* and *Victor, Victoria*, but there was no offscreen dalliance. Andrews might have been expected to strike sparks with Paul Newman, but when Hitchcock tried that combination in *Torn Curtain*, the stars fizzled instead of sizzled.

Because it is so difficult to judge whether actors will catch fire in a play or movie, directors have to rely on intuition and play their hunches. They don't usually like to admit that's what they're doing, however, and so they come up with all kinds of arbitrary "reasons" to explain a decision that they may not fully understand themselves. When you fail to get a role, it will quite often be because the director has a hunch that a different combination will work better. That can be frustrating. But rest assured that you will also get parts because of such hunches.

Coping with Rejection

The very fact that casting is a tricky and often mysterious process provides one key to coping with rejection when you are not cast. Always remember that failing to get a role can have as much to do with directorial intuition as it does with the relative talent of the person who gets cast and the person who does not. Never beat up on yourself unnecessarily when you don't get cast. Recognize that there may be reasons for your "failure" that have little to do with your real ability.

Not Necessarily Your Fault

In the course of this section of the book, we've noted a number of reasons why a failure to be cast may not be your fault. Let's review them:

1. You are physically wrong for the role in terms of the conventional approach to the characters.
2. You are too tall or too short to play opposite an actor whom the director feels must be cast.
3. You look too much like an actor chosen for another important role.
4. Another actor is an "audience favorite."
5. The director's intuition mandated a different choice.
6. The part you wanted was in fact pre-cast, even though you were informed that all parts were open.
7. The director or theater owner decides to play the lead at the last moment.
8. The director is sleeping with—or wants to sleep with—the actor who gets the role instead of you.

Let's add two more reasons, one very specific, and one unfortunately all too general. In the professional theater, actors sometimes get cast because someone has put up a great deal of money to back the show. "Angels," as the money people behind the scenes are called in Broadway parlance, do not always have the disposition of such heavenly creatures, and may wield their financial power to see that someone gets a role—their wife, mistress, son, daughter, whatever. This is far less likely to happen in amateur theater, where there's no such thing as a multimillion-dollar musical, but it can occur.

The final possible reason you didn't get cast is in some ways particularly discouraging: The director is a jerk. Estelle Parsons, who has both an Oscar and a Tony to her credit, was once asked during a television interview to name some good directors. She smiled and replied with her own question, "Are there any good directors?" She was not making a joke, and several famous actors tend to feel this way. But that is an extreme view. Most actors are quick to praise directors whom they respect, and can usually name several.

Performance Notes

No matter why you think you may have failed to be cast in a show, go see the production when it opens, if at all possible. Don't stay away out of pique or embarrassment. Seeing the show may make clearer the reason you weren't cast, and it may not reflect badly on you at all. If the actor cast instead of you is awful, you can gloat. If he or she is very good, you'll learn something.

Nevertheless, no one who makes a career of acting, and no one with wide experience as an amateur actor, will escape the occasional encounter with a stupid director. The world is full of incompetents; you can find them in every profession. Some of them manage to become quite successful. We could even name several jerk actors who regularly get their names above the title. An incompetent director will come your way, and you are bound to find yourself on stage with incompetent actors from time to time. That's life.

"I'll Just Work Harder"

At times, of course, you will fail to get cast because you didn't deserve to be. Even very talented actors have off days and give terrible auditions as a result. Your reading will be flat and stale, your high note will be flat or sharp, you will move around the stage like a zombie, or overact frenetically. You'll be awful. It happens occasionally to every actor.

And sometimes you'll bite off more than you are ready to chew. Your love of a certain role will lead you to audition for it before you are ready to do it justice. You may not yet have enough experience, or emotional maturity, or technical command to pull off the role. That's not the end of the world. In fact, any actor who really wants to improve should occasionally take a risk and audition for that great role that's a little beyond his or her reach. By all means, push yourself now and then. But if you take such a risk and fail, lower your sights a little next time, and go for a role you know you can do. With another two or three less ambitious parts under your belt, your confidence may be such that you're ready to take a risk again.

Backstage Tales

Liza Minnelli had already won a Tony Award for her starring role in the musical *Flora, The Red Menace*, when the same composers, John Kander and Fred Ebb, completed the score for *Cabaret* with Minnelli in mind for the part of Sally Bowles. But the director, the legendary Harold Prince, instead cast the British actress Jill Haworth, who was not well received by the critics. Liza Minnelli, of course, eventually won the Oscar for portraying Sally Bowles onscreen. She has always maintained that although she was crushed to lose out on the stage version, her rejection made her work all the harder, and resulted in a better performance when she did get her chance at the role.

When you fail to get the role you want, or are rejected altogether, take that as a reason to work harder. Trying and failing is a crucial part of eventual success.

You've Got the Lead!

The phone rings. You're expecting it to be a friend calling just to chat. Instead, it's the director of the show you auditioned for only yesterday. You're surprised to hear anything so quickly. Maybe he wants you for a call-back. But then you hear him asking you to play the lead. "You were terrific yesterday," he says. "This is the perfect role for you." You feel like yelling at the top of your lungs, but you swallow hard and keep your cool. You say, "thank you," and "that's wonderful," and even have the presence of mind to ask when and where rehearsals begin. And after you hang up, you stand there for a moment, muttering, "I can't believe it." It is, after all, your first lead. But even if it were your tenth, you'd be a bit giddy for a moment. There's nothing like the moment when a dream comes true.

And the Responsibility

After the first flush of excitement, however, a new reality asserts itself. The fact that you've got the lead means that a great deal of the responsibility for the show's success will fall on your shoulders. Some lead roles are particularly daunting. If you've been cast in a title role, whether it's Hamlet or Mame, Hedda Gabler or Sweeny Todd, the entire show depends on your talents. In many plays, a lead role is protected by several other roles of similar size, but if you've got a title role, you're fully exposed, and if you don't deliver, no one else can save the show.

It would be surprising if you didn't feel a bit nervous suddenly, when you think about that responsibility. Even actors who have "carried" a show numerous times are sobered by the fact that they must do it again. In fact, they may be even more nervous than the actor who's taking on a lead for the first time. If you're a veteran, you know in your bones how much work lies ahead.

Places, Everyone!

When you land a lead role, stop and think before calling everyone you know to tell them. Did some of your good friends audition for the same show? They may not know whether they've been cast yet. Some of them may have been told there's no part for them in this particular show. Give yourself time to calm down before talking to them, or you might make them feel even more anxious or upset.

Real Work to Do

If you've been cast in a lead role, the time to start working is immediately. With luck, you'll have some time before rehearsals begin, maybe a week, perhaps in community theater as long as a month. Don't waste any of that time. Read the play again, two or three times, paying as much attention to the other characters as you do to your own. If it's a period piece, you may want to do some research. Start learning your lines, and your songs, too, if it's a musical, right away. Get a move on. You've been given a great opportunity, but it is more than that. You've been entrusted with a major responsibility. Take it very seriously.

The Least You Need to Know

- Casting decisions are complicated, so don't be surprised if it takes time to be informed of your status.
- If offered a less important role than expected, don't hesitate to ask for 24 hours to think it over.
- Take the reasons given for not casting you with a grain of salt.
- Rejection may come for reasons beyond your control, but can also be a goad to greater effort.
- Don't let the thrill of getting the lead obscure the need for hard work ahead.

Part 4

Rehearsal Rigors

Some actors love rehearsing so much that they would be happy if that phase of developing a production could go on forever. In fact, some professional theater productions, usually experimental in nature, rehearse for months, even on-and-off for years, before settling on a final form. Some of the theater pieces of the great British director Peter Brooke have taken that route, and Al Pacino made a feature film of his lengthy rehearsals of Shakespeare's Richard III. *But most actors and directors view rehearsals as simply the preparation period for the opening night of a scheduled production a few weeks later. It is an intense period that usually seems all too short.*

In this section of the book, we will take you through a normal rehearsal period of a few weeks, step by step. You'll learn about everything from scheduling problems to the personal dynamics of a stage production. We'll show you how the nitty-gritty mechanics of stage movement and line memorization gradually evolve to the point of revealing the ultimate shape of the play or musical.

Chapter 17

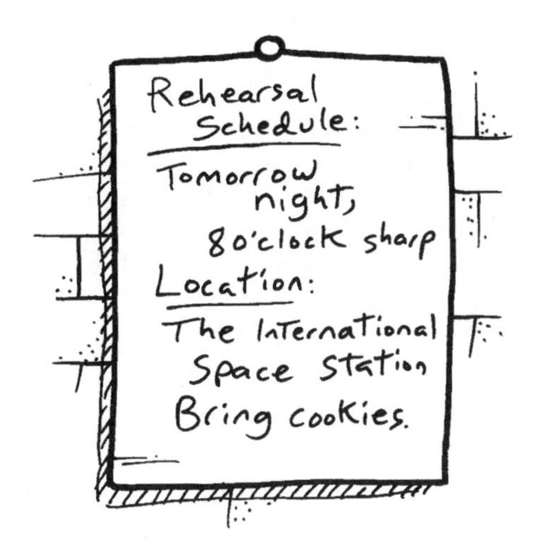

Scheduling Nightmares

In This Chapter

- Finding out how to negotiate a sensible rehearsal schedule
- Learning the ins-and-outs of transportation etiquette
- Recognizing the importance of avoiding scheduling conflicts

Once a cast has been assembled, the director or stage manager will create a rehearsal schedule. Broadway shows usually have at least three weeks of rehearsal, and a major musical can demand more, while at the other end of the professional spectrum, summer stock companies may put on a different show each week, rehearsing one while performing another. Amateur productions, whether at the school, college, or community theater level, generally have a fairly long rehearsal period, ranging from a month to as much as two months. This extended schedule is necessary because the cast members are either attending classes or have full-time jobs, and can meet only in the evenings and on weekends.

In this chapter, we'll take a close look at how a rehearsal schedule is put together. There are a number of approaches to scheduling, and they vary from one show to another, depending in part on the nature of the show and in part on the inclinations and experience of the director. No matter what approach your show takes, you'll find that problems inevitably arise, and we'll tell you how to deal with them. At the school and community theater levels, you'll probably often find transportation issues to cope with, since the cast members will need to get together at a central location at odd hours. We'll discuss both the practical and social aspects of this problem. In addition, we'll be detailing the kinds of conflicts between normal life and rehearsal hours that are bound to crop up in amateur productions.

The Long and the Short of It

Most actors feel that the longer the rehearsal period, the better it is for the show. However, even though too few rehearsals can mean a ragged production, a very extended rehearsal period can cause different kinds of problems. There is a developmental process built into a good rehearsal schedule that brings the actors to a peak—and that peak should coincide with the opening of the show. If the rehearsal schedule forces a premature peak, actors can suffer a psychological let-down that is difficult to overcome, and performances become stale. If the schedule is strung out over too long a period, the actors may lose the edge they've achieved in scenes that they rehearsed the first week of rehearsal.

Thus, devising a good rehearsal schedule is not merely a matter of practical organization. It also involves working on the play in ways that enable the actors to continually develop their characters. The challenge is to integrate the calendar with all the creative concerns so that they form a mutually supportive whole. It is not an easy task.

"Why Do I Have to Be There?"

Some directors prefer to rehearse a play in strict sequence, following the order of the scenes as they occur exactly. Others will work out of sequence, dealing with the most important scenes first, and then going back to put minor scenes in place. Both approaches have advantages and disadvantages in terms of creative development. They also raise different practical problems when it comes to scheduling.

Places, Everyone!

If you've been cast as a dancer or a chorus member in a musical, be aware from the start that you will be rehearsing, as a group, as much as those actors in the starring roles. Small parts in straight plays, on the other hand, usually require far less rehearsal time.

The nature of a particular show may demand one approach or another. A play like Harold Pinter's *Betrayal*, which tells its story backwards (starting in the present with each succeeding scene taking place earlier in time) requires a strict sequence, or else the actors can end up thoroughly confused about the emotional arc of the play. On the other hand, rehearsing a big musical cannot be done in sequence, because musical numbers involving many chorus members or dancers are the most difficult and time-consuming to stage. The director must start work early even on musical numbers that take place late in the show or there won't be sufficient time to polish them. More intimate scenes with a small number of characters need less rehearsal time and thus will be dealt with out of sequence.

Whether a director rehearses largely in or out of sequence, you'll be given a copy of the schedule before rehearsals begin or perhaps at the first rehearsal, which always includes the entire cast. Read this rehearsal schedule very carefully. You may be in for a shock, and the time to deal with problems is right at the start.

In most cases, the director or stage manager will create a rehearsal schedule by breaking down the production into scenes. You'll see a list of characters taking part in each scene next to each listing, followed by the date, time, and place of the rehearsal. If you're playing one of the leads, you can expect to see the name of your character appearing day after day. Even if a lead is not in every scene rehearsed on a particular date, his or her presence may be required for at least one of the scheduled scenes. This happens because the director may have scheduled all the scenes in which a secondary character appears for a single rehearsal. Even though that character has three scenes that you aren't in, there may be a fourth that includes you, making your presence necessary.

But suppose you are one of the secondary characters. If you see your character listed for date after date, something is wrong. Someone hasn't broken down the rehearsal schedule sensibly, or you would be required to show up only a couple of times a week. Some directors, usually inexperienced ones, have difficulty breaking down a play into sections, or scenes, in ways that give the secondary characters time off. The simplest problem to solve is the schedule that requires your presence for only one scene out of three listed. In cases like this, you should be allowed to show up at the start, do your scene and then leave, or come in later, at a time when your scene will, in fact, be dealt with.

Performance Notes

Don't complain before you know the score. Some directors will balk at actors coming in midway through rehearsals, just for their scene, protesting that it's hard to know how much time will be spent on earlier scenes and that your presence is therefore necessary throughout. Comply with this dictum once. If you are sitting around for an hour and a half before you are needed, you will then have better ammunition to use to change the director's mind about this issue.

Preparing a good rehearsal schedule is a complicated task. If the cast is large, working it out properly can verge on solving a three-dimensional puzzle like a Rubik's Cube. Some directors are very good at it; others are terrible. Those who recognize their deficiency in this area try to find an assistant or a stage manager with a knack for it. But sometimes a stubborn or inexperienced director will insist on proceeding according to his or her nincompoop arrangement. In such cases, it may be possible for several members of the cast with smaller roles to put their heads together and work out a better solution. Don't try this all by yourself, but if you can enlist three or four other actors and come up with a good solution, type it up and present it, as a group, to the director.

Backstage Tales

During his third year at Harvard, co-author John Malone was cast as Vendice, the central character in Cyril Tourneur's *The Revenger's Tragedy*, a play full of great poetry and typically horrific Jacobean mayhem. Vendice is an enormous 1,100-line role, longer than any in Shakespeare. John was prepared for a killer rehearsal schedule requiring his presence every day. To his delight, the schedule had been brilliantly worked out so that he got a break every few days. The director was Michael Ritchie, who, as noted before, went on to a distinguished career as a Hollywood director and producer. If it's possible to come up with a schedule that gives an actor playing Vendice time off, it can be done with any play. Are you listening, directors?

Changing Timetables

Once rehearsals are underway, the schedule is bound to undergo changes sooner or later. That's because some scenes prove to be more difficult to stage than the director anticipated or because one or more of the cast members turn out to have problems getting some scenes right.

Places, Everyone!

Go to rehearsals prepared to while away some time. If you haven't learned your lines, bring your script and study. If you know your lines, bring a book, work from the office, or have a knitting project—anything to occupy your time fruitfully.

Let's suppose that one scene involving only three characters is scheduled for the start of an evening's rehearsal, at seven o'clock. Two other actors involved in the next scene show up right on time to begin work on it, at 8:15. But they find the cast still working on the first scene. With luck, those working will sort out the difficulty quickly and the newly arrived cast members will only have to wait around for 15 minutes. But if the problems prove more complicated, they can wait much longer. Some directors will throw up their hands and move on. Others will persist with the troubled scene until they make progress. If the latter happens, the whole evening may slow down to such an extent that the director postpones the next scene—even if it has more characters—to another night.

Delays can occur when rehearsing dramas and also, especially, when staging musical numbers, fight scenes, or any scene involving large numbers of actors. Often, such delays will scramble any neatly organized schedule considerably. That means you must keep rehearsal periods open even if you aren't originally scheduled to appear. Don't lock yourself into other appointments on supposedly "free" days, or you'll end up with a new problem.

More Car-Pooling

Most college productions will rehearse at a central location on campus, and you'll be able to walk to rehearsals. But transportation can be a problem with both school and community theater productions. It can make it necessary for some members of the cast to hitch a ride at the convenience of the driver. That's likely to mean more time spent waiting around for your scene because, even though you are scheduled for 8:30, you can only get a ride to the theater an hour earlier.

Another Appointment for the Kids

Most parents are so used to car-pooling arrangements that they will know exactly how to make sure their kids get to rehearsals for a grade-school Christmas pageant or a high-school play. But sometimes problems crop up. If the rehearsals take place right after school, as is often the case, it may mean that a child can't take the school bus home as usual. And, at least toward the end, some rehearsals may take place at night, complicating things further.

A community theater production introduces new elements to the situation. If a kid is in a production, such as *Annie*, that has numerous other children, then the usual parental conferences will take care of getting everyone there, even if it has nighttime rehearsals. But a number of plays have just one child in the cast, from Enid Bagnold's *The Chalk Garden* to the musical *Camelot*. That means that
either a parent will have to make a couple of trips on rehearsal evenings or weekend afternoons, or work out an arrangement with an adult member of the cast who lives nearby.

Places, Everyone!

If a lone child is in a cast, ask the director to help arrange transportation before rehearsals begin. He or she will know where everyone lives, and can approach adult cast members more easily than a parent who may never have met any of the actors involved. Don't worry about being a nuisance. Good child actors are hard to come by, as anyone watching cute kids mumbling through television commercials will be aware.

Who Has Cars in the Cast?

Even adult members of a community theater cast may have transportation problems if their city doesn't have a good subway or bus service. For reasons that await a graduate thesis in psychology to describe, a surprising number of actors either don't drive or don't have cars. Others may drive and own a car, but have a spouse who works nights or a teenage child who has commandeered the family's second car. Among professional actors working in dinner theater or regional theater, the suspense is considerable in regard to which cast members will have a car, and how willing they will be to drive people around or loan out their vehicle. Even in community theater, this question can be important. Many community theater actors appear in productions in other small cities as much as an hour away from home, and transportation can be a real issue.

Gas Contributions

It shouldn't be necessary to say this, but the world is full of tightwads: If you need transportation, and some other cast member is willing to drive you back and forth to rehearsals, be sure to offer to share gas expenses. The tightwad rationale on this matter is that the driver has to go to rehearsals anyway, so it really isn't costing anything to cart you around. That is beside the point. Offer to share gas expenses as a matter of common courtesy. And if you're the driver and the offer isn't made, don't hesitate to ask for a contribution. Fair is fair.

Conflicting Responsibilities

Professional actors are sometimes given special status in terms of rehearsals for a stage play or when making a movie. If an actor appearing regularly on television does a Broadway play, the director of the play will arrange the rehearsal schedule around his or her needs, with actors not performing elsewhere making necessary adjustments to their own schedules. And if an actor is appearing on Broadway, but simultaneously making a movie in New York, directors and production companies will make similar concessions.

In amateur theater, there may also be an actor or two in a show with other commitments that they can't change—a college chemistry lab that takes place once a week, or a full-time job that involves occasional night duty on a revolving basis. That can complicate the rehearsal schedule and make it necessary for other cast members to rehearse at odd hours. Obviously, a show can't have more than one or two such individuals, or it will be impossible to create any kind of sensible schedule.

Quite aside from special scheduling problems, most people involved in amateur theater productions have other responsibilities, whether schoolwork, a full-time job, or caring for a family member. Conflicts in scheduling are inevitable. If that's your situation, take a hard look at your rehearsal schedule as soon as you get it. Pay particular attention to the final week of rehearsals, when your presence is imperative and dress rehearsals are bound to run overtime. Let's look at some common problems:

Backstage Tales

A friend of the authors who is a community theater actor in Pennsylvania works for a furniture company as a salesman. He's been there for 15 years. He also acts in at least three shows a year. His boss has been very understanding about Joe's theater activities. The store is open nights and Joe does his share of night duty during periods when he is not in a play. His boss lets him off for Wednesday matinees during the run of a show, not just because he is a nice guy, but because Joe is something of a local celebrity and brings customers into the store. Not all bosses are going to be so flexible, however.

1. If you are a teenage athlete, do you have a ball game scheduled for that same weekend? You can't do both. If you're a third-stringer who sits on the bench most of the time anyway, it may be that your coach will let you off that weekend. But find out immediately.
2. Does your grandmother's birthday fall on that weekend, with a big party held every year? Tell Grandma immediately that you won't be there this year.
3. Do you work in a store that has inventory scheduled for that crucial final week of rehearsals? You probably can't get out of that, so you'd better square it with the director if you have a small part, or drop out of this production if you've been given a larger role. (To tell the truth, you probably shouldn't have even auditioned for a show falling on those dates in the first place.)
4. Have you been asked to be a bridesmaid or best man at wedding that coincides with the end of the rehearsal period? This one crops up quite often and always creates bad feelings as the director's rage encounters the maid of honor's tears. More than one director has been moved to say, "It's too bad you can't give a performance that convincing onstage." Ouch.

There are a hundred variations on these conflicts. Whatever they may be, resolve them before rehearsals begin. If you wait and hope the conflict will go away, you'll just end up with everyone mad at you.

Parents of kids appearing in shows need to take special care in this regard. The rehearsal and performance period is NOT the time for your kid to get those braces for his or her teeth. Postpone that yearly shopping trip to the big city or visit to Uncle Jim and Aunt Flo. (Kids who are reading this book might consider asking their parents to take a good look at this chapter in particular.)

When You Can't Do Everything

Because rehearsal schedules are complex, and are subject to change as the needs of the actors and the production become evident, unanticipated hitches always arise. Add to that the myriad curveballs that life throws at us all, from dead car batteries and snowstorms to the flu. The result is that actors do miss rehearsals from time to time.

Broadway, Off-Broadway, and major regional theaters will have understudies to cover for actors who are ill or called away by an emergency, but this is seldom the case in amateur theater. Even dinner theater and summer theater productions usually don't have understudies. When an actor is missing from rehearsals in amateur theater, the usual recourse is to have someone with a small part, or even a stagehand, read the role with script in hand so that rehearsals can continue, although that is seldom a very satisfactory solution. The authors know of occasional situations, however, where the missing actor came to greatly regret his or her absence. The replacement, even with book in hand, was so much better in the part that the actor returned from a couple of days absence to find his or her part reassigned to the substitute. So, beware.

Backstage Tales

Co-author John Malone once went to see a prep school production of *A Midsummer Night's Dream* directed by a former teacher and good friend named Ralph Symonds, who was English, a five-foot-two bundle of talent and energy. Women from a nearby junior college played the female roles. But John was taken aback by the appearance of Helena. "What an unattractive girl," he thought. Then, "Wait a minute, that's not a girl, it's a man." And finally, "My God, it's Ralph." The girl playing Helena had been called away for her grandmother's funeral and Ralph stepped in to save the day. Although in Shakespeare's time boys always played women's roles, the playwright might have been a bit stunned by Ralph's hilarious appearance in the role.

If it's a true emergency—an unexpected, serious family emergency or a cold so severe that the actor really can't speak the lines—the director and the rest of the cast will be sympathetic and pull together to get through things as best they can. "The Show Must Go On," is a motto as old as the theater. However, when an actor misses even a rehearsal, never mind a performance, for reasons that are less than serious, he or she won't find forgiveness so easy to come by. A missed rehearsal sets back other actors. It is very difficult to play a scene at anywhere near the proper level of conviction when you're trading lines with a stagehand reading a script instead of with your regular acting partner. Although by definition amateur theater means that you usually don't get paid, it doesn't mean that unprofessional conduct is allowed. Missing rehearsals for anything less than a real crisis is unprofessional. When you audition for a play, you must have it clearly in mind that you are taking on a very serious responsibility.

Co-author Paul Baldwin once played King Arthur in a summer theater production of *Camelot* in which all the actors had been hired out of New York with one exception. Sir Pellinore's dog, Horrid, was played by a huge local mixed-breed named Mitzi. Because she was so big and hairy, even her owners didn't realize she was pregnant until after the three-week run opened. She gave birth to a litter of five on a Sunday evening; Monday was a day off. A substitute dog, cute but woefully small, had been located. But on Tuesday, at the time Mitzi usually left for the theater, she went out and stood by the family station wagon, barking. Her owners delivered her as always. Even Mitzi knew the show must go on!

Places, Everyone!

Take your child's commitment to a production seriously. Parents of school-age children participating in a play need to recognize that this activity is not just a "fun" extra. The lead in a school play has as strong a duty to show up on time and do his or her job well as that same child would if the boy was quarterback of his high school football team or the girl the center on her basketball team.

Acting is enormously rewarding. It expands your knowledge of the world, lifts your spirit, shows off your talents, and enables you to express yourself in a way that enriches the lives of other people who come to see you. The applause they give you comes from the heart. But acting is a discipline as well as an art, hard work as well as fun. And that discipline is particularly important during the rehearsal period. A schedule is a schedule. If the schedule is badly conceived, you have a right to try to get it changed. But once it is set, it is your duty to adhere to it unless serious unforeseen difficulties arise.

The Least You Need to Know

- It's fine for cast members to suggest some fine-tuning for a rehearsal schedule, but it must be adhered to after that.
- Settle all transportation problems early on, and don't forget to contribute gas money to car owners.
- Clear your calendar of engagements that conflict with rehearsals and performances.
- Always remember that appearing in a play involves duty as well as fun.

Chapter 18

The Early Stages

In This Chapter

- The importance of initial read-throughs
- Stage-blocking terms from A to Z
- The tricks of line memorization
- When and why to ask questions
- Moments of insecurity for everyone

Chances are, you'll find the early stages of rehearsal both exciting and confusing. You'll have new people to meet and establish working relationships with. As you listen to everyone reading through the play together, you might find the potential of the cast to put on a great show exhilarating. But you might also become a little overwhelmed when you realize how much work you have to do. The task of memorizing your lines will mean a lot of homework, and so will learning the blocking. And at moments you'll wonder if you'll really be able to remember everything, let alone bring your character to life.

In this chapter, we'll tell you how to get the most out of the group read-through of the play on the first day of rehearsals. We'll explain the technicalities of stage blocking, and give you tips on how to memorize lines. We'll clue you in on the best times and ways to ask the director and stage manager the many questions you're likely to have during the early stages of rehearsal. Finally, we'll reassure you as you face the doubts you're bound to feel when things go wrong, which they undoubtedly will!

The Reason for Read-Throughs

On the first day of rehearsal, it is traditional for the entire cast to gather and read through the play from start to finish. Everyone sits in chairs, sometimes at a table but more often in a semi-circle that enables everyone to have a clear view of each other. You'll all introduce yourselves, and the director will usually have a few words to say about his or her concept of the play. If the production is a musical, the music director will play a piano to accompany the songs, and the choreographer may attend also, as a spectator at this point. You'll get a few minutes of break between the acts of the play, and perhaps a couple of other breaks if the play is a long one.

Performance Notes

Don't worry if you can't remember everyone's name at first. If the cast is a large one, it is going to be almost impossible to commit everyone's name to memory on the first go-around. It's easier if you concentrate on first names, and wise to make a special effort to get the name of someone with whom you'll have a lot of scenes. But nobody's going to take offense if you have to ask his or her name again later.

Read-throughs are fairly relaxed situations. Actors will stumble over the occasional line or mispronounce a word. Perhaps one or two people in the cast will have played their roles before, and they will obviously be more assured at this early point. But even they won't be giving a "performance." This is a get-acquainted occasion, both in terms of the cast members and the play itself.

A Sense of the Whole

When you read a play for the first time on your own, aim to follow the plot and develop a good sense of what the characters are like, as well as to discover the play's themes and glean what the play "means" in a larger sense. Any good play—even a light comedy—offers some kind of message, and some plays are so dense with meaning that they continue to reveal themselves with repeated readings over the years. *You Can't Take It with You*, by George Kaufman and Moss Hart, is a knockabout comedy full of eccentric characters and explosions in a cellar, but it also has a strong message about the importance of individuality and respect for other people, even peculiar ones.

But no matter how much you think you understand about a play when you read it silently by yourself, you're bound to notice all kinds of new perspectives when you hear the words spoken aloud by a group of actors in a read-through. Plays are meant to be heard, and even a rough first read-through will give you a much greater sense of the play as a whole.

Identifying Problem Scenes

Directors hold read-throughs not only to benefit the actors but also to give themselves a chance to judge how the cast will work together. Which actors already seem to have a strong grip on the nature of the characters they are playing? Which ones are a little off base? Who is going to need extra help?

During your part of the read-through, you'll see the director scribbling notes. Don't let that throw you. Although some of the notes may be critical of what you're doing, many may also be positive. You may give an inflection to a line that the director particularly likes, and he or she will make a note of it so that he or she can make sure you keep that reading. Hearing the play read aloud for the first time by this new cast may also give the director fresh ideas about how to stage a certain scene.

It doesn't really matter at this point whether your director writes down positive or negative things—it's all to help you give the best performance possible.

Places, Everyone!

It's fine to laugh at the jokes during a read-through, but try not to laugh when someone mispronounces a word or makes a mistake—you may be the next one to do it. Sometimes an actor will mess something up, realize it, and make a funny face, which is an invitation to laugh. With a musical, an actor may do a stunning version of a famous song, like "The Impossible Dream" or "Everything's Coming Up Roses." If you feel like applauding, go right ahead. But do be sensitive to others' feelings.

Blocking Is Traffic Control

At the first rehearsal following the read-through, the director will start blocking the show. Blocking is the theater term for any stage movement larger than a gesture or a shift of weight from one leg to the other in the same place. An entrance or exit falls under the heading of blocking. If the director instructs you to move two steps to your right, to sit down or to stand up, or to cross the entire stage from one side to the other while going behind the sofa—that is blocking.

But smaller movements you make in place are a different matter. If the director tells you to raise one arm above your head, that is a gesture. If he or she tells you to sit down as you say one line, and then pick up a magazine on the next, the first action is blocking, while the second one is "stage business." In other words, blocking involves a shift in the placement of the entire body, a gesture is a movement of the arms while standing in place, and stage business means that a prop of some kind is being handled.

Blocking is essentially traffic control that moves the actors on and off the stage and around the set. But blocking can have several different purposes:

1. To move the action forward as dictated by the dialogue or stage directions. For example, a character might say, "Look at this letter," to another actor standing several feet away. One of the two has to move across the stage to make the transfer of the letter from hand to hand.
2. To give physical expression to emotions, from anger to joy to puzzlement.
3. To keep the audience interested.

The first purpose listed above demands blocking. If the script or dialogue indicates movement across the stage, there is no question about whether or not to do it. But the discretion of the actor or the idea of the director often governs the second and third purposes, and these may sometimes be in conflict. An actor may want to move around a lot while expressing great anger, but the director might feel it is more in character to stand in one place and yell, or vice versa. The greatest conflicts often arise when a director feels that too little is happening on stage, and fears that the audience will start getting bored. An actor may feel that a piece of blocking in this situation is arbitrary, and therefore want to know what his or her motivation is for such a movement. This kind of conflict can get heated, which we explain further in Chapter 20, "Taking Direction."

Stage Left and Stage Right

As a beginning actor, you may be bewildered when the director asks you to move stage left or stage right. Here's how it works: The director usually sits in a seat in the auditorium, looking at the stage from the audience's point of view. Stage right is to your right, and stage left to your left, as you face *downstage* toward the audience. Thus, the director gives instructions that are counter to his or her own perspective. However, there is a catch for the actor, too. If the actor is facing *upstage,* with his or her back to the audience, stage left is now to the right. It is a fixed direction, like north or south, and doesn't change if you have your back to the audience or are oriented sideways.

Stage Directions

Downstage is the front of the stage, nearest the audience. **Upstage** is the rear of the stage, farthest from the audience. This rule becomes fuzzy if you are acting on a thrust stage, with the audience on three sides, or in-the-round, where the audience surrounds the stage on all four sides and entrances are made down the aisles. In a theater-in-the-round situation, the director will either designate a right and left stage, or use clock terminology, with 12:00 noon being the "EXIT" sign marking the main entrance from the lobby.

When you read a play, it may or may not contain specific stage directions. If the play is being published primarily as literature, it usually will not have any stage directions. But if it is an "acting edition," like those published by Samuel French, the publisher includes the stage directions of the original production. In this case, SL means stage left, and SR means stage right. But directors often ignore these printed stage directions and devise their own instead. In fact, in the 1990s, when a small theater production adhered too closely to the original stage directions, the original director and stage manager filed suit. They claimed that they should have received program credit because it was their work, rather than the work of the local theater director, being presented.

That leaves us with one other term to cover: "Centerstage" is just what the words suggest. However, the set of the specific play determines the exact location of centerstage. If, for instance, there are raised platforms or a stairway at the rear of the stage, centerstage is further downstage than it would be if those sets were not there. Centerstage is the midpoint, from left and right as well as from upstage and downstage, of the main open playing area. Downstage center is equidistant from the left and right sides of the stage but closer to the audience than stage center, with upstage center being the reverse.

Writing It All Down

You must write down all blocking directions the minute you get them from the director or stage manager. Because blocking can—and almost always will—change as rehearsals continue, use a pencil, not a pen, and make sure you have an eraser with you. Keep the pencil in a shirt pocket, behind your ear, or stuck through your hair. You could also invest in a good clip-on pencil that you could attach to the script itself. But you need it with you at all times, not inside a bag offstage. Some young or beginning actors assume that they'll be able to remember blocking without writing it down. It doesn't work. You'll just end up confused.

Places, Everyone!

Everyone needs to make notes about the blocking or other scene directions—even the director. He or she will usually have an assistant or stage manager to do it. If you're confused, that's the person to ask for help. Everyone in the cast is likely to need such assistance occasionally, but if you ask for it too often, you might be scolded. Keeping track of your blocking is part of your job.

When Things Don't Work

One reason why a director changes blocking is that sometimes things just don't work. The director may have a beautiful stage picture in mind when he or she first blocks a scene. But in later rehearsals, it will become clear that getting everyone into place to complete that picture is creating too much moving around, and the scene will need to be simplified. Such changes will also occur when the set is finally in place, a problem we will deal with in Chapter 23, "Tech and 'Techies'."

Often the blocking changes when an actor finds a particular piece of blocking physically awkward, or feels that it is at odds with the lines he or she must speak. The problem can be an obvious one, such as simply a question of having to turn or walk too fast to get into place for the next line. But it can also be an almost subliminal sense that something is wrong. If you are dubious about a piece of blocking, try it two or three times. It may be that you just need to get used to the movement, or that with practice you'll discover that it works fine. But if you continue to be uncomfortable, talk to the director about it. Most directors will change something about which an actor feels uncomfortable, sometimes restaging it completely, or making an adjustment that amounts to a compromise.

Backstage Tales

The third time that co-author Paul Baldwin played Don Quixote in *Man of La Mancha*, the director, who had never staged the show before, had Don Quixote dancing around in a very clownish way during the song "Knight of the Woeful Countenance." The situation has its comic aspects, in that an innkeeper who merely wants to placate Quixote performs the knighting. But Paul quickly pointed out that Don Quixote is utterly convinced that he is indeed being knighted, and that it is the great moment of his life. If Don Quixote seemed to be joking around, then the point of the scene, and the essence of his character, would be spoiled. The director changed the blocking.

Memorizing Your Lines

Some actors memorize lines very easily, and for others it is one of the most difficult aspects of conquering a role. Younger actors generally find it easier to commit words to memory than older ones. Meryl Streep, now in her early 50s, has said that she finds it much harder to memorize now than when she was younger. Helen Hayes eventually gave up stage acting in her mid-70s because she could no longer remember lines well enough, although she continued to do some television work in which TelePrompTers were available. But even some young people find memorizing a problem. Actors who suffer from dyslexia, a learning disability that causes the brain to reverse the order of letters (Cher, among others, has this disability) must put a great deal of time and effort into memorization. But no actor, especially one with a large role, should underestimate the time memorization will take.

The Sooner the Better

We want to stress once again that you should begin the process of memorizing lines as soon as you're given a role, so that by the time of the read-through, you will have made a good start. If you haven't, then you'll have lots more work to do from the beginning of rehearsals on.

It should be obvious that the sooner you learn your lines, the better able you will be to give them full meaning. It is difficult to discover which word needs inflecting and which ideas need vocal underlining while you are still groping for the words themselves. You can't make gestures with real freedom and conviction until the script is out of your hands. What's more, when you memorize your lines, you must also learn the "cue" lines of other characters—the words they speak just before a line of your own. If you haven't got those down, disruptive pauses may occur when you fail to recognize that yours is the next line.

Places, Everyone!

Learn your lines, for your sake as well as for your fellow cast members. If you don't know your lines, you may give a garbled version of a cue line, confusing the actor whose line immediately follows. Or, you may leave out a crucial sentence in a speech—the very one another actor is supposed to reply to. Such problems slow the progress of other actors and thus will not make you popular.

In some amateur productions, particularly in grade school and high school, you'll have particular trouble learning lines because you won't have the entire script in front of you. Instead, in an effort to save money, the director will provide each actor with "sides." These xeroxed pages contain only your lines and the cue lines of the other characters in the scene that feed directly into your lines.

Although sides cut down on expenses (scripts can be expensive to buy or rent), they also cause problems. For example, another character may have a speech that goes on for half a page, but the side you've been given will often contain only the last line of that speech, the one that is the cue for your own line. In that situation, it can take a while before you get used to the fact that someone else is going to talk for two minutes between one line of yours and the next.

Tricks of the Trade

Performance Notes

If you find yourself given only sides, try to get hold of a full script of the play. Check the library. Xerox another actor's copy. Even if you have to pay for the copying, it's money well spent.

Actors approach memorization of lines in individual ways because there's simply no single best way to go about it. One actor may find it easier to learn lines written in verse—in Shakespeare, or a Molière translation—because the rhymes and rhythms of poetry act as a guide. But poetry can throw another actor who has little trouble with a modern script written in conversational prose. Such differences in mental focus also mean that a memorization technique used by one actor with great success will not work at all for another. But let's look at a few methods that could be worth trying.

Some actors learn their lines silently, reading them again and again, and then looking up from the page and running through them in their minds. But a greater number speak them aloud. (More than one wit has observed that when you see someone muttering to him or herself on the street in New York City, it is hard to tell if the person is crazy or just an actor—assuming, the wit will add, that there is any difference.) Still others take a middle course, finding it unnecessary to speak the words aloud, but moving their lips silently. These actors swear that "training" the lips to form the words is a great aid to memorization.

One widely used trick of the trade is to record the lines of the other characters in a scene, leaving a blank where your own lines will occur. You then play the tape, saying your lines when appropriate. It might be hard to work out how much quiet time to leave on the tape between lines, but some say that solving this technical problem is, in itself, an aid to memorization. Of course, if you can get the actor who shares a scene with you to record his or her lines while you do the same for him or her, it can make matters much easier.

Someone to Help

A great many actors call upon friends and family members to help them learn lines. For school-age actors, Mom and Dad or an older sibling are often willing to assist. Boyfriends, girlfriends, and eventually spouses will get called upon for line-reading duty. The family member or friend will read the lines of other characters—often just the cue lines—and correct the actor when a mistake is made. There's a fair amount of repetitive drudgery for the volunteers in these situations, but they often find it fun up to a point, since it gives them a vicarious taste of the theater world.

Backstage Tales

In 1997, co-author Paul Baldwin made a trip to New York to help out Carole Monferdini, who'd been hired to stand by for Mary Louise Wilson in the Off-Broadway hit *Full Gallop*. This was a one-woman show based on the life of the famous editor of *Vogue*, Diana Vreeland, and it required memorizing an entire full-length script. It was imperative for Carole to get it down quickly, since her contract called for her to take over the role once a month. (She subsequently starred in a touring production.) Carole and Paul have been pals since the second grade, and he was glad to help out, even though he was simply correcting any mistakes she made for what he describes with a laugh as "three days chained to a chair."

Legitimate Questions

During the early stages of rehearsal, you'll be learning so much, so quickly—about lines and blocking and the director's vision of the play—that you'll have little time for anything else. That's about all an actor can deal with. But when you're rehearsing scenes for the second or third time, you're bound to have some questions for your director or other colleague. Before you ask, you need to consider both if your question is legitimate and who is the best person to answer it.

When to Ask

In most cases, ask your questions before rehearsal begins or just after it concludes. The director, assistant director, stage manager (and later the technical people working on sets, lighting, and costumes) are usually available for a few minutes for just this purpose at those times. Some days, many people may have questions, in which case not all of them will get answered. If you have a real problem that needs answering before working on a scene scheduled for that rehearsal, then say so, but minor questions, or ones dealing with scenes that won't be dealt with that day or evening, can usually wait.

Asking a question in the middle of rehearsing a scene is sometimes necessary, but the question should be a serious one to justify bringing everything to a halt. If something really isn't working for you, whether it's a piece of blocking or a line reading, and you simply haven't had an opportunity to bring it up at the start of rehearsals, then go ahead and ask.

And it is always legitimate to ask a question if the director has given you a new line reading or a change in blocking and you don't entirely understand it. But don't waste time on the trivial or ask for unnecessary reassurance. For example, don't stop a scene to ask what kind of sandwich it will be that you're pretending to eat at this point; that's trivial. Nor should you ask if the director can hear you—if he or she can't hear you, you'll know!

Performance Notes

Be careful about asking questions in the middle of a scene that involve something another actor is doing wrong. The surest way to make an enemy is to turn to the director and say something like, "Is she always going to take so long to hand me the book?" Let the director worry about the other actors. If something another actor is doing is driving you crazy, bring it up privately later.

Who to Ask

You can save everyone time by asking questions of the right people. If you don't like the way you've been told to read a line, or are having trouble executing a piece of blocking, there's only one person you can ask—the director—because in the end, only the director can approve any changes of that sort. But if you've forgotten on which line you cross the stage, ask the stage manager or assistant director, whoever is keeping the master script. (Of course, you should have written down that in your own script in the first place.)

As rehearsals continue, you can ask a question of the set designer about the set, or the costume designer or head of wardrobe about a costume. Don't bother the director with it unless the person chiefly responsible for that aspect of the production fails to give you a satisfactory answer. If there's a traffic problem backstage that makes it difficult for you to make an entrance in time, bring it up with the stage manager. The stage manager is in charge of everything that happens backstage, and can often deal with a costume or set problem, as well, if the designer isn't around.

Don't Be Selfish

You will have quite a number of questions to ask in the course of rehearsals. But keep in mind that everyone else in the cast is going to have questions, too. Some actors, both beginners and old timers, always seem to have more questions than others do, and they may be legitimate. A young actor may indeed need more help, and some people are simply less secure than others are. But some actors also ask a lot of questions in order to attract attention. Don't be selfish that way. People will say awful things about you behind your back if you are.

"I'll Never Get This Right"

Insecurity is the actor's curse. Every actor goes through moments of despair, certain that he or she looks like a fool. It's perfectly reasonable to feel that way. Anyone who performs in public is going to be judged. The fact that you're an actor at all means that you have stronger nerves than most people do, and you have a perfect right to get queasy once in a while.

Inevitable Doubts

The natural insecurity of actors leads to inevitable doubts. Only the very worst actors are sublimely sure of themselves, because they are too stupid to know better. So, being a good actor, you're going to find yourself saying, at least silently, "This part is too much for me," or "How did I ever get into this?" or "I really sucked in that scene." Go right ahead and wail—it's good for you. Doubts are human, and they keep actors from getting too insufferably arrogant, and, most important of all, they mean you're in the process of learning something new, extending yourself, taking a risk in order to grow as an actor and as a person. Doubts are great teachers. Don't be afraid of them.

Backstage Tales

One sign of the exposed nature of the actor's life is a particular kind of nightmare known as "an actor's dream." In an actor's dream, you'll be onstage in the wrong costume for an entirely different play, or you'll start spouting lines from *King Lear* even though it's *Twelfth Night* you're supposed to be appearing in. Or, you'll be standing center stage with the entire cast staring at you, but have no idea why. You may also be standing stark naked at center stage in the midst of a memory lapse. Actor's dreams are ghastly and inescapable. Get used to them.

Solutions "Happen"

When you have doubts, work harder. Ask the director for help if you need it. Keep rehearsing. Keep practicing on your own. One day you'll still be thinking, "This is all wrong; this just isn't working." And, suddenly, the next day, it will work for the first time. You'll be able to feel it. You'll know it's right. That is one of the most exhilarating things that an actor can experience. It just seems to "happen." But, of course, it has happened because of all that work you've put in—and also because your subconscious mind was working on it even when you weren't aware of it. Breakthroughs, in all kinds of endeavors, sometimes seem like magic. "Eureka!" we shout, like Archimedes in his bath. "I've got it."

The greatest single stage performance co-author John Malone ever saw was in 1956, when he was 17, at a Saturday matinee in Boston. It was a pre-Broadway tryout of Jean Anouilh's *The Lark*, starring Julie Harris as Joan of Arc. She was luminous and magical to the point of incandescence. Two weeks later, after the play had opened to raves in New York, there was an interview with Harris in *The New York Times*. She said she had been having great difficulty with the role of Joan, but that it had suddenly all come together at that Saturday matinee in Boston. John had been very lucky, having gotten to see the breakthrough take place. When such a breakthrough occurs, the results can be extraordinary even for an amateur actor.

The early stages of rehearsal can be very tiring, and sometimes it will seem as though you're not getting anywhere. But keep in mind that those rehearsals are laying the groundwork for an eventual Eureka! moment.

The Least You Need to Know

- Read-throughs give the cast a sense of the whole play.
- You must write down all blocking instructions immediately, but in pencil.
- The more quickly you learn your lines, the better.
- Try to get questions answered at the start or end of a rehearsal, rather than stopping the flow during a scene.
- Remember that doubts are normal, and that you can have breakthroughs unexpectedly.

Chapter 19

Cast Dynamics

In This Chapter

- Exploring the world of personal relationships in the theater
- Understanding the importance of getting along with everyone
- Discovering how to deal with problem actors
- Learning the rules of backstage gossip

Personal relationships in the theater are often more important than those in other situations, such as work or school, and the rules are a bit different as well. Putting on a play is an intense experience. A successful show depends upon the input and collaboration of a lot of different people, both onstage and behind the scenes. A degree of "team spirit" is required that's more akin to what happens on sports teams than to most other group efforts. You need to be able to work with the other people involved while a show is being rehearsed and performed, regardless of how much you like them as individuals.

In this chapter, we'll explore the nature of cast relationships, both on and offstage. We'll give you tips on how to forge working relationships with people even if there's little personal sympathy between you. You'll learn how to deal with actors who are weak links, as well as with those who think the whole show is about them. And we'll spill some secrets about backstage gossip.

Who's My Friend?

In a grade school production, you're likely to know most of other kids in a show, but at a big high school you may well be meeting new people who are a grade or two ahead of or behind you. You may also discover that some fellow students you know very little about, and weren't much interested in, have a lot to offer. On a major college or university campus, you can do eight or nine shows during your undergraduate years and meet at least a few new actors every time. The pool of talent for a community theater is likely to be somewhat smaller, and over the years you will work again and again with many of the same people. That situation makes good relationships with fellow actors particularly important.

Buddies and Soul Mates

You can make a friend for life when you appear in a play or musical, discovering a soul mate whose life will become a part of yours forever, whether or not you ever appear together in a show again. But that's unusual. Nobody has room in his or her life for more than a few "best friends." You're very likely, however, to make a lot of buddies, more casual friends whom you'll always be happy to see when you run into them. As with friendships in general, the most lasting ones formed in the theater are usually between people who aren't in direct competition with one another. Thus, you're probably not going to become best friends with your main rival for the role of Romeo or Juliet, but rather with an actor who plays a different type of role. That's just human nature.

Strong friendships do sometimes develop between actors of the same type who are of different generations. For instance, a woman who played Juliet 15 years earlier and a young woman playing the role for the first time often find themselves with a lot in common. This kind of "mentoring" relationship, in which the older performer takes a younger one under his or her wing, can be deeply satisfying, and such friendships are common among professionals. Similar friendships can also arise between individuals of the opposite sex who are of different generations.

Places, Everyone!

To give a good performance, you must react to the character in the play rather than to the actor playing the role. That helps a great deal when it comes to playing scenes with someone you don't much like. Concentrate on the person the other actor is supposed to be in the play rather than on the person he or she is in real life. That's what you're supposed to be doing anyway.

One Big Happy Family?

Since the members of a cast must pull together to create a successful show, it would be nice to think that, in most cases, they manage to form an entirely cohesive unit, at least for the duration of the show. Sometimes that does happen. Everyone basically gets along well, and there are very few tensions between members of the company. But this situation is rare enough that when it does happen, the actors involved will remember it for a long time, and talk about it in later years. "That production of *Company* I did in North Carolina in the 70s," an actor will say, "was the most pleasant experience of my life."

More often, surface camaraderie disguises personality conflicts underneath. Two talented individuals, both of whom are seen by others as nice people, may not much like one another. In fact, they may cordially detest one another. But the key word here is "cordially." If there is someone you can't stand in a cast, the best way to deal with it is to be as polite as possible and keep your distance offstage.

Romantic scenes between two actors who dislike one another can be a severe test of acting ability, but good actors can persuade the audience that they're mad *for* each other even when they're mostly mad *at* each other. Vivien Leigh and Clark Gable managed it in *Gone With the Wind*, for example, even though Gable thought Leigh was extremely haughty and she regularly complained about his bad breath. It may have helped that the characters they were playing were involved in a love/hate relationship, but acting is, after all, about the creation of an illusion.

A company of actors is comparable to a family, but we all know families who have to grit their teeth in order to get through the Thanksgiving family reunion. The circumstances require a special effort, and the fact that the production of a play can mean an extended period of teeth-gritting doesn't make it any easier. But if the bad feelings spill over the footlights, the audience is going to be uncomfortable.

Backstage Tales

In the 1960s, there was a major Broadway production of Eugene O'Neill's *A Touch of the Poet*, starring Kim Stanley, Helen Hayes, and the renowned British actor Eric Portman. None of them liked one another, and stories got into the press about the feud between Stanley and Hayes, who came from utterly different schools of acting—Hayes being a traditionalist and Stanley a product of the Actor's Studio. Co-author John Malone saw the production during its Boston tryout, and the onstage tensions were so great that the audience was talking about them at intermission. The play got guarded reviews in New York and was not the hit expected with such a stellar cast.

Because an actor's livelihood is not on the line in amateur productions, as it so often is in professional theater, personal tensions are less likely to attain a fever pitch. Many producers who run community theaters will admit, however, that they make it a point to avoid casting certain feuding actors in the same production if it's at all possible.

"He's Just Awful"

Amateur productions are somewhat more likely than professional ones to be faced with the problem of an actor who's actively bad in his or her part. That usually occurs in a show with a large cast, when the number of roles to be filled exceeds the number of good actors available. Anyone who attends a lot of college or community theater productions has had occasion to ask in disbelief, "Where did they dredge him up?" While it may be true that there are no small roles, only small actors, a really bad actor can make a small role loom much larger than it ordinarily would. But as the audience sits slack-jawed at the sight of such ineptitude, you as a cast member may wish you were anywhere but playing a scene with the poor dolt.

Places, Everyone!

Seasoned actors know that there's only one way to play a scene with someone who's truly dreadful: Pretend that the actor in question is delivering his or her lines correctly. This is not always easy to do, but you're an actor, after all. You manage to act as though the stage gun is really loaded, so you ought to be able to convince yourself that a lousy actor is doing a good job.

The dreadful actor in the company creates problems both onstage and off. Not only do you have to struggle through your scenes with the person, you must also manage to keep a civil tongue in your head when talking with him or her offstage. You are not going to make things any better by telling the offending performer that he or she is ruining the play. Indeed, bad actors seldom seem to realize quite how awful they are. By their own lights, they often think they're doing a splendid job. They know they may not be ready to play Hamlet quite yet, but you can bet they'd give it a try if asked.

Things are made somewhat easier by the fact that bad actors are often quite sweet people. It takes a certain purity of spirit to appear on stage and make a complete fool of oneself. One very experienced community theater star we know says that she deals with truly bad actors by thinking of a favorite dog from her childhood, one that was never quite housebroken. "I think of dear Sparky, who stained the carpet occasionally for 13 years, and I get quite sentimental. It helps me overlook any number of human failings."

Worry About Yourself

Quite aside from just being a nice person, there are practical reasons not to let yourself get overly perturbed by another actor's bad performance. To begin with, you have your own part to worry about, and no one is perfect. Even the very greatest performances have their flaws. Any energy you expend on lamenting the quality of someone else's performance could certainly be put to better use improving your own, enabling you to get rid of as many weak moments as possible.

What's more, the bad actor is probably there on stage with you because the alternatives to him or her were even worse actors. Sometimes, of course, the director has simply made a terrible mistake, but it's not one that you can fix. The director no doubt recognizes the mistake, or laments the fact that there wasn't someone better to put in that role, and will do his or her best to compensate. That may mean giving the bad actor extra time, or using various directorial tricks to obscure the more stubborn deficiencies. Giving a faltering actor a prop to work with—a handkerchief to flutter, or a cigar to chomp on—can sometimes work wonders. In other circumstances, of course, getting any and all props out of the 10-thumbed hands of an actor can improve matters. But that's for the director to stay awake nights thinking about. Your job is to lie awake thinking about your own problems.

Performance Notes

It's easy to become so conscious of the weaknesses of another actor in a scene that you begin to lose sight of what you need to do to hold up your end of it. In some cases, playing opposite a bad actor can inspire the kind of scene-stealing that would ordinarily be inappropriate, but which is now justified as a matter of survival. But be careful not to get too out of hand, or instead of the bad actor getting all the notes, the director will be telling you to get a grip.

Helping the Weak Kitten

Although it's important not to expend too much energy worrying about what another actor is doing, especially if your concerns take a negative form, in other situations you can also do everyone some good by lending a hand. That doesn't mean taking over the director's job and bossing another actor around. There's a fine line here. But it is possible to bolster a weak actor's confidence, or to point someone in the right direction, by praising anything the actor does get right. Sometimes the inexperienced actor, or the plain bad actor, doesn't even know it when he or she finally does something effective.

If, for example, an actor who's particularly stiff loosens up enough to make a natural gesture during rehearsal—unconsciously straightening the books on a table, say—tell the actor you liked that moment. Praise usually works much better than criticism. If an actor has been delivering a line very flatly, and inflects it slightly during one rehearsal, say, "I like the way you read that line about the sunset today." You may have to repeat the reading yourself to get the point across, but such small compliments can have a real effect. Noting progress can lead to more improvement.

Although professional actors love to tell funny tales about inept people they've worked with, they can also get almost misty-eyed relating stories about fellow actors who were having great problems and then finally began to get the hang of a role. The theater is about transformations, and it can be very moving to watch someone who didn't seem to have a clue blossom into adequacy.

Backstage Tales

When co-author John Malone was attending Andover, he had a classmate who tried out every year for the Shakespeare play. He was a good-looking guy with a deep voice, but he had grown to over six feet very quickly, and he alternated between gangly and stiff. He did a decent job as the rustic, playing Wall in *A Midsummer Night's Dream*, but otherwise had only small roles as messengers. Lo and behold, he later matured into a fine actor with numerous important stage credits and starring roles in television movies and series. Frank Converse proved that you should never judge a teenage actor by his or her first attempts.

Star Trips

In professional theater, if you get to be a big-enough star, your name goes above the title in order to sell enough tickets to guarantee a strong advance sale for a play. Even back in the days of silent pictures, movie moguls knew that "stars put fannies in the seats." That certainty goes back at least to the days of Shakespeare, when the playwright inserted comic characters even into his tragedies in order to make use of the audience-pleasing talents of Will Kempe at the Globe Theatre.

Amateur theater productions seldom put anyone's name above the title, but that doesn't mean that there are no stars, or that stars don't get special treatment in that venue. Stars get more attention from the director, more expensive costumes, perhaps a dressing room that they share with only one or two other actors instead of a dozen (depending on backstage space), and, of course, they get to take the final bows.

Often, stars deserve all of this attention. Stars have to work harder than anyone else, and they (usually) have the talent to back up the attention and accolades they get. A lot of actors who almost always play lead roles are terrific people. Both authors have met a number of professional stars who were household names but still managed to be kind, generous, and fun. And the same can be said of many leading actors in amateur productions. But starring roles do go to some actors' heads, and they can behave badly as a result.

The Prima Donna Lead

There are prima donnas of both sexes. The term is borrowed from the world of opera, where it denotes a star soprano with a very great voice. Originally intended as a term of respect, it has increasingly come to suggest an outsized temperament to go with the voice. And since there is no comparable term for male singers, it gets derisively applied to the tempestuous tenor as well. In the theater, prima donna behavior can infect some leading ladies and leading men. They treat everyone else as though they were hired help, and throw tantrums whenever things don't go as planned (or just their own way). Depending upon their mood, they can be aloof or just plain snotty. Prima donnas will openly criticize your acting during rehearsals, and in performance they will do their best to make the audience look at them, instead of you, during your big speech. They are, in short, monsters.

Performance Notes

If you're frequently cast in lead roles, just being polite engenders respect and affection from your fellow actors. Always say hello to everyone, never scream at anyone (even the director), and make the occasional joke at your own expense. Such politeness and modesty are so at odds with the stereotypical star image that you will be widely admired. Such behavior will also help get you many more starring roles.

If you have the misfortune to work with a prima donna, how should you handle the situation? First, there is no point in arguing with monsters. They are not open to reason and can almost certainly yell louder or get far nastier than you can—they've had years of practice. Under no circumstances should you try to charm them or cuddle up to them. They will simply use you by pitting you against the rest of the cast to protect themselves, and then throw you away when you are no longer useful. Treat them like that terrifying fourth-grade teacher you once had: with the great respect born of abject fear. If they think you're afraid of them—even if you aren't—they may actually start referring to you as that "nice boy" or "sweet girl."

Monsters, as you may already know, are usually quite frightened themselves.

Small Part, Big Ego

Fortunately, monsters are almost as rare in amateur theater as they are common in professional theater. But you can be sure of encountering a different kind of scourge in amateur theater: the actor with a small role who is convinced that the entire play is really about his character or her performance. These creatures are tiresome but no threat. It's best to just let them rattle on about their own self-importance. They're talking for their own benefit, on the whole, and don't really expect confirmation. If they get too annoying, or you are trying to do something else like work on your lines, say, "Oh, get over yourself, Susan," or, "Get a grip, Bobby." They will say, "Why are you so mean?" and go bother someone else. And don't worry about offending them. They'll soon be back to prattle about themselves some more.

Backstage Gossip

Back in 700 B.C.E., the Greek farmer/poet Hesiod wrote, "Gossip is mischievous, light and easy to raise, but grievous to bear, and hard to get rid of." Nothing has changed during the ensuing millennia, and among human endeavors, only politics has proven as fertile a ground for gossip as show business. If show business gossip were banned, dozens of magazines would be put out of business and the television schedule would have huge holes in it. The lives of the actors in a college or community theater production may seem very quiet compared with those of movie stars, but that doesn't slow the flow of gossip for a moment.

The theater term for gossip is "dish." Once upon a time, half a century ago, a beautiful young person of either sex was often referred to as a dish, and the word gradually evolved to describe gossip about romantic activities in general among the show business set. Almost every cast has at least one "town crier," whose main job (aside from playing a role) is to march breathlessly into a room and announce, "Have I got some dish for you."

Places, Everyone!

Gossip is inevitable because it appears that most actors are born with a "flirting gene." The job of actors is to seduce audiences into identifying with the characters they play. That's often true even when you're playing a villain; Shakespeare's Richard III is nothing if not a seducer. Any character, whether male or female, that the audience "loves to hate" is always a good one. If you don't have a seductive bone in your body, you don't belong onstage.

Fun Gossip vs. Mean Gossip

Dish about other actors is, of course, fascinating and great fun—"easy to raise," as Hesiod put it. Dish about yourself, however, is hard to bear. But those of you who are just starting out will get used to it, trust us. You have no choice. Fueled by a strange combination of affection and envy, dish keeps everyone updated on the slightest sign of mutual attraction between cast members. Dish can be flattering in the sense that everyone is so interested in every secret smile you exchange with another actor, mischievous in that it often exaggerates the situation, and quite mean when it suggests that someone is cheating on someone else.

A lot of theater gossip is harmless enough, more an occasion for giggles than gasps. But when it does induce gasps, you're getting into treacherous territory. Meanness is one step away. Repeating giggle gossip isn't going to hurt anyone, but repeating gasp gossip is an exercise in putting someone else down. You know the difference—we all do. There's an all-purpose answer to mean gossip that helps to slow down the person repeating it: "Oh, who cares?" Scolding the person spreading mean gossip just encourages him or her, because they've gotten your attention. A dismissive "who cares" tends to put a damper on things.

If you're being gossiped about, you have two choices: Ignore it totally or make a joke of it yourself. The second approach works best because it says you can take it with a smile. But ignoring it is better than confronting it, because if you get angry, then they'll be gossiping about that, and will take it as confirmation of the original slander.

When to Keep Your Mouth Shut

Because rehearsing and performing a play is so collaborative, it creates a special kind of intimacy among the cast members. You get to know new people more quickly than in most group endeavors because the creative processes involved demand emotional exposure of a kind you're unlikely to encounter in most classroom or office situations. That intimacy means that if another cast member finds you a sympathetic person, he or she is likely to confide in you more easily than might otherwise be the case. But the fact that someone has confided in you also means that they trust you not to spread around what they've said.

The ingenue who tells you she's got a crush on the leading man (or vice versa) doesn't want you to rush off and say, "Boy, have I got some dish for you." Indeed, if you turn a confidence into gossip, you're not going to be very popular. If you spot the ingenue and the leading man kissing in the hallway, you might be wise to keep that to yourself, too, but at least it's not a confidence with which you've been entrusted.

Backstage Tales

It's important to understand the difference between gossip and a really good story. Co-author Paul Baldwin has fond memories of a pretty and talented young woman making her professional debut in a musical he starred in. She became romantically involved with an actor in the cast. Although everybody knew it, no one spoke much about it because she seemed to want to keep it to herself. But then she lost the gold locket she wore around her neck. She was very distraught, and everyone helped her look for it, but it couldn't be found. The following day it turned up—in the middle of her long, very curly, very red hair. Now that story made the rounds of the cast in about 10 minutes, and is still talked about a quarter-century later. Theater romances are a dime a dozen, but lockets lost in your own hair are not.

Theater gossip can be great fun or quite cruel. Couples get involved with one another and break up, sometimes quite badly, and it's greatly tempting to discuss the situation in ways that only make it worse. But there's a safer outlet for the gossip instinct—gossip about other shows, with names left out and details exaggerated. But this is gossip that has been transmuted over time into a "theater story." Such stories keep everyone entertained, and can help satisfy the theater world's unquenchable appetite for "dish."

The Least You Need to Know

- Try to get along with everyone in the cast of any show, but recognize that such a goal may take some work.
- Worry about developing your own role instead of wasting energy complaining about the deficiencies of others.
- Learn how to take both the tantrums of prima donnas and the boasting of secondary actors in stride.
- Remember that it's all too easy for theater gossip to cross the line into meanness.

Chapter 20

Taking Direction

In This Chapter

- Recognizing that you're one among many
- Finding out when it's okay to object to direction
- Learning the importance of taking complete notes
- Discovering how to deal with good and bad directors

Part of being a good actor is taking direction well. Some famous actors have a reputation for being "difficult," which means that they argue with the director all the time. You can only get away with that if you're very good and very experienced, and even then it can damage your reputation. If you're unwilling to even try something the director asks you to do, you'd better have a very good reason for causing trouble. The director is in charge, and when you resist direction, you are not only undermining his or her authority, but also taking valuable time away from other cast members who also need the director's attention. That doesn't mean you can't ever object to a line reading or a movement that makes you uncomfortable, but you'd better know how to explain what your problem is and when to discuss it.

In this chapter, we'll be looking at two different aspects of the actor/director relationship. We emphasize the importance of understanding that you're part of a group, even if you're playing a title role. To do your job properly, you need to do your best to follow the director's lead. That means taking precise notes when the director gives you instructions, and we'll give you some tips on how to make sure you've got everything straight. But actors and directors can also disagree sometimes, and we'll explain what to do when you feel a director is off base.

You're Part of a Larger Picture

Whether you're performing a play with a relatively small cast like *The Odd Couple,* or a big musical like *On the Twentieth Century,* you're always part of a larger picture, and the director must always keep that larger picture in mind. While you may feel as though you aren't getting as much attention as you deserve or need at times, the director will have a better sense of who needs help the most.

Sometimes the biggest roles cause a director less concern than a couple of much smaller ones. The man playing Ravenal in *Show Boat,* or the woman starring as Mame, may have played their roles before, or be so talented and experienced that they require little direction beyond the initial blocking. At other times, an actor is such a natural for a role that even though he or she doesn't have a great deal of experience, the director still doesn't have to worry much about them. At the same time, an actor with a very small but crucial role may need more attention, even if he or she has very few lines to deliver.

Backstage Tales

Co-author Paul Baldwin had already played Charlie Anderson in *Shenandoah* five times when he was hired over the phone for a new summer theater production. The musical is Charlie's show, and Paul quickly understood why the director had wanted someone who knew the role inside out. The rest of the cast had been at the theater all summer, playing a variety of roles in musicals with modern settings. They were far from ideally cast in a period show like *Shenandoah,* and the young women playing Charlie's daughter and daughter-in-law had special problems: Their singing voices were right for the roles, but in physical appearance and temperament, each should have been playing the other part. Paul got almost no direction at all as a result.

The Squeaky Wheel

An old saying applies to what happens during rehearsals for a show: "It's the squeaky wheel that gets the grease." What this saying implies is that while other wheels may need lubrication, too, it's the one making actual noises of distress that gets attended to first. The director begins to get a clear idea during the first read-through which actors will require his primary focus, although potential problems may have suggested themselves even during auditions. This isn't a matter of the actors asking for special help. Some may not even grasp how much work they're going to have to do. But any experienced director can spot an actor in trouble very quickly.

Up to a point, you should take as a compliment the fact that a director isn't giving you many notes. Some directors will tell an actor he or she is doing a great job, but the majority of them do not. One director may be wary of inflating an actor's ego by being too effusive, another simply forgetful, and still another may think an actor knows perfectly well that things are going well, making comments unnecessary. Whatever the reason, if you're not being guided or corrected much, generally take that as good news. You're doing fine; just keep it up.

Places, Everyone!

When it comes to a director's attention, the watchword is "silence is golden." If the director tells you very little, you're probably doing just fine. Don't go fishing for compliments, but if you need direction on a line or a scene, feel free to ask for it.

"Hey, I'm Here, Too"

At times, however, it's necessary to let out a squawk and be a deliberately squeaky wheel. Say you're playing Bill Sykes, the villain in the musical *Oliver!* The director has a lot to worry about because the actor playing Fagin has a tendency to overact, and Nancy sings beautifully, but she's an inexperienced actress. And while the kid playing Oliver is amazing, some of the other kids need a lot of work. The director has a full plate, and he keeps skipping over Bill Sykes's big song, "My Name," largely because the music director says you sing it well. But you're not used to playing villains, and although you're fairly tall, you're not a beefy type. Is anyone going to believe you in this tough-guy role?

It's the last week of rehearsal, and you've never had the chance to perform the song with the full company on stage reacting to you. It's time to squawk. Go to the director and say you're really worried about how you're going to come across in this song, which is crucial to the balance of the show. If Bill Sykes isn't convincingly threatening, the whole end of the show can fall apart. In a situation like this, it's fine to say, in effect, "Hey, I'm here, too."

Working It Out for Yourself

At other times, however, you should try to solve your problems on your own. Are you having trouble with the rhythm of a long speech? Think about what may be wrong. Are you perhaps getting too emotional too quickly? Or does the middle part of the speech seem to sag? If you can identify the problem to that extent, you're halfway to solving it. Often you'll be able to discover your own answer to the problem. And that, in the long run, is more helpful than having the director hand an answer to you. What you discover for yourself usually carries greater conviction.

Performance Notes

Directors do not have immediate answers to every little question. If they're very familiar with a play, or perhaps played a role themselves at some point, they may be able to give an instant line reading. But in many cases, all they will be able to do is suggest things to try. And those suggestions may not be as right for you as something you eventually come up with on your own.

Places, Everyone!

If you think you've come up with a solution to a problem on your own, perform it in rehearsal without telling the director first unless it involves a change in blocking. If you ask permission to do it, some directors will say, "Well, let me think about it." If you just go ahead and do it, and it works, the director will probably accept it immediately.

The legendary Tallulah Bankhead, who originated the roles of Sabina in Thornton Wilder's *Skin of Your Teeth* and Regina in Lillian Hellman's *The Little Foxes*, once put out a recording of sketch material. One of them consisted of instructions on the many ways to read a line. In her much-imitated husky drawl, Tallulah gave four readings of the single line, "What are you doing?" Each reading emphasized a single word, as in "WHAT are you doing?" and "What ARE you doing." It was very funny, as she meant it to be, but it also makes a good exercise for actors who are having trouble with a line. Go through the line, trying one emphasis after another. It can be great fun, plus you will learn a lot—and it may solve your problem without bothering the director.

When to Argue

Sometimes the director will have you deliver a line or move across the stage in way that doesn't feel right to you. You may feel uncomfortable with a line reading or with the emotional pitch of a speech, sensing that it's out of character. Or you may find some piece of blocking very difficult to bring off, or even dangerous.

It's time to make your objections known. It's true that directors love actors who seldom complain or argue, but that doesn't mean you should be a doormat when you're convinced that something doesn't work. In fact, if you're generally a very cooperative actor, you'll have a greater impact when you do speak up. You'll get a more serious hearing from the director than the constant complainers ever will.

"It Doesn't Feel Right"

Actors use the phrase "it doesn't feel right" so often that it's sometimes the subject of satire. Since the phrase can come across as an all-purpose whine, try to be more specific. But sometimes you truly will not know what's wrong, only that something is off kilter. Then "it doesn't feel right," vague as it is, comes as close as you get to properly expressing the problem.

Often this phrase is directly connected to another rehearsal cliché: "What's my motivation?" You may find that a way of saying a line, or the blocking or stage business that accompanies the line, may seem out of character. You simply don't believe that the person you're trying to bring to life on stage would speak or act in quite that way. Asking the director to explain your motivation is a shorthand way of indicating the nature of the problem.

Performance Notes

Directors who are sympathetic to method acting, as it is taught at such institutions as the Actor's Studio, will welcome motivational questions. But there are those who are impatient with this approach, and such directors have been known to reply, "Your motivation is that I told you to do it. Now get on with it." If you run into such a director, try using more down-home language, perhaps saying, "I don't think my character would do this."

If something doesn't make sense to you in terms of the character you are playing, it may mean that you and the director have a different concept of the role. The greater the role, the more interpretations it is subject to. With Hamlet, for example, the question of whether he is going mad or just feigning madness has been debated for centuries, and that's just one aspect of this complex character that allows for different approaches. Even the minor characters of Rosencrantz and Guildenstern, Hamlet's friends from university, can be played as silly, as conniving, or as bewildered.

Usually the director has cast a play in accordance with his or her concepts of the characters—he or she assigns actors certain roles because their auditions had the quality the director was looking for. But unexpected disagreements can and do crop up, and if that happens to you, you'll have to hash them out with the director.

"It's Too Dangerous"

While there are times to speak up and times to try to work out problems on your own, you (and every actor) have the right (even the duty) to question any blocking that he or she feels is physically dangerous. Whether the action involves a sword fight, throwing a plate at someone on stage, tumbling down a flight of stairs, or merely tripping over a rug, if it isn't working right and it seems possible that you or another actor could get hurt, bring it up immediately.

A surprising number of actors have been directed to fall down flights of stairs on stage. Laurence Olivier did it in *Coriolanus*, Alan Alda in *The Apple Tree,* and Carol Burnett in her famous *Gone With the Wind* parody. Whether done for comic or serious effect, it never fails to wow an audience. But nobody should be asked to do this before he or she receives special training by an expert, a great deal of rehearsal, and sets and costumes constructed to protect the actor. A great many actors would refuse to even try this stunt, because it makes them too nervous or because they simply don't have the kind of physical agility it requires. Just say no to dangerous blocking unless you feel completely confident you can do it safely.

Backstage Tales

Harry, the character that co-author Paul Baldwin played in *Company,* is required to engage in a karate contest with his wife—it's written into the dialogue. She's taking lessons, and Harry ends up on the floor. Paul was assured that he would have a mat during rehearsals and special training from a professional. He didn't get either. Because it was his first professional role aside from summer stock, he didn't complain. He should have. At the end of the 10-week run, he had to have a swollen elbow drained of fluid, and his back has never been the same. Take warning.

"Okay, I'll Try It"

Unless it's something dangerous, you should at least attempt to do what the director asks of you. Whether it's delivering a speech twice as fast as you think right, or engaging in a tricky wrestling match with an overcoat as you dash for the door, give it your best effort two or three times before saying you just can't do it that way. You'll be surprised how many things work out just fine.

Actors have been known to deliberately sabotage directorial instructions that obviously won't work. A director asked one actor playing Shakespeare's Henry V to lead a group of soldiers up a 15-foot ladder behind a high platform while wearing a helmet and carrying a sword. On reaching the top, he and those behind him were supposed to leap up onto the platform, stand erect, and then swarm down the ramps on either side. He and the other actors discussed this bit of derring-do while waiting to try it for the first time. Everyone thought the idea was crazy. There was no way to "spring" gracefully from the rung of a ladder to the platform. The actor playing Henry V said he'd fix it. He got to the top of the ladder and fell flat on his face on the platform, his sword skittering out of his hand and falling to the stage below. That was the end of that nonsense.

When something is truly idiotic, a bit of sabotage may be the best way out. But in most cases, giving an idea a try is the best approach. Often enough, it will work.

Notes, Notes, and More Notes

We've repeatedly emphasized the need to take notes about anything the director tells you, whether the subject is a line reading or blocking, and ultimately costumes and makeup. As the rehearsal period goes on, and you know most of your lines, the director will usually interrupt scenes less. After you've run the scene, the director may call for a pause so that he can give notes about it, and you should have your script, notebook, and sharpened pencil handy. Other directors may run several scenes before giving notes, and in the final week may not give them until the end of the rehearsal. But always be prepared to write down what's said, and go over your notes as soon as you get home, if possible, and certainly before the next rehearsal.

Places, Everyone!

It is common to write down blocking instructions and acting notes in the margins of the script. But if you have a larger role, you may want to take the script apart, attach the pages to ruled paper, and keep it all in a loose-leaf notebook. This will give you much more room for notes. Unless you have two scripts, you'll need to glue each page along the left-hand side only, so that you can turn over the script page to read the other side.

Gracious Notes and Tough Notes

Directors have different styles of giving notes. Some are very gracious about it, phrasing criticism gently and taking an actor aside when they have something stern to say. Others like to joke around a bit, teasing actors about their failings in a good-humored way. And then there are the task-masters. The task-masters can be rude, even cruel, and may make a 40-year-old feel like a grade school kid. Such directors believe that embarrassing actors in front of the entire cast will ensure that the note is paid attention to. It's no fun to hear a director tell you, "Ed, you're still playing that third-act confrontation with Bob as though you've discovered you're out of toothpaste. Your mother has been arrested for murder! React, for God's sake."

Is this kind of note-giving just nasty, or does it serve a purpose? A little of both, probably. But be ready for it. You've no doubt heard of "hanging judges" who always give the maximum sentence. Well, there are directors from the same disciplinary school and you're bound to run into one sooner or later. You will notice, however, that such a director spares no one, and the best actor in the cast may well get clobbered the hardest. Console yourself with the knowledge that everyone's in it together.

You Forgot?

If you take proper notes and go over them carefully, you should be able to remember any changes in blocking or line-readings that the director has given you. But when the director makes changes late in the rehearsal period, the original movement or line reading may be so ingrained that you will forget a change. That kind of lapse can make a director scream. If that happens, don't get upset or go into a long explanation about why you forgot. Just say, "Sorry," and do it right.

Changes in blocking late in rehearsal can throw off a lot of actors. An actor may remember the change in movement, but forget the next line or two. That's because it's common for actors to link line memorization with blocking. A change can short-circuit the connection between the two. The only remedy is to go over the blocking change and the lines surrounding it again and again, until you firmly establish the new connection.

Backstage Tales

Amateur actors seldom have to deal with the wholesale last-minute changes that Broadway professionals do. New shows about to open in New York, especially musicals, can be in a state of chaos up until—or even after—opening night, with speeches and entire scenes being cut, even as entirely new songs are being put in. Co-author John Malone saw a dress rehearsal of the musical *Purlie* with Melba Moore, who was making her Broadway debut. She sang a terrific song that John was astonished to learn had only been put in the show the day before, an addition made because Moore was so good in the role. That song, "I Got Love," became the show's big hit and helped net Moore a Tony.

Getting It Right

As we've noted before, the fact that you're not getting a lot of notes from a director usually means that you're doing just fine. Some directors are more forthcoming than others in terms of praising actors, and you have to make the assumption that no news is good news. But sometimes an actor who is indeed playing a role well will suddenly reach a new level, or make a breakthrough in a particular speech, scene, or song that exceeds the director's fondest hopes.

If you surprise a director in this way, even those who are usually stingy with their praise will get excited. You've not only gotten it right, but "nailed it," and the director will tell you so, because he or she wants to be certain you keep doing it that way. Actors usually know when they've nailed something, and gone beyond what they expected of themselves. The exhilaration such moments bring can exceed anything created by opening night bravos.

But such breakthroughs can also be scary. In the previous chapter, you read about the breakthrough Julie Harris made as Joan of Arc during the Boston tryout of *The Lark*. We should add that Harris cried for two hours in her dressing room between the matinee and evening performances that day. She knew what she had done, but it had taken so much out of her that she was afraid she wouldn't be able to repeat it. The director's job in that situation was to say, "Of course you can." And Harris did indeed find a way to retain the effect on the audience without tearing herself to shreds doing it.

Places, Everyone!

Pace yourself. Towering roles make very large demands on actors. It is impossible to play a title role like Joan of Arc or Willy Loman in *Death of a Salesman* without fighting a running battle with exhaustion. You'll have to find a way to simulate emotions night after night without tiring yourself out.

Good Directors and Bad Directors

Anyone who does a lot of acting will end up working with both good directors and bad directors. A director can be "bad" for a number of reasons: A director may have a fine track record in general but still occasionally mess up a show. A director can be wrong for a particular play or musical; he or she may have been a big success with *The Sound of Music* and *Hello, Dolly* but can't manage a hard-edged show like *Sweeny Todd*. A director who works wonders with Shakespeare may run into trouble with Arthur Miller, and vice versa.

Even the Best Make Mistakes

Even the very best directors encounter problems they can't solve on occasion. We all have blind spots, and a director who has done a splendid job on almost every scene in a play may still mess up on a single important one in the second act. If that scene happens to be a major one for you, you may decide the director is just awful when almost everyone around you thinks he or she is terrific.

It can also happen that a director who is very good with one actor has trouble communicating with another. If you're the one he or she has trouble with, you're likely to have a low opinion of the director. But keep in mind that the problem may be as much yours as the director's. Personality conflicts occur even between people with a great deal of ability.

Even the Worst Get Some Things Right

Very few actors or directors get everything right or everything wrong. Even bad directors and bad actors get things right occasionally. Indeed, mediocre directors and actors can have surprisingly successful careers provided they stick to the kind of thing they know how to do fairly well.

If—or rather, when, because it will happen—you get stuck with a bad director, it's easy to get very discouraged. You know rehearsals are going badly, and you're afraid you'll embarrass yourself in performance. Don't sink into that mood, but instead look for the things that are going right, even if they seem few and far between. Use what's going right to keep yourself afloat. If you get so upset with the situation that you can't even recognize a good moment when it happens, you're lost. On the other hand, if you keep yourself open to the good moments, you'll be able to build on them to achieve others.

Picking Up the Slack Yourself

Don't waste your time or energy going around bad-mouthing a director to everyone else in the cast. That only makes things worse. The fact that your director isn't the best means that you'll all need to put extra energy and time into working on your own to compensate for the flaws in the direction.

A good cast can overcome a great deal if they put enough effort into it. Great casts have managed to turn plenty of second-rate plays into terrific productions. A good cast can also go a long way toward compensating for weak direction. Work on scenes with other actors privately. The best revenge on a bad director is to give a terrific performance anyway, even if that means the director ends up getting accolades he or she doesn't deserve. You and the rest of the cast will know to whom the credit really belongs: to all of you.

The Least You Need to Know

- A successful show is a collaborative effort, and no matter how large or small your role, you're still part of a bigger picture.
- Don't try to hog the director's attention, but do speak up when something seems seriously wrong.
- Whether a director gives gracious notes or tough ones, it's your duty to carry them out with dispatch.
- Always try to live up to good direction and surpass bad direction.

Chapter 21

Making Progress

In This Chapter

- Learning how to nail down your lines
- Exploring voice projection and scene pacing
- Understanding why less can be more
- Discovering the secrets of stage give-and-take

The start of rehearsals is always exciting, but then comes the hard work of learning your lines and memorizing the blocking. Around the middle of the rehearsal period, you may go through a brief period of frustration, feeling that things aren't moving ahead fast enough. But there will come a point when you'll sense that both you and the entire production are making real progress. It is then that you'll take some of the most important steps toward a complete performance.

In this chapter, we'll discuss those crucial steps forward on five different fronts: becoming fully secure with your lines, using your voice properly, pacing your scenes, avoiding the pitfalls of overacting, and establishing onstage connections with your fellow actors. You'll discover ways to deal with memory lapses. We'll also be giving you tips on vocal technique, and clues to good pacing. You'll learn why overacting can hurt your performance, and how to cope with scene-stealing by other actors. And we'll show you why being a giving actor will enhance the performances of other actors as well as your own.

Getting "Off Book"

At an early rehearsal, sometimes even the first one, the director will say that he or she wants everyone "off book" by a certain date. This means that the cast needs to be able to rehearse without a script (the "book") in hand. The director may give two or three actors in leading roles a little more time because their parts are so large. Unfortunately, it's even more important for the lead to be off book as soon as possible exactly because of the size of their roles. Lead roles, as we have noted before, carry greater responsibilities, and those who have been cast in them are expected to put in much more time learning their lines for that reason.

Performance Notes

Don't fall down on the job—even if you're very talented. Indeed, ironically, actors who are exceptionally talented sometimes have a lazy streak. They're sure they can always pull things together at the last moment. But they make life much more difficult for everyone else, and get a bad reputation. Eventually they fail to come through in the clutch, and nobody feels very sorry for them when they do fall on their faces. If you're very good, live up to your talent with hard work. That way no one will begrudge you your successes or celebrate your failures.

Jenny was cast as the young bride in a high school production of Neil Simon's *Barefoot in the Park*. She was talented and pretty, and everybody said she looked a lot like Jane Fonda, who played the role opposite Robert Redford in the 1969 movie version of the play. She was so "right" for the role that she didn't bother to spend the necessary amount of time learning her lines. After three weeks of rehearsal, with only a week remaining, she was still carrying her script around. The teacher who was directing the play suddenly marched up on stage, tore the script out of her hand and screamed, "Say goodbye to your security blanket!" Jenny burst into tears, but the director was utterly unsympathetic. "See," he bellowed, "with the book out of your mitts we finally get some real emotion!"

If you think the director who yelled at Jenny was being mean, keep in mind that Jenny simply wasn't doing her job. Her director had told her to be off book at the end of the previous week and, because she still didn't know her lines, she wasn't making nearly as much progress as the rest of the cast.

The boy playing her husband consoled her, but was actually pretty pleased with what the director had done. Although the actor suspected Jenny was more talented than he was, he had already moved on to another phase of mastering his part, and Jenny wasn't there for him; she wasn't responding at a level that matched the one he had achieved. She was holding him back, too.

When Lines Become Real

The reason that directors want a cast to be off book as soon as possible is that new things start happening when scripts are put aside. For one thing, the physical aspects of a role, from the development of gestures to the handling of props, can't be fully realized with a script in your hand. Good acting is a whole-body endeavor, and with that script in your hand, you're depriving yourself of an instrument of expression.

Backstage Tales

"Staged readings" are performances in which actors use scripts in full view of the audience. Such events may have only a single performer impersonating a famous person, as Hal Holbrooke did with Mark Twain and Emlyn Williams with Charles Dickens. Co-author John Malone had a chance to talk to Williams after he had given one of his famous Dickens performances standing before a lectern and reading from the author's works, as Dickens himself had actually done on tours of America. The book on the lectern was simply a prop—Williams knew every word he spoke in the course of the evening by heart.

Even more important, however, is that lines start to become real in a new way when you're fully secure with them. At a largely subconscious level, lines become part of you instead of words on a page once you've memorized them. You inevitably speak them with new conviction, because they are an instantaneous response to what other characters say to you. When you no longer have to glance down at the page, you begin to more fully inhabit the character you're playing. You stop being Ron and Julie, college kids trying to remember lines, and start becoming two other young people named Romeo and Juliet falling in love in the moonlight of a Verona garden. It is a mysterious, sometimes almost magical, transition from one reality to another, the essence of what makes acting a "calling" for those who truly love it, amateur or professional.

Performance Notes

When they first get off book, many actors find themselves paraphrasing some lines—they get the general sense across but change the word order or choice of words from what appears in the actual script. This is fine up to a point, but the director will eventually tell you to get it right. If you go on paraphrasing, the director may stop you in mid-sentence. The other actors get their cues from you, and if you change the words, you'll cause problems for everyone.

Memory Lapses

When you first get off book, you will certainly have moments when your next line completely eludes you. Even in rehearsal you'll find it embarrassing to stand there with a blank look on your face as your brain searches frantically for that missing mental file card. But it happens to everyone, and the worst thing you can do is to get upset about it—then the following lines will vanish from your memory, too.

During rehearsals, someone—often the stage manager, but sometimes an assistant to the director—follows the script at all times. It is his or her job to write down any blocking instructions, or changes to blocking, that the director gives, as well as to cue actors who have forgotten or simply skipped a line. If your mind is blank, say: "Line, please," and this person will read the line to you. Occasionally, you'll be so confused that you'll find it necessary to pick up your script and look at it, but that breaks everyone's concentration to a much greater degree than calling for a cue. Always try to get back on track by calling for a single line first.

The fact that you're off book does not mean that you can stop going over your lines. Memory lapses and paraphrasing are signals that you're not secure with your lines, but most actors keep on reviewing them between rehearsals even if they haven't made a mistake. The more deeply ingrained those lines are, the less likely it is that you will have a memory lapse during an actual performance.

Backstage Tales

As much as possible, it is wise to know the lines of other actors as well as your own. That protects you from being badly thrown if another actor forgets to say a line. Co-author Paul Baldwin once played Oscar in a production of *The Odd Couple* in which he and the entire cast had to learn Felix's lines, because the actor playing the role was very undisciplined and sometimes skipped whole pages, or answered "yes" when he was supposed to say "no." The production was a success because everyone else did double work to cover for Felix, who was funny when he got it right.

Louder, Please

When a play or musical has been fully blocked, and the cast is off book, you will often find the director disappearing from the front row where he or she has spent most of the time up to that point. Where did the director go? Up to the balcony, if the theater has one, or to the very back row of the first level. And from those dim recesses of the theater, his or her voice will come: "Louder, please."

Even experienced professional actors will hear those words on occasion. That's because every theater is different, not just in size and shape but also in terms of the kinds of material from which it is constructed, right down to the fabric on the seats. All of these environmental features affect the *acoustics* of the theater, and even very experienced performers may have to adjust their voices to their new surroundings.

Stage Directions

Acoustics, derived from the ancient Greek word for "heard," *akoustos,* is the science of sound. In some ways, it is a lost science. Outdoor Greek amphitheaters, dating back to 300 B.C.E. often have extraordinary acoustics, enabling the audience to hear the slightest whisper on stage from hundreds of feet away. Some modern theaters, on the other hand, such as Avery Fisher Hall at Lincoln Center in New York, are plagued by sound problems that no one seems to be able to completely fix. Any element of the theater's construction may affect the way an audience hears sound, and actors must learn to adjust their voices to the circumstances.

The Science of Projection

Projecting your voice so that it fills a theater involves both the strength of the vocal chords and the use of proper breathing techniques. The vocal chords, two bands of flesh within the voice box, or larynx, are controlled by a complex set of muscles. The vocal cords vibrate in resistance to the pressure brought to bear on them by an exhaled breath.

The muscles that control the vocal chords are strengthened by use, just like any other muscles in the body. Some lucky people are born with strong voices (although their parents may not consider themselves as fortunate when a baby has a wail that can be heard for a block). But anyone can strengthen his or her voice through practice. It is best to perform long speeches when attempting to strengthen your voice.

Because it is the exhalation of breath that causes the vocal chords to vibrate, it is important that you learn to breathe from the diaphragm, the lower part of your lungs that fill the abdominal space just below the ribs. Inexperienced actors or singers sometimes make the mistake of thinking that they will produce more breath by expanding the chest when just the opposite it is true. Our chests normally expand

Performance Notes

Don't overdo it when practicing. Overuse will strain the vocal chords, just as too much exercise will strain the muscles of the legs or arms. You don't always need to use your voice at full volume during rehearsals, either. For example, there is no need to project your voice when you're in the midst of blocking a scene—the focus is on movement, not on what the actors are saying. Similarly, you can use less-than-full voice when the lights are being set during technical rehearsals.

Performance Notes

Let's clear up a myth about whispering here. If you're losing your voice due to overuse or a cold, don't speak in whispers offstage to "save" your voice. In real life, you whisper using only your vocal chords (not with the support of the diaphragm), thereby straining the chords even further. If your vocal chords are tired, there's only one way to rest them: Shut up!

when we are out of breath. All the muscles of the upper body, including the shoulders and neck, tighten under these conditions, constricting the voice. If you watch professional singers closely, you will notice that their chests and shoulders remain relaxed, while their abdomens move in and out.

Proper projection is also aided by good diction, the use of the lips and tongue to enunciate consonants, especially the letters "d," "p," and "t," which so often come at the ends of words. If your consonants are crisp and clean, your words will carry further with less effort.

That Doesn't Mean Shout

Inexperienced actors sometimes confuse projection with shouting or yelling. In real life, we only shout when we're very angry, or yell when trying to attract attention from someone quite far away. A shout is a loud but also coarse sound that quickly becomes grating. It's almost impossible to modulate a shout or a yell, and only by modulating your voice will you be able to give full meaning to a sentence by raising the volume slightly on one word, and dropping it on another, to emphasize ideas or emotions. Just as music played at too high a volume on a stereo system sounds distorted, so yelling on stage risks the loss of meaning. It becomes sheer noise.

Shouts and yells are certainly used on stage, but only in special circumstances such as Shakespearean battle scenes. Actors may also use them in a more domestic drama at particular points. In Tennessee Williams's *A Streetcar Named Desire*, character Stanley Kowalksi yells up to his wife, bellowing "Stella," at the top of his lungs. Marlon Brando, who originated the role on stage and then played it in the movie, used that yell to establish the crass, bullying aspects of Stanley's nature. But Brando didn't shout his way through the entire role. Like any great actor, he could also convey menace in low, even silky tones. Shouts and yells should be used on stage sparingly, or they lose their effect.

Backstage Tales

When it comes to diction, the late George Rose, who won Tony Awards for performing in both musicals and straight plays, was a real champ. As a young actor, he practiced speeches with marbles in his mouth (DON'T SWALLOW!), just as the Greek orator Demosthenes was known to have practiced by walking up and down the beach declaiming with a mouth full of pebbles. Most actors don't go to that extreme, but you can emulate Rose in another way. He often used Gilbert and Sullivan patter songs, like "I Am the Very Model of a Modern Major General," from *The Pirates of Penzance*, to practice his diction. Gilbert and Sullivan patter songs are tongue-twisters that must be delivered with great speed, and they are terrific for diction practice. You don't even have to sing them—just reciting them can be a big help.

The Stage Whisper

The stage whisper is not the same as whispering in real life. The diaphragm supports a stage whisper just as it does any other stage utterance. But if you want to whisper on stage, give a "breathy" quality and lower the volume of your speech. To help the audience understand what you're saying at this lower volume, use exaggerated lip movements, as a visual aid, to form the words.

Picking Up the Pace

Pace—the speed at which a scene plays—is crucial to any good performance. If a scene moves too slowly, the audience will get restless, and you'll hear more coughing and rustling. A rushed pace, on the other hand, can leave an audience confused because things happen too fast for them to follow the action. In any play or musical, the pace of different scenes can quite properly vary considerably. A scene involving an argument, for example, usually demands a fast pace, while a love scene may require a much slower one. But the audience should never feel that a scene is "dragging," or that what's happening is taking so long that it can be described as having "a snail's pace."

Once the actors are off book, the director will start paying a lot of attention to pace. He or she will be concerned about three different aspects of pace: cues, dramatic pauses, and the speed at which actors get on and off stage.

It's Your Cue

Unless and until the actors know their lines well, it's difficult for the director to set the pace of scenes. The principal way to speed up the pace is for actors to pick up their cues instantly. The instant one actor finishes a line or speech, the actor with the next line should begin speaking, unless there is good reason for a pause (we'll talk more about pauses in a minute). A couple of seconds may seem like nothing between one actor's line and the next, but over an entire scene, a lot of slow responses can add up to two or three minutes, and the scene will drag.

Places, Everyone!

Picking up the pace does not mean stepping on another actor's lines. If you begin to speak before the final word of another actor's speech or line, the audience will lose both the end of the other actor's line and the beginning of your own. This is true even when the script calls for an interruption. The actor being interrupted must sound as though he or she has more to say, while the actor interrupting must cut in very fast without stepping on the last word of the previous line. It takes practice.

The Deadly Pause

Sometimes taking a pause between lines is not only called for but crucial. If a character is supposed to be astonished at what another is saying, for example, if the situation calls for a pause as the character takes in the startling statement, then he or she shows the initial surprise registering on the face before putting it into words. This is called a "take," or, in comedy, "a double take." Such facial expressions, however, are really substitutes for words. Something is still happening on stage even though it isn't verbal. Indeed, in a comedy, some of the biggest laughs are likely to come from facial double takes. Lucille Ball was famous for her double takes, as John Lithgow is today on the television sitcom *Third Rock from the Sun*.

Some actors, however, have the false impression that it is more dramatic, or funnier, to pause between every line. Nothing could be farther from the truth. Pauses lose their meaning when there are too many of them. John Lithgow's double takes, for example, are even funnier because the rest of the time he picks up his cues with great speed. A pause for its own sake is almost always deadly.

Snappy Entrances

Inappropriate pauses can be deadly, but nothing sucks the pace out of a play more completely than slow entrances. Even if you're playing a character who enters a scene in a state of exhaustion, dragging himself through the door, you need to be absolutely on the button in terms of timing that slow-motion entrance. If you aren't, and other actors are onstage already, they'll be left standing around looking foolish while you get you butt onstage. The lapse of mere seconds can drain the life out of a scene, and you'll all have to work hard to breathe some life back into it.

Backstage Tales

British dramatist Harold Pinter wrote pauses into his scripts—long pauses. Pinter is so famous for them that you will hear directors saying, "Forget the Pinter pauses," when actors use them inappropriately, whether in a Neil Simon comedy or a Shakespearean tragedy. Pinter constructs his plays around the pauses, and it takes actors with extraordinary timing to make them work. The authors have fond memories of watching Rosemary Harris play the pauses in Pinter's *Old Times* and Sir John Gielgud and Sir Ralph Richardson work their magic in *No Man's Land.* Such supreme actors can make these pauses vibrate with tension. But we have also seen lesser talents turn them into very boring evenings. Few stage techniques require more experience and ability than sustaining long pauses.

Whether your cue for an entrance is a line spoken by someone already onstage, a musical cue from the orchestra, or simply a change in the stage lighting, you should enter instantly on that cue. That need is especially evident in a farce, in which characters miss encountering one another by seconds and inches.

Even in a very serious play, a slow entrance can dissipate carefully built-up tension. When Shakespeare's King Lear appears carrying the corpse of his daughter Cordelia, crying out "Howl, howl …," he has to stagger in at precisely the right moment. In fact, with a famous play, precise entrances take on even greater importance: Numerous people in the audience will know Lear is supposed to enter at that particular moment, and any delay will start them thinking, "Where is he?" Or worse, "Can't he lift her?"

Ham on Wry

The long running Off-Broadway show *Forbidden Broadway* has survived for more than a decade by updating its parodies of Broadway musicals every year. One of its most successful numbers has been a send-up of the song "I Am What I Am," from *La Cage Aux Folles*. The parody is called "I Ham What I Ham," and its a very telling swipe at *ham acting* and all those actors, professional and amateur, who seem compelled to take the term "larger than life" to its extremes.

Stage Directions

Ham acting is overacting. This slang term originally derived from a nineteenth-century Negro song called "The Hamfat Man." Ham acting is too rich to be fully digestible, marked by broad gestures, exaggerated facial grimaces, and unnecessary vocal excesses.

When Less Is More

Some famous actors, great stars like Peter O'Toole, the late Zero Mostel, Zoe Caldwell, and Carol Channing, have made a career of "chewing the scenery." They win awards and delight many people, but they are also very controversial. Such stars are beloved by some and loathed by others. Critics, too, are of two minds about such actors—when the material is right, they review these actors well, but when the play or movie can't sustain their mugging, the reviews can be hostile. And they are sometimes intensely disliked by other actors who appear with them, who can feel as though they've been run over by a steamroller. Please note, too, that it's only because these hammy stars have immense talent that they can get away with antics lesser talents couldn't pull off.

Audiences cherish many of the greatest actors for their ability to convey a great deal with very economical means. Anthony Hopkins, for example, admits to hamming it up in his early career, but didn't become a true star until he learned to tone down his performances. In the movie *The Remains of the Day,* his performance was almost deafeningly quiet, yet you couldn't take your eyes off him. In a very different role, as the cannibalistic serial killer in *Silence of the Lambs,* he underplayed a role that many actors would have taken over the top, and was rewarded with an Academy Award for Best Actor. Like Kevin Spacey, another Oscar winner, he keeps demonstrating that less can be more.

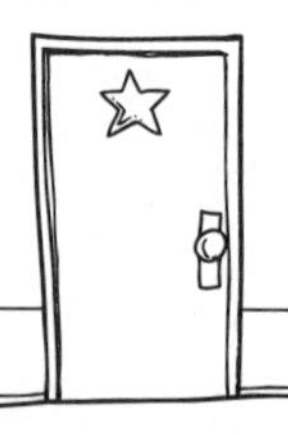

Backstage Tales

Shirley and Dan were college sweethearts, both majoring in drama. They could hardly believe their good luck when they were cast as George and Martha in Edward Albee's *Who's Afraid of Virginia Woolf* (parts for which they were far too young, but in college that is often the case). Shirley, however, took to playing Martha in the most brazen way possible, seeming to take over the play. But instead of competing with her braying, Dan wisely gave a performance of quiet intensity, making her look phony. He got the good reviews—and they were no longer sweethearts.

Some roles have a degree of hamminess built into them. Shakespeare's Falstaff, for example, who appears in both *Henry V* and *The Merry Wives of Windsor* is an over-the-top, clownish character who "play-acts" for his friends. Such scenes can be, indeed should be, imbued with a quality of excess. But Falstaff also has moments of great poignancy, as when his old friend Prince Hal (now Henry V) rejects him. If an actor fails to play those scenes with great sincerity and control, a major aspect of the character's significance will be lost. You can't ham a sense of loss and shame and still expect to move an audience. Thus, even when playing a genuinely hammy role, the actor must know when to pull back and communicate his or her feelings in a very different way.

Dastardly Upstagings

There are two kinds of upstaging, and no good actor should indulge in either of them. The less blatant kind involves moving upstage of another actor while engaging in a dialogue, thus forcing that actor to turn his or her back on the audience. This is an underhanded trick that may make you the focus of audience attention for the moment but will infuriate the other actor.

The second kind of upstaging, which occurs most often in musicals, is an even cheaper ploy. A minor character stands upstage of a lead actor singing a major song, all the while making faces behind the lead's back to attract attention. Such upstaging may work well if it's planned, as was often the case in skits involving Tim Conway and Harvey Korman on *The Carol Burnett Show*. But otherwise it is despicable.

Backstage Tales

A legendary theater story about upstaging involves Gertrude Lawrence and Danny Kaye in the Kurt Weill musical *Lady in the Dark.* Lawrence was one of Broadway's greatest stars, while Kaye was a newcomer at the time. Kaye, who was noted for hamming it up during his entire career (sometimes to great effect), started making funny faces behind Lawrence during one of her most important songs. She was the star, and could have had him fired, but she took another course. His big number was the famous song in which he reeled off the names of dozens of Russian composers in two minutes flat. At the next performance, Lawrence strolled out on stage during his number, sat on a stool, and crossed and uncrossed her legs while he sang. Danny Kaye learned not to try to upstage Gertrude Lawrence.

The Giving Actor

Whether you're the star of a show or have a minor part, acting is always a "give-and-take" situation—or should be. The more the actors give to one another by communicating as fully and directly as possible while on stage, the more convincing the scenes of the play will seem to the audience. What's more, this kind of mutual support helps everyone to give a better performance. It enables all the actors in the scene to believe in one another's characters more completely.

Is This a Soliloquy?

The selfish actor refuses to give other actors anything to work with in the scenes, behaving as though every speech were a soliloquy, communicating only with the audience (or with the camera in movies and television). Jane Fonda once commented that when she made *Walk on The Wild Side* with the late Laurence Harvey, it was "like acting with myself." Harvey gave some striking performances, but he was not well liked by other actors because he behaved as though they weren't even there, leaving them with nothing to react to. Everything was about him.

That kind of selfishness not only makes you unpopular but, in the end, also undermines your own performance. Harvey was always at his best when playing utter cads because the self-regard of his acting technique was in tune with the character he was playing. When he tried to play more sympathetic characters, he often failed to impress.

Places, Everyone!

Watch *Inside the Actors Studio* on Bravo and you'll hear many actors stress the importance of listening. This program is both a delight and a learning experience for any actor. It is always fun to see a favorite like Julia Roberts or Harrison Ford talk about their careers for an hour, instead of for the few minutes allowed on talk shows when they are promoting a new movie. It often has surprises—Roberts and Ford are both much funnier than most people would expect, for instance. But there are also numerous tips about acting that even the beginner can make use of. Tune in.

The Art of Listening

When professional actors talk about their technique, a great many of them single out the art of listening to other actors as particularly important. Simply standing there and waiting for your cue cuts off the possibility of creating electricity on stage. You should listen to the other actor as though you are hearing the words he or she is speaking for the very first time, whether it is the second performance or the hundredth.

When an actor truly listens to what another character says, special things begin to happen. In a long run, actors may vary the way they say a line slightly from evening to evening, feeling something a little differently each time. And if the actor to whom they speak truly listens, he or she will hear that slight variation and change his or her performance in reaction. That keeps a performance fresh and alive. But you have to be listening in order to pick up on such variations. Listening—being receptive to nuances—is half the battle when it comes to acting.

Emotional Truth

Once you're off book, you can begin to make real progress. Projecting your voice, picking up your cues, and making entrances on the button, as well as finding the appropriate level or style of performance, all begin to fall into place. As you gain control over these largely technical matters, you'll also be able to interact more fully with the other actors in a form of "give and take" that creates emotional truth on stage. You are now ready to "become" your character, to inhabit the skin of the person you are portraying. And the play itself will begin to come alive.

The Least You Need to Know

- The sooner you get off book, the more time you'll have to make real progress in becoming your character.
- Proper breathing and good diction are essential to projecting your voice so that it fills the theater.
- Picking up your cues, whether in terms of lines or entrances, ensures that scenes have a lively pace.
- Hammy acting, unless the script calls for it, is bad acting.
- Upstaging other actors is a cheap trick that often backfires.
- The giving actor gets a great deal in return, and everyone's performance benefits.

Part 5

"We Open Next Thursday"

The first song in Kiss Me Kate, *Cole Porter's backstage musical about a production of Shakespeare's* The Taming of the Shrew, *is called "We Open in Venice." That's Venice, Italy, of course, but whether you're on the verge of opening a show in that other Venice in California, or in the town of Paris, Maine, or London, Ohio, the final week of rehearsals is a heady time. The cast members know their lines (hopefully), and are in the process of fine-tuning their characterizations. But now there are a lot of new aspects of the production to concentrate on.*

Costumes are being completed, you're rehearsing on the actual set, and lights are being set. Final run-throughs of the complete play take place, followed by the rigors of technical and dress rehearsals. And then, at last, comes the thrill of opening night. The production is up and running. This section of the book will take you through the excitement and hard work of that final week of rehearsals and the subsequent run of the play.

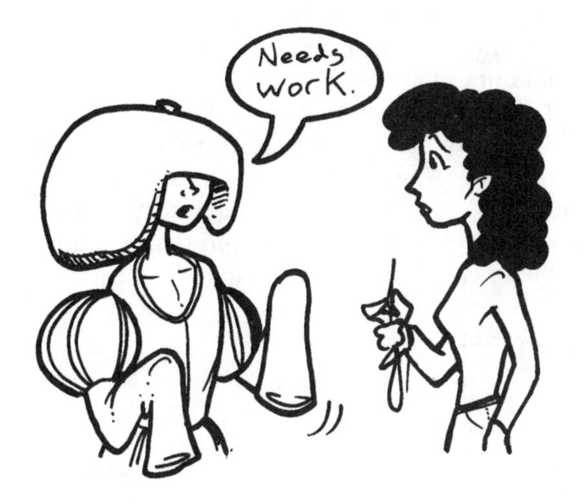

Creative Costuming

In This Chapter

- Learning how to make sure your costume fits
- Discovering the pluses and minuses of providing your own costume
- Exploring how and when to complain about costumes
- Recognizing when a costume will be needed early
- Understanding how costumes help shape a performance

All actors, young or old, amateur or professional, find themselves getting a bit excited when it comes time to try on their costumes for the first time. It can be an exhilarating experience. It can also be deflating, and sometimes hilarious. In this chapter, you'll learn the ins and outs of costuming as we detail several kinds of specific problems that can arise with costumes and we explore how to cope with them. In amateur productions, actors are sometimes asked to provide their own costumes, or accessories for them, and we'll tell you how to deal with that situation. Some costumes require extra time to get used to, and we'll give you tips on how to make sure you have it. Finally, we'll explore the ways in which costumes enhance your feel for the character you're playing, providing new insight and improving your performance.

Fitting Stitches

Needless to say, costumes must fit properly. It's not just that you will be up on a stage with an audience noting every detail of what you're wearing. Nor is it necessarily a matter of looking good with all those people staring at you—sometimes your costume should be frayed or in bad taste because it suits the character you're playing. If, for example, you're playing the role of an old bum in clothes seemingly rescued from the trash bin, the costume must still be constructed in a way that makes it comfortable for you to perform in. It must give the illusion of being ill-fitting without hampering your ability to move around the stage with ease. A pair of trousers can be baggy and frayed at the cuffs, but the legs can't be so long that they trip you up unexpectedly. At the other extreme, a form-fitting, sexy costume mustn't be so tight that it causes breathing problems or makes it impossible to carry out your blocking.

Backstage Tales

There are special situations in which you may use costumes that constrict movement. In the original production of the musical *Follies*, for example, for which Florence Klotz won a Tony Award for her costumes, there were sequences in which young counterparts of the middle-aged former showgirls at the center of the story moved across the rear of the stage like ghosts of their youth. These showgirls wore very tight costumes with feather fans projecting from the hips, as well as enormous headdresses. It was impossible to sit down in these costumes or to move with any speed. But the chorus members wearing them were not required to sit down on stage, and they were choreographed to move in slow motion. Thus, these very constricting costumes were not a problem. Backstage, between entrances, they could temporarily remove the headdresses and feathers.

Too Big and Too Small

It might seem too obvious to mention that costumes should be the right size, neither too big nor too small. But in college and community theaters, where the budget is small and costumes from earlier shows tend to get recycled, you should be ready to insist that the costumer actually take your measurements. If he or she simply asks for your dress size or your collar and waist measurements, our advice is to say that you're not sure, even if you are. That way, you'll force him or her to get out a tape measure, something a truly responsible costume designer or maker should do as a matter of course. If not, a memory lapse on your part is called for to ensure that things are done right. Occasionally, it's very smart to pretend to be an idiot.

When the costumer asks you to try on a costume, take your time about testing it out. Raise your arms above your head to make sure there's enough room in the shoulders.

Walk around to check the length of skirts or trousers. Are the sleeves the right length? A sleeve that's too long or too short will not only drive you crazy, but also spoil your gestures on stage. If the costume doesn't fit properly in any way, make clear what the problem is. And ask when you should come back for a fitting.

Places, Everyone!

Costume people in amateur theater—and in professional summer theater, too—are often overworked and don't have as big a budget as they need. Because of these problems, costumers can be the touchiest of all the technical people working on the show. Be sympathetic. Tell them you know that they have too much to do, but also keep checking back to make sure your problem is being taken care of. If nothing happens, go to the stage manager or the director and let them know you're not getting action. When it comes to costumes, you have to look out for yourself.

The Cloak That Chokes

Gary was playing King Arthur in a production of *Camelot*. He had been told that he would be wearing a long black cloak in the final scene, but it didn't show up until just before he went onstage for that scene at the dress rehearsal. It was a splendid cloak, but the material was heavy, and a thick gold chain secured it at the neck. Once he got onstage, he realized that the cloak was choking him. He could barely speak. Since it was dress rehearsal, he didn't want to stop the show, and simply removed the cape and laid it on the stage floor beside him. He never saw it again after that night.

There are a couple of lessons here. The first is that an actor should never wear a costume onstage unless he or she tries it on beforehand. Gary should have refused to wear it at all when it was thrust at him at the last minute. But once he was onstage with it, he did the right thing. If a secondary piece of your costume gives you problems while onstage, get rid of it as quickly and unobtrusively as possible. Struggling with it while trying to act is all too likely to make you look ridiculous, and the audience may well start laughing—a disaster in something like the moving final moments of *Camelot*.

The Hat That Deafens

Hats, whether worn by a man or a woman, can give the final flair to a costume. What would "The Ascot Gavotte" in *My Fair Lady* be without picture hats? Top hats for gentlemen may be required for many debonair roles, or 1930s fedoras for hard-boiled detectives or gangsters. Helmets for warriors, 10-gallon hats for cowboys, wimples for nuns, and feathered head-dresses for showgirls—hats can make the costume. But they come with built-in problems.

Most obviously, hats are given to falling off. If a hat is too loose and the actor has to make sudden, quick moves, the hat may fly right off his or her head. In small theaters, the stage door to the outside may be only a few feet offstage, and if it opens unexpectedly on a blustery day, a surprisingly strong wind can sweep the stage. Many a hat has taken off on its own, under such circumstances. So, if you're going to wear a hat, make sure it fits snugly. Women in picture hats or headdresses have to go further and make sure to anchor the hat with hairpins.

There's another problem that most actors don't think about until they experience it. Hats can block your ears, making it hard to hear other people's lines or even the music for a song when the orchestra is small. Confining headgear, like the helmets worn in some classical plays, or the nuns' wimples in *The Sound of Music,* can be a particular problem, as can a more ordinary hat that's so large it covers even one ear. If you're going to be wearing a hat, check it not only for how it looks and how it fits, but also test your hearing while wearing it.

Places, Everyone!

If the script (or the director) requires that you remove a hat while on stage, be sure to start practicing with it long before dress rehearsals. Work on this maneuver at home in front of a mirror. Can you get the hat off without messing up your hair too much, or worse, dislocating a wig or hairpiece? If taking off your hat (or putting it on, for that matter) is supposed to get a laugh, you will need to work on your timing. Start early.

"Can You Provide Your Own?"

In amateur theater, actors are often asked to provide their own costumes, especially if the play is a contemporary one. That request comes out of small budgets and the need to conserve funds for productions that require period costumes. In the old Mickey Rooney/ Judy Garland "let's put on a show" movies, there were always problems raising enough money to mount the production, but in the end the costumes always looked like a million bucks—MGM bucks, of course. That's not the way it works in real life, unfortunately, and a lot of costumes come straight out of the home closets of the actors.

Boots, Shoes, and Accessories

Boots and shoes are expensive, and you're particularly likely to be asked to supply them yourselves if you possibly can. Women are usually able to come up with an appropriate pair of shoes. Those who do a lot of acting keep boxes of old shoes that they wouldn't necessarily wear on the street, but which they could dye or re-heel for use in a play. It's a little trickier for men. They can use black dress shoes in many productions, of course, but boots are a different matter. You can use cowboy boots in some shows, but they aren't going to work for Shakespeare. When they buy new boots for their own regular wear, men who act a lot often look for the plainest kind of boot possible, since an undecorated boot can pass muster when used with costumes from many periods.

Accessories are usually of more concern to women than men. You can often buy them cheaply or borrow them. Liz, for example, found a perfect pair of "cat eye" glasses at a flea market when she was performing in *Grease*. Dina's grandmother opened her big box of costume jewelry and said to use whatever was needed. When Dina came down the staircase as Dolly Levi in a community theater production of *Hello Dolly!* she was dripping in Grandma's diamonds—the rhinestone kind, of course, but they looked great.

Places, Everyone!

Dancers, amateur as well as professional, are generally expected to own the kind of dance shoes appropriate to the choreography, from tap shoes for a production of *My One and Only,* to toe shoes for the occasional ballet sequence. Both women and men who do a lot of chorus dancing in musicals should have black dance slippers (Capezio is the most famous brand). These can also come in handy for both sexes in productions of Shakespeare or Restoration comedies. Don't expect them to be bought for you—they're basic equipment.

The Whole Shebang

For many modern plays, both men and women may be asked to provide a complete costume, even several for a woman playing a role that requires elegance and a number of changes. As with shoes, it's always wise for a performer to save old clothes, especially those that are in good condition but out of fashion—they may be exactly right for a play a couple of years later. When you're asked to provide an entire costume, it's wise to take a couple of alternative outfits in for the costume coordinator to look at. You may think you know exactly which dress or suit is right for your character, but the final choice may depend on what other actors are wearing. The director may not want two women in the same color or two men wearing virtually identical suits. Women need to keep in mind that if they're playing secondary roles, the perfect outfit may not work because it's too similar to something the leading lady wears. The star comes first, in this and many other matters. It's simply the way of the world.

Advantages and Drawbacks

You'll find two major advantages to wearing your own clothes on stage. First, you won't have to worry about the fit. That's particularly true of shoes. Many small theaters keep boxes of old shoes, but the fit can be problematic, and there's nothing worse than wearing shoes that don't fit. A second advantage to providing your own costumes is that you can start wearing them earlier in rehearsals, and even take them home to practice in. You'll be spared extra fittings and last-minute problems that lead to being sewn into an unfinished costume for dress rehearsal.

The great drawback to wearing your own clothes is that you will probably wear them out in the course of the play. Most people tend to sweat a good deal under hot stage lights, which is hard on clothes. They will also get makeup on them. And since acting is a very physical activity, the general wear and tear is likely to be greater than what would occur in everyday life. So, you should probably leave your favorite dress or suit at home in the closet.

Performance Notes

Some people use a part in a play as an excuse to go out and buy new clothes for the show, with the expectation, or at least the hope, that they can then wear them in their regular lives. That is usually a false expectation because of the hard wear the clothes will get. Therefore, if you're going to buy clothes for your own costume, it makes more sense to look for them in thrift shops, where you can often discover great finds at low prices.

"I Look Like the Goodyear Blimp"

Actors can be vain about how they look on stage. That's as true of males as it is of female performers. One of the things that distinguishes character actors from "stars" is the willingness of the former to look awful. When a star is willing to look frumpy, he or she—and particularly the women—can get a lot of credit for doing it. In 1954, Grace Kelley was at her most staggeringly beautiful and glamorous in *Rear Window*, but also allowed herself to appear with little makeup, an unfashionable hairdo, and wearing old cardigan sweaters as the wife of the alcoholic actor played by Bing Crosby in *The Country Girl*. The contrast was startling, and it helped gain her an Oscar as Best Actress for *The Country Girl*.

But if you're playing a character who is supposed to look terrific but must wear an unattractive costume, there's every reason to be unhappy. A lot more than vanity is involved in such cases—your very ability to create a convincing character is being sabotaged. Similarly, a costume should disguise rather than accentuate a leading lady's big hips or leading man's skinny legs. And while you can't expect a limited budget to allow for the elaborate silks and satins of Broadway, the amateur performer still has a right to demand a costume that is at least suitable to the character.

The Disastrous Costume

Sometimes even a fairly simple costume can be a disaster. Marcie, for example, was cast as the sports reporter Gloria in the musical *Damn Yankees*. Her big number was the show-stopper "Shoeless Joe from Hannibal Mo." That's a very strenuous song and dance number in which the baseball players toss Gloria back and forth in the air. She was given a white pleated skirt to wear. Although she was quite slim, the cut of the skirt made her hips look very heavy. Worse, the material was slippery, and during the first run-through while wearing it, she was dropped twice. Unattractive is one thing, dangerous quite another, and Marcie didn't even have to complain. The director immediately said, "You're getting a new costume." If he hadn't said that, she would have caused a ruckus, quite rightly.

Complaining Too Late

If a costume is a disaster, say so as soon as you realize it, or you're likely to end up stuck with it. On a big musical or a play with period costumes, nobody is going to be working harder than the people—often unpaid volunteers—sewing the costumes. They almost never have as much time as they need, so the sooner you speak, the more likely you are to get action. If you make your special needs clear at an early stage, it's possible that the costumer can fix the problem altogether. A slightly raised waistline can disguise big hips, for instance, and the use of boots or a long cloak can disguise a man's skinny legs, clad as they are in tights. If you're allergic to some kinds of fabrics, the costumer can choose others. You should discuss all these solvable problems at the start of rehearsals. Don't wait for things to go wrong before speaking up.

If you do discover a problem late in the game, it had better be a serious one. The skirt that's causing you to trip or the sword you can't easily slip out of its sheath are real problems that could louse up a performance. Details of color or style that you don't like, on the other hand, are a matter of taste, and opening day is not the time to bring them up. There are too many more important problems to deal with; you should have said something much sooner.

Performance Notes

Because the people making costumes are so often overworked, you'll get a lot farther being pleasant and polite than you will by yelling or ordering them around. Ask if you can get anyone some coffee or a soda. Do you have some unused cloth at home, or a trunk in the basement full of your grandmother's hats? Offer them for use. If you're making a day trip to the nearest big city, ask if you can pick up anything in the way of supplies while you are there. Anything you can do to help out will pay dividends in getting your own needs addressed.

When to Rebel

As we've already suggested, quickly take care of any costume problems that affect your ability to breathe or move properly. The same is true of costumes that have ripped. If the costumer isn't responding to these problems, go to someone with power—the stage manager, the director, a producer, even a theater board member—and make your case.

Another situation that calls for rebellion is the costume that isn't ready for dress rehearsal. Everyone in the cast should have a costume for dress rehearsal, even if it's unfinished, with no buttons up the back so that the actor has to be pinned or even sewn into it temporarily.

Co-author John Malone played the role of Agamemnon, the King of the Greeks, in a production of Shakespeare's *Troilus and Cressida* that opened the new multimillion-dollar Loeb Drama Center at Harvard University in 1960. Because this was a major production inaugurating a new theater, Robert Fletcher, a graduate who had gone on to

Performance Notes

Beware of putting your foot down with too much force. Threatening not to go on unless you get your way is a dangerous step. In the professional theater, it can get you fired unless you are a very big star. On Broadway, of course, everyone has understudies, but that's seldom true in amateur theater, which means that actors have a greater responsibility to the rest of the cast to show up and go on no matter what.

design costumes for Radio City Music Hall and many Broadway productions, volunteered his services. The costumes for the Greek and Trojan warriors were short, form-fitting tunics that had numerous patches of leather sewn on them as decoration. As of dress rehearsal day, John's costume was not finished, and he was told to go on in street clothes. Since there was an invited audience of nearly 150, including a number of his friends, he was not happy, and became even more upset when he learned that his costume was, in fact, finished except for the decorative patches and the clasps that held it together in the back.

John rebelled. Since he was supposed to be bossing around all the other Greek warriors, including Achilles and Ulysses, he thought he would look extremely foolish doing so while they were in costume and he was in chinos and loafers. He went to the director and said that if he didn't have a costume, he would go on naked or not at all. He didn't raise his voice, but his choice of words drew a grudging smile from the director. He was sewn into his undecorated costume and sallied forth to command the Greeks.

Everyone should have at least the semblance of a costume for dress rehearsal. If you don't, get tough.

Early Requirements

Most productions don't have costumes fully ready to wear until dress rehearsal, and even that may be dicey. If you'll be wearing your own clothes in a contemporary play, you are, of course, a step ahead. But even in plays or musicals that require period costumes, some situations and roles virtually demand having a costume long before dress rehearsal. If you're going to change your costume in full view of the audience, for instance, or if the costume itself presents special difficulties in terms of movement, you need to have it as early as possible.

Changes in Audience View

The classic example of changing a costume onstage takes place in the first scene of *Man of La Mancha*. As the musical opens, the writer Miguel de Cervantes arrives at a prison with his faithful servant Sancho Panza. They have been accused by the Inquisition of refusing to pay church taxes, and are to remain in prison while awaiting trial. The other prisoners threaten to burn the manuscript Cervantes clutches to his chest. To preserve it he agrees to act out the story it tells about the "mad knight" Don Quixote, and to use the other prisoners in various roles as the plot unfolds.

At this point, the actor playing Cervantes must sit down and transform himself into Don Quixote. It is a "beat the clock" situation, since he must accomplish the transformation while he delivers a musically underscored speech introducing the new character he is assuming. The actor must apply a beard, mustache, and false eyebrows, as well as daubing on age lines. Before he finishes his speech, Sancho also helps him into Don Quixote's armor. The transformation, done correctly, leaves audiences amazed, but it's a very difficult feat to pull off, taking a lot of practice and rehearsal long before dress rehearsal. In addition to plays in which an onstage change is made clear in the script itself, you may find yourself in a production in which the director has decided upon onstage changes to keep the audience amused, or to heighten some symbolic aspect of the play. Greek tragedies are often played with masks, and those, too, will be needed early, since they change the very sound of your voice and may require a different kind of gesturing to compensate for the fact that your face is hidden. Both situations demand that you have the costumes or masks early.

Armor and Hoop Skirts

The donning of armor on stage by Cervantes/Don Quixote is a special situation. But even if you will always be putting your armor on offstage before making an entrance, its use means that you should have it earlier than other costumes. While stage armor is usually fairly lightweight and is not made of metal, it is always somewhat cumbersome and constricting. You will need to rehearse with it considerably before dress rehearsal because it will alter the way you move.

The same is true of hoopskirts. Anna in *The King and I* must learn to handle incredible yardages of fabric sustained by stiff hoops. If she doesn't have it soon enough, she's likely to knock some of the King's smaller children off their feet while singing "Getting to Know You." And then, of course, there is the waltz with the King, while wearing a skirt of truly epic proportions. This is the highlight of any production of the musical, and Anna will need to have at least an approximation of her costume to work with, starting early on. That applies to any costume, male or female, that affects basic movement.

Places, Everyone!

The smart actor not only gets a head start on learning his or her lines before rehearsals begin, but also pores over the stage directions to find any hints about possible problems with costumes, props, or makeup. Make a list of any questions you have, and bring them up with the director or stage manager at the earliest opportunity. Forewarned is forearmed, in the theater as well as in battle.

Clues to Character

Many actors find that even though they think they have a good understanding of a character, and are doing quite well in rehearsal, they may gain an entirely new perspective when they finally get their costume. It may be the way a skirt swirls that gives the leading lady a fresh sense of the sexiness of her character, or the cut of a suit that gives the leading man a greater authority. Spike heels or a pair of actual nurse's shoes can be the final touch that makes a woman feel as though she is inhabiting, instead of just acting, the role she is playing. The padded shoulders in a suit can make a man feel more thoroughly at home in the role of a 1940s gangster. Costumes provide the final clues to a character that can inspire a terrific performance instead of just a good one.

The Padded Stomach

Shakespeare's Falstaff always comes to mind when thinking about padded stomachs on stage. True, many actors playing the role may be somewhat heavy-set to begin with, but few can resist adding a few more pounds for good measure. Falstaff is, after all, referred to again and again as a "fat old man."

But plenty of roles call for a woman to wear stomach padding as well. A famous example is the heroine of the play *My Fat Friend*, a role originally played on Broadway by the young Lynn Redgrave. In the first act, she wore a "fat suit." When she appeared minus her fat suit in the second act (her character having gone on a strenuous diet), suddenly tall and beautiful, the audience was so thrilled, performance after performance, that it erupted in spontaneous applause. For that to happen, of course, the "fat suit" must be utterly convincing, and the actress wearing it must have enough time to rehearse in it so that her movements become heavier in their every aspect.

Many roles call for women to wear padding to appear pregnant, perhaps most famously Agnes Gooch, the secretary to Auntie Mame. The first sight of a hugely pregnant Agnes negotiating the descent of a staircase was a hilarious tour-de-force that made Peggy Cass's career. You can be certain that she'd been wearing that padding almost from the start of rehearsals.

The Crucial Handkerchief

In Shakespeare's Othello, a handkerchief, which Othello had given to his wife Desdemona, is stolen by her maid, Emilia, at the request of her husband, Iago. Iago uses the handkerchief to trick Othello into believing that Desdemona has been unfaithful to him. That handkerchief is the most crucial costume accessory in all of dramatic literature. And because it passes from hand to hand among all these characters, it is essential that they have it almost from the beginning of rehearsals.

Many plays have important costuming elements that change hands in service of the plot, leading to misunderstandings that may be either comic or tragic. When reading a play before rehearsals, always make note of any such instances, and ask about getting the crucial item early on. That also goes for *props*.

Stage Directions

Technically speaking, a **prop** (short for *property)* is any portable object that an actor carries or uses during the course of a play. It can be a bouquet of flowers or a sword, a letter or a pen, a book or a wastebasket. A chair moved by a character is not just a piece of furniture (part of the set), but by virtue of being moved by the actor it becomes a prop as well. And a prop can be a costume element, like Desdemona's handkerchief.

"Now I Feel It"

Costumes are not just something to wear that is appropriate to the character. They have psychological importance for the actor as well. Any experienced actor will tell stories about the times he or she had problems with a role that just getting into costume solved. The right costume can provide the actor with a new insight into the character being portrayed. Suddenly, the sound of a long skirt rustling or the tilt of a hat over the forehead enables the performer to make a deeper connection with the role. "Aha," the actor will say, "Now I feel it!"

The Least You Need to Know

- You need to make certain that your costume fits properly, including shoes and hats.
- Providing your own costume can solve fitting problems, but the costumer still needs to approve your choices.
- If a costume causes you difficulties onstage, or makes you look bad, say so immediately.
- Costumes that affect how you move, or that you must change into onstage, need to be ready early.
- A costume is one key to your performance, and you need to list potential problems with it as you first read the play.

Chapter 23

Tech and "Techies"

In This Chapter

- Learning to appreciate the importance of "techies"
- Discovering how to make sure your props are always ready
- Exploring the mysteries of stage lighting
- Finding out how to keep your footing onstage

When audiences attend the theater, they usually leave talking about the actors and how good or bad they were, about the story that has been told in the course of the evening, and about the songs if they saw a musical. They'll also talk about the sets and costumes, particularly when the show involves a certain amount of spectacle. Almost always, however, the actors get the most attention, especially from the audience, since it is only the actors who get to take bows at the final curtain. (At Broadway opening nights, the author, composer, and director may take a bow, but that is a special circumstance.)

But the actors couldn't take their bows if there wasn't somebody to turn up the lights, raise and lower the curtain, provide sound cues, make sure the actors have the right prop for the right scene, assist in costume changes, move scenery around, and generally make the show "run."

Be Kind to Techies

Even though the audience usually pays little attention to the names listed as technical staff (known as *techies* in theater slang), the actors in the show know better—or at least they should. Actors who treat techies coolly, or even with disdain, are asking for trouble. Not only are techies essential to a smooth-running show, but also in some situations an actor's physical well-being rests in their hands.

Stage Directions

The technical staff of a theater is known as **techies.** Techies run lights, change scenery, and handle props, among other tasks. Many stage managers go on to become directors, and a person listed as a stage carpenter may one day be a Tony-winning set designer.

Offstage but Vital

To demonstrate the importance of techies, let's look at what happens on stage in one of the most famous sequences in dramatic literature, the balcony scene between Romeo and Juliet. Here we have a situation involving only two characters, but many things can go wrong if the techies haven't done their jobs right.

To start with, there is the balcony itself. Techies will build it, either unionized stage carpenters if it's a Broadway production, or the set designer and anyone he or she can round up to help out in an amateur production. The balcony must be strong enough to support Juliet's weight as she stands on it. The railing must be secure enough so that it doesn't give way as she leans on it. It must support Romeo's weight as he climbs up to touch hands with Juliet. Often Romeo uses a vine to hold on to as he climbs, and that vine must also be securely anchored, and strong enough to support his weight. If the balcony rail is flimsy, Juliet will have to worry as much about her safety as delivering her impassioned speeches. If the vine comes loose, it can send Romeo tumbling to the stage floor, getting a misplaced laugh and spoiling the scene.

Most of the stage is dimly lit during the balcony scene, which takes place late at night. At the same time, Romeo and Juliet must be lit well enough that the audience can see their facial expressions. Techies are the ones who hang the lights in the right places, and who put the colored gels (sheets of transparent film) over the lights to give the effect of a moonlit night. The techies also control the brightness of the lights. In the scene, Juliet is worried that someone will discover her meeting with Romeo. A few offstage

Performance Notes

Don't panic, but accidents do happen onstage. Sometimes they are the performer's fault, particularly in the case of dancers, where a misstep can mean a broken ankle. But accidents also occur because of a loose board or piece of carpet, an improperly secured light that crashes to the stage, and numerous other problems that are the responsibility of the technical crew. Your safety depends upon their expertise and thoroughness.

noises, provided by—you guessed it—techies, to which she reacts with nervousness, help convey that tension. Techies also provide any musical underscoring you hear at the beginning or end of the scene. The Nurse calls out to Juliet from offstage at the end of the scene, and an assistant stage manager is responsible for seeing that she is there on time to say her line.

Without good work by the technical staff, lots of things can go wrong with the balcony scene, ruining its magic. And this is actually a relatively simple scene. It doesn't involve any of the several props that might be essential in a Neil Simon comedy scene, or such sound-effect complications as ringing phones or doorbells, an offstage gunshot, or the sound of thunder that may be required in other plays. Techies may be offstage and invisible to an audience that doesn't care who they are. But the wise actor had better care.

Respect Pays Dividends

One of co-author Paul Baldwin's leading ladies once said to him, "Paul, you're too nice to techies." She was very talented, but she couldn't be bothered to learn the stage crew's names, or say hello when she ran into them on the grounds of the summer theater where she and Paul were performing. Paul looked at her and said, "They work even harder than we do and our lives are in their hands. I think it's smart to give them the respect they deserve."

Backstage Tales

There is a legendary theater story about a great Metropolitan Opera soprano who received a devastating comeuppance in the 1950s. She had once been very beautiful, but had gotten extremely heavy as the years passed. She was also famous for her backstage temper tantrums. In one of her final Met performances, she appeared in the title role in Verdi's opera *Tosca*. At the end of the opera, Tosca flings herself to her death off the parapets of the Castel S. Angelo in Rome. The large soprano was used to landing on a pile of mattresses and pillows backstage, but the fed-up stage crew substituted a trampoline. The audience broke into howls of laughter as the lady bounced back into full view. She wasn't hurt in the least physically, but her pride was deeply wounded. And the story made clear the ultimate power of techies.

Techies do work hard, and a smile and a "How's it going, Stan?" can pay a lot of dividends. No self-respecting techie is going to take revenge by making a mistake that can cause real injury. They're too responsible for that, and of course they not only could get fired but even be sued for that kind of behavior. But an actor who treats techies badly may discover that the lights are getting a little dim during a big number, or that an onstage phone is ringing a beat too late, causing an uncomfortable pause. Niceness, in the theater, as in life in general, is not only the right approach, but can be self-protective as well.

"Where's My Sword?"

The backstage areas in a theater are dimly lit, so that no light spills over onto the stage to interfere with the effect of the onstage lighting. There's usually a lot of traffic backstage, as actors mill around waiting for their entrances or cross behind the set for an entrance on the other side of the stage. Even in a two-character show like the musical *I Do, I Do!*, a number of stagehands and other technical people will be backstage. It gets crowded quickly, and in a small theater there will be inevitable traffic jams.

This is the kind of environment in which things get easily misplaced, and props have a way of vanishing as easily as car keys or reading glasses at home. That's why prop tables are at either side of the stage, where all props are supposed to be kept, and a prop manager is there to oversee the tables. But problems still occur. The desperately whispered cry, "Where's my sword?"—or letter, teapot, candy box, or gun—is too often heard.

Backstage Tales

Props must work to be effective. Co-author Paul Baldwin once played Bill Sykes in a summer theater production of *Oliver!* After murdering Nancy, he was supposed to be shot by the outraged mob of citizens. The gun didn't go off and they decided to rush him and push him down the flight of stairs from the platform he was standing on. He suffered a broken finger, but survived to write this book. It's often necessary to improvise lines to cover a missing prop, but improvised combat can be dangerous.

All-Important Props

Props are often crucial plot elements. Obviously, Hamlet and Laertes can't have a sword fight if the latter is missing his sword. You can't make a big deal of hiding an incriminating letter without a piece of paper to hold behind your back or to stuff under a pillow. You can't pour a poisoned drink with no bottle and glass—and the liquid in the bottle will have had to be replaced with a fresh supply between shows.

Your Responsibility, Too

Having a good property manager is essential to a smoothly running show. And they are often very good—it's a position that can lead to being the stage manager next time around, so they tend to try hard. But every actor still needs to keep a constant check on his or her own props. You should always check the prop table before a performance to make certain that everything you need is there, on the correct side of the stage. Look in that bottle of "poisoned" liquor—did someone refill it with fresh weak tea or whatever else you're using as a substitute for real liquor? Make sure that any fresh foods the cast consumes on stage are changed every day, so nobody in the cast gets ill. Cap guns used on stage must have been freshly loaded. Is a prop letter or telegram getting too frayed in the course of the run? If so, ask for a new one. The more responsibility you take for checking on your own props, the less possibility of errors.

Having a good property manager provides a cast a great deal of confidence, but no matter how reliable he or she is, the smart actor always double-checks everything.

Places, Everyone!

Mark your props by placing your name on them, especially if it's something individual to your character or to you personally. For example, fencing foils used in stage sword fights can have quite different weights, and you'll want to use the one you're most familiar with during the performance; otherwise, you risk being thrown off balance, which can be both unsightly and dangerous.

The Light and the Dark of It

Every year, not only are Tony Awards awarded to the artist who provided the Best Costumes and Best Sets, but also for the Best Lighting. Indeed, stage lighting isn't just a matter of making sure the audience can see what's going on. It's an art form that can greatly enhance the emotional impact of a scene. In addition, a gifted designer can create lighting that can act as a substitute for elaborate sets, creating atmosphere as surely as wood and canvas do. In "symbolic" plays, ranging from Greek tragedies to Thornton Wilder's *The Skin of Our Teeth* and the works of Samuel Beckett, lighting is far more important than scenery.

On Broadway, or at important regional theaters like the Mark Taper Forum in Los Angeles, computerized lighting systems are marvels of technological flexibility. In amateur theater, the technology is usually far less modern, depending on old-fashioned switches and dimmers. But because light is such a flexible medium, a good designer can create extraordinary effects, subtle or spectacular, even with a minimum of equipment.

Finding Your Light

When light floods the stage in a big musical number, for example, actors don't have to worry about the lighting. It's everywhere, and if you're on stage, you're bathed in it. But in smaller scenes, even in musicals, some areas of the stage will be bright and others will be dim. In these situations, the actor must know how to "find" his or her light. Being able to do so is partly instinct and partly learned skill.

Backstage Tales

Some actors have such a finely tuned instinct for lighting that even lighting designers look to them for input. Elizabeth Taylor is legendary in that respect. She could walk onto a movie set (where lighting problems are particularly complex because they must take film exposure into account) and immediately know if there was a problem. She could tell a grip exactly which light he or she needed to adjust, and how. While speaking out on this subject might be annoying from an actor who was simply concerned with vanity, lighting designers greatly valued Taylor's expertise. She saved time and trouble for everyone.

Judging light on stage is not a simple matter for an actor. Things look different when you are in the middle of the stage than they do from the broader and more distant perspective of the audience, particularly when you're supposed to stand in only a small pool of light at a particular moment. You are unable to judge how the well the light covers your whole body, from head to toe, especially if you are tall, so that the light hits your face.

In some productions with complicated lighting, the director or lighting designer may mark the stage with strips of tape that indicate exactly where you should place your feet. But that is not always possible. Actors must learn by experience to find their light. For one thing, they'll know whether the light is on their faces because they can feel its heat on their skin. Some people have more sensitive facial skin than others and will pick up this clue quite quickly. It may take more time for those with less sensitive skin to discern the difference between the general heat of stage lights and that of a particular light that is focused directly on them. One kind of light will find you, rather than you finding it: the *follow spot*.

"Can I Be Seen?"

Sometimes an actor gets the feeling that he or she is not properly lighted, usually when he or she is far downstage at the curtain line, or far upstage, perhaps on a staircase or on a raised platform at the back of the stage. There may be a valid reason for keeping that character somewhat in the shadows, but if you think you're getting so little light that you're practically invisible, don't hesitate to ask the director or a lighting technician if the audience will be able to see you. It may be that with so many other problems to deal with, you've been left in the dark by mistake.

But if you ask this question, be prepared for the director to tell you that the lighting level is correct. Directors sometimes get arty ideas about having a virtually disembodied voice emanating from the gloom. If so, you're likely to be stuck in the dark. Few things are more difficult than talking a director out of a favorite arty idea, even if it's a dumb one. If you are stuck in the dark, be sure to raise your volume and speak with particular clarity—the human voice is capable of making an impact even in deep shadow.

Stage Directions

A **follow spot** focuses a circle of light on a particular character on an otherwise dark stage. As its name implies, this light follows an actor as he or she moves. Usually placed at the side or rear of a balcony and mounted on a swivel, they are operated by hand by a member of the light crew. While that appears to mean that all responsibility lies with the person operating the follow spot, the actor must, in fact, stick to the same exact movements at each performance, or else lose his or her light.

Getting Offstage in the Dark

Many people have some degree of "night blindness." They simply do not see as well as others in the dark, and the problem is often at its worst when they go from bright lights into darkness. Since it is common for many theater scenes to end with a "blackout," with all the stage lights extinguished simultaneously, it can be a nightmare to get offstage in one piece. Judy Holliday, who won an Oscar when she repeated her stage role as Billie Dawn in *Born Yesterday*, had severe night blindness. When she subsequently starred in the musical *Bells Are Ringing* on Broadway, several blackouts followed musical numbers. A stagehand had to rush on and lead her off by the hand. (Of course, when the stage lights were up, her charisma succeeded in making the lights seem dim.)

If you do have night blindness, make your problem known early on, so that either another actor with good night vision or a stagehand can practice lending you a hand.

Performance Notes

If you have night blindness, don't take on the responsibility of taking props off the stage at the end of the scene. Make it very clear that you aren't a good prospect for such tasks, since you'll need as much help as the chair in making an exit in the dark.

Obstacle Courses

Set designers, like architects, can get so carried away with the "look" of things that they forget human beings are going to have to inhabit one of their sets or buildings. (The number of major theaters built without adequate cloakrooms or restrooms is legion.) High platforms, steep stairs, and stage living rooms filled with enough furniture to stock a warehouse are just a few of the obstacle courses set designers ask actors to navigate. What's more, actors often begin rehearsals in a big studio room with nice flat floors and only lines of tape on the floor to indicate what the set is like. Encountering the actual set can be a real shock, so let's go over some of the major hurdles you may have to leap.

Platforms and Steps

Platforms are a big favorite of set designers. A platform raised above stage level provides visual interest to a set design, as well as a separate playing area that can help keep a play moving. As one group of characters completes a scene on the stage proper, the lights can be brought up on a raised platform where a new scene begins with virtually no interruption. Some productions, if the stage is big enough, may have two or three raised areas.

Platforms can be fun for actors, too. Unless you suffer from vertigo—in which case the theater is probably not where you belong in the first place—being up there above the stage is often exhilarating. If you're playing a character like Mark Antony in Shakespeare's *Julius Caesar*, the height on which you're standing will certainly add conviction to your rendition of "Friends, Romans, countrymen, lend me your ears." Platforms can offer a definite psychological lift to the actor.

But they can also be a problem. To start with, they are often fairly small areas, which means that you can't take great strides in any direction and must always be aware of the edges of the platform. That can be as inhibiting as the height itself is commanding. You will need to spend extra time getting used to the particular space you have to work with.

Places, Everyone!

Spend extra time practicing on both the platforms themselves and the stairs that lead to them. Come in early for rehearsal or stay afterward, and go up and down the stairs and around any platforms until you could do it in your sleep. Then, no matter how unnatural the set may have seemed at first, you won't trip or fall during a performance.

Platforms also mean steps, or stairways, leading to them. All actors soon discover that stage steps and stairs seem to have been designed for creatures from Mars. The tread may be very wide or exceedingly narrow, the riser exceptionally high or very low, but somehow the combination often defies the normal human gait.

The production of *Troilus and Cressida* in which co-author John Malone played Agamemnon had a set designed by a good friend of his who was an architecture student. It had a very steep stairway at centerstage, which John was supposed to descend while giving a speech to the Greek warriors below him. The set designer came into the theater a few days before the opening and found John walking up and down the stairs again and again. The designer asked what he was doing. John replied, "Learning how to walk in your new universe."

A friend of ours once played the blind hero in the play *Butterflies Are Free* at a summer theater. The night the set was finally in place, he stayed for more than an hour after rehearsal and walked around stage without a single light in the theater except for the mandatory exit lights. This helped him give an extremely convincing performance, since he knew the set as an actual blind person would his own apartment. But, in fact, any actor should spend the time getting to know a set so well that it is as familiar as his or her own bedroom in the dark.

Raked Stages

In elementary or high school productions, you will find yourself working on a normal, flat stage. But in college or community theater you are likely to encounter something very different: the dreaded *raked stage*, which is a tilted platform.

To the inexperienced actor, a raked stage can be intimidating, even frightening. It is all too easy to feel that the slightest slip will send you crashing into the orchestra pit. And once you get over that fear, the question still remains: How do you cross the stage from left to right when one foot is lower than the other without looking like you're limping?

Walking with confidence, and looking normal doing so, on a raked stage takes practice. In essence, you must lean slightly against the tilt, whether forward, backward, or to one side or the other. While it may sound difficult, thousands of actors have not only walked successfully on a raked stage, but have also danced or had sword fights on them as well. And, ultimately, actors look good performing on a rake because, when they're standing still, they must inevitably bend one knee, which creates an attractive pose.

Stage Directions

A **raked stage** is essentially a tilted platform, with its lowest end toward the audience and its high end at the rear of the stage. The rake is the degree of the tilt, seldom more than about 15 percent. Still, you will be performing on a surface with a pronounced downward slope, similar to the gradient on a wheelchair access ramp. For aesthetic reasons, most raked stages are either oval or round.

Balky Doors

Few experienced actors haven't encountered a door in a stage set that refused to open or close properly. Everyone has a story about this problem, including both authors of this book. In a high school production of Agatha Christie's *Ten Little Indians*, John played the role of the mad judge who has invited nine strangers to an island mansion in order to take retribution against them. At the end of the play, the judge is supposed to lock all the doors and then shoot himself offstage, leaving one

Places, Everyone!

Learn to improvise! When the scenery starts falling apart or refuses to function properly, you'll have to think on your feet. Fortunately, it is moments like this that make live theater truly live, and audiences are not only forgiving but usually feel they've been given a special treat. Don't panic; just use your common sense. At least you'll have a good story to tell at dinner parties.

character all alone in a house littered with corpses and a noose hanging from the chandelier. Unfortunately, another character had pulled too hard on a door at one side of the rather flimsy set a few minutes earlier, leaving an entire wall supported only by that partially open door. John decided to just pretend to close and lock that one (after all, the judge had already been revealed as bonkers), and the audience was so caught up in the plot that no one even laughed.

Paul played Sweeny Todd in a professional production of the Stephen Sondheim musical of that name. At his final exit he was supposed to slam a door hard behind him at the back of the stage. The door led to a wooden cubical with no way out. When it came time to take his curtain call—the last person to do so—the door wouldn't open. He gripped it firmly, tore it off its hinges, set it to one side in full view of the audience and walked forward for his centerstage bow. The audience loved it, of course, and his solution to the problem was at least in tune with Sweeny's character. The stage manager, however, was none too happy.

"What's That Chair Doing There?"

Realistic sets with a good deal of furniture can turn into a real obstacle course. Directors may have to change blocking that actors have followed since the start of rehearsals because an easy chair or sofa turns out to be bigger than expected. Or, if a play has more than one set, an actor may discover a chair placed where it shouldn't be, thanks to a mistake by one of the techies. In this situation, the actor can either move the piece of furniture out of the way at an opportune moment, or if it's too big for that, improvise new blocking to deal with the problem.

Sometimes, when the cast finally gets onto the set, the placement of furniture can be a surprise. One friend of ours was playing the role of the debonair Beverly Carlton, based on Noel Coward, in a community theater production of *The Man Who Came to Dinner.* The character has to sit at the piano and sing his own latest songs while accompanying himself. Our friend discovered, to his dismay, that the piano had been placed so that his back was to the audience when he sat down at it. The stage manager claimed there was no other way to fit the piano on the set, but our friend finally persuaded the director to swing the piano around just enough so that he was at least in partial profile to most of the audience. No actor can be blamed for complaining when the placement of furniture spoils his or her big moment.

Backstage Tales

When the new Metropolitan Opera House opened at Lincoln Center in 1963, the composer Samuel Barber was commissioned to write an opera especially for Leontyne Price, based on the story of Antony and Cleopatra. The massive set included a huge pyramid on a turntable at centerstage, which was to swing open to reveal the resplendent Egyptian queen. At dress rehearsal, not only did the turntable totally break down, but the pyramid wouldn't open either. Leontyne Price was trapped in it, in total darkness, for more than half an hour. Fortunately, you're unlikely ever to be that unlucky!

The Least You Need To Know

- Always treat "techies" with respect, not only because they deserve it but also because they're crucial to your own success.
- Take responsibility for checking your own props before every performance.
- Know how to find your light so that you're not left in the dark, and discuss any lighting problems with the director.
- Be aware of potential problems with the set and learn how to cope with them.

Chapter 24

Dress Rehearsals

In This Chapter

- Preparing yourself for new problems that crop up during run-throughs
- Learning about the world of makeup
- Understanding the tech run-through
- Exploring the dynamics of curtain calls
- Finding out how to survive a dress rehearsal

The night before a show opens, you'll have a dress rehearsal with the cast in full makeup and costume. Ideally, a director and his or her company will treat the dress rehearsal as if it were an actual performance, with no stopping, no matter how many small problems occur. But sometimes things go so wrong at some point that you'll have to straighten the mess out. Many productions have more than one dress rehearsal for exactly that reason, and in such cases a small invited audience may be present for the final one, the night before opening. That enables the actors to get a feel for how a paying audience will respond, particularly important when the show is a comedy.

In the final days before opening night, the play will have at least one full run-through every day, sometimes two on a Saturday or Sunday. In this chapter, we'll explore the frustrations of run-throughs, including the tech rehearsal in which you'll deal with scene changes and lighting glitches. We'll also guide you through the creative and technical process of applying stage makeup. And since you'll soon be taking a bow for your performance, we'll explain what you can expect in terms of a curtain call.

Run-Through Frustrations

A run-through is supposed to be exactly what the term implies—a rehearsal during which the play proceeds in order, from the first scene to the last, in approximately the length of time an actual performance will take. Because plays are almost always rehearsed out of sequence at first, run-throughs may be the first time the cast truly gets a sense of the whole arc of the play. But doing that may trigger the director to make changes, and making changes means taking a break to work them through. In addition, things have a tendency to go wrong in run-throughs, as we will see, and that also means stopping. Thus, the goal of getting straight through the whole play is often frustrated.

Everything That Can Go Wrong

During run-throughs, you're likely to be dealing with many props and other aspects of the set for the first time. One person will forget to put something down; another will forget to pick it up. Because you'll be walking down unfamiliar steps, you may find yourself arriving at your spot either too soon or too late. Somebody is bound to drop something or spill something. If any food is being consumed onstage, somebody will have his or her mouth full at the wrong time and be unable to say a line. And, of course, several of these problems are likely to cause laughter, which will break everyone's focus, slowing things down even more.

Backstage Tales

Sir Alec Guinness, one of the greatest stage and screen actors of the twentieth century, noted in both interviews and his autobiography that his early stage career was nearly derailed by a tendency to dissolve in giggles, not just during rehearsals but during performances. Laughing on cue is difficult, and many actors have to work hard to develop a natural-sounding stage laugh. But real laughter at inappropriate moments is all too easy to succumb to, and sometimes hard to control. Guinness felt that, in his case, it was a sign of nervousness, and he got over it as he became more secure as an actor.

Although everyone supposedly knows his or her lines by the time run-throughs begin, memory lapses will suddenly start spreading like the measles at this point. That's because there are so many new things to take into account, in terms of props and sets, that concentration tends to become diffused. Don't get panicky about such memory lapses; things will settle down again soon enough.

Performance Notes

Don't reveal your annoyance with fellow actors who have a lot of problems during a run-through. They're flustered enough as it is, and the last thing they need is nasty comments, or even "free advice" from anyone else. Don't tease anyone when they make a mistake, either. Save the jokes for another time, when everyone can look back on the chaos and laugh together. You're bound to make a mistake of your own soon enough.

The Three-Hour First Act

Because of the combination of new things to deal with, run-throughs can drag on interminably. Instead of getting through the whole play in three hours, it's common for just the first act to take that long. This is frustrating for everyone in the cast, as well as for the director. Musicals are especially likely to go slowly during a run-through because the choreographer will also see new problems, and the music director may have to call a halt because either someone onstage or someone in the orchestra is making a hash of things. So, keep in mind that run-throughs might better be called crawl-throughs, and that's nothing unusual.

If the director (or choreographer or music director) makes a change during a run-through, pay very close attention to what he or she says. As soon as you get offstage, write the change into your script, and if you have any doubts, consult the assistant to the director or the stage manager after rehearsal. If things are going relatively well, the director won't stop the run-through for every little thing, but instead will give notes at the end of the rehearsal. You should always have your script at hand when he or she gives these notes.

Places, Everyone!

Each director has a different style of giving notes. Some will be pleasant and upbeat. Some will be very somber, looking as though they're in the White House dealing with an international crisis. And some will be sarcastic. Don't let the somber ones scare you, and learn to take the sarcastic ones in stride—they don't really hate you, or think you're lousy; it's just their way of getting a point across.

Makeup Crises

As you approach the date for the first dress rehearsal, the issue of makeup will come to the fore. How much and what kind of makeup will be necessary varies according to the kind of theatrical production you're involved in and the kind of character you're playing. Let's break things down by age groups first.

- **Grade School:** A teacher or volunteer parent is likely to apply the makeup at this level. But pay attention: The more you learn when you're young, the sooner you'll be able to do your own makeup.
- **High School:** If you're 17 years old and playing the lead in a musical, you won't have all that much to worry about. If you're a girl, you only have to enhance the makeup you might wear on a date. If you're a boy, you'll have to learn the art of basic stage makeup, but that isn't terribly complicated—generally it's just some base makeup, mascara, and eyeliner (and, yes, you have to wear it, or else risk looking like a dead fish under the stage lights). The director will be able to help if your role requires anything more complicated.
- **College:** If you need help with your makeup in this venue, a fellow performer with more experience will probably be able to help you. Again, pay attention; the sooner you learn to do your own makeup, the better.
- **Community Theater:** Some well-funded community theaters may hire a professional makeup artist for a play that requires a lot of character makeup. But even if you're expected to do your own, you'll probably be able to get some help from a cast member or the director if you're stumped.

Performance Notes

Don't overdo it, even if you're playing an odd character like a Shakespearean clown or a sleazy one like a Kit Kat Girl. You need to create a heightened effect in the most economical way possible, so that your facial muscles remain expressive. If you study Joel Grey's makeup in *Cabaret* closely, you'll notice that although the overall effect is bizarre, it doesn't violate the planes of Grey's own face, which remain sharply defined.

Too Much and Too Little

People generally have fairly strong and immediate opinions about makeup in real life, quick to comment that one woman looks cheap because she's wearing too much rouge and lipstick, and that another looks extremely drab because she refuses to wear any makeup at all. We all make such judgments about male politicians when they appear on television. Most experts agree that Richard Nixon suffered in his first presidential debate against John Kennedy because he didn't wear enough makeup, which led him to appear wan and slightly sinister. In the first presidential debate in 2000, many commentators thought that Al Gore wore too much makeup. Stage makeup, on the other hand, is a little more difficult to judge.

To begin with, how much or how little makeup to wear is not a matter of taste but rather depends on the character. When a woman plays the virginal Isabella in Shakespeare's *Measure for Measure*, she should have just enough makeup to look lovely under stage lights, but not enough to contradict her chaste nature. At the opposite extreme, the Kit Kat Girls in *Cabaret* need to overdo the makeup because they're portraying characters of easy morals in a sleazy nightclub. The Master of Ceremonies at the Kit Kat Club, for which Joel Grey won both a Tony and an Oscar, is a bizarre character who must wear a lot of makeup, as is also the case with most of Shakespeare's clowns.

Young actors often get carried away with age makeup, adding so many lines to the face that they end up looking more like a city road map than a person. Fewer lines, in the right places around the eyes and on the forehead, combined with shadows to hollow the cheeks, are all that is necessary to convey age across the footlights.

Occasionally, a character actor may play a role that calls for quite extreme makeup. The Witch in Stephen Sondheim's *Into the Woods* or the "monstrous" Caliban in Shakespeare's *The Tempest* for instance, can require pulling out all the stops, such as false noses, warts, and other facial deformities. But even in this kind of part, the makeup should never become a layered mask that inhibits facial expression. Lon Chaney, Hollywood's "man of a thousand faces" in the 1920s and 1930s, often wore extreme makeup, but made certain that he never obscured his very expressive eyes.

My Nose Won't Stay On

A review in *The New York Times* of an Off-Broadway production of *Cyrano de Bergerac* in spring 2000 noted that the actor playing the title role lost his famous long nose in mid-performance. The reviewer complimented him on the way he handled this actor's nightmare, reporting that he put it in his pocket, and when referring to his nose from then on, would sometimes pat his pocket, getting nice laughs from the audience. This was certainly a clever bit of improvisation, but it is safe to suggest that he will be having bad dreams about that performance for years to come.

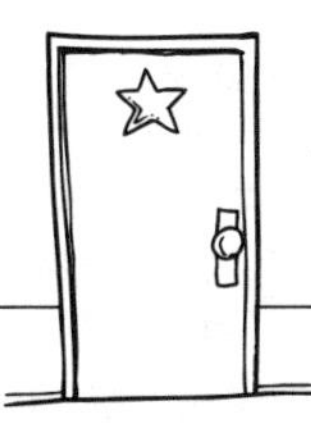

Backstage Tales

Sir Laurence Olivier was regarded as a genius with makeup, and like many geniuses, he had an obsessive quirk. He liked to change the shape of his nose for every character he played, and it wasn't just a matter of shaping a hooked beak of a nose for Richard III. He wore false noses shaped with putty for Hamlet and Henry V, as well as for Heathcliffe in *Wuthering Heights*. Changing the shape of the nose, especially in the subtle ways he did, requires the skill of a sculptor and great technical know-how. Most fake noses, especially in the movies, tend to look fake. One can admire Olivier's daring and skill, but few actors of even the greatest talent are tempted to emulate him in the nose department. It's too much work and too chancy.

Noses that come off, wigs that slip, rubber jowls that suddenly droop—these are put into the category of makeup catastrophes by all actors. (Dealing with facial pieces that must be applied with spirit gum requires help from someone with a lot of experience with this kind of applied makeup.)

Doing Your Own

Almost all actors greatly enjoy doing their own makeup. It can be time-consuming and laborious when the role requires heavy character makeup, but even then it involves a degree of fun. It's a creative task, and all of us have a bit of childhood "mud-pie" joy left in us no matter what our age. More important, doing your own makeup helps you to better understand your character. You must transform yourself into someone else while on stage, and applying makeup helps to get that process going in the hour before the curtain rises. You'll be sitting in front of a mirror, after all, literally re-making your own image into that of the individual you'll play in just a few minutes. A few actors take to doing their own makeup so naturally and easily that they might have been born to the calling. For others, it will be a learning process. If, in the beginning, other people apply your makeup, watch what they do, ask questions about what kind of makeup they use, pay attention to how different colors work with your skin, and pick up any technical tricks you can. In time, even people who consider themselves klutzes can learn to do most of their own makeup. It may take work, but the ultimate rewards are well worth it. There are a number of books on makeup. Get one out of the library, or buy one and teach yourself.

The Personal Makeup Kit

Once you're acting in college productions or beyond, you'll probably start putting together your own makeup kit. Although there are a number of different brands of theater makeup, Bob Kelly being the most famous, actors often find products manufactured by the large commercial beauty and skin-care companies extremely useful. Gradually you'll find yourself adding different brands of base cover, lip coloring, rouge, eyebrow pencils, eye shadow, and mascara to your kit, along with sponges of various sizes and textures, and numerous other special items. Women will also collect hairpieces, and men may want to add false mustaches and beards.

Once you do start building your own makeup kit, it's not only acceptable but also correct to insist that it is yours and yours alone. In an emergency, you might lend another cast member an eyebrow pencil or some mascara, but generally you should refuse to do so. Stage makeup is expensive, for one thing, and it is also very personal. In fact, it is unhygienic to share certain makeup items, particularly lipstick and mascara. Every amateur cast has its habitual borrower, and nothing is wrong with firmly saying, "No, I'm sorry, but I don't lend my makeup to anyone." Say it, and stick to it.

Backstage Tales

When co-author Paul Baldwin was cast for the second time as Don Quixote in *Man of La Mancha*, he decided to buy his own false beard. Since he had to take that beard on and off in full view of the audience at each performance, it needed to stand up to a considerable amount of wear and tear. Paul paid quite a lot for his beard, but because he took very good care of it, cleaning and combing it after every performance, and storing it away in a foil pouch inside a plastic bag, it lasted him through not only that production but four subsequent ones.

The Tech Run-Through

The tech (or technical) run-through is not conducted primarily for the actors' benefit. Its purpose is to make sure that all the light cues and sound cues are correct, and that set changes can occur with speed and efficiency. The cast must be present in order to make certain that the timing of cues is integrated with individual performances. Lights will undoubtedly have to be refocused while the actor stands on stage in the exact place that a speech will be delivered in performance.

Places, Everyone!

Be aware that tech rehearsals can last into the night. Directors will take school and family schedules into account during tech rehearsals at the grade school or high school level, but that may not be the case in community theater productions. If your child is involved in such a production, expect that a tech run-through can mean a very late night.

The actors also must recite their lines during a tech run-through, and they need to do so at the pace they expect to use in performance in order to make the cues exact. But there is no point in using full volume or trying to achieve a dramatic high during a tech rehearsal. There will be a lot of stopping and starting again during a tech run-through, and long pauses while the techies make corrections. It's boring, and at times chaotic. But that doesn't mean you can goof off. If you don't pay close attention, someone will set a light or sound cue wrong that may end up making you look bad in actual performance. If you think something isn't right, definitely speak up. That may mean stopping again, and some people will groan, but this is the time to nail down any details involving the physical aspects of the production.

Sometimes a broken piece of stage machinery will bring the tech run-through to a complete halt. Perhaps a set won't lower into position correctly, or a small revolving turntable won't turn. The problem may be so complex that the only solution is to proceed with the rest of the run-through and to have the cast come back earlier than expected the following day, after the problem has been fixed, to go through that scene again. For that reason, all cast members should clear all scheduling conflicts during the last days before a production opens. This is not the time for a dentist appointment or a big birthday party.

Curtain Call Confusion

Directors often leave the blocking of curtain calls to the last moment, such as the end of the tech run-through or just before the dress rehearsal. There are reasons for this delay, but they're not always good ones. It may be that he or she simply had too many other problems to solve.

Or, a director may want to wait to see who is really delivering among the secondary members of the cast, so that he or she can devise an order that will reflect the likely applause level from the audience. Last minute blocking of the curtain call can create problems, though. Curtain calls mean a great deal to the cast that has been working so hard, and they're important to the audience, too. In fact, audiences often see curtain calls as very much a part of the show. A sloppy curtain call can be a downer on both sides of the footlights.

Backstage Tales

The best solo curtain call we've ever seen was accorded to Glenn Close, who has won Tony Awards for *Death and the Maiden* and *Sunset Boulevard.* The curtain call was for *Crucifer of Blood,* a play based on the tales of Sherlock Holmes. She played a beautiful woman who, to Holmes's regret, turned out to be a jewel thief. The other characters took their bows except for Close and John Wood, who played Holmes. The curtain came down and rose again on Glenn Close, alone at centerstage. She had changed her costume to a very dark red gown, and she looked over shoulder with her back to the audience. Her hands were bound behind her back with the stolen diamond necklace. The audience went wild.

Traffic Jams

Curtain calls tend to create backstage traffic jams. While there are few times even during a big musical that everyone in the cast has to be ready to go onstage, that's exactly the situation during a curtain call. In order for this to go off smoothly, people must form lines instead of milling about like penned cattle. If the space is small, those lines on each side of the stage may have to snake around one another. It's like waiting for your table at a very popular restaurant. People are not always good about forming lines (as anyone who has tried to get on a subway car at rush hour knows), but during a curtain call, they are essential.

As each cast member goes onstage, the line must immediately move up. This is not the moment to start conversations about what has gone right or wrong with that performance. The show isn't over until the curtain has come down for the final time—and that's after everyone takes his or her bows. Good curtain calls demand speed and precision. That's particularly true for chorus members and secondary characters who bow to the audience as a group. Generally speaking, cast members taking group bows should already be on stage as soon as the group before them finishes bowing, and move very quickly into place. Only those in the two or three lead roles can take their entrances at a slower pace, and even they should move with dispatch.

Fast-moving curtain calls actually create an atmosphere that produces more applause, not less. If some cast members dawdle, the applause will die down a bit as the audience waits for the straggler to take a bow. When everyone zips into place, the applause is not only more sustained, but builds to a stronger climax. Dawdlers are really stealing audience energy from the others that follow them, often the more important characters. Sustained applause ends up making everyone in the cast feel more exhilarated in the end.

Bruised Egos

In a modern play with a small cast of characters, curtain calls are quite straightforward. There's almost never any question about the order in which people should take their bows. But in a musical or a Shakespeare production, there's such a big cast that someone will inevitably feel that he or she should have taken a bow later than someone else, either because of role size or the quality of the performances. "Vanity, vanity," is a favorite theatrical mantra, for good reason.

In some cases, the order of the bows is virtually set in stone. Take *Hamlet*, for example. Polonius, the father of Ophelia and Laertes, takes his bow before Ophelia, but after Laertes. It doesn't matter if the actor playing Laertes is absolutely brilliant in a not-terribly-rewarding role, while the actor playing Polonius is nothing more than adequate. Polonius is one of the most famous roles in Shakespeare, and the speech in which he advises, "To thine own self be true," is one of the most quoted in the language. Even badly played, Polonius gets the later and more important bow as a matter of course.

Performance Notes

Take it easy when taking your bows. Egos can get out of hand when actors take curtain calls. Some actors practically turn handsprings trying to draw more applause, which may annoy not only the other actors but even the audience. Most actors take their curtain calls in character, as the fictional person they are playing might do, but that shouldn't be overdone.

But the fact that someone takes a later bow doesn't guarantee that he or she will get more applause. A special burst of applause often rewards a brilliant performance in a smaller part. It may well be stronger applause than some actors in more important roles get later—meaning that you've stolen the show to some extent. The actor in the bigger role will know full well that you've registered better with the audience. That should be sufficient ego gratification. Order of appearance during a curtain call isn't everything, and the audience always has the last word.

"Just Run It"

There comes a time, hopefully before the actual dress rehearsal, when the director will say, "Just run it tonight." That means that as much as he or she may feel like charging up on stage and shaking people in the middle of the run-through, he or she is going to keep hands off, and leave it to the actors to get through it as best they can. It's an important psychological moment. Now the cast is almost on its own.

Places, Everyone!

Learn to cope when an actor is slow to enter in a scene. Every actor has to deal with this calamity sooner or later. You may have to deliver a few lines on your own, or to make a big deal of rearranging the flowers in a vase or of looking at the books in a bookcase.

No Stopping for Anything

If the director tells the cast to just run it, that means no stopping for anything. If you forget a line, make something up if you can, or just plunge ahead to whatever comes next and hope that the other actors can pick up the pieces. If your wig falls off, pick it up off the floor and keep going. Like that Off-Broadway Cyrano mentioned earlier, you may have to stuff your errant nose in your pocket, but to keep going remains the goal.

"We Got Through It Alive"

With luck and hard work, final dress rehearsals, with or without an invited audience, can be thrilling because everything finally falls into place. But sometimes just the opposite occurs, and everything seems to fall apart. There is an old saying in the theater that a bad dress rehearsal means a good opening night. And it can work out that way. With luck, both will go well, the dress rehearsal good enough but with room to improve, and opening night managing to do just that, with everyone attaining new heights.

When the dress rehearsal is truly a mess—and that does happen—don't despair. Just say, "Well, we got through it alive." You're still standing, after all; no limbs were broken, and that means that, as Scarlett O'Hara so famously said in *Gone With the Wind*, "Tomorrow is another day." Another day to get it right.

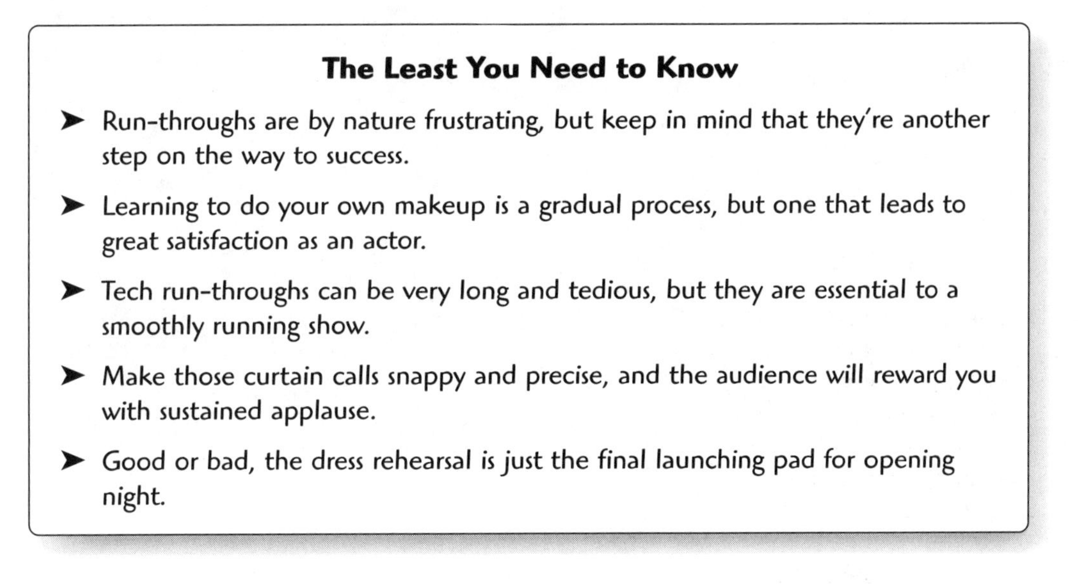

The Least You Need to Know

- Run-throughs are by nature frustrating, but keep in mind that they're another step on the way to success.
- Learning to do your own makeup is a gradual process, but one that leads to great satisfaction as an actor.
- Tech run-throughs can be very long and tedious, but they are essential to a smoothly running show.
- Make those curtain calls snappy and precise, and the audience will reward you with sustained applause.
- Good or bad, the dress rehearsal is just the final launching pad for opening night.

Chapter 25

Opening Night

In This Chapter

- Coping with opening-night anxieties
- Focusing yourself for the big night
- The magic of a real performance
- The art of accepting compliments

Even if you performed for an invited audience for the final dress rehearsal, you'll find that the opening night of a play is always a very special occasion. In most cases, you'll play before a paying audience, so you're expected to make that outlay of cash worthwhile. If critics are attending, you and your colleagues must persuade them that they should recommend this performance to the general public. All of these factors contribute to a sense of excitement and tension.

In this chapter, we'll take you through the pleasures and rigors of the opening night experience from start to finish. We'll give you tips on dealing with pre-performance nerves; an opening-night performance creates a new state of mind for any actor, and we'll explore the ways it will affect you. Finally, we'll discuss how to react to compliments—or the lack of them—after the show.

"I Feel Sick"

Feeling ill on opening night is more common than you can imagine. A combination of excitement and nervousness can trigger weird bodily responses ranging from upset stomachs to dizziness. Such physical reactions can affect even people who are usually quite calm, and can strike out of the blue. Genuine stage fright, on the other hand, is a condition that some actors must deal with throughout their lives. The good news is that you can learn to deal with whichever challenge you face: either the temporary and often-surprising case of opening-night jitters, or the more deep-seated afflictions of stage fright.

Adrenaline Butterflies

Adrenaline is the popular name for the hormone epinephrine, a natural body chemical. Released by the adrenal glands in situations of tension or fear, adrenaline causes your heart to beat faster, your muscles to tense up, and your lungs to dilate. All of these reactions occur to prepare you to either flee or fight when you perceive danger, which is why scientists call it the "fight-or-flight" response. "Perceive" is the operative word here. Obviously, going out onstage to perform is not dangerous in the sense that a battlefield situation is—or even a skidding car. But you may well perceive it as full of potential danger. Will you remember your lines and your blocking? Will your voice crack on the high note of your big song? Will the jerk playing the burglar finally get the timing right when he pulls out his gun or will you have to improvise? Did the stage manager fix the door you're supposed to slam? Will the phone ring when it's supposed to in Act Two? The things that can go wrong onstage are legion, and it's all too easy to start imagining the worst.

As queasy as it might make you feel in the minutes before the curtain rises, the flow of adrenaline can be your friend onstage. It can heighten your responses in ways that give added zip to your performance. But in the last few minutes before you go onstage, adrenaline can have adverse effects. You don't need it yet, since there's no immediate use for it, and it can cause butterflies in the stomach or light-headedness because you don't have the outlet of performance to use it up. Some actors rarely get truly nervous, but they are the lucky minority. Most get butterflies once in a while. Even someone quite experienced, who's never felt anything other than normal excitement on opening night, may still succumb to nerves under new circumstances. If you've always played secondary roles and are finally playing the lead, you may feel an opening-night tension you've never experienced before. Perhaps, after appearing in several productions, you will find yourself speaking the initial lines of a play for the first time. That can be particularly daunting if you are going to be onstage alone: for example, as the narrator, Chorus, who gives the first speech of Shakespeare's *Henry V*.

Places, Everyone!

Learn to let go. You can control how well you know your role, but by the time you've reached opening night, the last thing you should be thinking about is what other people—actors or technicians—might do wrong. You have no control over that.

Actors have devised dozens of ways to calm down before opening nights, many of them quite odd. One leading man we know would place empty coffee cans behind the sets at either side of the stage on opening night, in case he needed to throw up. In fact, he never did, and claimed that just knowing the coffee cans were there seemed to make them unnecessary. One of co-author Paul Baldwin's leading ladies kept a cooler filled with ice in her dressing room, and would put a piece in a washcloth and press it to the back of her neck under her hair. Others don't need physical props. One friend used to repeat Lewis Carroll's nonsense poem "Jabberwocky" over and over in his head on opening nights. He said that doing so kept him from thinking about the performance to come.

If you're given to butterflies on opening nights, by all means devise your own ritual or distraction to help settle yourself down. Don't worry about seeming peculiar. One way or another, almost all actors behave strangely on opening nights.

Real Stage Fright

Genuine stage fright can be so severe that it makes it impossible for people with considerable talent to perform in public at all. In such cases, the person may feel calm enough beforehand, but once in front of an audience he or she finds it literally impossible to speak. Sometimes a professional therapist can help an actor conquer this kind of affliction. But some very famous performers suffer from serious stage fright and yet still manage to have extraordinary careers. Barbra Streisand suffered greatly from stage fright throughout most of her career, which is one reason why she did so few concert tours; she says that in recent years it has become much less of a problem. Dame Judi Dench has admitted to having stage fright before every performance. Both Dench and Streisand are nervous wrecks before they go onstage, but once they are in front of the audience, they're fine. It's an anticipatory stage fright, rather than the destructive kind that occurs onstage.

If you suffer from the kind of stage fright that occurs before every performance, but which disappears once you're onstage, you'll soon discover personal techniques for getting through it. As with Dame Judi Dench, the joy you experience onstage will more than compensate for the queasiness that precedes it.

Performance Notes

Never leave the backstage area unless you tell the stage manager first. You may be tempted to find some quiet away from all the hubbub, but don't go far if you risk either missing a cue or running into an audience member while you're in full costume.

Personal Space

Most of your fellow actors feel just as nervous as you do before a performance, and they, too, will develop personal routines to get them through it. Unfortunately, some personal routines naturally clash: Some actors fight off opening night jitters by talking a blue streak, while others need quiet to focus on a mundane task that requires considerable concentration. This can be a particular problem in a group dressing room. The actor who needs quiet and wants to work on a crossword puzzle may be troubled by the one who needs chatter, so everyone should be willing to accommodate. If you're the chatty one, talk to cast members willing to listen, but give those who need to be left alone some personal space. Don't try to rope them into the conversation.

Curtain Up!

Although sometimes there isn't a curtain at all—the ancient Greek amphitheaters had no curtains, nor did London's Globe Theater—the expression "curtain up" always means that the show is about to start. You can find velvet or brocade curtains that rise vertically into the space behind the proscenium arch in opera houses and in large professional theaters. Many other theaters, from high school auditoriums to smaller community theaters, have stage curtains split in the middle with two panels that pull back horizontally to either side of the stage.

Thrust stages that place the audience on three sides, and in-the-round theaters with the audience completely surrounding the stage, will have no curtains at all. In these cases, the lights coming up on the stage signify the rise of "curtain," as is true when the director chooses to raise the curtain before seating the audience. But whatever the conditions at a given theater, or for a specific show, the words "curtain up" mean that the play is beginning. And on opening night, those words signal the start of a new adventure for actors and audience alike.

Backstage Tales

The curtain had already been raised when the audience began to take their seats for the original Broadway productions of the musical *Sweeny Todd* and the drama *K2*. The sets for these shows were so different and spectacular that the directors wanted the audience to get used to them before the show began. Both the vast steel set for *Sweeny Todd* (constructed from the structural skeleton of an actual factory) and the mountainous wall of ice for *K2* won Tonys for their respective designers, Eugene Lee and Ming Cho Lee.

Concentration Aids

On opening night, the director usually asks the entire cast to assemble an hour before the show starts to clear up any last minute problems with costumes, makeup, or the set. As the run of the play continues, everyone will have to be present and accounted for a half-hour before curtain. In some cases, the director may give an actor who appears only in the second act permission to arrive later than that. Others, particularly those with complex makeup to put on, may arrive long before the stage manager calls "half-hour." Actors have a variety of ways to prepare for the curtain to rise. Some may do almost no preparation at all. Cool as cucumbers, they are capable of interrupting a whispered conversation about a new movie to enter directly onstage, turning on their performance mode and slipping into character almost instantly. Other actors often envy these performers and regard them with considerable annoyance. At the other extreme, some actors spend the final half-hour before going onstage slowly working themselves into character. That process often begins as they look into the mirror to apply their makeup. The changes that they make to the contours of their faces help them attune themselves to the mindset of the characters they're playing. The very act of making up serves as a concentration aid.

Still others may wait until the stage manager calls "10 minutes" or "five minutes" before settling down and working themselves into character. All that many actors need do at this point is to go over an important speech in their minds or simply play their first scene through in their heads, paying less attention to the particular lines than to the emotional arc of the scene.

In some cases, an actor may not even consider the scene as a whole, but rather ease into the mood of his or her character at the start of the scene. Some moods are easier to attain than others. If you're playing a character like Dapper in Ben Jonson's *The Alchemist*, for example, it's not difficult to start feeling that character's great anticipation, since it is so in tune with the excitement of making a splashy comic entrance. On the other hand, someone playing Viola in *Twelfth Night* may have more difficulty in capturing the mood of a person amazed to be alive after a shipwreck but fearful that her beloved brother has drowned.

Backstage Tales

Some actors go to considerable lengths to get into character. One actor we know who was playing the antisocial Judd in *Oklahoma!* at a summer theater, went outside and rolled around in the dirt before each show. Some other members of the cast thought that was a bit silly, but it worked for him.

You're on Your Own

Although directors usually try to get through the final dress rehearsal without a stop, the show is often brought to a halt once or twice by technical glitches. Thus, opening night may be the first time a show truly runs straight through from beginning

Performance Notes

Never try to anticipate problems onstage. If another actor has been having difficulty with his or her lines in a scene, it's tempting to think about how you would handle the situation. But if that actor does forget a line, it will inevitably be the one you thought he or she had down cold, and hadn't prepared for. What's more, anticipating such problems can lead to confusion on your own part. Improvising in advance doesn't work.

to end. Although backstage personnel, from the stage manager to the prop manager, will be doing their best to keep everything moving smoothly, if something goes wrong onstage it's up to you to struggle through as best you can. If you forget a line, another cast member may know the scene well enough to feed it to you in a whisper, but you can't count on it. You may have to improvise if you or someone else drops a line.

You can't allow a missing or malfunctioning prop to bring the show to a stop, either. You just have to figure out a way around the problem.

A stage performance can be compared in some ways to driving a car. Even if you do everything correctly, another driver (actor) may make a mistake. So, you must always be ready to adjust your driving (performance) to what's happening around you at the time. For example, suppose Susan has a two-minute speech just before you enter a scene. If she suddenly drops a couple of sentences, and 30 seconds, from the speech, you still need to be ready to make your entrance on the cue line—or, if she drops the cue line itself, to enter anyway. That means paying close attention to what's happening onstage as you wait for an entrance. If Susan drops 30 seconds and you enter 30 seconds late, it becomes your fault as well as hers. In fact, audience members might not even notice Susan's dropped lines, but they will notice that there's a strange gap before your entrance. In that situation, you'll get the blame. You always have to look out for yourself.

Sudden Magic

Despite all the nervous tension that accompanies opening nights, that first performance before a full house is always magical. There is nothing like a live audience. If you're in a comedy, the sound of laughter will lift you into another realm. You will suddenly feel "home free." All that hard work is paying off, and some part of you will want to echo Sally Field's famously effusive Oscar acceptance speech: "You like me! You really like me!"

If you're acting in a serious drama, you won't have laughter to give you wings (although some dramas do have funny moments as well), but you will be able to sense the rapt attention of the audience. Onstage, you can sense the concentration and emotional empathy of an audience. When a scene is working perfectly, the audience seems to breathe as one. Hundreds of people hang on your every word, and that, too, will help lift the level of your performance. There is an emotional give-and-take between actor and spectator that increases the depth of the experience for both.

Backstage Tales

Opening night audiences are special unto themselves. On Broadway, critics are often invited to attend any of several final previews so that they can meet their deadlines with more ease. But the critics still come on opening night to college and community theater productions, adding to the cast's desire to shine. More important, however, real theater lovers turn out for opening nights. They want to see the show regardless of what the critics end up saying, and their enthusiasm for live theater is infectious. Opening night theater audiences are almost always good audiences.

Alive in the Moment

As scene after scene flows by on opening night, the actors can often feel the play or musical coming alive in a new way. Things that had never quite jelled before become seamless. A new sense of the whole develops, and the stage reality fully asserts itself. You, the actor, are another person in a different world, living out a story that seems fresh and urgent. Even the little things that do go wrong on opening night—and there are usually a few—are surmounted by what seems an amazing ease. You are, at last, completely in the moment. There is nothing quite like it; it's a reward in itself, greater than any amount of subsequent praise can equal.

Places, Everyone!

Giving opening-night token gifts to fellow cast members is a tradition that many actors follow (though don't feel obligated). However, choose your gifts with care: Some people are allergic to certain flowers, and chocolate coats the throat, sometimes causing vocal problems.

Accepting Compliments

The general public usually suspects that actors are vain and greedy for both attention and praise. They balance this suspicion by a tendency to idolize those actors with star charisma. Audiences may admire even supporting actors for their talent, at all levels of the theater, from grade school to Broadway. "I could never do that," the fan thinks, looking upon the actor with a degree of awe.

Actors themselves face a much more complex reality. Some who demand worshipful attention are, in fact, very insecure. They need the praise to offset their own self-doubt. But many other actors have trouble accepting praise, especially face-to-face.

In a few cases, this may be a matter of genuine modesty. Sir Alec Guinness was as noted for his modesty as Sir Laurence Olivier was for his lack of it. But the main reason why many actors have trouble accepting praise is that they aren't fully satisfied by what they've achieved. They know they gave a good performance, but feel that it could have been better. That makes it difficult to be gracious when fans come backstage and fawn over them.

And then there is another problem. Some actors really are shy. Onstage, they may seem like the most outgoing people in the world. They appear utterly in command. But offstage it's different. They have no lines to speak, no character to play, and are thrown back on themselves. They feel ill-at-ease with people they don't know well, and they want to hide. For such actors, accepting compliments can be more of an ordeal than the performance they have given onstage.

Tired as You Are, Smile!

Even for the star actor who doesn't lack in self-esteem, receiving the public after a performance, especially on opening night, can be a trial for the simple reason that the actor is exhausted. Performing any lead role takes a great deal out of an actor. It may be obvious to an audience that playing King Lear has to be extremely tiring, but that role is no more taxing than playing Fanny Brice in *Funny Girl*, which requires singing 16 songs.

Backstage Tales

When Emlyn Williams' semi-autobiographical play *The Corn Is Green*, which is about a remarkable schoolteacher in a Welsh mining town, began its Broadway run in the late 1930s, the opening-night audience gave it a standing ovation that went on for 20 minutes. The play's star was the legendary Ethel Barrymore, who gave one of her greatest performances. After she had taken 16 solo curtain calls, Miss Barrymore held up her hands for silence and uttered a few words that sum up what many actors feel at the conclusion of an opening night. "That's all there is," she said quietly. "There isn't any more."

After an opening-night performance, family and friends will come to congratulate you. Some people you don't even know might rush up and congratulate you. Praise is wonderful, of course, but if you have played a large role, you may wish everyone would simply vanish. You probably still have an opening-night party to go to and you've very tired already. But, in fact, you still have another performance to give.

It's now your job to smile and to say, "Thank you," and "I'm so glad you enjoyed it," and, "Yes, it's a terrific part." Some actors, as we've noted before, love all this stuff, and can hardly get enough of it. But those of you who are shy offstage, or hardly know what to say when people tell you they've never been so moved, must pull yourselves together and be gracious. It's expected; it's actually part of your job. Some very good actors hate dealing with compliments so much that they practically snarl at the well-wishers, but that's not only rude, it's also unprofessional. So smile, even though you'd like to scream.

"What Did She Mean by That?"

Of course, not everyone who comes backstage is going to heap praise on you. Sometimes the performance hasn't gone well (yes, that happens to everyone eventually). Sometimes the play really is pretty awful. But there your friend Muriel, or your co-worker Stan, stands anyway. They know that you expected them and so they're backstage to say ... something. And what comes out of their mouths may not be exactly what you want to hear. For example, you may hear this:

1. "You were really pretty good." (And you think, "Did he expect me to be bad?")
2. "I could hear every word you said." (And you think, "I would hope so, sitting there in the second row.")
3. "You were so pretty up there that I hardly recognized you." (And you think, "Yes, Aunt Doris, I know you think I'm the plain one.")
4. "It's too bad you didn't have a better part." (And you think, "Yeah, tell that to the director.")
5. "Well, that was a learning experience, wasn't it?" (And you think, "Oh, please get me out of here.")

Few of the people who say such things mean any harm. Sometimes they're trying very hard to say something nice because they really did think you were good, but it comes out wrong. So, once again, smile and say "Thank you for coming." That's a lot easier than pursuing the subject. Occasionally, if you're feeling very alert, you can get away with a comeback. A friend of ours playing Oscar in *The Odd Couple* was told by an uncle, "You were pretty good, but I'll still take Walter Matthau." Since Matthau had died the month before, our friend replied, "Yes, it's too bad he's not available anymore."

Never Apologize

You've just played the lead in a new play written by a local playwright. When you first read it, you thought it had possibilities, but the author didn't want to change

Places, Everyone!

Keep your own experiences in mind when you see a friend in a play and you pay them a backstage visit afterward. Tallulah Bankhead claimed to have an all-purpose opening-night comment. "Dahling," she'd purr, "I've never seen anything like it." That covered everything from sheer genius to utter catastrophe.

anything, and the director was a numbskull. Half the actors were miscast and you know you've never been worse. But now the curtain has come down on opening night, and people actually applauded, and to your dismay, a number of people you know are waiting to say hello. Some of them manage to say quite nice things, picking out a moment here and there that, in fact, went fairly well. Even so, your inclination is to start apologizing for how dreadful everything was, including you. Don't do it.

No matter how bad you thought that you—or the play—or the performance—was, keep that fact to yourself. Friends and family, even strangers, have taken the trouble to come back and offer congratulations. Accept them. Remember to say thank you. Remember to smile.

That also holds true if you have had an "off night" in a fine play in which you are, in fact, very good. Don't reply to compliments by saying, "Well, I'm sorry you had to see this performance." Or, "I wasn't at my best tonight." To begin with, the audience may not have noticed the little things that upset you. As far as they're concerned, you were terrific. Don't spoil it for them. In addition, if you start putting down your own performance, most people will feel that they have to compensate by praising you even more, which will only make you feel worse if you did, in fact, have an off night.

Compliments are compliments. Even if they are badly phrased, and sound backhanded, or even if you don't think they were deserved, take them as they were intended. It's opening night, after all.

The Least You Need to Know

- It's not unusual to feel queasy on opening night, and you'll be fine once you're onstage.
- Try different methods to focus before going onstage, and stick with whatever works best.
- Open yourself up to the special magic of an opening night performance.
- Always be gracious when someone compliments you on your performance, no matter what the circumstances.

The Run of the Play

In This Chapter

- Learning how to cope with reviews
- Exploring the dynamics of backstage behavior
- Discovering ways to sustain a high performance level
- Getting the low-down on audience reactions, good and bad

Grade school and high school productions of plays may have only one or two performances, but college and community theater shows are likely to run for at least a couple of weekends, and can often involve an eight-performance-a-week run similar to a Broadway show. In addition to the work involved, you're likely to receive some extra attention: Even high school actors may find themselves reviewed in the school paper, and sometimes the local daily paper as well, while college and community theater productions may receive several reviews from different publications. Both multi-performance runs and the publication of reviews introduce new elements into an actor's life.

In this chapter, we'll give you tips on how to handle the problems reviews can create. It's not only bad reviews of a show, or of a particular actor, that can be upsetting. Good reviews that fail to mention some actors, or lavish praise on just one or two, may cause hard feelings, and we'll tell you how to deal with such situations. When a show has multiple performances, little things can start to get on people's nerves, and we'll discuss ways to keep the backstage atmosphere congenial. We'll make some suggestions about how to keep your performances on a high level during a longer run. Finally, we'll give you some clues about how to adjust your performance for different audiences.

Good Reviews/Bad Reviews

Anyone who performs in public will receive some bad reviews at one time or another, and that includes even the greatest actors, singers, and dancers. Actors who are particularly popular with the public are likely to have piles of bad reviews because critics can't resist taking them down a peg. (The same is true in any of the arts.) You'd better get used to bad reviews, no matter how good you are, because they're inevitable. Fortunately, you'll also receive some rave reviews as well, filled with extravagant praise for your talents. Ironically, you'll often be both praised and panned for your performance in the very same production.

Some actors, including quite a lot of famous ones, claim that they never read their reviews. Usual translation: They have someone else read the reviews to them. Even if an actor truly doesn't know what the reviews have said exactly, he or she will have a good idea of whether they were positive or negative by the way other people behave. Good reviews mean congratulations, while bad ones often result in deep silence on the subject. You really can't escape knowing whether you've been saluted as a genius or dismissed as an incompetent.

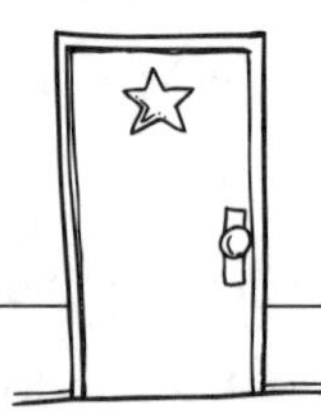

Backstage Tales

As long as they're sufficiently witty, dreadful reviews can become legendary. Journalist and wit Dorothy Parker responded to one of Katharine Hepburn's early Broadway performances by telling her readers that she "ran the gamut of emotions from A to B." The esteemed *New York Times* theater critic Brooks Atkinson loathed Tallulah Bankhead and always seemed to be looking for new ways to insult her. His most famous pan was of her performance as Shakespeare's Cleopatra: "Miss Bankhead barged down the Nile as Cleopatra last night, and sank." That kind of review becomes a collector's item, and is likely to outlive the actor by decades.

It's a Personal Opinion

The most important thing you need to remember about a review is that it reflects just one person's opinion. Whether the critic is a part-time writer for a local paper or a world-renowned journalist, what he or she writes is just that individual's view of things. It's worth keeping in mind that George Bernard Shaw spent years writing theater criticism, and constantly tore Shakespeare's plays to pieces. A bit of jealousy or an excess of competitive zeal, perhaps? And when it comes to reviewing actors, theater, movie, and television critics have their favorites and those they can't stand, just like everyone else. They never stop trying to promote their favorites and debunk the talents of those who rub them the wrong way, and sometimes they do it just because they know there are other critics who disagree with them.

Don't think for a minute that things are any different when it comes to reviews of college or community theater productions. The small-city critics also have their prejudices, which can affect how they review the play itself or a cast member. What's more, local critics sometimes steal from reviews that appeared in major publications when a play first opened on Broadway. They may swipe a positive phrase here and there, but more often it's a negative one. Co-author Paul Baldwin once appeared at a North Carolina dinner theater, in a musical that a local critic referred to as a "so-so sandwich." Paul knew exactly which review of the original production that the local critic stole it from.

Places, Everyone!

After you get a bad review, just move on. There's no point in writing a letter to the editor complaining about a review, either because it seems biased or because it has "borrowed" from an earlier review. The local critic will always have an excuse—and is likely to slam the letter writer even harder the next time they have a chance to do so. Don't pick fights with critics: They're almost unwinnable.

Because theater reviews are personal opinions, you need to learn to take them with a grain of salt. That goes for the good ones as well as the bad ones. Many actors actually learn to cherish certain bad reviews. When co-author Paul Baldwin starred in a very successful production of the musical *On the Twentieth Century* at a summer theater, all the reviews were good. But one critic, knowing that the musical was based on a 1930s movie starring John Barrymore and Carole Lombard, remarked that although Paul acted and sang the role splendidly, he looked more like Lionel than John Barrymore. Since Paul was tall and slender like John, rather than heavy-set like Lionel, he was able to find this funny, and is more likely to repeat it than any good review he ever got. A sense of humor about reviews is valuable to any actor.

You Weren't Even Mentioned?

Some actors would almost rather get a bad review than not be mentioned at all. Critics necessarily pay close attention to the production's lead actors, but strange things happen when it comes to secondary characters. Let's say you have the third largest role in a play, but a critic doesn't say a word about you, instead giving a sentence or two to cast members with much smaller roles. This happens all the time. Often it's because an actor is playing a largish but essentially thankless role. In reviews of *Hamlet* for instance, critics seldom mention Horatio even though he appears in numerous scenes, while they almost always recognize the Gravedigger, who appears in only one, in their reviews. While it's dispiriting to play a sizable role and be totally ignored, there's no use fretting about it. Look at it this way: You obviously did your job or the critic would have said something nasty, calling you "a weak link," or worse. There is a school of thought that there's no such thing as bad publicity, but it's wiser to adopt the view that "no news is good news."

Uh-Oh, They Liked You Best

Any actor wants a good review, and one that says you were the best in the show is even more exciting. But getting the best reviews for a production can create tension as well as joy. It's one thing to get the best review if you're the star of the show or one of several leads, all of whom were well received. But things change if you are singled out as the "only member of this cast who got the Noel Coward style right," for example. Or you might have a fairly small but showy part and be touted for "stealing the show," while the rest of the cast gets middling notices. Such situations can spell trouble with other cast members.

It's not that any of your colleagues will blow up at you. Most cast members will congratulate you on the good review. But at least a few people might get their noses out of joint. They may feel that they were just as good as you were and, thus, can't understand why you were singled out. They may be annoyed that you're getting so much attention for a small part when they've worked much harder in far more difficult roles. As a result, you may get teased: "Ah, here comes the real star," someone will say.

Just smile if that happens. Don't try to flatter the person who's teasing you by saying that everyone knows how good he or she is, and that the reviewer must be crazy. He or she isn't likely to believe it, even if you're sincere. A shrug and a smile work much better.

Life Isn't Fair

You gave a terrific performance as Laurey in *Oklahoma!* and the actor playing Curly opposite you was just as good. And that's not just vanity; people who'd seen the show stopped both of you to tell you how wonderful you were. But as far as the reviewers were concerned, the main reason to see the production was the girl playing Ado Annie. She was certainly funny, if you like mugging, but come on! It's just not fair that she got so much attention!

Come on, yourself. Ado Annie is a classic scene-stealing role. If somebody is good in it, she's always going to walk away with the reviews. The fact that she has about a fifth as much to do as the actors playing Laurey and Curly is beside the point. They've got to sing beautifully but, like many romantic leads, they're not wildly interesting characters, and Ado Annie is fascinating. Life isn't fair. If you're going to be an actor, you need to get used to that fact.

Backstage Tales

When *The King and I* originally opened on Broadway, its star was Gertrude Lawrence. She received splendid notices as Anna, but the most ecstatic reviews went to Broadway newcomer Yul Brynner as the King of Siam. Lawrence soon became ill with inoperable cancer. When she informed the producers of her illness, Lawrence said she would stay with the show as long as possible on one condition: When she left, Brynner's name would appear above the title with whomever took over her role. She played Anna until her strength gave out, and died two weeks after leaving the show. Brynner had not been told how ill Lawrence really was, and was astonished when his name went up in lights along with that of the new Anna, Patricia Morrison. Forever after, he paid tribute to the class, courage, and generosity of Gertrude Lawrence.

Dressing Room Decorum

The show is up and running. Opening night went amazingly well. The reviews were good, even if some people did get more than their fair share of the glory. You've got three weeks of performances ahead of you. If you're going to get through that period smoothly, you need to keep a few things about backstage behavior in mind.

Having been through rehearsals with the cast, you will know most of your fellow actors fairly well. But there may be a few people you remain unacquainted with, especially if you're in a large cast. In addition, the cramped backstage of most theaters creates an enforced intimacy that is quite different from the rehearsal atmosphere. Crammed into a small space, it's all too easy for people to get on one another's nerves in unexpected ways.

Little Annoyances

Some actors get so wired before a performance that they talk incessantly, tell tired jokes, laugh too loudly at tired jokes, and generally behave like braying donkeys, which, needless to say, can get tiresome in tight quarters very quickly. If you have a tendency to indulge in such shenanigans, try to get a grip. Otherwise you're going to get told to please shut up, and the please may soon be left out if you don't.

Then there are those who prefer musical air pollution, but be warned: Boom boxes are not welcome backstage. Even if you use earphones but keep the sound too high, there are plenty of singers whose voices will spill over into the room. Aretha Franklin is a great singer, but most people aren't going to want to hear her screaming "Respect" while trying to get into character for a performance. Show a little R-E-S-P-E-C-T yourself.

Every cast seems to have at least one habitual borrower. Borrowers have forgotten to bring their script, and ask to see yours so they can check the line they stumbled over last night. (Of course, they should have done this long before getting to the theater.) Or they're out of eye shadow and want to borrow yours. Can they have just a sip of your diet soda? Will you lend them your hairbrush, since theirs has disappeared?

We all forget to bring things, or run out of something, on occasion. And most actors are very generous about helping out. But if you make borrowing a habit, you're going to make yourself unpopular.

Backstage Tales

One of the productions of *Man of La Mancha* in which co-author Paul Baldwin played Don Quixote was such a hit that the producer decided to cancel another show and repeat *La Mancha* after running one intervening show. Paul agreed to come back on two conditions: One was a modest raise in salary; the other was an agreement that he didn't have to share a dressing room again with the actor playing Sancho, who borrowed everything in sight and often forgot to give things back. The woman playing Aldonza was willing to share Paul's dressing room instead, and that worked beautifully. Sancho's feelings were hurt, but Paul simply said, "I'm sorry, but my mustache comb is mine." Sometimes you have to be blunt.

Neaten Up

Some people are neatniks, while others are slobs. But in a shared dressing room situation, everyone has to be neat or chaos will ensue. You can't leave your shoes or your pants or your purse in the middle of the room. Some people may have to make quick costume changes during the show, and there mustn't be anything for them to trip over.

In a shared dressing room, you'll likely have a chair at a long table with mirrors on the wall; that's where you'll do your makeup. The table space allotted to you may be little more than the size of a large place mat. You should have a kit or a box (even a shoebox will do) at one side of that space to keep your makeup in. Some actors take their makeup home with them between performances because, every now and then, makeup gets stolen. A friend of the authors likes to tell the story of Ralph, who was nicknamed the "makeup raccoon." Ralph loved makeup, not just to put on but also to eat. He would stay behind after the other actors left and help himself to greasy snacks. People kept wondering why their makeup was dwindling so fast until another actor went back for something he forgot and caught Raccoon Ralph in the act.

Performance Notes

If your costume needs washing or cleaning, take it to the costume manager (or the assistant stage manager in charge of such matters) right after a performance. The same goes for a costume that has a rip in it and needs to be repaired. Don't wait until just before the next performance to show up with a torn hem or a shirtsleeve that's coming loose. If a prop is falling apart, tell the property manager about it immediately as well (the moment you come offstage if possible).

After the curtain comes down at the end of a performance, you'll have some chores to do. Straighten up your makeup space and hang your costume up in the spot you've been allotted for it. Put any costume shoes right under it. Taking such care will save wear-and-tear on the costume itself, and make things easier for you and everyone else the next day.

If you have any costume changes to make in the course of a show, have everything neatly laid out in the dressing room before the performance begins. If it's a quick change you make just offstage with someone's help, it's still your responsibility to see that everything is ready before the show starts. Neatness is imperative when it comes to costume changes. You don't want to go onstage with only one shoe because you've misplaced the other.

If you're going to need props quickly during the show, you can place them just offstage in the same place before each performance. But be sure to pick a spot where no one else is going to trip over them while making an entrance. Remember that keeping the backstage neat and safe is everyone's job, and you have to do your part before and after every performance.

Decibel Levels

We've already talked about keeping the noise level down in the dressing rooms. That's a matter of not driving other cast members crazy. But once the show is under way, it's also vital to keep offstage noise to a minimum. How much whispered conversation you can conduct backstage will depend on the particular set and the acoustics of the theater. A full living room set that has actual doors will obviously muffle offstage noise more a set with little or no furniture and mere side curtains. If someone tells you a whispered joke just offstage, don't laugh out loud because laughs carry especially easily into the audience. Hang on tight to props offstage, too; a dropped sword will make a clatter that startles the audience and disrupts the scene that's taking place. We know an actor who used to blow his nose just before going onstage. He sounded like a foghorn in a waterfront drama, which was hardly an appropriate sound effect for *Camelot*. Avoid making any noise, especially any that are at odds with what takes place onstage at that moment.

Warming Up

Voices are instruments, and just like violins, they need to be tuned. However, while an orchestra is permitted to make final adjustments onstage or in the orchestra pit after the audience is seated, actors do not have that luxury. Obviously, the cast of a musical is going to have to do more to warm up their voices than will be necessary for the actors in a straight play. But warming up the voice is often wise for any kind of production, and an actor playing a big role in a Shakespearean play or a highly emotional modern drama may have to do more work in this regard than most.

Keeping the Engine Tuned

If you are a singer, you will have to learn to warm up *a capella*, without music. If everyone played tapes of their music while warming up, the competing tunes would throw you all off. Using earphones would defeat the purpose, since you wouldn't be able to hear your own voice. Some singers vocalize using scales, while others prefer to sing verses of songs. You may find another cast member with whom you can warm up, throwing notes back and forth, but don't count on it—warm-up exercises tend to be a bit particular to the singer. Some actors in straight plays find that they can warm up their voices sufficiently simply by talking in a normal voice, but others like to run through a few lines in a projected stage voice. Another technique is to do "hums." That means humming from the diaphragm right up through the nasal passages. It's a quiet way of readying yourself vocally. Taking very deep breaths, holding them, and then letting them out several times over can be helpful, regardless of any other techniques that you use. The deep breaths open the lung passages and get the blood flowing.

Places, Everyone!

Warm up your voice before leaving the dressing room for the immediate backstage area so that the sound doesn't carry into the audience; it's better to do it earlier than later. With several actors warming up simultaneously, it will add up to a considerable cacophony, but that's something you have to get used to.

It's Crowded Back There

Dancers and actors playing roles that require a great deal of physical activity will need to warm up their bodies in addition to their voices. The generally cramped spaces backstage make it difficult to do anything more than stretching exercises. For that reason, many dancers get to the theater early so that they can use the stage itself to warm up with actual dance movements before the doors open to the audience.

Good Audiences/Bad Audiences

During the run of a play, expect striking variations in audience response at different performances. First, different people make up each audience, creating a different dynamic. Second, even if the same people filled the same seats at two different performances, chances are they would be in different moods or see things in a different way. And actors also have their good and bad days, and some performances simply work better than others. But even a fine performance can get a lackluster audience response while an off-kilter one seems to go over extremely well. You never know what will happen.

All kinds of things can affect how an audience reacts. Bad weather that made the trip to the theater difficult may cause an audience to be unresponsive at first. But that same audience, once it has settled in and decided that the trip was worthwhile, can prove particularly attentive.

Audiences also can be initially cool when it's a new play or one they've heard little about. In such cases, it's up to the cast to sell the production. But a play or musical that's had a lot of hype can lead to inflated expectations, in which case the response may be excited at first but then less so as disappointment sets in. That kind of audience may eventually realize that they were expecting too much, and then warm up again.

If the audience is made up of theater parties—groups that often travel together to see plays—they may exhibit a herd instinct. And while a Tuesday night audience may be smaller, it can also be especially enthusiastic because it consists of people who really want to see the show, while a Saturday night full house can be distracted, perhaps a trifle inebriated, and difficult to please. The variations are almost endless, and present a continuing challenge to the cast.

Places, Everyone!

Take into account audiences that have special needs such as hearing loss. Sometimes, an expert will stand at the side of the stage and sign the dialogue for a deaf audience, for example. The audience may be a beat slower in laughing under such circumstances, but these theatergoers can ultimately prove to be particularly enthusiastic. It's a very special event for them.

They Paid Their Money

Regardless of how an audience reacts, actors must always remember that these people paid good money to see the show. It's your job to give the best performance you can in any situation. Just because one audience doesn't laugh at the jokes as much as others have, you can't decide to slack off. Nor does an audience's constant rustling and coughing at a serious play give you an excuse to "walk" through your role with less-than-usual intensity. You need to keep in mind that the difficult audience will later tell their friends what they thought of the show. If you keep the performance at a high level, that word-of-mouth may be better than you might expect.

In addition, quite a number of people in what seems to be a bad audience may be having a very good time and are very impressed. Some of them may be important—people with clout who can influence ticket sales. Even the least responsive audience will have some members who are right with you. Perform for them—they're always there someplace, and they deserve your best.

Matinee Blahs

Matinee audiences are different from evening audiences, and mid-week matinee audiences are often not at all like Saturday or Sunday matinee audiences. That can throw actors, especially inexperienced ones.

Midweek matinees often have a large number of older women in the audience. Someone in the cast will say, "A lot of blue-hairs today," referring to the blue rinse that was once so popular with women whose hair had turned white. This is more of an affectionate term than a put-down, since older women are often a very good audience, particularly for comedies. New actors may start out thinking that older women make a boring audience to play to, but they soon discover that a group of women will laugh more often and more loudly, particularly at risqué jokes, than they will if their husbands are with them. Still, there can be a letdown in the level of a performance at midweek matinees, simply because you and your cast will have performed the previous night and will have to give another one that evening. That problem also develops at Saturday matinees, which are likely to have numerous family groups, sometimes including quite young children. Families also like Sunday matinees, and since that's the last performance of the week, with a day off coming up, actors sometimes slack off for those as well.

Places, Everyone!

Give it your best at every performance, evening or afternoon. Both authors have attended all too many matinees, even on Broadway, when it was clear that the cast was just going through the motions, and not working very hard. It's always a big disappointment when a star you admire seems to be performing at half-wattage. You came to see a 150-watt performance, not a 75-watt one. Keep that in mind when you perform a matinee.

While sheer fatigue may cause a less-than-vibrant matinee performance, sometimes the problem stems from the fact that some actors feel that a matinee audience doesn't really deserve their best. That's dead wrong. Not only did those people pay to see the best show you can give, but also, those kids who attend the

Saturday and Sunday performances are the adult theater fans of the future. Baseball great Joe DiMaggio was once asked why he hustled so much on the field even at the end of his career, when he was often playing with injuries. He replied that he thought about the kid in the stands who was seeing him for the first time, and did his best for that reason. Actors should take that lesson to heart.

Adjusting the Performance

Because audiences differ from performance to performance, actors must learn to adjust their own work based on each audience's reaction. This is fundamentally a matter of instinct, although it requires technical assurance to make it work. Some actors have such a strong instinct for adjustment to the audience that they can do it almost from the start. Others must learn how to do it as they become more experienced.

You should keep some basics in mind, however. If audience reaction seems flat, and the jokes aren't getting their usual quota of laughs, for example, it usually means that the cast needs to pick up the pace. You'll have to eliminate the pauses that would ordinarily occur after laugh lines, and pick up your cues more rapidly. Even the speed with which longer speeches are delivered should be increased slightly, so that the play zips along. That in itself can wake up an audience. The same thing holds true when an audience seems restless at a serious drama. Is a lot of rustling of programs and coughing going on? Pick up the pace.

Conversely, if an audience is really with you, it may be necessary to allow longer pauses after laugh lines, because it will take longer for the audience to settle down and pay attention to the next line. This is tricky, because if you don't keep the level of intensity high despite the longer pauses, you can lose an audience. A longer pause for a laugh means that the next line must be hit a little harder than usual. With a serious play, a raptly attentive audience makes it possible to put extra nuances into your performance. When the audience is truly with you, subtleties can score, which another audience might miss.

When a show opens, it's "set," which means no further changes in blocking or role interpretations will occur. (In a long-running Broadway hit, of course, things may change some when new actors join the cast as replacements, but that is seldom a concern for the much shorter runs of amateur productions.) But the fact that a show is set doesn't mean that it's set in concrete. Any production of a play or musical is a living organism, and it must have room to breathe.

Performance Notes

Whenever it's possible, and affordable, actors should make an effort to see productions they like more than once. Watching a show for a second time with a different audience can be an important learning experience. Not only will you understand more clearly why certain actors are particularly effective in their roles, but a second viewing will also give you a chance to see how the cast adjusts to the responses of a new audience.

You will always cross the stage on a certain line during the run of the play, and your character will always have the same outlines. But within that structure, you'll make small changes in emphasis from performance to performance. You and the rest of the cast will take some scenes faster because of the audience response, while you'll slow down others; you'll find that it's a constant give-and-take between actors and spectators on each particular day. Such subtle changes not only fine-tune the performance for a given audience, they also help keep the entire production fresh and seemingly brand new, from the first performance to the last.

The Least You Need to Know

- Always remember that reviews are personal opinions.
- During the run of a show, do your best to observe the rules of decorum that keep backstage a happy place.
- Make sure to warm up properly so that you keep your performance on the same high level.
- Learn how to adjust your performance to the responses of each new audience.

Part 6

What Is a Professional?

Although many amateur actors are perfectly content to be just that from start to finish, others think quite often about the possibility of becoming a professional. The temptations of fame are present at any age. Even grade school kids may look at a television show in which children are at the center of things and think, "Hey, I could do that." In high school, teen-oriented movies are likely to trigger fantasies of stardom. If you're a leading actor on a college campus, everyone (including you!) will wonder if you'll take the risk of heading for New York or Hollywood. Most community theater actors made the decision to remain an amateur some time ago—but every now and then you may think to yourself, "What if …?"

In this final section of the book, we'll explore the pros and cons of trying to make a career of acting. But we're not going to give you any false hopes here. Professional acting is a tough life, and talent alone is no guarantee of success. So, we'll also be talking about what it really means to be a professional, and why so many amateurs rightly consider themselves to be pros. If you still think that acting as a career is the right answer for you, we'll present the basic information that can get you started on your way. The choice, of course, is up to you.

Experience and Dependability

In This Chapter

- Finding out when an amateur is really a professional
- Understanding the true meaning of acting excellence
- Exploring the pleasures of local stardom
- Recognizing the benefits of audience loyalty

Strictly speaking, being a professional actor only means that you belong to a union and get paid to perform. It doesn't guarantee that you'll get your name in lights on the theater marquee or above the title in the program. Plenty of professional actors haven't played a starring role since college, if then. More importantly, some professional actors aren't very good, and a lot of amateur actors performing in college or community theater productions are absolute dynamite. Professionalism, when you look at the broader picture, is about a lot more than a union card and a paycheck.

In this chapter, we'll tell you what it means to be a true professional in amateur theater. You'll learn why so many amateur actors are told they're as good as—maybe even better than—the "name" who plays on Broadway. In fact, being an amateur has some distinct advantages, especially as a star or a character actor, and we'll explain why that's so.

A Lifelong Avocation

A vocation is what you do for a living. An avocation is something you do on the side because you love it. A surprising number of people have become more famous for their avocations than for their day-to-day work. Poet Wallace Stevens and composer Charles Ives, both considered major American artists of the twentieth century, were important insurance executives, for example, but their immortality stems from their creative sidelines. You're not going to get into the cultural history books as an amateur actor, of course—few enough professional actors achieve that status—but thousands of amateur actors do become leading lights in their own communities, widely known and deeply respected.

What's more, an avocation can bring a kind of self-satisfaction and self-respect that's particularly meaningful. Being a good bank teller or a good lawyer is nothing to sneeze at in our complicated world, but being a good actor as well lifts the spirits in a different way.

The Amateur Pro

Plenty of community theater actors are professionals in everything but the name. They behave professionally: They're always on time for rehearsals, they learn their lines with dispatch, they take direction well, and they quickly grasp what a director wants. In terms of acting technique, they're as experienced and proficient as most professionals. They can always be counted on to give a good performance and often an exceptional one. They don't let anyone down, including the audience.

Backstage Tales

As noted before, co-author Paul Baldwin played Don Quixote in *Man of La Mancha* in numerous productions. He was fortunate to have a fine Sancho Panza at his side in all of them. But the very best of them was in a community theater production for which he was hired as an Equity Guest Artist. The Sancho was played by Joe Centini, who worked a full-time job with a supply company but had been acting for 20 years. He was extremely talented, very experienced, and, with huge saucer eyes and great comic timing, born to play Sancho. It was one of the happiest experiences of Paul's career. He was sharing the stage with an amateur who could do it all.

Day-Job Security

Why wouldn't an actor whose talent and responsibility rise to professional levels want to at least give acting a try as a full-time career? The answers to that question vary a good deal, but they tend to fall into three main categories:

- The person has something else he or she wants to do more.
- The person loves to act but not on a full-time basis.
- The person wants a life with greater security.

Let's look at each of these considerations in turn. Many people excel in several different fields of endeavor. Good as they may be on the stage, they have even greater interest in making the most of an entirely different talent. They often make this choice in college—they may star in several shows on campus, but they remain focused on becoming a doctor, a lawyer, a writer, or a research chemist. If you've always had a number-one professional goal, and you have the skills and discipline to achieve it, then you should go for it. With luck and planning, you'll be able to make time to act in community theater productions. If not, it will be because the field you choose will give you great satisfaction and won't leave any time for acting. You had your time in the spotlight in college, and you'll always cherish those memories, but you'll have different priorities to pursue.

If you fall into the second category, you may be certain you'll continue to act in community theater productions throughout your life because you love it so much, but you simply don't want to make acting the central focus of your life. That's common in respect to many talents. Most people know someone who's an extraordinary cook, for example, and it's easy to say, "You should have your own restaurant." But as much as such people love to cook, they don't want to have their lives revolve around it. Thanks, but no thanks, they say. As someone who loves to act, you may feel the same way about an acting career.

Places, Everyone!

Every now and then, someone sets off to New York or Hollywood from college, gets a good role in a week, and is a star within a year. Meryl Streep landed five important roles her first year in New York, but she knows she was lucky. Another Oscar-winning actress, Jessica Lange, spent a lot of time waiting tables at a Greenwich Village restaurant called The Lion's Inn. Don't be fooled into thinking success comes easy by the occasional overnight success story.

The largest group of amateur actors probably consists of people who cherish a degree of security even more than performing. They don't want to spend years working as waiters or temporary office workers while they wait for that big break as an actor. What's more, they're aware that even the best and most popular actors can spend a lot of time out of work. Eileen Heckart won the 1972 Best Supporting Actress Oscar for *Butterflies Are Free*, and said she got a terrific round of applause the next day "from all my friends in the unemployment line." If you think that's very funny but not something you want to be in a position to say, you have a lot of company. For many amateur actors, job security comes first.

As Good as Anyone in the Part

One of the dirty little secrets of the acting business is that some amateur actors are more talented than a surprising number of professionals. A professional career depends on luck, perseverance, and a tough skin, in addition to talent. Some of the most brilliant actors the authors have ever known got nowhere as professionals. When co-author John Malone was at Harvard, he knew a Radcliffe student who bowled over the entire campus with a series of extraordinary performances. Her Rosalind in *As You Like It* remains the finest John has ever seen, even 40 years later. She dropped out of college after two years and headed to New York. Everyone expected to her to have a Tony Award in her pocket within a couple of years. But it didn't happen. She was playing a secondary role on a tour of *The World of Suzie Wong* when the Chicago theater they were playing in burned down. That did it. She dropped out of show business. There are a lot of stories like that, and it doesn't usually take a theater in flames to persuade a young actor to throw in the towel, either. Just plain discouragement will do it.

Others don't even take the chance on a professional career. There were two young women at North Texas State University during co-author Paul Baldwin's college years whose talent he still marvels at, but they didn't even try to turn professional. They do, however, appear in community theater productions.

Better Than Broadway

Because so many people don't take the chance on a professional career, or give it up too soon, the amateur level has an extraordinary pool of acting talent. At community theater intermissions, we've often heard members of the audience say that an actor in the cast was better than the person who played the role when they saw the show on Broadway—and sometimes that means a major Broadway star. It happens all the time. That's one reason why community theaters have such loyal audiences. You never know when you're going to see a performance that takes your breath away.

For the actors good enough to make that kind of impression, hearing such accolades from a local fan brings great satisfaction, of course. But most of them are sensible enough to recognize that there are many reasons why another actor has his or her name above the title on Broadway, and that plenty of people saw the original production and thought the star was the cat's meow.

Talent Is Talent

No one wants to be diagnosed by an amateur doctor or be represented in court by an amateur lawyer. Those are professions that require years of graduate study to excel. But there are many other areas of expertise where natural ability can be every bit as important as formal training. We all know people who have a "gift" for something, whether it's redecorating a room or designing a beautiful garden, cooking an unforgettable meal or building the perfect bookcase. They're just plain talented to start with and they seem to be able to learn their craft by some kind of osmosis. Many actors are like that. Some become professionals; many do not. But they've got it. If you're one of those people, your talent will shine on any stage and it doesn't matter where the stage is located or how many people it seats. You're one of those special individuals whose talent erases the line between amateur and professional.

Performance Notes

If someone tells you that your performance was better than what he or she saw on Broadway, don't argue. You may have seen the show on Broadway, too, and while you know you're very good, you still think that New York actor was terrific. There's no way to get that across without sounding like you're putting yourself down, so just take the compliment and run.

The Local Star

Some stars become household names across the country and around the world, but it takes movies, big movies and important movies, to create the kind of star whose name stays front and center for decades, often well beyond the actor's lifetime. Some television stars become extremely well known for a while, but a couple of failed series can turn them into has-beens in a hurry. There are Broadway stars, but if they generally stick to stage performances, they're often not known by a wider audience. Cherry Jones and Donna Murphy are both Tony-winning Broadway stars of immense talent, but they're only beginning to be known to a larger audience through television and movie appearances.

Off-Broadway stars exist, too, such as Larry Pine, who's something of a legend among New York theatergoers but little known to the general public. And there are local stars, community theater actors whose names and faces are instantly recognized within their city or town, but not known beyond a small geographical area.

The fact that your star shines only in community theater—or Off-Broadway, for that matter—doesn't necessarily mean that you have less talent. Talent is talent, and a star is a star wherever it appears.

Backstage Tales

The biggest names are not necessarily the best actors. Clark Gable and John Wayne are legends, and both won Oscars, but even they knew that their range was fairly narrow. Basically, they played themselves, something that works much better on movie and television screens than it does on stage. Most Hollywood actors of that period recognized that James Mason was a far better actor than either Gable or Wayne, but he didn't enjoy the same kind of popularity, and he never won an Oscar, though he received several critics awards.

Big Fish/Little Pond

We have a friend who's played a wide range of roles in community theater, from Nicely-Nicely Johnson in *Guys and Dolls* to Falstaff. As you might expect of an actor who has played these roles, Jack is a heavy-set man. An appreciative theatergoer once said to him, "This may be a little pond, Jack, but you're certainly the biggest fish in it." Jack smiled, patted his hefty belly, and replied, "What do you mean, fish? I'm a whale."

Jokes aside, Jack is a big fish in his community. It's more lake than pond—he lives in a city with a population of 100,000—and he's perfectly content with his situation. "So many people have urged me to turn professional over the years," he says. "But it's an ocean out there, and even someone of my size can get lost in it pretty easily." Jack doesn't have to fight to get roles; the local directors fight over who's going to get him in a production next, and sometimes a producer will delay a play with the right part for him until he's free.

Beyond having less competition in a smaller pond, you're also likely to get the chance to play more great roles than most professionals. Take the case of Linda. In her 40s, she's a very attractive woman, but, as she puts is, "Michelle Pfeiffer I'm not." Recently she had one of her favorite years. She played, in order, Blanche Dubois in *A Streetcar Named Desire*, the title role in the musical *Mame*, and Gertrude in *Hamlet*. "No professional actress is going to get the chance to do all those roles in single year," Linda notes. Admittedly, Linda is exceptionally talented and versatile, and not every year is that exciting, but she doesn't pine for the "big time" in the least. Would you?

Character Credentials

In community theater, most actors play roles of varying sizes and importance in different productions. If you're the star of one show, you're likely to take a character role in the next. This happens largely because it's important to offer a variety of plays and musicals to the local audience. But such scheduling also means that actors who have a particular gift for Shakespeare or contemporary comedy are likely to play a lead in plays that reflect their strongest suit, and play a secondary character in another kind of play. (Do note that Linda, whose special year we talked about a moment ago, played each of her roles with a different theater group.)

In community theater as on Broadway, however, there are also actors who almost always play character roles. Good character actors have the ability to make a sharp impression with only limited time onstage.

Performance Notes

Actors in their 20s and 30s should take note that in community theater the opportunities to play major roles can increase just at the age when professional actors begin to lose out to younger performers. In the world of community theater, younger actors are often too busy with their careers and families to do as much acting as they'd like, giving middle-aged actors a better shot at the starring roles.

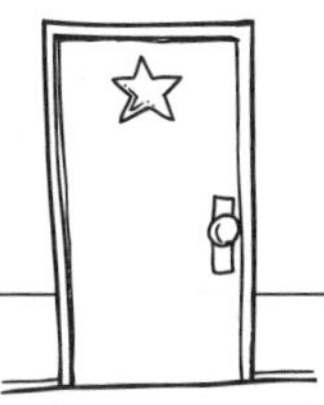

Backstage Tales

Several actors have won Academy Awards for supporting roles that were remarkably small. Judi Dench was onscreen for only eight minutes as Queen Elizabeth I in 1999's *Shakespeare in Love,* but made an indelible impression. In 1976's *Network,* Beatrice Straight had about 10 minutes and only two scenes in which to establish herself as William Holden's embittered wife. Such actors win awards for these tiny roles because people recognize what great skill it takes to give a memorable performance in a very small role. Some stars would never be able to pull it off.

If you're primarily a character actor, community theater is an excellent place to make the most of your skills. Not only will you get parts in a wide range of dramatic styles, in plays set in many different periods, but you'll also engender special audience affection.

Audience Recognition

Because the tickets for community theater productions are a lot cheaper than those for Broadway shows, and because smaller communities have fewer events to draw people away from the theater, you'll probably see many of the same faces in the audience at play after play. That has the happy effect of increasing audience familiarity with, and loyalty to, character actors.

As a character actor, you'll find that you, too, have fans, just like the local stars. People will stop you on the street to say how much they enjoyed your performance just as they do with the leads, although many professional character actors find themselves to be considerably more anonymous. Audiences remember the faces of professional character actors, but are often uncertain of their names. You won't suffer that kind of anonymity in community theater, however, because so many members of the audience will see you in different productions year after year.

Always a Job Well Done

While a small cadre of New York theatergoers have the time and money to see everything that opens on Broadway, most people pick and choose what they will see. Stars draw people to Broadway, and so do hit shows, especially musicals. But New York theatergoers can also be extremely picky. They will avoid a certain show because they can't stand one of the stars (and that can be anybody, since even the most famous and popular actors have their detractors). The "sophisticated set" may boycott certain shows because they regard them as corny. We know a lot of New York theatergoers, for instance, who resolutely refused to see *Shenandoah* during its two-year Broadway run, despite its Tony-winning lead performance by John Cullum. It ran for so long because out-of-towners loved it. (Having played that role many times, co-author Paul Baldwin found that audiences in states like Pennsylvania and North Carolina, where the Civil War has a more immediate historical presence, appreciated it more than those in states farther north.)

Places, Everyone!

Never acknowledge applause unless you're taking your bow at the end of the show. Like the big stars, of course, you will need to hold for a moment before speaking your next line, while the applause dies down. But never break character to acknowledge such applause.

As an actor in community theater, you'll encounter less of this kind of hoity-toity resistance to certain kinds of shows. That doesn't mean that every community theater production will play to full houses. Live theater has hits and misses wherever it is produced, and one production of a particular play or musical can meet with great success while another a few years later does not.

Generally speaking, however, the community theater audience is a remarkably steady and loyal one. If you peek out from behind the curtains shortly before the house lights go down, you will almost always see faces you recognize. They are smiling as they look at their programs because they see the names of actors with whom they're familiar—you among them. They settle back and relax. "Oh good," they say to one another, naming an actor or two, "So-and-so is in this one." Seeing those names—not necessarily in the lead, but playing in some role—they know they're in good hands. They may even applaud a character actor's first entrance.

Because audiences for community theater come to know local actors so well, and come to cherish their experience and dependability, the long-time community theater actor enjoys a special relationship with that audience. You are very much a "somebody" to that audience, even if you usually play smaller roles. It is much more difficult for the professional actor to establish that kind of warm rapport with theatergoers. Certainly, the best-known professional actors have fan clubs; indeed, you can find many such clubs on the Internet these days. But there is still a certain distance between that celebrity and his or her fans. When you're a celebrity in your hometown, however, the experience has a personal dimension that adds immeasurably to the satisfaction of being a first-rate amateur actor, a professional in all but name.

The Least You Need to Know

- Being an amateur actor doesn't mean you can't have every bit as much skill as a professional.
- Local audience members can be quite correct when they say that you were better than the actor was on Broadway.
- Being a big fish in a small pond has real advantages.
- The relationship between the community theater actor and his or her audience can have special warmth to it.

Chapter 28

Getting Paid

In This Chapter

- Getting paid for community theater
- Dealing with professional guest stars
- Negotiating for pay

The two primary differences between amateur and professional actors are union membership in Actor's Equity and payment for work. However, some community actors do, in fact, get paid, though it's usually very little. When a community theater actor gets paid, however, Actor's Equity, the union that represents stage actors, has nothing to do with it. Actor's Equity requires producers to pay actors certain minimum amounts depending on a number of factors, including the kind of theater involved and the category of contract they sign. Above the minimum sum, the actor, or more often his or her agent, can negotiate for a higher salary. We deal with Actor's Equity rules in more detail in Chapter 30, "Getting a Union Card." Here we're concerned with the occasional payments made to amateur actors who have no union affiliation.

In this chapter, we'll explain why, when, and how some community theaters pay their actors. We'll tell you how to defuse any tension that might arise when a few actors are getting paid while others are not. Because some community theaters occasionally hire a professional star through an arrangement with Actor's Equity, we'll look at the different dynamics this creates within the company. Finally, we'll tell you how to negotiate payment or other compensation for performance.

The Community Theater Pittance

No community theater ever pays an actor much, so you should consider the sums more symbolic than realistic. But there are good reasons why paying its actors is far from the theater company's first concern. First, most companies are barely able to pay their bills. A few long-established community theater groups have boards of local citizens who contribute funds toward the yearly budget. Lucky theater groups may have a modest endowment fund, thanks to bequests made to them in the wills of wealthy theater-lovers.

Places, Everyone!

Corners have to be cut anywhere it's possible at community theaters. That's why some actors may have to make do with "sides," pages that contain only their lines and cue lines, instead of a full script. You may also be asked to pay for your own scripts if possible. Don't complain about these things; the production company has good reason for them.

Most community theaters, however, must struggle to make ends meet largely on box-office receipts. That's not easy, and the physical costs of producing a play, especially a musical, tend to eat up what money there is. The cost of sets, costumes, and lighting, even when volunteers do the majority of the work, add up quickly. In addition, they must pay royalties for the right to produce the show in the first place, as well as for scripts and musical scores to purchase or rent.

Who Gets Paid and When

Among professionals, the star always gets paid a lot more than anyone else does. When there are two stars, one may have more perceived box-office clout than another, and thus can demand a higher salary. Although this tends to be the case for the few people who get paid in community theater as well, it doesn't always work that way. Some actors may be very well off, and never ask for money at all, no matter what kind of role they play, which is their way of making a contribution to the theater group. But the producers may pay someone not so well off, even if he or she is not the star. That's especially likely to happen if that actor will have to give up overtime pay in order to attend rehearsals. So, while professional actors are paid according to their perceived ability to sell tickets and in accordance with Equity rules, matters are more flexible in community theater.

Long Service Counts

In general, if you're a young actor starting out in community theater, or even an older one without much previous experience, you're not going to get paid at all. After all, you have a full-time job. Acting is an avocation, not something you do to put food on the table. Those who run community theater companies would like to keep it that way as long as possible, and some simply state flat out that they do not pay actors, period. Others will state that they almost never pay actors, which means that occasionally they do, and you could be one of those so favored.

Backstage Tales

The amount of money paid to professional stars often ends up published in the newspapers, which almost never happens in community theater. One of the most famous mistakes ever made by Broadway producers concerned the contract they signed with Louis Jourdan to star in *On A Clear Day You Can See Forever.* He wasn't working out in the role and left the show during the Boston tryout. A clause in his contract guaranteed him $5,000 a week, whether he was in the show or not, until he got another movie or stage role. Thus, the producers couldn't afford to pay a new star. Jourdan's understudy, John Cullum, took over for very little money, but that role set him on the path to genuine stardom that would eventually bring him two Tony Awards.

Actors who have "paid their dues" with a company, working for free in parts large and small for several years, often eventually end up with a little pay for each show they do, especially if they play the starring role. "Something" is unlikely to be more than $500 altogether—for the rehearsal period as well as for the two to three-week run of the play. Community theater rehearsal periods, as noted before, can last for several weeks, which means that it breaks down to about $12 a day. And the established local actor playing a small but crucial role isn't likely to receive more than $150 tops for the same lengthy period.

You may wonder if such paltry sums are worth worrying about. But even $150 will buy a couple of theater books and several CDs of Broadway musicals. To many community actors with well-paying regular jobs, this is "mad money" that they can spend on whatever frivolity comes to mind. For others who earn less, even a small sum can help plug holes in a budget stretched to the breaking point. One friend of ours who sometimes gets paid very modest amounts says, "I regard those checks

Performance Notes

When the company "almost never pays actors" but chooses to pay you, the producers will probably ask you not to reveal your compensation to others in the cast. Basically that means you'll have to lie, which may make you feel uncomfortable. You'll have to decide that issue for yourself. Some actors look at it this way: If people are rude enough to ask if or what you're being paid, they deserve a lie.

in the same way I did the 10 bucks in a special money envelope I got from my grandmother when I was a kid. Oh, goody!" Another friend, with a more ironic wit, says, "Hey, anything that keeps me from shoplifting."

Places, Everyone!

Keep the IRS in mind when you receive payment for your work in the theater. Some small companies will give you a wad of cash rather than a check. The powers that be in the company don't want any record of such a payment. For legal reasons, including tax considerations, they consider the money a gift, not a payment. If you're paid in cash, view it as a gift, but if you receive a check, you must report it as income on your tax return.

But there's another aspect to getting even these small payments for your work as an actor. Most people in the cast aren't getting anything. They're performing just for the love of it. And although you feel that way, too, and have put in a lot of hours for your love of the theater in the past, it's nice to have some recognition of your efforts. The money itself isn't the important thing—it's hardly enough to get excited about—but the spirit behind the payment means a lot. Getting paid anything at all in community theater is a tribute. It says you're important. It's not so much about the cash itself, but the symbolism that counts.

Working with Equity Guest Stars

As a community theater actor, you may have the chance to evaluate your skills by occasionally working alongside a professional brought in to play a major lead role. (This can also occur at some colleges once in a while, often involving a graduate of the institution who has turned professional.) Actor's Equity allows its actors to work with amateurs under special contracts because that creates more work for members of the union. And the amateur company hopes that having a professional in the starring role will not only draw bigger audiences but also give its actors exposure to the work of an experienced professional.

Sweethearts and Prima Donnas

Equity Guest Artists almost always give a fine performance when they head the cast of an amateur production. They've usually played the role before, and the fact that they know the play or musical so well can be a great help during the rehearsal period. Because they already have a secure sense of what they're doing, it means that you and the other local cast members will have a virtually finished product to play off during rehearsals, which can help speed up your own mastery of a role. In addition, because the director doesn't have to spend as much time working with the guest star, he or she can give the rest of the cast greater attention than usual. The result is usually a superior production, justifying the money spent on the guest artist.

However, not all local casts adore Equity Guest Artists. There may be some resentment at first that the visiting star pulls down a professional-level salary while everyone else gets little or no pay. That usually abates as you recognize the value of having a pro in the cast who knows exactly what he or she is doing. In addition to pay, sometimes problems can arise because of the personality or attitude of the visiting star. Most are glad to have the work—even the best professionals often go through periods of unemployment, as well as recognize that local actors can themselves be extremely talented. Unfortunately, a few will behave as though they're too good for local theater, issue prima donna demands, and end up making themselves quite unpopular.

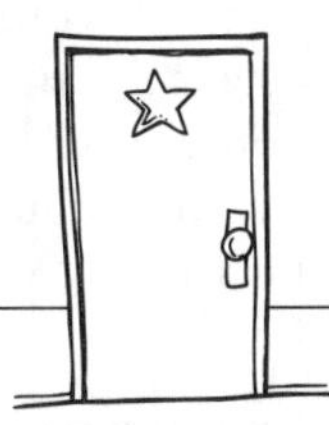

Backstage Tales

The best Sancho Panza co-author Paul Baldwin ever worked with was in a community theater production that he had joined as an Equity Guest Artist. The members of the company treated Paul wonderfully, asking him to their homes for meals, showing him around the lovely Pennsylvania countryside and making him feel very much at home. He told a couple of cast members how grateful he was, and they both replied that they were very grateful, too. It seemed that the previous Equity Guest Artist had been snooty, snotty, and an all-round pain. "You're being treated so well," one of the cast members said, "because you're treating us so well."

A Professional Relationship

Equity Guest Artists are professionals, and they're going to expect you to be, too. Many will be happy to give advice if they know the answer to a question. Since they've usually performed the show before, they may have some tips on creating a scene. You need to be careful, however, not to put them in the position of debating with the director on your behalf. If you don't like something the director asks of you, don't try to manipulate a professional guest into taking your side against him or her. They know better than to do that. It's not professional to play that kind of game.

A guest actor will also expect you to be at your most responsible by showing up on time, learning lines, and getting things right. In the professional theater, actors must follow Equity rules in a number of areas. For example, rehearsals aren't allowed to go on beyond a given time without a break. A halt can be called to rehearsals that extend too late into the night, unless the cast votes to continue. Every professional production has an Equity Deputy, elected by the cast, whose job it is to enforce such rules and to call a cast member on the carpet if he or she gets out of line.

Places, Everyone!

While a guest artist will be delighted if you ask him or her to your home for Sunday lunch before rehearsal, make sure that you plan the afternoon so that everyone will get to rehearsal in plenty of time. And if you offer an invitation that the visitor declines because he or she wants some time to work on a scene alone, or even just to take a nap, don't be miffed.

Professionals are, therefore, used to having things organized well, but they also realize that an amateur production needs to have some leeway in certain matters. Even when they're in a professional show, Equity actors may find it a bit silly to call a vote about continuing when there's only half a scene left to get through. So, they'll accommodate themselves to the fact that community theater rehearsals often run long, especially in the days just before opening. They're not going to stalk off stage just because things are running overtime. But, in return, they have every right to expect that you and other cast members will do your jobs.

Working with a professional guest is a great opportunity. You're certain to learn things, and your own performance may be lifted to a new plane because you're getting so much support and inspiration from the visiting professional. It's quite possible that you'll form a friendship that will last for years beyond the production—that happened to co-author Paul Baldwin several times. But if a member of Equity treats you like an equal, be sure to be just as professional yourself.

How to Negotiate

You've been acting with a community theater for years, playing both leads and smaller roles. You may have worked with an Equity Guest Artist or two, and you've been impressed by them, but they've also told you how good you are. Audiences always give you an enthusiastic response, and you have a lot of fans in the area who've let you know how much they enjoy your work. You've more than paid your dues. Isn't it time you became one of those favored few who sometimes get paid something for playing a role?

You know budgets are tight. But other actors do get paid something sometimes. Isn't it your turn? If only you had an agent to negotiate for you—but you know that's not possible. Agents charge fees for the work they do, a percentage of every contract they negotiate for a client, and they're not going to be interested in the nickels and dimes you're talking about. That means you're going to have to negotiate for yourself.

How Much Do They Need You?

Since you do have to negotiate for yourself, what's the best approach? A lot of adages are concerned with how to get ahead in the world. "Nothing ventured, nothing gained." "It can't hurt to ask." But, in fact, it can hurt to ask, and an ill-timed request can bring about a loss rather than a gain.

Before you decide to ask for some kind of payment for the next community theater show you do, you need to ask yourself some questions. First, are you really at the head of the line in terms of contributions to the company and length of service? Are there other actors who've been around even longer who aren't getting paid a dime? If so, you're not in a good position to make any requests yourself.

Performance Notes

If you don't make much money at your regular job, or have to take time off to rehearse, bring it up with the producer or director. Genuine need is a powerful argument, even if you don't have a long track record with the company.

The second question you need to ask yourself is whether the new role you've been asked to play is important enough, or difficult enough to cast, so that you might have some leverage in asking for a fee. Are you playing a secondary role in this show? Then wait until you've got another starring role. Have you indeed been cast in the lead, but had to fight hard to get it? If you've been called back to audition several times because the director can't make up his or her mind between you and someone else, then you couldn't possibly pick a worse time to bring up the subject of money. The director has someone else to fall back on, a person who's probably terribly disappointed that he or she may not get the starring role. That person will jump at the chance to play it, and won't ask for a dime—the director or producer will tell that other actor that you've requested money in order to prevent him or her from doing the same.

If you aren't negotiating from strength, you'll probably not only fail to get what you want, but spoil your chances of getting a lead for some time to come. When Jack and Jill want money, and producers view them as being out-of-line in asking for it, there's a great temptation to teach them a lesson by offering them only small parts for a while.

There's a third question to ask yourself that is less practical but extremely important. Is the part you've been offered one you've wanted to play for many years? If you finally get your chance to play one of your dream roles—Shakespeare's Richard III or Ibsen's Hedda Gabler, say—this may not be the right time to negotiate, even if you think you're the only one around who can manage the role. Other people will certainly know that this is your dream role—you've been going on about it for years—and that gives the theater the upper hand. The producer can always say, "We thought this role was just what you wanted. We're doing the play as a favor to you. And you

Places, Everyone!

Never assume that a community theater is going to do a play just because it announces it in advance, and even if subscriptions to the entire season have been sold. Even major professional theater organizations that depend heavily on subscriptions, like New York's famous Roundabout Theater, sometimes have to postpone or cancel a production because of a wide range of problems. That's why the ads say, "Plays subject to change without notice."

want money as well?" Or, he or she could also deliver an ultimatum: "Okay, in that case we'll do a different play. This cast would be terrific for several other things."

Let's review the questions you should ask yourself before requesting payment:

- Are you really at the head of the line in terms of length of service?
- Can someone else easily step in to play your role?
- Is this a dream role that you don't want lose, no matter what?

With these exceptions to worry about, is there really any good time to ask for payment? Certainly. If you've been acting with a community theater for a long time, and you're asked to play a starring role that interests you but it isn't one that you couldn't forego if push came to shove, then it's time to bring up the subject of money. A woman we know—let's call her Helen—was asked to take the role of the Mother Superior in John Pielmyers's *Agnes of God*. It was certainly a good role; Anne Bancroft had been nominated for an Oscar for it. But it wasn't a role Helen really coveted. She knew she could do it and that it might be a problem to find someone else locally who was right for it, but she wouldn't feel devastated if it went to another actor. So she said, "I don't know. Of course it's a terrific role and I think I could do some good things with it. But life is a bit busy these days."

The director started trying to sell her on it. Helen listened, and then said, "It's a small cast, isn't it? One set, basically? So it won't cost that much to produce. Is there any chance of getting a little money for this one?"

There was a long pause, followed by a "Maybe," followed by a "Can I get back to you on this?" In the end, Helen played the part and received $250 for it. Very little, really. But it established a precedent, and she now gets $400 for lead roles, some of which she very much wants to play. She picked the right time to ask.

We know a number of other people who get paid a little, $100 to $150, for playing relatively small roles that are difficult to cast. Roger, who's very busy—and everyone knows it—also happens to be as fine an actor as can be found in his locality. He has a special genius for comic roles that require an actor to take over the stage for a scene, such as the Gravedigger in *Hamlet* and the husband of Roxie Hart who sings "Mr. Cellophane" in the musical *Chicago*. Roger has been an audience favorite for two decades in his hometown. He seldom plays anything but secondary roles, but he always gets applause when he comes on stage. The audience knows that they're in for a good time, and word of his always-hilarious performance spreads quickly. He may only be onstage for 10 minutes, but he sells tickets. Therefore, he gets paid every time.

How did Roger start getting paid? Roger said, "No, I don't have time." Know your own worth.

Let's spell out some of the ways to start getting paid:

- Be sure you're really needed.
- Be good enough to be needed.
- Be ready to say no and not regret it.

A Free Program Ad for Your Business?

There's another way of getting paid that won't either upset other actors or risk the wrath of directors and producers. If you're a valued actor who owns his or her own business—a flower shop, a printing shop, a hardware store—ask for a free ad in the program for your business. This kind of "in-lieu-of-payment" arrangement gives you something of value for your time without straining the budget of the theater. Although most programs are filled with ads from local companies who pay for the ad itself or who help to underwrite the theater season, there's usually room somewhere in the program for another small ad for a business owned by a member of the company. Make sure to ask that the ad be run in the program all year, whether you're in a particular show or not.

Backstage Tales

The Barter Theater of Abingdon, Virginia, was founded at the height of the Great Depression in 1933. Robert Porterfield had an idea: What if you opened a professional theater in rural Virginia that the local farmers could buy tickets for with their produce instead of with money? It would put a number of actors to work and provide entertainment for ordinary folks living through very grim times. Vegetables were the usual commodity, but one farmer brought a cow, milked her in front of the theater until he'd met the ticket price, and then sent her home while he went to the show. In later years, Gregory Peck, Patricia Neal, and Ernest Borgnine all appeared at the theater, as did Carole Monferdini, who wrote the foreword to this book.

Persuading a community theater to compensate you by putting an ad for your business in the program for a whole season's worth of shows is barter at its best. The theater gets your terrific performance, and you get some free advertising.

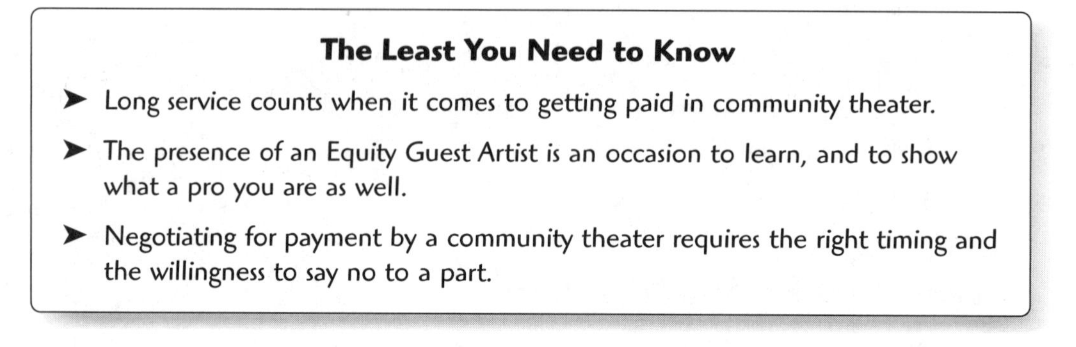

The Least You Need to Know

- Long service counts when it comes to getting paid in community theater.
- The presence of an Equity Guest Artist is an occasion to learn, and to show what a pro you are as well.
- Negotiating for payment by a community theater requires the right timing and the willingness to say no to a part.

Chapter 29

Should You Turn Pro?

In This Chapter

- The life of an occasional professional
- The possibilities of non-Equity summer theater
- The lifestyle of the professional actor
- The financial risks of being a professional
- Judging your readiness for an acting career

Some people know they want to be professional actors at a very young age—and may even start their careers as child actors. Others love acting but know they don't want to make it a career. A third group is tempted but uncertain. This chapter is addressed primarily to the latter group, people who sometimes think they would like to act professionally, but aren't sure they're ready to make that big leap.

In this chapter, we'll discuss some of the factors you'll want to think about as you make a decision to turn professional. We'll also suggest some ways to explore the world of the pro without making a full-scale commitment. You'll learn how to break into the world of local television commercials and the possibility of working at summer theaters that hire non-union actors. We'll talk about the lifestyle of the starting professional actor and the insecurities that are part of it. Finally, we'll show you how to evaluate whether you've got what it takes, in terms of talent and—especially—drive to take a chance on turning pro.

Making Local Television Commercials

Some community theater actors take a small step toward a professional career by appearing in local television commercials. Most often, these are low-budget commercials featuring the company owner making the basic pitch. Actors are sometimes used to play satisfied customers or people with a problem that the local company can solve. You see them on television all the time, especially on local news shows.

Extra Income

Appearing in a local commercial can be fun, but it won't pay much, and you'll receive no residuals—the payments made to professional actors every time a commercial appears on television. You won't have to join a union to appear in such a commercial, but you will have to sign a release stating that you do not belong to a union and won't make any further monetary claims, no matter how often the commercial appears. So, this is strictly a one-shot deal. Local commercials sometimes feature union actors, but not often because it adds to the expense.

If you turn out to be very photogenic, or have a funny bit that attracts attention, the same producer or another might ask you to appear in other commercials. Or, an agent who sees your commercial might be impressed enough to offer to represent you as a professional. That doesn't happen often, but it does occur.

Places, Everyone!

If you do appear in a local commercial, ask if you can have a tape of it. The people who hired you aren't required to do that, but some can be nice about it. If they refuse, tape it yourself, even if that means recording the entire local news for two or three nights until your commercial shows up. It could come in handy later as an audition tape if you decide to pursue that line of work more seriously.

A Sometime Pro

If your appearance in a commercial is a smashing success, suggesting that you have a knack for that kind of acting, you may want to join AFTRA (American Federation of Television and Radio Artists). Doing so will make it possible to appear in commercials that are distributed to a number of markets. That kind of work is more lucrative, and you will get residuals. But be sure to work out the math. Do you think you have a sufficient chance at getting enough commercial work to make payment of union dues worthwhile? (We provide more details about AFTRA in Chapter 30, "Getting a Union Card.")

Non-Equity Summer Theater

Summer theater has a long tradition in the United States. In the decades before television came on the scene in the 1950s, great stars like Gertrude Lawrence and Tallulah Bankhead graced the stages of summer theaters such as Cape Playhouse at Dennis, Massachusetts and Theater-by-the-Sea at Matunick, Rhode Island. These theaters featured new plays potentially on their way to Broadway. Now, far fewer straight plays appear on Broadway, and their route to New York is through year-round regional theaters rather than through summer theaters.

But summer theater still flourishes. New productions of old hits, generally musicals and comedies, tour from one theater to another, but seldom with major stars. Shakespeare productions and musicals are mounted in city parks across the country. Many small theaters in tourist areas put on a season of a half-dozen shows, often cast with non-Equity actors. These theaters can be a good place for the young actor to get some credentials on the path to winning an Equity card, and for others to see how they like the actor's life.

Getting Your Feet Wet

Summer theaters that hire non-Equity actors come and go like fireflies. They often pop up in out-of-the way towns that attract tourists for the scenery or for activities like golfing, fishing, or antiquing. Some last just one season, a few for several seasons, but not many last very long. They advertise for actors in theatrical trade papers like *Backstage*. To audition for them, you'll often have to travel to New York for East Coast productions or to Dallas or Chicago for those in other locations. Producers also will place ads in local papers, so a few actors and technical workers may live close enough to commute.

Such non-Equity summer theaters usually pay a small salary, as well as offer room and board. By small salary, we mean as little as $75 a week, although a few will offer more than twice that amount, and actors in starring roles may even get a few hundred dollars a week. You'll probably have to share the room they give you, even if you're a star, and sometimes with two people. The food can vary from decent to truly awful, and unless you know someone who's worked at that theater before, it's impossible to know what the living and eating conditions will be in advance. Prepare yourself for the worst.

Backstage Tales

An actor we know worked at a theater that had a large communal kitchen where cast members could cook. The refrigerator was stuffed with paper bags labeled with the names of various actors. The second summer our friend worked there, he decided that the refrigerator badly needed a cleaning out, and set to work. At the back of a shelf he found some carefully wrapped cheese bearing his own name. It had been there for a year.

The general lack of amenities at many summer theaters goes largely unnoticed by the actors for the simple reason that they are either working, sleeping, or spending an exhausted hour unwinding at a local bar. We've performed with summer theater colleagues who had also spent a summer working on a ranch or a year working with the Peace Corps in the jungle. Ask them where they worked the hardest and they will quickly answer, "The summer theater."

Summer theater isn't for slackers. At night you'll perform one play, and during the day rehearse the season's next play. In the course of seven weeks, you may have to learn the lines and blocking for six plays. At times, you'll wonder how you can possibly stand up on stage, never mind give a performance. Just to make sure you don't get bored, many of these theaters also put on half-hour shows for children every Saturday morning. These plays are never written down, fortunately, because you couldn't possibly fit another line into your head. You'll have to improvise, although you'll usually have a single hour of rehearsal that begins at the crack of dawn.

Backstage Tales

Co-author Paul Baldwin's first professional job was at a summer theater in the hills of western Connecticut. The plays were performed in a nineteenth-century opera house with a condemned balcony. The company of about 20 actors performed one-week productions of *My Fair Lady, Man of La Mancha, Fiddler on the Roof, Hello, Dolly!, Funny Girl,* and *Gypsy,* plus six children's shows. By the end of the summer, everyone looked as though they had scurvy from lack of sunlight, although the performances were amazingly good. That was in 1974, but Paul is still friends with the music director, the Dolly, and the Fannie Brice. Listening to them reminisce is like watching an episode of *Survivor,* but a lot funnier.

If you can survive such a summer, you will learn a great deal. You'll test the limits of your technical skills, your personal strength, and your range as an actor. You will discover how close it's possible to come to a nervous breakdown and still go on stage and be rewarded with a standing ovation. You will learn how to improvise when another actor does have that nervous breakdown, and how to rescue yourself when you not only don't know your next line, but aren't even sure what play you're performing. You'll find out, in other words, if you truly want to be—or are cut out to be—a professional actor.

Enough Fame for Many

One season of summer stock can be enough to persuade some actors, no matter how talented, that a professional career isn't for them. Obviously, an actor who goes on to get his or her Equity card and moves up the ladder will get beyond the rigors of one-week stock soon enough. But he or she may spend years working at theaters that do a new play every two or three weeks during the summer season, and that's not easy, either. If you can't take one-week stock, you probably don't belong in the business. Quite a few actors decide that once is enough when it comes to summer stock, and stick to community theater from then on.

Places, Everyone!

If you're working in summer theater, be sure to warn your parents and friends how hard you work. You don't need them telling you how pale and sickly you look when they first arrive!

Plenty of actors greatly enjoy summer stock (especially when the shows run for two or three weeks). It does keep you on your toes and can be very exciting. Some actors do non-Equity summer stock while holding down regular jobs the rest of the year. Of course, your "regular" job has to be one that allows you the summer off, but some teachers, people who work at ski resorts during the winter months, or those who are fundamentally self-employed anyway, can manage that. Non-Equity summer stock can bring enough fame to some actors, a chance to strut their stuff for a couple of months each year.

Lifestyle Decisions

Needless to say, if you become a professional actor, you'll be living a very different kind of life than if you had a nine-to-five job. First, you'll probably have to live in one of the two meccas for actors, New York or Los Angeles. New York is the chief destination for those who want to be stage actors. Los Angeles attracts those who want to break into the movies or television, although some films and television series are made in New York, and Los Angeles has its share of legitimate stage productions. Stage actors often go on to work in movies and television, but the reverse is much less common. Hollywood puts a premium on looks, of course. On stage, you don't have close-ups and can wear more makeup, so it is quite possible for a stage actor with attractive but not spectacular looks to appear very handsome or beautiful on stage. The camera is less forgiving.

But whether an actor heads for New York or Hollywood, several aspects of the acting life are distinctly different from those that come with regular employment in a nine-to-five job.

Backstage Tales

There are numerous examples of actors who have eventually made a great success in the movies after honing their skills in the New York Theater. Kathy Bates is a prime example. She starred on Broadway in Marsha Norman's Pulitzer Prize winning *'night Mother* and had a big Off-Broadway hit in Terrence McNally's *Frankie and Johnny in the Claire de Lune*. Those roles went to Sissy Spacek and Michele Pfeiffer when the movies were made, but Bates got smaller roles in a dozen movies, and then walked off with the Best Actress Oscar for her stunning performance in 1990's *Misery*. Attractive but never slender, it is doubtful that Bates would have succeeded as well if she had started out in Hollywood.

Professional "Gypsies"

The Gypsies of Europe have been a nomadic people since the Middle Ages. They seldom stay in one place long, though they may often return to it. In some periods, they did not even need passports to travel between countries, long before the existence of the European Union. Professional actors say that they live the gypsy life because they, too, must so often uproot themselves for extended periods of time. They usually have a home base, an apartment in New York or Los Angeles, but they are constantly leaving it to appear in a play or to shoot a movie someplace else. Stage actors travel the country to appear in summer stock, at dinner theaters, at regional theaters, or to go on tour with a Broadway hit.

If you're going to be a professional actor, you almost certainly must be a gypsy, too. Many young actors share apartments because rent is high in New York and Los Angeles, and those who have tiny apartments of their own often sublet them when they go on the road. Someday, if you become a star, you might be able to afford a home in Connecticut, like Joanne Woodward and Paul Newman, or in Montana, like Robert Redford. But, in the meantime, your living quarters are likely to be cramped, far too expensive for what you're getting, and home to a stranger when you're away. Unlike the real Gypsies of Europe, you won't be able to take your home on wheels everywhere you go. (Having your own RV won't work, because there are no trailer parks in New York City.)

Backstage Tales

The gypsy life of the stage actor is symbolized and celebrated by the Gypsy Robe of Broadway fame. This robe is passed on to each new musical that opens on Broadway by the cast of the previous one to open. Each new show adds a cloth patch to the robe, and a ceremony is held on stage opening night, with a chorus member who has been elected by the cast parading the robe for all to see. Sometimes the robe will remain with one cast for weeks, even months, but it has also been known to change hands within a 24-hour period—it depends on the scheduling of new shows.

Living the Actor's Life

When they're not performing in a show—which can be the majority of the time—actors still have to make a living. That means jobs that have a steady turnover, like waiting tables, or those that you can pick up and leave behind at a moment's notice, like temporary office work. There are plenty of such jobs—you won't starve—but it also means needing to have additional skills. The more computer skills you have, and the faster you can type, the better. You might think anyone could wait on tables in a restaurant, but you need skills for that as well. Being a good waiter is no cinch. Some actors prefer waiting tables because they enjoy interacting with people all the time, while others prefer office temp work exactly because they don't have to deal as much with people.

As a professional actor, you will have special expenses that constantly eat into your budget. You'll probably want to get new resumé pictures quite often, and not only are they expensive in themselves, but they usually mean a trip to the hair salon as well. You'll also have your personal makeup kit to maintain, and that can require a considerable outlay of cash, especially for character actors, who require a greater variety of makeup as well as special items like beards. Your subway, bus, and taxi fares will be higher than for most people, because instead of going to one location and staying put the entire day, you are likely to find yourself going back and forth to auditions or rehearsals for a showcase production that pays you nothing. Many actors try to squeeze enough money out of their budgets to join a gym. You'll need to keep in shape, not only to look good, but also because acting is a very physical profession. You'll need to have an answering machine so that you don't miss any messages relating to work, and many actors also have an answering service as well. And then there's that agent. He or she will help get you work, but when you work (in the theater, that is!), you pay a percentage of your paycheck to him or her.

Places, Everyone!

If you're seriously thinking about becoming a professional, there are two songs you should listen to. Get hold of the original cast recording of Stephen Sondheim's *A Little Night Music* and put on "The Glamorous Life"—"cracks in the plaster, tra-la-la." And see if you can get your hands on a recording of Noel Coward singing his famous ditty, "Don't Put Your Daughter on the Stage, Mrs. Worthington." Both songs give fair warning.

You have to be well organized to be a professional actor. You must be on time for all auditions in cities where transportation snarls are commonplace. You need to be adept at handling red tape because you'll have to examine theater contracts with a fine-tooth comb (even if you have an agent to do so), and have sublet agreements to draw up, and, perhaps most important, have unemployment forms and procedures to deal with. You'll need to have everything in your life set up so that you can put down the phone, pack a suitcase, and head to Maine to take over a part for an actor who's broken a leg.

Ninety Percent Unemployed

It's been said that Actors' Equity is the only union in the world in which 90 percent of its members are unemployed. This may be a slight exaggeration, but there's no question that the majority of professional actors are out of work at any one time. Even in the summer months, when employment shoots up, a lot of actors are sitting in New York bewailing the fact that they're not performing somewhere, anywhere.

A Very Insecure Profession

Being unemployed doesn't necessarily have anything to do with the amount of talent an actor possesses. The most famous actors on the planet are unemployed a good deal of the time. In fact, stars can have a particular problem because they must wait and wait for the new musical or movie a writer or producer tailors just for them finally to be in good-enough shape to be worth doing. They may have an additional wait while the money is raised to produce the show. Stars can't go off to South Carolina to appear at a dinner theater while they wait, either, since that would greatly devalue their special standing. From that point of view, the little-known actor actually has more choices—provided you get cast in that South Carolina production, of course.

Even stars sometimes wonder, "Will I ever work again?" especially after a show or a movie turns out to be an utter flop. Less-established actors wonder this all the time as they wait for the phone to ring. Professional acting and insecurity are almost synonymous. That's why a tough hide, great self-confidence, and the ability to persevere no matter what are at least as important as talent. In truth, these qualities may be even more important than blazing talent. You're not going to make it if you're a no-talent, of course, but many people with moderate talent succeed because they persevere, while some with extraordinary ability decide they just can't take the tension any more and give it up.

Fallback Plans

A lot of actors listened to their parents and went to college before attempting to become a professional. "I think it's terrific you want to be an actor, kid, but you'd better have a fallback plan." And many of them are ultimately very glad they did have a college degree or some other form of fallback plan, such as joining Dad or Mom in the family business. One friend acted professionally for a few years, working as often as most, but not really getting anywhere. Her father had died some time earlier and her mother was running the family business. When her mother finally said she thought she needed some help (she was nearly 70), our friend went home to the Midwest without real regrets. She'd at least taken her shot. She runs the business and still acts regularly in community theater productions.

Performance Notes

Never underestimate the importance of sheer luck. Luck is a crucial, if amorphous, element in the lives of professional actors, as well as a host of other professions. Being in the right place at the right time is something we can't organize or predict, but it counts for a great deal in show business.

Some actors refuse to think in terms of fallback plans, feeling that having one will jinx them in some way, or cause them to try less hard than they otherwise might. People like that do sometimes have the perseverance it takes to become a success as a pro. But others are kidding themselves, and when they do give up on acting, they have to scramble to figure out what to do with the rest of their lives. All we can say to those who resist having a fallback plan is, "Good luck. I hope you make it."

Are You Really Good Enough?

Throughout this book, we've emphasized that many actors in college and community theater are as good as most professionals. True as that is, you should consider some other factors. You may be very talented, but is there an established actor who looks a lot like you, has the same kind of manner and bearing, even a similar voice, someone who makes you think, "I could be playing that part," every time you see the actor perform? If you're very much like an established actor, you can be in for trouble. Directors and casting agents will notice the similarity, too, and they can react against you for that very reason. They'd rather have the "real thing," or someone quite different, instead.

This problem can arise for so-called "niche actors" as well. We have a very talented friend who's tall and heavy, with red hair. He's very talented indeed, and he did quite well in summer theater and dinner theater. But another actor looks almost exactly like him who became better known because he was in a number of national commercials. And our friend began to get an unsettling reaction, "Oh, yes, I've seen you … but that's not you, is it?"

Backstage Tales

There are some famous Hollywood examples of "carbon-copy" actors who never quite got to the top. Lizbeth Scott was put into movies because she reminded everyone of Lauren Bacall. But her career never got much beyond the B-movie level for the same reason. Michael Parks was supposed to be "the new James Dean," but it quickly became apparent that no one much wanted a second James Dean, and although Parks continued working through the years, he never became an A-list star. Both Scott and Parks were talented young actors, but they didn't have the excitement of the originals they reminded everyone of. Good, in their cases, wasn't quite good enough.

Little Fish/Big Pond

In Chapter 27, "Experience and Dependability," we mentioned the heavy-set actor we know who self-mockingly describes himself as a "whale" in the community theater pond. He also once said that one reason he didn't turn professional was that he much preferred being a very big fish in a little pond over being a miniature whale in the big pond of professional acting. That professional pond is way overstocked with fish of every kind, and there isn't enough food in that pond, or even enough oxygen in that water, for all of them. Certainly, a few will get to be very big fish in the larger pond. But those few also take up a lot of room, and consume a lot of the available food. The little pond can therefore prove more satisfying for many actors, and much more secure, as well.

The Least You Need to Know

- Making local television commercials can be a first step toward turning pro.
- Summer stock is a good way to get your feet wet, and will test whether you're cut out for professional acting.
- The actor's world requires you to adapt to a different way of living—it's a gypsy life.
- Keep in mind that acting is a very insecure profession, emotionally and financially, so think hard about fallback plans.
- Talent isn't all you need to make it as a pro—not by a long shot.

Chapter 30

Getting a Union Card

In This Chapter

- Finding out the facts about the various actors' unions
- Exploring possible routes to getting a union card
- Recognizing that as a pro you'll enter a whole new world

Working in summer stock or at a dinner theater is a professional job, even though the theater does not work under union rules or offer union contracts. But all Broadway theaters, major Off-Broadway productions, and the best-known regional theaters operate according to Actors' Equity Association rules, so in order to act in such productions you will have to be a union member. All studio-produced and most independent feature films, as well as television soap operas, series, and movies, require that you be a member of a different union, the Screen Actors Guild (SAG). The American Federation of Television and Radio Artists (AFTRA) shares some jurisdiction with SAG, but also represents a wide range of professionals, from newspersons to magicians. SAG is the primary union for live television performers of many kinds, including actors.

In this chapter, we'll show you how these three major unions operate, and the steps you'll need to take to gain membership. We'll give you some tips on various routes to getting a union card as well as dispel some myths about the subject. And we'll have some final words about what it means to begin a professional acting career.

Facts, Not Hearsay

All unions are somewhat mysterious to nonmembers. They set forth very specific requirements for becoming a member, which can vary considerably, not only among unions in different fields but even between unions involved in very similar work, like carpenters and plumbers. What's more, unions have some rules that protect the union member with respect to employers and working conditions, and other rules that the members themselves must follow. To the uninitiated, then, unions can seem like secret societies, and myths abound that confuse matters further.

We're going to give you the basic facts on the three most important unions governing actors. We can't cover everything—that would be a book in itself—but you'll have a much clearer idea about how to proceed if you want to become a card-carrying professional actor. (You can get more detailed information from the unions themselves. All have Web sites; just enter the name of a union in a search box.

Actors' Equity Association

In conversation, actors almost always refer to the Actors' Equity Association simply as Equity, and that's what we'll do here. Stage managers as well as actors belong to Equity (many stage managers are also actors, in fact). The union has more than 40,000 members, a number that makes clear both the allure of the acting profession and the reason why there is such great competition for every acting job.

Places, Everyone!

No two members of Equity can have the same name. With such a large number of members, if your name is a common one, you are likely to have to change it, taking a new professional name. Many young actors have been stunned to discover this fact. Think about this possibility well before you apply for membership, and have at least two alternative names ready. That's the name that will be going up in lights on Broadway someday.

You can become an Equity member by three ways:

1. By getting hired for a show operating under a standard Equity contract
2. By compiling 50 weeks of work at any of the theaters that have been accredited by Equity to administer the union's Membership Candidate Program
3. By being a member in good standing in one of Equity's sister unions—SAG, AFTRA, AGVA (American Guild of Variety Artists), or AGMA (American Guild of Musical Artists)—a policy called Open Door Admissions

Let's take a closer look at each of these membership options. The first category might be called "the big break." You've arrived in New York straight from college or a graduate drama program. You're extremely talented and also very lucky. Your natural talent, the technique you have developed through hard work, the quality of your voice, and your looks all happen to coincide exactly with what a director needs for a particular role. The director auditions numerous actors who are already members of Equity—perhaps for years—but you, the unknown newcomer, fit best into the director's concept of that particular role. You're hired, and because it is an approved Equity production, the union grants you your membership into Equity as soon as you sign your contract.

This miracle does happen. It happens to people like Meryl Streep, who had just graduated from the Yale program when she joined an Equity production, and then went on to become one of the most respected, honored, and famous actors of her time. It also happens to people who have a brief flash of fame, but who quickly give up professional acting. Getting your Equity card through a "big break" scenario doesn't happen to all that many people, and even when it does occur, it's no guarantee of a long and remarkable career.

Backstage Tales

We know an actor who arrived in New York from college, got a lead role as a replacement in a long-running Off-Broadway show within weeks, and thus became an instant member of Equity. Within another year, he was playing the central role in an important new Broadway show. He got mostly good reviews, but the show was a flop. He went on working as an actor for another 10 years, mostly Off-Broadway or in touring shows, and then retired from acting. He's not at all bitter about his experience. "I was the perfect juvenile lead," he says. "I looked like a juvenile for quite a while, but when I didn't look like that any more, it was over. I'd always known that would happen. I'm just glad I had what I had."

Big breaks are wonderful when they happen, and they make everyone else you know a bit jealous. But they do not make a career—they're just the lucky start to a potential career. It is perfectly possible for an ultimately more remarkable career to begin with the harder route to an Equity card offered by the second option, the Membership Candidate Program. Because you must put together 50 weeks of work as a non-Equity actor in accredited theaters, that means you will have to win a lot of roles.

The plays or musicals you appear in during this period may run as few as three weeks or as many as seven. You'll also receive credit for the rehearsal periods, which are likely to be two weeks each. But, as a matter of simple math, that means that, at best, it will take you six or seven shows to reach your 50-week total, which can take two, three, even four years. You will, of course, improve your resumé and your skills with each show you do, and it's always possible that after putting in 20 weeks, or 35, you'll get your own big break with the offer of an Equity role. That's fairly common.

The third option, the Open Door Admission, can seem on the surface to provide a shortcut to an Equity card. Television and the movies have more roles to fill than stage productions do. Drama series like *The X-Files* use a lot of actors in relatively small roles, and even if you have five lines before you're eaten by a mysterious fungus in the teaser before the opening credits, it counts as much as a lead role in terms of completed work. Such roles are not as easy to get as you might imagine, however, and SAG has its own membership criteria, as we'll see in the next section. What's more, you must be a member in good standing of the sister union for at least a one-year period before you can even apply for Equity membership.

Performance Notes

Don't think you can buy your way into Equity. You can't get around the membership work requirements stated here by paying a higher initiation fee. That's a myth.

No matter which of these three options you pursue, an Equity initiation fee is $800. You don't have to pay it all at once, though. Within three months of filing an application, you must pay a minimum of $300 of the fee, and for that you receive full membership. You then have to pay the remaining $500 of the initiation fee within two years. You'll also owe union dues: $39 paid twice a year. In addition, when you're working, the union deducts 2 percent of your salary, which adds up to $13 on a $650-a-week contract, $16 on an $800-a-week contract, for example.

Once you're a member of Equity or any of the other performing unions, you'll have to abide by the rules of that union. That means keeping up with your dues and accepting the instructions of the Equity deputy on union matters connected with any show you're in. Above all, it means that you agree not to accept a role in any production not governed by Equity protocols. You can't join a union and then go back to acting in nonunion productions just because you haven't landed a union job. Equity does make it possible, as we've discussed in earlier chapters, for its members to act with community theaters and other nonprofessional groups under an Equity Guest Artist agreement. But if the union says you can't take such a job, that's it. Being a union member brings new responsibilities as well as opportunities.

SAG (Screen Actors Guild)

As with Equity, SAG membership does not in any way guarantee work. According to the union's own statistics, more than 85 percent of SAG's 90,000 members earned less than $5,000 in 1996, for example. What's more, the SAG initiation fee and annual dues are higher than those of Equity, although the amount withheld from the paychecks of working actors is slightly less.

The initiation fee for SAG, at this writing, is $1,234, plus the first payment of regular dues, which are $100 per year, paid in two semi-annual installments. Percentage dues withheld from paychecks are 1.85 percent of all SAG earnings up to $200,000, and 0.5 percent on earnings from $200,001 through $500,000.

SAG does not have a membership candidate program like Equity's that enables you to amass working weeks toward eventual membership. You can join SAG only if you present proof of employment—a signed contract, payroll check, check stub, or letterhead statement—from a production company that is itself a SAG signatory company. You may have already completed the job, or the job might be scheduled to begin within two weeks from the date of your application. In most states, the Taft-Hartley Law allows you to work for a SAG signatory company for 30 days without joining the union, but after that you must join before accepting any further work with such a company. It should be noted that SAG also has agreements with its sister unions that can facilitate becoming a member.

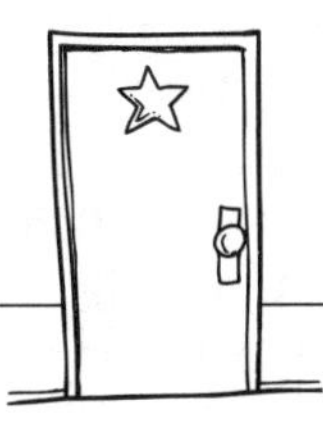

Backstage Tales

As is the case with Equity, no two union members can have the same name. In some cases, the old Hollywood studios changed people's names to more appealing ones. Frances Gumm became Judy Garland, and Marion Morrison became John Wayne. But even in the old days, actors were sometimes forced to change their names because another actor already had his or her real name. A young British leading man who made his first film in 1938 had the same name as an American actor who had already made a number of films, but who had broken through to stardom that same year with *You Can't Take It With You*. His name was James Stewart, and the British actor had to become Stewart Granger, even though his friends always called him Jimmy.

AFTRA (American Federation of Television and Radio Artists)

AFTRA represents broadcasters and newspersons at more than 300 radio and television stations, as well as actors making radio and television commercials and appearing on entertainment programs. It also represents musical recording artists and actors who record talking books. Although in 1997 they set a standard initiation fee of $1,000, dues still vary from one union local to another, although the union expects to implement a uniform standard in coming years. Dues are paid on a semi-annual basis, as is the case with Equity and SAG.

Eventually, many actors belong to all three unions. As SAG emphasizes in its literature, to earn a living wage from performing alone, actors often have to work in several different arenas—stage, screen, and commercials, for example. Some performers may have such varied careers that they will also want to join one or both of the remaining sister unions, AGVA (American Guild of Variety Artists), or AGMA (American Guild of Musical Artists). AGVA represents nightclub and cabaret performers, as well as comedy showcases, dance revues, and even amusement park shows. AGMA represents singers and dancers who appear in operas or other classical musical productions.

Several Routes to Follow

Because the five sister performing-artist unions fully recognize the work an actor does as a member of any of them, and that makes it easier for a person who is a member of one union to join the others, there are several paths to becoming a full-fledged union professional. The route you take can be partly a matter of choice, but the nature of your talent may suggest one as well. For example, many fine actors have little or no musical talent. If you're such an actor, your path is unlikely to begin with membership in either AGVA or AGMA, which place particular emphasis on musical ability. If you're a fine actor but don't have a face that the camera loves, your route is more likely to be through Equity rather than through SAG.

Backstage Tales

Few things about show business are more mysterious than why the camera loves some faces and not others. There have been several famous cases of people who were very beautiful or very handsome, but who still did not film well. Suzy Parker was the top of glamour model of her time. In still photographs she was stunningly beautiful. But on film, her face tended to look inexpressive and not nearly as lovely. On the other hand, Ellen Barkin has had a fine career in films, and has sex appeal to burn onscreen. Her face is unusual, with a slightly crooked nose and odd planes to it, but although she is far from conventionally beautiful, the camera loves her. It's simply a mystery why such differences have the effects they do.

Chance can also affect the path you take toward union membership. One actor we know had a voice that recorded extremely well, and he had a gift for reading books aloud. Because he had a cousin who was blind, he started recording books while still at college. That meant that his first union was AFTRA, and it was not until later that he joined Equity and ultimately SAG. If a combination of talent and happenstance puts you in a position to gain entry to any of the five sister performing unions, jump at it. While your main interest may be stage acting, membership in another union will ease your way into Equity.

Job Brings Union Card

As you should know from reading this chapter, the clearest path to getting a union card is to get a job with any producing entity that abides by the rules of the union governing your area of entertainment. If you're hired by such an entity, the union will grant you membership. The catch here is that you might not have the opportunity to audition for Equity productions in the first place because many are open only to Equity members. That catch is one reason why many actors use Equity's Membership Candidate Program. By getting jobs with theaters that do hire non-union actors, but that take part in the Equity program, you can gradually work your way toward full union membership.

Chance can also enter the picture here. Some movies and stage productions actively seek new young talent by advertising an open call, which means that casting agents or directors will see anyone who shows up. Famous Broadway shows that conducted open calls include *Hair, Annie,* and *Rent.* If you go to an open call, know that actors start lining up at dawn, the lines will go around the block, and you may be very tired by the time you get to audition yourself. But actors do win roles at open calls and become overnight professionals.

Places, Everyone!

If an agent does contact you, be sure to check out his or her credentials. The various unions have directories of accredited agents, which can be obtained by contacting the union. No legitimate agent accepts or asks for a fee in advance. As SAG literature warns, stay far away from any agent who tries to send you to a particular photographer to take your pictures.

What About an Agent?

Here again you'll run into a catch. Most agents are not interested in representing anyone who doesn't have a union card. There are exceptions, however. Occasionally an actor appears in a non-Equity play, perhaps Off-Off-Broadway, and the show gets the kind of attention that brings agents to see it. An agent impressed with your performance may be willing to take you on as a client.

If you have a good friend who has both a union card and an agent, ask him or her to recommend you to the agent. If your friend is convincing enough about your talents, the agent may grant you an interview. An agent can sometimes get you auditions with Equity productions even though you don't yet have a union card. He or she will be anxious to get you into an Equity production, because the more money you make, the more he or she will earn as your agent. The standard percentage an agent earns is 10 percent of an actor's wage.

Finding exactly the right agent for you can take a long time. You may become a client of several before you find the one who has a special understanding of, and an appreciation for, your abilities. But any accredited agent will at least get you started, and may help you a great deal.

Special Connections

Do actors sometimes get into a union because they have special connections? Yes, but that's not just a matter of an important person picking up the phone and demanding that you receive a union card. What sometimes happens is that a producer who invests a lot of money in a show will see to it that a young relative or friend gets a small part in an Equity show, which earns him or her the union card. That's favoritism, of course, but as far as the union is concerned, it's all legit: You've been offered a role in an Equity or SAG production.

A major director or actor can sometimes make a similar arrangement. But such cases are exceptions, a matter of knowing or being related to the right people. If you get a union card that way, you'll still have to deliver a good performance, and, as already noted, just having a union card doesn't mean you'll get future work. In the end, you'll still have to prove yourself with your work.

Starting Over in a Different World

Belonging to a union makes you a professional in the technical sense. But it doesn't increase your natural talent or magically enhance the skills you've acquired. It may help you to get jobs that will further develop your skills, but professional status is not the equivalent of success. You're now just one of 40,000 members of Equity, or 90,000 members of SAG. It will be up to you to nurture your talent, to grow as an actor with each new role, and to develop new skills and hone the ones you already have to a fine edge.

As we discussed in Chapter 29, "Should You Turn Pro?" if you're a professional actor trying to build a career, you'll live a different kind of life than most people, a gypsy life to a considerable extent. You'll probably make a lot of friends, because professional actors are often gregarious people who are a great deal of fun to be around. But all actors go through rough patches, professionally and personally—we could say, "Just like anybody else," but that's not altogether true. Actors are not like everybody else. You know that already, no doubt. You have a special talent that makes you stand out and that opens new vistas only glimpsed by non-actors.

You're an actor. Whether you choose to use that talent in the amateur world of community theater or try to build a strong career as a professional, perhaps even to attain stardom, we wish you the very best of luck. Or, as theater superstition decrees, we'll voice our good wishes this way: "Break a leg."

The Least You Need to Know

- Membership in any of the five sister performing unions can open doors for you as a professional actor.
- Belonging to a union brings new responsibilities as well as greater opportunities.
- In the end, it is your own talent and hard work, not union membership, that will bring you the success you want.

Appendix A

Stage Directions Glossary

acoustics The science of sound as applied to theaters, relating to how sound travels and reverberates.

acting bug The slang term used to indicate that someone of any age has been infected with a great desire to be an actor.

actor A person who performs on stage, in the movies, or on television.

anti-timing A failing of some actors who seem to be too slow or too fast in responding to action or dialogue onstage.

audition As a noun, the opportunity for an actor to display his or her talents when seeking a role in an upcoming production of a play; as a verb, to give a brief performance at such an occasion.

backstage The entire area behind the stage of a theater, including dressing rooms.

blocking Stage movements by actors, including entrances, exits, and any steps taken in any direction across the stage.

body language Bodily movements, large or small, which indicate what a person is thinking or feeling.

breaking-up Out-of-place laughter by an actor on stage.

Broadway A major thoroughfare in New York City on which many theaters are located; used as a general term to describe productions at large New York theaters in the Times Square area of midtown Manhattan.

bus-and-truck tour A low-budget tour of a play or musical, often presented in smaller cities for only a few nights.

call-back A request that an actor return for an additional audition.

cattle call An audition open to anyone, regardless of experience.

character role A supporting role with pronounced or eccentric characteristics.

chemistry A mysterious element that creates excitement when two actors appear together.

cold reading Delivering a speech or acting a scene at an audition without having read it beforehand.

community theater A local theater group in a city or town.

cue A line of dialogue, action, or sound, onstage or off, that tells an actor it is time to enter, exit, move across stage, or—most commonly—begin speaking.

curtain up The start of a performance, whether or not an actual curtain exists in front of the stage.

cuts Lines, speeches, songs, or any other element in a printed script left out of a particular production.

diaphragm The lower part of the lungs, filling the abdominal space, that supports the voice when actors and singers breathe correctly on stage.

diction Clear, sharp pronunciation of words, especially of consonants.

director The person charged with staging a play or musical, who coordinates all on-stage aspects of the production, including the performances of the actors.

double-take An exaggerated facial response to another actor's words or actions, usually used for comic effect.

downstage The area of the stage closest to the audience.

Equity The commonly used short term for the main stage actors' union, Actors' Equity Association.

finding your light An actor's ability to sense when he or she is properly placed in respect to stage lighting.

flop A theatrical production that fails to draw an audience, regardless of whether the critics liked it or not.

ham An actor who gives a very broad or exaggerated performance.

high note The highest note sung in a particular song, which varies according to the musical key of the song.

in-the-round A theater in which the audience is seated on all four sides of a central stage.

larynx The human voice box, containing the vocal chords.

makeup Any material, from eye shadow to a false beard, used to heighten or change an actor's appearance on stage.

mannerisms Gestures, facial expressions, and vocal tricks that a particular actor uses again and again in different roles.

Method acting An internalized form of acting that uses experiences from an actor's personal life to help produce onstage emotion.

mimicry An actor's ability to sound and/or look like someone else, usually a famous person.

monologue A speech used by an actor to demonstrate his or her ability at an audition.

notes Instructions, usually regarding changes in an actor's blocking or performance, given after a rehearsal by the director, music director, choreographer, or stage manager.

Obies Annual awards for Off-Broadway theatrical productions in New York City.

off-book When an actor knows his or her lines and no longer needs to carry the script.

offstage The area immediately behind or to the sides of the stage area; also used more generally to talk about an actor's everyday life.

oldie but goodie An expression used to describe a top-notch song from a past era.

pace The speed at which a scene is played.

pan A very bad review from a critic.

pausing for effect A deliberate pause within or between lines, used by an actor to call special attention to a moment.

picture The photograph actors leave with the director when they audition, along with their resumé.

Places, everyone! The warning given by the stage manager that a performance is about to begin.

presence An actor's ability to command attention onstage, even when surrounded by other actors.

projection An actor's ability to use his or her voice so that it can be clearly heard in the back rows of a theater; also used in reference to the emotions an actor wishes to convey.

props Any movable object, from a letter to a sword, used by an actor during a performance.

proscenium stage The classic theater arrangement, with a curtained stage facing an audience on one side.

raked stage A tilted performing area, usually specially constructed, with its upstage space raised higher than the downstage space.

range The vocal extent of a singer's voice, from its lowest note to its highest.

rave An extremely good review from a critic.

read-through Actors reading the entire play aloud while seated, generally at the first rehearsal.

rehearsals The period during which the actors' performances are developed and hopefully perfected by repetition.

resumé The printed record of an actor's experience, presented at auditions, along with a picture of the actor.

Screen Actors Guild The chief union representing actors appearing in movies and on television, commonly referred to as SAG.

set As a noun, the physical design of the stage area within which the actors perform; as a verb, to make permanent the way in which a scene is being played.

sheet music The pages containing the music and lyrics to a single song, as opposed to a score containing all the music for a show.

sides Pages containing only the lines and cue lines of one actor, instead of an entire script.

signature song A song that is primarily associated with a single famous singer, as "My Way" was with Frank Sinatra.

stage left The side of the stage that is to the actor's left as he or she faces the audience.

stage right The side of the stage that is to the actor's right as he or she faces the audience.

thrust stage A stage that projects outward, with the audience seated on three sides.

Tonys The nickname for the Antoinette Perry Awards, given annually to Broadway productions.

typecasting Assigning a role to an actor on the basis of his or her surface appearance or personality.

typed-out The elimination of an actor during auditions because of such obvious features as height, weight, or age.

understudy An actor, often playing a small role, who learns another role, so as to be able to perform it if the regular actor is ill.

upstage The rear area of the stage farthest from the audience; also used to describe an actor's attempt to distract audience attention from what another actor is doing.

walk through To perform a role at less-than-usual intensity, such as during a technical rehearsal; also used critically, as in "he walked it," for a lazy performance at a matinee.

Acting School Directory

Check your local Yellow Pages to find one of the hundreds of acting classes offered across the country, in both large and small communities, usually by teachers from local schools or colleges. High school students with an interest in acting who are applying to colleges will find that a great many offer drama courses of several kinds, and will also find that a number of them grant degrees in the performing arts. Several guides to U.S. colleges and universities are on the market—check them out.

The acting schools in the list below cater largely to those who are interested in pursuing a professional acting career. Several, however, offer intensive two-week workshops or summer programs in which the enthusiastic amateur would feel at home. Others are happy to welcome adults with full-time jobs who nevertheless want to improve their dramatic skills.

Please note that neither the authors nor the publisher are in any way endorsing these schools. The quality of such schools can vary from year to year because the teaching faculty is subject to change. In addition, a school that may be just right for one person can be wrong for another. But these are all well-known programs, and most can claim several alumni who have succeeded as acting professionals.

Act Now Acting Academy
6065 Roswell Road, N.E. #1414
Atlanta, GA 30328
Phone: 770-216-9339

The Acting Studio, Inc.
P.O Box 230389
Phone: 212-580-6600

Actor's Asylum
4841 S. State Street
Murray, UT 84107
Phone: 801-262-5245

American Academy of Dramatic Arts
120 Madison Avenue
New York, NY 10016-7089
Phone: 212-686-9244

American Academy of Dramatic Arts
600 Playhouse Alley
Pasadena, CA 91101-5218
Phone: 323-464-2777

Beverly Hills Playhouse
Milton Katsela Scene-Study Classes
254 S. Robertson Boulevard
Beverly Hills, CA 90211-2827
Phone: 310-855-6886

CAST
4030 Central Avenue, N.E.
Columbia Heights
Minneapolis, MN 55421-2916
Phone: 612-789-2353

Circle in the Square Theater School
1633 Broadway
New York, NY 10019-6708
Phone: 212-307-0388

Creative Arts Theater
1100 W. Randol Mill Road
Arlington, TX 76012
Phone: 817-861-CATS

DreamWrights
Youth and Family Theater
100 Carlisle Ave.
York, PA 17404
Phone: 717-848-8623

H.B. Studio, Inc.
120 Bank Street
New York, NY 10014-2126
Phone: 212-675-2370

Lee Strasberg Theater Institute, Inc.
115 E. 15th Street
New York, NY 10003-2101
Phone: 212-593-5500

Margo Manning Entertainment
14800 Quorum Drive, Suite 200
Dallas, TX 75240
Phone: 972-239-2882

Neighborhood Playhouse School of the Theater
340 E. 54th Street
New York, NY 10022-5017
Phone: 212-688-3770

Stella Adler Conservatory of Acting
419 Lafayette Street
New York, NY 10003-7033
Phone: 212-260-0520

Theater of Arts
4128 Wilshire Boulevard
Los Angeles, CA 90010
Phone: 213-380-0511

TVI Actors Studio—Los Angeles
14429 Ventura Boulevard
Sherman Oaks, CA 91423
Phone: 818-784-6500

TVI Actors Studio—New York
165 West 46th Street
New York, NY 10036
Phone: 212-302-1900

The Working Actor's Studio
6820 Benjamin Road
Tampa, FL 33634
Phone: 727-464-0530

Additional information about many of these schools, others like them, and numerous college programs, is available on the Internet at www.thespiannet.com. This site provides information on a variety of topics of interest to actors.

Play and Sheet Music Sources

Plays and Scripts

Many anthologies of plays, as well as recently published new plays, will be available at your public library or at large chain bookstores. Some local independent bookstores may have special sections devoted to dramatic literature. To acquire scripts for use by an entire cast, or just for yourself, there are two principal sources, used by both professional and amateur actors for decades: Samuel French, Inc. and Drama Bookshop.

Samuel French, Inc. is the foremost publisher of play scripts in the English-speaking world, with publishing offices in both England and America. It publishes thousands of titles, from Broadway hits to plays specifically written for production at schools and in local theaters. The scripts, in thin paper covers that you can easily bend back while holding during rehearsal, are relatively inexpensive, and you'll see them lying around wherever actors congregate. You can buy them the Internet at www.samuelfrench.com or order them from the following offices:

Samuel French, Inc.
45 West 25th Street
New York, NY 10010-2751
24-hour FAX: 212-206-1429
Phone Orders: 212-206-8990

Samuel French, Inc.
7623 Sunset Boulevard
Hollywood, CA 90046-2795
24-hour FAX: 323-876-6822
Phone Orders: 323-876-0570

Samuel French, Inc.
100 Lombard Street
Toronto, Ontario M5C 1M3
24-hour FAX: 416-363-1108
Phone Orders: 416-363-3536

The **Drama Bookshop** is a New York City institution where stars and chorus gypsies mingle quietly in the search for plays new and old. The Drama Bookshop stocks or can find almost any play in print. It is located in Manhattan at Seventh Avenue and 48th Street, if you want to visit in person on a trip to New York. Here is its full address:

Drama Bookshop
723 Seventh Avenue
New York, NY 10019
FAX: 212-730-8739
Phone Orders: 212-944-0595

Sheet Music

Sheet music for show tunes and popular hits used to be available everywhere, but it has become increasingly difficult to find in many localities, even in large cities. You can probably turn up almost anything you want at one of the three following sources, however, which maintain Web sites as well as responding to mail and phone orders:

Sheet Music, Etc.
14149 Twin Peaks Rd. #12A
Poway, CA 92064
Phone: 858-513-2558
FAX: 858-513-2578
Web Site: www.sheetmusicetc.com

Sheet Music Online
5830 S.E. Sky High Ct.
Milwaukee, OR 97267
Phone: 503-794-9696
Web Site: www.sheetmusic1.com

Sheet Music Plus/Musician Store
1322 Pacific Avenue
San Francisco, CA 94109
Phone: 1-800-480-6041
FAX: 415-931-8819
Web Site: www.sheetmusicplus.com

Two Web sites offering information and links to obtain free sheet music—chiefly old music out of copyright—are also of interest:

The Free Sheet Music Directory, www.musicaviva.com (This site has been given a ChildSafe Q.S.E. Award.)

The Free Sheet Music Guide, www.rainmusic.com

Appendix D

Further Reading

Some of the books listed here are classic works about acting technique or the world of the theater. Others are more recent books, widely discussed and recommended by many actors. Take note that some of these books represent very different views of acting. For example, the book by Pulitzer-winning playwright David Mamet is an attack on the teachings offered in the book by Lee Strasberg, founder of the Actor's Studio. You can learn a lot by reading both and making up your own mind.

Boleslavsky, Richard. *Acting: The First Six Lessons*. Florence, KY: Routledge, 1987.

Caine, Michael, with Maria Aitken. *Acting In Film: An Actor's Take on Movie Making*. New York: Applause Theater Books, 1997. (Paperback)

Callow, Simon. *Being an Actor*. New York: St. Martin's Press, 1995.

Goldman, William. Introduction by Frank Rich. *The Season: A Candid Look at Broadway*. Wilmington, DE: Proscenium Books, 1984. (Paperback Reissue)

Guernsey, Otis L. *The Best Plays 1999-2000*. New York: Limelight Editions, 2001. (A series of editors have compiled this annual anthology since 1920, most famous among them John Gassner. Most public libraries will have at least some of the past editions, which comprise an invaluable record of twentieth-century American theater. Please note that until the mid-1990s, the series was titled *Best American Plays* and was published by Crown.)

Hagen, Uta. *A Challenge for the Actor*. New York: Scribner, 1991.

Hagen, Uta, and Haskell Frankel. *Respect for Acting*. Saint Paul, MN: Hungry Minds, Inc., 1973.

Harrington, Laura (Editor). *100 Monologues: An Audition Sourcebook from New Dramatists*. New York: Mentor/NAL, 1992. (Paperback)

Hooks, Ed. *The Audition Book*. New York: Back Stage Books, 1996.

Kelley, Thomas A. *The Back Stage Guide to Stage Management*, 2nd Edition. New York: Back Stage Books, 1999. (Paperback)

Mamet, David. *True and False: Heresy and Common Sense for the Actor.* New York: Vintage, 1999. (Paperback)

Rodenberg, Patsy, and Ian McKellen. *The Right to Speak: Working with the Voice.* Florence, KY: Routledge, 1993. (Paperback)

Rodenberg, Patsy, and Judi Dench. *The Actor Speaks*. New York: St. Martin's Press, 2000.

Schulman, Michael (Editor), and Eva Mekler. *Great Scenes and Monologues for Actors.* New York: St. Martin's Press, 1998. (Paperback)

Shurtleff, Michael, and Bob Fosse. *Audition*. New York: Bantam, 1980. (Paperback)

Sonenberg, Janet. *The Actor Speaks: Twenty-four Actors Talk About Process and Technique.* New York: Crown Publishing Group, 1996. (Paperback)

Spolin, Viola. Paul Sills, Editor. *Improvisation for the Theater: A Handbook of Teaching and Directing Techniques (Drama and Performance Studies)*, 3rd Edition. Evanston, IL: Northwestern University Press, 1999. (Paperback)

Stanislavsky, Constantin, et al. *An Actor Prepares*. Florence, KY: Theater Arts Books, 1989. (Paperback Reissue)

Strasberg, Lee. *A Dream of Passion: The Development of the Method.* New York: NAL, 1990. (Paperback Reissue)

Two newsstand publications offer on-going news about acting, actors, and the American theater:

American Theater is published 10 times a year by Theater Communications Group, 355 Lexington Avenue, New York, NY 10017. Phone: 212-697-5230. E-mail: atm@tcg.org. It includes a listing of upcoming productions at theaters across the country.

Playbill—The National Theater Magazine is a monthly publication from the publisher of programs for Broadway and Off-Broadway theaters, Playbill, Inc., 52 Vanderbilt Avenue, New York, NY 10017. Phone for subscriptions: 1-800-533-4330. E-mail: mamsterdam@playbill.com.

In addition, many public libraries subscribe to *Variety*, the venerable trade paper of the entire entertainment business, published weekly.

Index

A

B

C

D

E

O

P–Q

R

S

T

U

V

W-Z